'For a small regional charity like ours, this is a vit
diversifying our income strategy. This comprehen:
not only helped us broaden our supporter base wi
also improved our approach and retention plans.'
Matthew Cornish, Fundraising and Development Manager, The Severn Trust

'A fantastic overview of the key areas of community fundraising. Highly recommended, especially for new or sole fundraisers. A handy guide to be referred to again and again throughout your career.'
Sarah Goddard, Chair of Institute of Fundraising Community Fundraising Special Interest Group

'Focusing on all aspects of modern-day community fundraising from strategy and planning to people management, audiences and techniques, this guide provides practical advice and insightful case studies throughout. Community fundraising is on the march – and this book will be of value to anyone looking to grow their knowledge and develop their community fundraising portfolio.'
Luke Mallett, Associate Director, Supporter Engagement, CLIC Sargent

'Written in a no-nonsense and engaging way by expert practitioners, this is a fascinating look into the gratifying world of community fundraising. Anyone new to fundraising, or wanting to develop their knowledge further, will find it valuable. Whether it is the up-to-date techniques and practical tips or the case studies and useful templates, there is something here for all community fundraisers.'
Lucy Squance, Director of Supporter-led Fundraising, Alzheimer's Research UK

'With a growing interest among professionals in community fundraising and so few resources out there, there couldn't be a better time for the new edition of this book. Drawing on established wider research but applying it in a pragmatic approach to the subject, this comprehensive guide will make essential reading for all community fundraisers.'
John Trampleasure, Director of Fundraising and Communications, RAF Benevolent Fund

The Fundraising Series

Second edition

Community Fundraising

Edited by
Sam Rider

dsc
directory of social change

In association with:

Published by the Directory of Social Change (Registered Charity no. 800517 in England and Wales)

Head office: Resource for London, 352 Holloway Rd, London N7 6PA

Northern office: Suite 103, 1 Old Hall Street, Liverpool L3 9HG

Tel: 020 7697 4200

Visit www.dsc.org.uk to find out more about our books, subscription funding websites and training events. You can also sign up for e-newsletters so that you're always the first to hear about what's new.

The publisher welcomes suggestions and comments that will help to inform and improve future versions of this and all of our titles. Please give us your feedback by emailing publications@dsc.org.uk.

First published 2002
Second edition (print and digital) 2019

ISBN 978 1 78482 034 3 (print edition)
ISBN 978 1 78482 035 0 (digital edition)

British Library Cataloguing in Publication Data
A catalogue record for this book is available from the British Library

Cover and text design by Kate Griffith
Typeset by Marlinzo Services, Frome
Print edition printed and bound in Great Britain by CPI Group, Croydon

To all the hardworking unsung professional community fundraisers out there, dedicated to facilitating the differences that their organisations and supporters are committed to making.

Contents

About the Fundraising Series

Despite paid fundraisers having existed in some form since the middle ages, fundraising as we know it today is still an emerging profession. The Institute of Fundraising has only been in existence since 1983 and it took a further decade for academics to begin to take an active interest in the science behind giving to others.

A vitally important element of any profession is its body of knowledge – this is what enables members of a profession to grow, learn and reflect. Immersing oneself in that knowledge is, arguably, what makes one a professional fundraiser.

This series is an important part of bringing together fundraising's body of knowledge. It combines the best of the practical knowledge of experienced fundraisers with, increasingly, the expanding body of academic knowledge around giving and asking.

The series seeks to address the full range of fundraising activity and techniques. Each volume addresses a key element in the spectrum of fundraising techniques. As fundraising techniques evolve and develop, new titles in the series are added and old ones revised. Each title seeks to explore a fundraising activity within its historical, ethical and theoretical context, and relate it to current fundraising practice as well as guide future strategy. The series offers something for anyone who is aspiring to be a professional, whatever the size or type of their organisation or the stage of their career.

The Philanthropy Centre is proud to partner with the Directory of Social Change in the series' production. Furthermore, the series would not be possible without the input of many dedicated professionals involved in its writing and production; we thank everyone who has contributed to its development.

Adrian Sargeant PhD
Claire Routley PhD
The Philanthropy Centre

About the Directory of Social Change

The Directory of Social Change (DSC) has a vision of an independent voluntary sector at the heart of social change. We believe that the activities of independent charities, voluntary organisations and community groups are fundamental to achieve social change. We exist to support these organisations in achieving their goals.

We do this by:

- providing practical tools that organisations and activists need, including online and printed publications, training courses, and conferences on a huge range of topics;
- acting as a 'concerned citizen' in public policy debates, often on behalf of smaller charities, voluntary organisations and community groups;
- leading campaigns and stimulating debate on key policy issues that affect those groups;
- carrying out research and providing information to influence policy-makers, as well as offering bespoke research for the voluntary sector.

DSC is the leading provider of information and training for the voluntary sector and publishes an extensive range of guides and handbooks covering subjects such as fundraising, management, communication, finance and law. Our subscription-based website, Funds Online (www.fundsonline.org.uk), contains a wealth of information on funding from grant-making charities, companies and government sources. We run more than 300 training courses each year, including bespoke in-house training provided at the client's location. DSC conferences and fairs, which take place throughout the year, also provide training on a wide range of topics and offer welcome opportunities for networking.

For details of all our activities, and to order publications and book courses, go to www.dsc.org.uk, call 020 7697 4200 or email cs@dsc.org.uk.

About the authors

Susannah Forland

Susannah is currently Head of Income Diversification and Growth at the WEA, the adult learning organisation, and has over ten years' experience of working in various areas of fundraising within local, national and international charities. She has also worked for Maggie's, JDRF and National Deaf Children's Society.

Susannah has managed national, regional and local fundraising teams and led on national partnerships, campaigns, products and events. She also has extensive experience in devising and developing new fundraising strategies, budgets and plans for charities that have wanted to grow and diversify their income and portfolios.

Jane Galloway

Jane is a consultant and trainer in the not-for-profit sector and a Senior Lecturer at the University of Chichester on the UK's first Charity Development Degree BA (Hons).

Having initially worked in the private and commercial sectors, Jane started fundraising in 1988 for a museum in West Wales. She then worked for Macmillan on a capital appeal and subsequently on a £3 million appeal for a London teaching hospital. In all these roles, volunteer management was pivotal in raising money and awareness.

Prior to setting up her own consultancy business, Jane was CEO of a national conservation charity and now assists a wide range of organisations with their ongoing strategic development and training needs, including working with the Association of Jersey Charities on raising awareness of the Charities (Jersey) Law.

Liz Haigh-Reeve

Liz has over 25 years' experience at a senior level within the voluntary sector. She was Director of Fundraising and Communications at The Children's Trust for 14 years and was also, among other roles, Director for Fundraising and Capital Appeals at RSBC, Director of Income Generation at Demelza Hospice Care for Children. Prior to that Liz led fundraising at the National Society for Epilepsy, the CF Trust and Leukaemia Research Fund.

In 2015, Liz established Fundraising Works Ltd and her growing team provide strategic and operational support, insight and fundraising development to organisations of all sizes.

Lianne Howard-Dace

Lianne is an experienced fundraiser with a specialism in community and events fundraising. She began her career as a hospice fundraiser and has worked for Depaul UK, RSBC and Christian Aid. Lianne now works with a variety of organisations to help them make the most of their community fundraising and is particularly interested in innovation, stewardship, and learning and development in the charity sector.

An MSc graduate of London South Bank University, Lianne is also co-author of *The Complete Fundraising Handbook* (seventh edition) and speaks regularly at conferences and events on the subject of community fundraising.

Gill Jolly

A psychology graduate, Gill has been involved in professional fundraising since the mid-1980s as a fundraiser, manager, director and trainer of fundraisers and support teams. She has worked at a senior level in a number of charities and since 2000 has had her own consultancy, Achieve Consultants Ltd. She also works as a trainer, coach and consultant as well as working at a senior level on an interim basis.

Working across the UK and beyond, Gill's experience spans charities of all different sizes, shapes and causes. She loves the challenges and thrills of helping organisations achieve their fundraising goals. She has also sat on a number of grant-making boards and awards panels.

Having worked for years with both the Directory of Social Change and the Institute of Fundraising, where she helped develop the qualifications programme, Gill was honoured to be named a Fellow of the IoF in 2012.

Michelle Martin

Michelle has over 20 years' experience working in fundraising. Her career has mostly been spent in various roles in events, regional and relationship fundraising at Macmillan Cancer Support. She currently heads up the

Development and Implementation team, helping grow Macmillan's income from regional fundraising, challenge events, philanthropy and supporter events and corporate partnerships.

Michelle is passionate about delivering a brilliant supporter experience. She led the development of supporter journeys and the implementation of CRM systems and champions using the best data and insight to make great decisions. She is an advocate for grassroots fundraising and leads the regional fundraising volunteering team at Macmillan.

Andrew Peel

Andrew is an award-winning fundraiser and consultant with over 25 years' experience in the UK charity sector. Having led fundraising teams at Help the Aged, the British Red Cross and Sightsavers, he set up Peel Consulting in 2007 and has now worked with more than 100 charities, including the British Heart Foundation, Diabetes UK, Guide Dogs, Saltdean Lido, TB Alert and a wide range of hospitals and hospices.

Andrew specialises in corporate and trust fundraising, and in developing impactful proposals, applications, pitches and strategies for clients. He is also a trustee of two charities in Brighton. A full member of the Institute of Fundraising, Andrew received its Professional Fundraiser of the Year Award in 1997.

Hannah Redmond

Hannah is an award-winning marketer and innovator with 12 years' experience of leading fundraising, marketing and innovation strategies for leading charity brands in the UK.

Hannah has developed some of the most successful new products in the sector, including Brave the Shave and Go Sober for Macmillan Cancer Support, as well as growing the charity's flagship fundraising event, The World's Biggest Coffee Morning, from a £10 million to £30 million annual initiative.

Sam Rider

Sam is overall editor of the new edition of *Community Fundraising* as well as contributing several of the chapters. She has 30 years' experience of fundraising and change management, including roles as a fundraising director and leading charities as a CEO. Working for national, international and regional charities, in sectors ranging from homelessness and criminal justice to hospices, the environment, education and the arts, she has devised and delivered transformational growth strategies.

Her work now focuses on educating a new generation of fundraisers. This involves writing and delivering undergraduate and postgraduate degrees in charity and philanthropy and teaching as a course leader for the Institute of Fundraising's Academy team. Through her consultancy work, she helps charities to identify the best ways in which they can deliver their mission by strengthening their fundraising and income-generation programmes.

Claire Singlehurst

Claire joined Macmillan in 2012 and is the Director of Relationship Fundraising, with responsibility for teams specialising in raising funds – through corporate partnerships, major gifts, challenge and special events, and regionally based fundraising – for people living with cancer. Prior to joining Macmillan, she worked in the private sector, latterly at Boots and predominantly throughout her career in leadership roles in target-oriented environments.

Having lost her sister to cancer in 2010, and experiencing first-hand Macmillan's support for families affected by cancer, Claire became a volunteer and took part in their challenge event to trek along the Great Wall of China. Following this trip, Claire put her skills and experience to use professionally within Macmillan and is now responsible for a team of around 400 people and hundreds of volunteers across the UK.

John Tasker

John is a passionate believer in the potential of events to inspire and engage people to do amazing things and support inspirational causes.

As a founding partner of massive, a specialist events agency, he works with charities in the UK and overseas to improve their results from new and existing events. So far, he has worked on more than ten of the UK's 25 biggest and most successful campaigns and also on events projects for Adidas, Jack Wills, London Marathon, parkrun, Great Run Company and the BBC.

Previously, as Head of Events for Cancer Research UK, he oversaw the UK's largest and best-known mass participation fundraising event, Race for Life, turning around a decline in both contribution and overall participation and set up an innovation team which developed three £2 million+ campaigns which are still fundraising today.

Debbie Warren

Debbie has worked in the not-for-profit sector for over 25 years, most recently setting up her consultancy, Inspired Fundraising, in 2011 to deliver first-class strategic planning and services to the not-for-profit sector. This has involved working with household names such as Macmillan, the Eden Project, WWF and Centrepoint, and helping smaller charities set up new fundraising programmes.

Debbie has a particular interest in digital fundraising and how communications can be used to encourage giving from individuals. Past projects involving product development, strategic planning and data analysis have helped to raise millions of pounds for the sector.

Acknowledgements

The first edition of *Community Fundraising* was published at the start of the new millennium and it is a testament to its editor, Harry Brown, that the book served its readers so well for many years. The fundraising landscape has moved on significantly in recent years, and so it has taken sterling efforts to prepare this second edition for the next generation of community fundraisers.

For their expert and wise advice, plaudits go to both the chapter contributors and the individuals who have advised on the content. Many thanks to them for sharing their extensive knowledge and experience.

We are grateful to Virginia Henley and Chris Knight of Hewitsons LLP for their patience and diligence in offering their legal opinion on the content of the book. We also thank Paul Ticher for his advice on data protection, Martin Bates for explanation of mathematical formulae and Hazel Bird for her expert copy-editing.

We are also indebted to those who have offered case studies and permission to re-use copyright materials. Specifically, we acknowledge the following:

- **Various chapters:**

  – Permission to use and adapt the following material from Sargeant and Jay's *Fundraising Management: Analysis planning and practice* (3rd ed.), Routledge, 2014. An adapted version of fig. 2.1 on p. 18, paraphrased text from pp. 30–32 including table 2.4 and fig. 2.5, paraphrased bullet points from p. 96, paraphrased text from pp. 98–117 on the structure of the fundraising plan, paraphrased bullet points from p. 10, quoted text and a footnote from p.234.

  – Beth Breeze for sharing the early findings of her book, *The New Fundraisers: Who organises charitable giving in contemporary society?*.

- **Chapter 1:**

  – A quotation from *Community and Growth* by Jean Vanier published and copyright 1989 by Darton Longman and Todd Ltd, London. Used by permission of the publishers.

  – Alzheimer's Research UK for permission to reproduce promotional text from its Running Down Dementia campaign.

– Permission to reproduce fig. 1.31 'The chain of contributors' from p. 13 and fig. 1.3 'The gift-exchange continuum' from p. 18 of James Isaacs, T. O'Sullivan and Robert. Paton, *Resources from Individuals*, Open University, 2007.

- **Chapter 2:**

– Mike Hudson for permission to reproduce 'How the elements of strategic direction fit together' from p. 47 of *Managing without Profit*, DSC, 2017. Thanks also for his advice on strategic aims.

– 'Sample plan for logging, managing and monitoring risks' from p. 14 of *Risk Management*, DSC, 2009, reproduced with adaptations courtesy of Elizabeth Gray-King.

- **Chapter 3:**

– The Ansoff matrix adapted and reprinted with permission from 'Strategies for Diversification' by H. Igor Ansoff. *Harvard Business Review*, September 1957. Copyright 1957 by Harvard Business Publishing; all rights reserved.

– The 'Tactical considerations model' reproduced courtesy of Claire Routley.

– 'Gantt chart for a local pub quiz campaign.' Design, with thanks, based on GanttProject (www.ganttproject.biz).

- **Chapter 4:**

– JDRF UK for the 'JDRF UK – tweaking the supporter journey' case study.

– MIND for permission to use a Pinterest board for their Crafternoon project and for the case study 'How Mind used digital to grow Crafternoon'.

- **Chapter 5**: Macmillan Cancer Support for the 'World's Biggest Coffee Morning' case study and also to David Waite for permission to use the letter from his wife Elizabeth and himself in the case study.

- **Chapter 6:** Diabetes UK for the 'Gamification of Diabetes UK's virtual event Swim22' case study.

- **Chapter 7:**

  – Alzheimer's Research UK for permission to reproduce its 'I fight Dementia' DIY fundraising option.

  – Elizabeth Kessick for confirming the details of her presentation at the Institute of Fundraising Event Fundraising Conference on 19 May 2014.

- **Chapter 8:**

  – massive for permission to reproduce the 'massive top 25'.

  – Macmillan Cancer Support for the 'How the World's Biggest Coffee Morning was revitalised' case study.

- **Chapter 9:** Rob Jackson, Mike Locke, Dr Eddy Hogg, Steve McCurley and Rick Lynch for their concepts and guidance, in various volunteering publications published by DSC, which have helped to shape this chapter.

- **Chapter 10:** Children with Cancer UK for the 'Children with Cancer UK – increasing income for schools and children's groups' case study.

- **Chapter 11:**

  – SOFII for permission to quote from Sam Butler's 'The Collection Tin'.

  – Marie Curie for the 'Marie Curie Great Daffodil Appeal' case study.

- **Chapter 12:** Age UK for the 'Age UK and Innocent's Big Knit – corporate partnership with participatory fundraising' case study.

- **Chapter 13:** Macmillan Cancer Support for 'Macmillan Cancer Support's approach to developing its community fundraising team' case study.

Foreword

As a respected community fundraising consultant said to me when I was starting out, 'People give to people. We thrive on our connections with others'.

As far back as you care to look, people have been raising money and volunteering to help others. It's that desire to engage with others and passion for a purpose that makes community fundraising what it is and makes me proud to be a part of it. Civil society is founded on grassroots mobilisation and looking out for others. Generosity has always fed the spirit!

Fundraisers exist to connect people with causes. We are a conduit or a means to an end, not an end in itself. Human stories, the experience of making a difference together with others, are what drive people to engage. Something to remember lest we become too occupied with our brand, our bottom line, our size and our return on investment.

And, as the world changes, so do our routes to engage with one other. The ability to connect through digital has transformed the possibilities of community fundraising exponentially. It offers organisations of all sizes a new means to engage, to reach and to scale in ways previously impossible. The most democratic and social form of fundraising, digital technology now provides people greater freedom to shape and share their fundraising as they mobilise their peers through localities, interest groups and in specific activities.

As always, focus is key to success. What you don't do is as important as what you do. So, this book provides a comprehensive route map for anyone, in a small or large organisation, wanting to set up and scale a community fundraising operation both sustainably and efficiently. It also offers a fantastic opportunity to learn from others who have trodden the path before.

I hope you enjoy it and relish your career in community fundraising. I have never felt more passionate about the roles I have had than those that have been at the heart of a community. Be proud of what you do and the difference you make.

Tracy Griffin, Executive Director of Marketing, Fundraising and Communications, Scope

CHAPTER ONE

Community fundraising in context

Sam Rider

> One of the marvellous things about community is that it enables us to welcome and help people in a way we couldn't as individuals.
>
> Jean Vanier, *Community and Growth*[1]

Introduction

Community fundraising is often the public face of a charity, comprising the wide range of participative activities that are most visible in communities. As a means of mobilising large numbers of supporters, it can raise substantial sums, as well as awareness of and engagement in a charitable cause.

Community fundraising provides opportunities for anyone to be a fundraiser and is often our first experience of supporting a charity as children. Most people prefer to give by cash,[2] typified by the public's preference for giving cash via collecting tins or buckets.[3] Over a third of people say they have sponsored someone in the past 12 months, and 23% have fundraised through an event.[4] Over recent years there has been an increase in large-scale community fundraising campaigns[5] – such as Go Sober (Macmillan Cancer Support) and Christmas Jumper Day (Save the Children) – and community fundraising has proved itself relatively recession-proof. The innovations of online giving platforms and the ease with which people can solicit and share support through social media are key factors in this growth. Charities are also embracing new technology, such as contactless donation devices, and using supporter data to gain insights to design activities that better reflect supporters' behaviours, experiences and motivations. The greater difficulties and costs of traditional donor recruitment have further shifted many charities' focus towards participatory methods of fundraising.

Community fundraising is taking a more central position within many charities' fundraising portfolios, with a benchmarking report showing that 87% of charities saw their community fundraising income grow between 2015 and 2018, and with 71% planning to continue to invest in the area.[6]

This chapter first looks at the history of community fundraising to see how it has evolved and how it is an embedded part of our human activity as social animals. It then seeks to define community fundraising by examining:

- what constitutes fundraising communities and networks;
- the participatory nature of community fundraising;
- the power of peer-to-peer recruitment, including:
  - how individuals engage people in their personal and professional networks to give and recruit others to support an activity (known as 'chains of contributors');
  - how individuals' giving of time and money propagates the contributions of others (known as 'contribution multipliers');
  - how being asked by others influences individuals' giving and participation.

The chapter next explores the multiple motivations of community fundraisers and the scale of community fundraising in the UK, and concludes by examining the benefits and challenges that can arise in this fundamental form of fundraising.

A brief history

Since the start of recorded history, people have asked others to help strangers through gifts of time, money and goods. Much of the documented history of giving is biased towards great gifts given by individuals of wealth. Although less is written about collective participatory low-level giving, there is evidence that it has its own heritage, with many recognisable forms of community fundraising stretching back through the centuries.

As Redmond Mullin points out in his chapter in *Thoughtful Fundraising*, collections are a recurrent historical theme in Europe. Donation boxes have been used since antiquity and the weekly church collection became commonplace in England in the sixteenth century, thanks to Henry VIII's declaration in his Beggars Act that all religious leaders in the country should use every effort, especially through their sermons, to elicit contributions from their congregations to go to people in need.[7] Major historical appeals, such as the building of Milan Cathedral between 1386 and 1391, not only relied on major gifts but also engaged local communities with jumble sales, street and house-to-house collections, and sponsored events. There is even evidence of a sponsored bell-ringing at Rouen in the Middle Ages.[8]

As outlined by Beth Breeze in *The New Fundraisers*, with the Age of Enlightenment in the eighteenth century came a gradual democratisation of giving and asking. Then the spread of wealth generated by the Industrial

Revolution, which started around 1760, coincided with more widespread mass fundraising activities.[9]

As early as the eighteenth century, funds were raised through selling bespoke fundraising merchandise, such as slave medallions, designed and produced by Josiah Wedgwood and worn by people in support of the Society for Effecting the Abolition of the Slave Trade.[10] Then in the nineteenth century in Britain jumble sales and fairs provided significant funds for the Anti-Corn Law League's campaigns, with one such event raising £25,000 (about £2.5 million in today's money) in 1845.[11] And, in England, charity dinners, gala events, street collections and public collections were essential to voluntary-funded hospitals.[12] Fundraising through fairs and events was not just a Victorian phenomenon. Fundraising had been a component of some of the oldest English events, and in the twelfth and thirteenth centuries both St Bartholomew and Sturbridge Fairs raised hospital funds, through proceeds from alcohol and amusements.[13]

The RNLI is credited with the first mass street collection in 1891 when Sir Charles Macara organised a cavalcade of horse-drawn lifeboats through the streets of Manchester.[14] By 1894 this form of mass fundraising via volunteers had been recognised by the RNLI as a means of raising vital unrestricted funds that could contribute towards running costs.[15] Agnes Morrison's 1914 flag day for wounded First World War soldiers involved 3,600 collecting tins and raised £3,800 (the equivalent of £350,000 today), which took 60 volunteers two days to count. Morrison recognised the benefit of accessing existing networks to recruit collectors and partnered with the Boys' Brigade and Boy Scouts.[16] Devolving tasks to volunteers was a key feature of these fledgling participatory fundraising initiatives. During its early days, the NSPCC relied on a loyal band of female collectors. By the end of the nineteenth century, around 6,000 women – organised by local districts – were volunteering to collect for the NSPCC.[17] Volunteer committees played a critical role in the Duke of Gloucester's Red Cross and St John Appeal during the Second World War. Raising the most funds ever in UK history, the appeal tapped into third-party networks such as schools and associations, and inspired social fundraising events from dog shows to concerts by the stars of the day.[18] And, although Band Aid's £8 million sales of 'Do They Know It's Christmas?' in 1984 was groundbreaking, performances in 1899 of Rudyard Kipling's 'The Absent-Minded Beggar', written and put to music to raise funds for Boer War soldiers, generated the equivalent of £25 million today.[19]

In the second half of the twentieth century, community fundraising expanded from volunteer-led jumble sales, coffee mornings, committees and collections to more centralised campaign management. In 1966 Oxfam pioneered a series of local sponsored walks that raised £50,000,[20] and in the 1980s national charities began to employ paid local fundraising staff to deliver schools programmes, co-ordinate fundraising by churches, and support individuals and committees raising funds in local communities. By the 1990s charities had recognised the value of developing lower commitment, centrally driven mass participation campaigns, with Macmillan's World's Biggest Coffee Morning recruiting 300,000 people and raising over £250,000 in 1991[21] and Cancer Research UK holding its first Race for Life in 1994.[22]

Charities have also continuously embraced new technologies and communication methods. Children in Need was shown on television for the very first time in 1955 and, thanks to wider telephone access, the charity reached and engaged new audiences by adopting the telethon format in 1980. This raised the profile of individuals' DIY fundraising efforts and heralded celebrity fundraising on a new scale.[23] JustGiving was launched in 2000, followed by a number of other online giving platforms; these provided fast and easy ways for people to collect donations and personalise their sponsorship pages. By 2006, Facebook had become available to anyone with an email address; it enabled charities to communicate with their supporters at a lower cost and with greater immediacy, meaning that new audiences could be reached. It also gave individual fundraising participants a simple mechanism to promote their activities and requests for support. In 2014, £60 million was donated via JustGiving from Facebook referrals,[24] and on the day of the 2017 London Marathon 88% of visits to JustGiving sites were via mobile phone or tablet.[25] The ability to seamlessly share stories across different social channels enabled the first successful viral mass participation campaigns in 2014: the Ice Bucket Challenge (to raise money for research into amyotrophic lateral sclerosis) and the #nomakeupselfie campaign (for Cancer Research UK).[26]

As the social media revolution enabled charities to engage new and younger participants, so the nature of their participation changed. According to JustGiving, from 2013 to 2015 there was a 200% increase in participation in MOB (mud, obstacles and beer) and experiential events. MOB events include tough mudders (which appeal mostly to young men), where participants run endurance obstacle courses. Experiential events (which mainly attract young women) include electric runs (night-time events where participants wear glowing necklaces and bracelets) and colour runs (where runners are doused in coloured powder).[27] These are as much about the social, fun and party atmosphere as the physical challenge, and the nature of the activity may be more important than the cause. These hypervisual events offer participants many opportunities to snap photos and selfies along the way, positioning fundraising as a great form of personal shareable social media content. Social media has also allowed people to sometimes reach far beyond their personal networks and immediate communities, as exemplified by individuals such as Caroline Jones and Jack Henderson (see box below).

In 2015, following the loss of her mother to breast cancer, Caroline Jones wore a different outfit every day, entirely made up of clothes from Cancer Research UK's charity shops. Caroline posted pictures of her ensembles on social media and by December 2015 had raised nearly £40,000.[28]

At the age of six, Jack Henderson started drawing pictures of people in return for donations to the Royal Hospital for Sick Children in Edinburgh, where his younger brother had received care.[29] By promoting his campaign through social media, he raised £64,000.[30]

In more recent years we have seen the evolution of virtual events such as Cancer Research UK's Walk All Over Cancer and Alzheimer's Research UK's Running Down Dementia. Without the costs of physical venues, weather restrictions or geographical boundaries, virtual events build on charities' growing experience of using social networks to reach new audiences and offer a flexible community fundraising product that can be delivered efficiently.

While community fundraising has evolved with social and technological changes, the desire of people to come together to make a difference through the power of mass, low-value donations – generated through peer-to-peer solicitation and volunteer support – has, and continues to be, a sustained feature of philanthropic endeavour.

Towards a definition of community fundraising

Attempting to define community fundraising is hampered by inconsistencies in charities' classification of different fundraising activities. For some, the term is used for the management of regionalised structures of fundraising, which may encompass all locally raised funds. For others, it encompasses only those activities undertaken by local fundraising groups and DIY fundraisers. Even the terms used for the different types of fundraiser and their activities can vary from one organisation to another.

Early twenty-first-century definitions of community fundraising highlight the central role of volunteers: 'fundraising carried out by volunteers in their local community'.[31] More recent descriptions consider the broader components: 'a wide range of participative events and activities all of which are visible within the local community, raise funds from individuals within that community and usually involve a volunteer workforce'.[32]

Fundraising communities and networks

While there is a tendency to frame the idea of community in the context of locality, communities can be defined more broadly as groups of people connected by shared interests, identities and perspectives, which may not relate to location.

Fundraising communities can be:

1. communities of **place**, such as the local neighbourhood, suburb, village, town, region or nation;
2. people with a shared **identity** based upon, for example, religion, ethnicity, age, gender, social or political views, or family;
3. people connected by a shared **interest**, need or behaviour, such as a sport, hobby, issue or activity;
4. communities that are based on **organisations**, from informal voluntary associations to formal entities such as businesses.

People operate in multiple communities. Some may have strong connections and others loose, and one community may intersect with another. Within communities, members may be part of social networks, interacting around a common interest through a multitude of media from online exchanges to face-to-face conversations, and in various environments from the workplace to social and leisure settings. The role of community fundraisers is to identify the networks within communities and to develop and support the fundraising activities that meet their members' needs.

Participatory fundraising

Community fundraising is characterised by its participatory nature. It is a people-intensive form of fundraising and depends on mobilising people within networks to participate in or organise profitable fundraising events and activities. This participatory form of fundraising is one of the three pillars of fundraising, as described by Robert Paton. It is distinct from the category of individual giving, which is triggered by an ask via mass media for a personal donation, and the more structured, policy-led methods of institutional giving from companies, foundations and government.[33]

Participatory fundraising activities can be classified into two basic groups:

1. individuals securing sponsorship or soliciting income for something they are doing: runs, walks, bike rides, head shaves, diets, skydives, etc.;
2. individuals volunteering to organise or facilitate participatory fundraising activities: collecting, organising events on a volunteer basis, selling event or raffle tickets, sourcing tombola prizes, etc.

There are several categories of networks through which participatory activities might be developed, such as:

- individuals' social networks;
- charities' own volunteer groups;
- membership bodies such as Rotary Clubs, Women's Institute and retirement clubs;
- activity, sports and hobby groups;
- businesses;
- churches and faith groups;
- schools and universities.

The power of peer-to-peer fundraising

People are more likely to contribute to a charity when they are asked.[34] In order to ask as many people as possible for support, community fundraising uses peer-to-peer methods, where individuals solicit donations from their friends and family on behalf of a charity.

The power of peer-to-peer fundraising rests on the impact of being asked by someone we know and feel connected to. The probability of giving is higher when we are asked by a peer,[35] and research from Ipsos MORI indicates that over a quarter of people have donated in response to a sponsorship request from friends or family.[36] Moreover, in the context of online sponsorship, most donations to a fundraising page come from the fundraiser's existing social group.[37]

Seeing how others give can also influence how much someone gives. Fundraising platforms such as JustGiving provide a public setting for donations where donors know that their donations will be seen by others. This environment shapes peer-to-peer giving behaviour, as donations made in this public way tend to be larger than donations made in private, and donations that follow a large donation are on average significantly greater than the donations that came before.[38] This method of asking by proxy can reach more people, in a potentially more efficient and effective way than only asking via a professional paid fundraiser.

The average non-profit needs to email 1,667 supporters with a fundraising message to win just one donation,[39] whereas a peer-to-peer fundraiser only has to ask between four and seven (depending on the activity) of their friends for a donation by email to get one.[40]

Chains of contributors

Peer-to-peer fundraising activities can be described as creating 'chains of contributors', where individuals are recruited by a charity to act as its agents to enlist other people's support. In turn, these people engage more individuals, who each engage others, creating exponential growth in support.[41] Figure 1.1 illustrates this idea using the example of a school undertaking a sponsored fundraising event for a charity.

FIGURE 1.1 THE CHAIN OF CONTRIBUTORS[42]

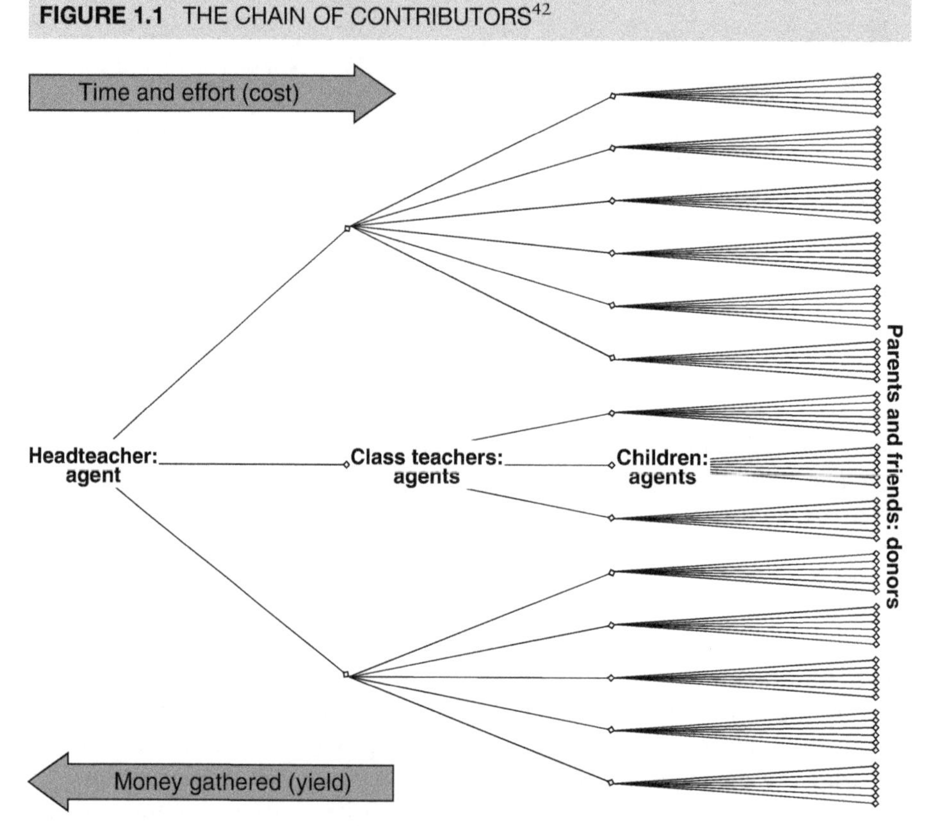

Within the chain, participants contribute in different ways, through a structured cascade of roles, tasks, activities or donations. In figure 1.1, a paid fundraiser recruits the headteacher to act as an informal agent of the charity to enlist class teachers; the class teachers act as agents to organise a sponsored event; the children are event participants but also agents who ask their family and friends for donations; and the family and friends are then the donors who sponsor the children's activity.

Contribution multipliers

Peer-to-peer fundraising activities are also 'contribution multipliers',[43] meaning that the time and money spent by a charity in finding agents to initiate an activity may be small, but, as people along the chain of contributors contribute their time and money individually, the overall resources invested in and generated by the event can add up to a large amount. In the case of the schools event in figure 1.1, the fundraiser might only spend a couple of hours recruiting and supporting the headteacher and spend limited resources on materials. However, the members of the chain each donate many hours of time and individually give or generate multiple cash gifts from the chain. Thus, the paid fundraiser can maximise the return on investment (ROI) on the activities undertaken by the people in the chain of contributors. Evaluating the ROI in this way can help you to determine the profitability of fundraising activities and assess the balance of staff time and volunteer time involved in organisation and delivery.

TABLE 1.1 EXAMPLE OF A CONTRIBUTION MULTIPLIER EFFECT

	Paid staff	**Agents**
Time	2 hours cultivating and meeting headteacher 1 hour guidance and thanking Total = 3 hours	3 teachers, each spending 3 hours on arranging the event 60 children, each spending 2 hours participating and seeking funds from their family Total = 129 hours
Money	Salary costs = £60 Materials costs = £100	Sponsorship income = £2,000
	Profit resulting from sponsorship income minus staff costs = £1,840	

Motivations for participating in community fundraising

The variety of roles in the chain of contributors reflects the variety of motivations to participate in community fundraising activities. According to researchers from the Open University, motivations for participation vary by individual along a continuum, from an altruistic gift to a straightforward exchange for something of value. In the case of a pure exchange, the cause may be irrelevant as the support is a conditional payment for a private benefit, such as the chance to win a prize or own some merchandise. As illustrated in figure 1.2, participants may have a wide range of motivations – and individual participants may have multiple motivations – along this continuum, including:

- **therapeutic** benefits, such as personal worth or alleviating loneliness (e.g. belonging to a charity's friends group);
- **developmental** benefits, such as acquiring new skills, experiences or intellectual enrichment (e.g. learning how to organise an event);
- a sense of personal **achievement,** by demonstrating a competence or seeking a particular result (e.g. running a marathon);
- **recreational** motivations of fun and relaxation (e.g. attending a charity music event);
- **approval** and status (e.g. leading a fundraising group).

FIGURE 1.2 THE GIFT–EXCHANGE CONTINUUM[44]

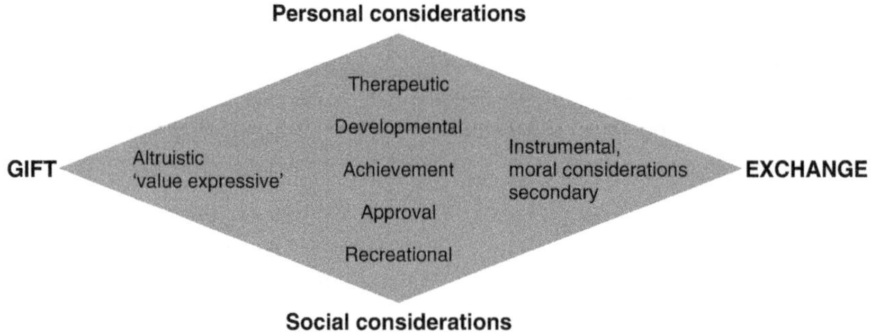

Personal considerations

GIFT

Altruistic
'value expressive'

Therapeutic
Developmental
Achievement
Approval
Recreational

Instrumental,
moral considerations
secondary

EXCHANGE

Social considerations

The idea of a developmental benefit motive is backed up by research that looked into reasons people participate in US charity sports events.[45] Researchers found that a driving factor for taking part was the desire to increase knowledge and learn new things. Other common motivators found by the researchers included:

- the sense of camaraderie that can come from a shared experience;
- a desire to escape the daily grind;
- feelings of reciprocity where the participant or their family and friends may have benefited from, or may anticipate benefiting from, the charity's work – this can often be the motivating factor for those who support hospice and health-related charities.

Furthermore, New Philanthropy Capital identified eight categories of motivation in the context of fundraising events:[46]

- **Philanthropic:** where the charitable cause itself is meaningful to the participant.
- **Purely private:** where a one-off event offers something of value to the participant, such as a glamorous night out or opportunities to form new business connections.
- **Prestige:** where the participant is motivated by the exclusivity of the event and/or the types of people (e.g. celebrities or people of a certain social group) attending it.
- **Leadership:** where the participant values opportunities to show their generosity and in doing so encourage others to engage with the charity or give a donation.
- **Relationship with the charity:** where the participant wishes to give back to the charity as a result of their or someone close to them having benefited from its work in the past (or anticipating benefiting in the future).
- **'Warm-glow giving':**[47] where the participant feels good about themselves as a result of giving to the charity.
- **Associated warm-glow giving:** where the participant's friend or family member has organised the event and the participant feels good about themselves by supporting that member of their social group.
- **Peer pressure:** where the participant is encouraged to attend by somebody else who is involved with the event or already attending.

To put some of these into the context of the school fundraising example introduced in figure 1.1, the headteacher might be motivated by the prestige achieved through positive publicity for the school; the teachers might seek the achievement of curriculum outcomes; the children might want the recreational benefits of a fun event; and the parents may give as a consequence of both the associated warm glow of supporting their child and a feeling of reciprocity towards the school.

Researchers have elaborated on the idea of associated warm glow to introduce the concept of 'relational warm glow'. This describes being motivated by the care the donor feels towards the person fundraising[48] and by experiencing a 'warm glow' from the amount of money that is raised by the person they care about.[49]

Fundraisers with small social circles raise as much as those with large social circles,[50] which may happen for two main reasons:[51]

- People in larger groups may give less than they would in a smaller group because they think everyone else in the group is giving. However, it is thanks to their concern for the fundraiser and how much they raise, and the fact that they care about the charity, that they give rather than not giving at all.

- A fundraiser with a small social group is likely to have stronger connections with the members of that group. As a result, the members of the group experience a higher level of relational warm glow towards the fundraiser than they would towards a fundraiser with a larger social circle.

The scale of community fundraising in the UK

In the UK there is a paucity of both academic research and survey data about the scale and contribution of community fundraising, with little benchmarking of trends across participatory fundraising activities. This section draws on a range of sources to provide some indication of the value of community fundraising in the UK.

- THINK's Community Forum 2015 benchmarking survey estimated the total size of the UK community fundraising market to be £4.4 billion, representing 42% of the total donated to charity by UK adults in 2014.[52]

- Some of the UK's largest national charities raise significant funds from community fundraising. In the financial year 2017/2018 Marie Curie raised £4.7 million from its local groups and Cancer Research UK raised £47 million from fundraising events.[53]

- Analysis of JustGiving data has found that 38% of fundraising pages are for mass events organised by charities (such as Race for Life), 45% are for mass events organised by non-charities (such as the London Marathon) and 17% are for people who choose their own event and charity.[54]

- Of the charities surveyed by Blackbaud in 2018, 69% received donations through peer-to-peer fundraising.[55]

- The UK's 25 most successful sports fundraising events collectively enabled charities to fundraise over £150 million in 2018.[56]

A key feature of these community fundraising methods is that they attract relatively low-value cash donations from large numbers of people. While there are exceptions, national benchmarking studies in the UK record community fundraising as achieving the lowest ROI of all fundraising methods, generating £1.57 for each £1 spent.[57] Other data suggests higher returns of £5.70 per £1 among hospices,[58] and THINK Consulting's 2018 survey gives the figure of £3.10 per £1.[59] The lower efficiencies of community fundraising are affected by:

- the need to develop personalised relationships with diverse supporters who are undertaking a wide range of activities;
- difficulties in predicting the frequency and volume of DIY fundraisers' activities;
- the resource requirements of servicing and supporting multiple low-value donations;
- the anonymous nature of some cash gifts, such as collections and sponsorships, which limits the potential for developing ongoing relationships and repeat support.

The benefits of community fundraising

Given these relatively low returns, why do charities continue to invest in community fundraising?

Awareness-raising

The visibility of promotional activity and the physical presence of an event, collection, fete or other endeavour can contribute to greater awareness of the charity within its communities. Extensive fundraising across multiple community networks provides the frequent contact that makes a charity more recognisable. An iconic event, media coverage, peer-to-peer asks, and the participation of friends and family all intertwine to build brand recognition and understanding of a charity's cause. An example of this effect was shown in research a hospice commissioned into prompted and unprompted awareness it had within its local area. Surveys in eight towns local to the hospice found a direct correlation between high levels of spontaneous awareness and the locations of flagship community fundraising events and active friends groups.[60] The influence of a charity's awareness levels on people's intended and actual giving is well documented in fundraising research,[61] with the likelihood of people supporting a charity increasing according to how well they know that charity.[62] By increasing awareness of charities in these ways, community fundraising may therefore indirectly support other income streams.

Recruitment

Fundraising activities that require low-level gifts and commitment can recruit new audiences. Research by Blackbaud, for example, found that 71% of all DIY volunteer fundraisers at a US fundraising campaign were first-time supporters.[63] Community fundraising may also be the only suitable means of engagement where people have a limited capacity to give and/or low levels of philanthropic motivation.[64]

Indirect recruitment

Community fundraising stimulates supporters to fundraise through their own networks, and these supporters may also influence members of those networks to move beyond simply sponsoring them. For example, 40% of people fundraising through JustGiving reported that since they had started fundraising, at least one friend or family member had also started fundraising, with over half of them choosing to support the same charity.[65]

Engagement

Community fundraising activities can secure participants' cognitive, emotional and behavioural investment in a charity. By understanding potential participants' motivations, fundraisers can design activities to provide experiences that are personally significant. Researchers have also argued that events can achieve a more profound level of engagement when they meet fundamental human needs, such as the need for:

- opportunities to make a difference;
- self-determination;
- positive relations with others;
- personal growth;
- a sense of personal purpose;
- self-acceptance.[66]

Creating opportunities to participate in activities that generate high levels of psychological well-being enables people to feel good about both the cause and themselves.

Retention and development

Research in 2015 found that 92% of event participants would consider supporting the same charity again and just over a quarter would consider other forms of support, such as donations to one-off appeals. Nearly one in five would consider volunteering or becoming a regular donor.[67] Some evidence also suggests that, while the cause may not be the primary motivation for participation, the more engaged in a cause a participant becomes during the experience of participation, the greater their intent to get involved in additional activities.[68] Most people who volunteer also give money to charity, which includes those who help to organise community fundraising activities.[69] It is also worth noting that high-income donors show a greater preference for ad hoc giving (such as giving at fundraising events or sponsoring someone), and 75% of high-income donors have reported sponsoring someone in the previous year.[70] Careful cultivation of supporters therefore has the potential to generate both additional and higher-value gifts.

A platform for corporate partnerships

Participatory fundraising activities provide platforms and communication channels that can help companies to reach existing and potential customers and employees. This can create corporate sponsorship and cause-related marketing opportunities for charities. For example, Macmillan's World's Biggest Coffee morning provides a focus for Homepride's product promotion of a donation to the charity on sales of special edition packs of flour.[71] Fundraising products offered in the community may equally suit employee fundraising or be integrated into Charity of the Year partnerships. See chapter 12 for details on engaging with business in the community.

Unrestricted income

Community fundraising participants are usually happy to donate to a charity's work in a general sense. So, while community fundraising's ROI may be lower than that of other forms of income generation, its ability to generate unrestricted income is of particular value at a time when reductions in charity funding from local authorities,[72] continued and planned cuts to local government funding (with an expected £7.8 billion funding gap by 2025),[73] and onerous government contracting and procurement processes are leaving many charities struggling to cover their core costs.[74]

Local relevance

Research carried out by the Charities Aid Foundation in 2016 found that 64% of people agree that local charities make a valuable contribution to their local community and 54% believe they are trustworthy.[75] Similarly, according to Open University research commissioned in 2016, 43% of people in the UK trust local charities, while only 29% trust national charities.[76] Fundraising based in a community can emphasise a charity's local nature and relevance. Given this greater level of trust in local charities, and the importance of trust to charitable support, the local nature of many community fundraising activities may positively influence the likelihood of gaining support.

Delivering charitable objectives through community engagement

Community fundraising can build networks through which charities can foster a dialogue with their communities. Some community fundraising activities also help to deliver charitable objectives, such as education and changed behaviours. For example, Cancer Research's Dryathlon raises awareness of the health and cancer risks associated with alcohol, as well as challenging people to take action by abstaining for a month.

Wider benefits of social connections and well-being

Many people's lives have become more solitary – there has been an increase in single households, especially among people aged over 45,[77] and more isolated virtual (rather than face-to-face) communications in the workplace. In this environment, participatory fundraising can provide opportunities for social contact. Indeed, there is much research that shows volunteering and participatory fundraising activities are associated with social connectedness and feelings of well-being (although it is not always clear whether socially well-connected people with good mental health are simply more likely to volunteer or participate).

An NCVO overview of volunteering research[78] highlights research which offers some evidence, particularly regarding older people, that indicates volunteering directly improves mental health in the long term and that feelings of social connectedness contribute to these improvements.

For example, a study in the US which compared data from the 1980s and 1990s[79] found that older volunteers were less likely to experience feelings of depression than non-volunteers. It also found that older volunteers were more likely to attend meetings at groups or clubs than non-volunteers, which helped reduce depressive symptoms.

Research on older volunteers in England that looked at changes in their well-being from 2004 to 2006 found that those who felt appreciated for volunteering reported more life satisfaction, more of an improvement in their quality of life, fewer feelings of social isolation and more of a decrease in feelings of depression since starting volunteering than nonvolunteers.[80] These benefits continued for those who were still volunteering in 2006, whereas they were no longer seen in those who had stopped volunteering after 2004.[81] In addition, one study in the US in 2017 found that volunteering for two or more hours a week helped widowed volunteers to feel less lonely than before they began volunteering.[82]

NCVO's briefing also highlights studies that indicate volunteering can help increase young people's sense of well-being. For example, one evaluation of young people in the US between 1994 and 2008 showed that young volunteers (who volunteered regularly and had freely chosen to do so) felt fewer symptoms of depression when surveyed 6 and 13 years after the start of the study.[83] Another study surveyed participants in a UK youth volunteering programme in the summer of 2016 and again in autumn of the same year and found that they felt reduced levels of anxiety and higher levels of life satisfaction as a result of participating.[84] This study also found evidence of young people feeling more comfortable about mixing with others from different social backgrounds, ethnicities and sexualities[85] and of greater social mobility as a result of the volunteer programme, which was measured using metrics such as feeling more confident in being a team leader and in meeting new people, and having the skills and experience to get a job in the future.[86]

Taking part in sporting and cultural events and activities can also make people feel more socially connected and like they belong. This has been shown to particularly be the case for those who are among groups of people who are from similar backgrounds, but there is also some limited evidence that sports participation promotes greater understanding of others from other social backgrounds.[87] For example, young volunteers aged 14 to 19 who took part in a UK sports programme reported that they experienced an increased sense of social connectedness with a diverse network of people.[88]

Wider economic benefits

Community events and activities can bring economic benefits and employment, from contracting local suppliers to use of local transport and community facilities, and increased footfall in retail areas. Consideration of these wider economic benefits may be helpful for many charities in demonstrating their contribution to society when seeking funding from government or grant-making charities.

The challenges of community fundraising

Alongside an awareness of the many benefits of community fundraising and the growth in some of its forms, most notably mass participation events and DIY fundraising, fundraisers developing participatory fundraising programmes need to consider some of the challenges they may face.

Recruiting and retaining volunteers

Over a third of community fundraisers cite a lack of volunteers as a significant internal challenge (i.e. a challenge originating from within the workplace).[89] The 2018 Community Life Survey reports that levels of formal volunteering have gradually decreased since 2013/14 across most age groups but have levelled off since 2015/16.[90] Given this drop in time commitment, community fundraisers may need to consider how to re-engage these groups.

Research carried out by NCVO's Institute for Volunteering Research in 2013 showed that, owing to both a change in expectations and the greater unpredictability of people's lives, there has been an increase in demand for flexibility and short-term volunteering.[91] Whether or not such a change would increase commitment by providing flexible options for volunteering that offer people more control over the time they give, such options may attract people who may not otherwise have volunteered.[92]

Recruiting and retaining fundraising staff

Over a quarter of charities find it difficult to secure suitably skilled community fundraisers, with over half of fundraisers leaving their role within three years.[93] The demand for event fundraisers outstrips the supply, with rising numbers of community and event fundraiser vacancies.[94] The fundraising skills gap is particularly acute in small charities,[95] while at the officer/executive level, community and event fundraisers continue to be paid less than their colleagues in corporate, trust, individual giving and major gift fundraising.[96]

Competition and dominance of larger charities

There are indications that the gap between larger and smaller charity brands' fundraising is widening, partially because bigger organisations can be better equipped to use their profile, data and resources to grow their events. In 2018, the ten highest income-generating events accounted for nearly 80% of the top 25 charity-owned mass participation events.[97] Given the dominance of these charities in the mass participation event market and the resulting competition to recruit event participants, it is hardly surprising that the biggest challenges community fundraisers identify are achieving high levels of brand awareness and recognition, and a lack of internal marketing support.[98]

Sustaining growth

Many charities and third-party suppliers are starting to find it harder to fill their events and fewer people are reported to be sponsoring fundraising participants.[99] Some charities are testing new event formats, focusing on more extreme types of experience, using humour, making events virtual, creating product extensions (such as the Race for Life Hike) or targeting niche markets. The risk, of course, is that new ideas can be quickly copied and differentiation lost. Others have concentrated on building events more slowly, with a focus on their cause and their core supporters (for example, Tommy's Splashathon).[100]

Adapting to new technology

Charities can find it particularly challenging to keep up with the speed at which technology changes and how it affects participants' expectations around engagement, event format and experience. For example, reports from 2018 found that half of charities surveyed cited a lack of digital skills[101] and only 42% of charities are confident that they have adequate technology in place to grow online and digital fundraising.[102] A 2019 survey, however, found charities to be digitally savvy, with four out of five charities overall stating that they have a digital strategy (although this dropped to three in five in the case of small charities).[103] In any case, developments such as online auctions, Facebook fundraisers, the rise of the app economy, contactless donation devices and smarter real-time analytics mean that there are more opportunities than ever to improve charities' reach, ease of giving and ability to provide personalised experiences for supporters. Charities need to rise to this challenge by investing, testing and applying these new tools to participatory fundraising programmes.

Conclusion

Community fundraising is the most social and democratic of all forms of fundraising, with its low-level entry points and the freedom individuals have to determine how and when they support the causes that matter to them. Compared to other forms of fundraising, it has perhaps benefitted disproportionately from the rise of social media and new technologies, and it has now evolved from being the poor relation of fundraising departments to become a key way for charities to attract and engage supporters.

While community fundraising can be difficult to define, it is characterised by its participatory nature and by the fact that it takes place within a community. A community, however, is not defined in purely geographical terms, but as a group of people who are connected by shared interests, identities and perspectives.

Community fundraising presents its own challenges, including the ability to retain volunteers and fundraising staff (although not all of these challenges are unique to this form of fundraising). At the same time, it offers far-reaching benefits both inside organisations and beyond them. For instance, community fundraising can both help a charity to raise awareness of its brand and increase supporters' engagement. In the wider world, its participative nature can have effects that other forms of fundraising do not, not least promoting a sense of social connectedness and feelings of belonging in a world where people are feeling increasingly isolated.

Notes

1 Quoted in 'Meet our founder' [web page], L'Arche Ireland, 2018, www.larcheireland.org/?t=o7ucn2bdc9gg3koknvm1j64rj4&tto=1ebaf4ff, accessed 20 August 2018.

2 *CAF UK Giving 2018: An overview of charitable giving in the UK* [PDF], Charities Aid Foundation, 2018, www.cafonline.org/docs/default-source/about-us-publications/caf-uk-giving-2018-report.pdf, p. 5, accessed 13 August 2018.

3 See Claire Bennett, 'Cashless Innovations – keeping up as cash goes digital' [blog post], nfpSynergy, https://nfpsynergy.net/blog/contactless-charity-donation?utm, 7 February 2019; and Briony Gunstone and Gavin Ellison, *Insights into Charity Fundraising* [PDF], Institute of Fundraising and YouGov, 2017, www.institute-of-fundraising.org.uk/library/insights-into-charity-fundraising-final-report, p. 20, accessed 19 March 2019.

4 *CAF UK Giving 2018: An overview of charitable giving in the UK* [PDF], Charities Aid Foundation, 2018, www.cafonline.org/docs/default-source/about-us-publications/caf-uk-giving-2018-report.pdf, p. 15, accessed 13 August 2018.

5 'Trends in mass participation fundraising events' [web page], massive, 2017, www.wearemassive.co.uk/insight/trends-in-mass-participation-events-fundraising, accessed 13 August 2018.

6 'Community fundraising benchmarking 2018' [web page], THINK Consulting, 2018, www.thinkcs.org/community-fundraising-benchmarking-2018, accessed 17 September 2018.

7 Redmond Mullin, 'Two Thousand Years of History' in *Thoughtful Fundraising*, edited by Jill Mordaunt and Robert Paton, Milton Keynes, Routledge, 2007, pp. 14–15, citing Joseph Tanner, *Tudor Constitutional Documents, AD 1485–1603*, Cambridge University Press, 1930, pp. 480f.

8 *Ibid.* pp. 12–13.

9 Beth Breeze, *The New Fundraisers: Who organises charitable giving in contemporary society?*, Bristol, Policy Press, 2017, pp. 45–47.

10 *Ibid.*, p. 42, citing David Owen, *English Philanthropy 1660–1960*, London, Oxford University Press, 1965, p. 13.

11 *Ibid.*, p. 42, citing Frank Prochaska, *Women and Philanthropy in Nineteenth-Century England*, Oxford, Clarendon Press, 1990, p. 54.

12 *Ibid.*, p. 37.

13 Beverly Gordon, *Bazaars and Fair Ladies: The History of the American Fundraising Fair*, Knoxville, University of Tennessee Press, 1998, p. 8.

14 Beth Breeze, *The New Fundraisers: Who organises charitable giving in contemporary society?*, Bristol, Policy Press, 2017, p. 40, citing the RNLI's 'Origin of the Lifeboat Saturday Movement' sourced from a photocopy from archives (no publication details available).

15 *Ibid.*, citing James Dibdin, *The Book of the Lifeboat: With a complete history of the Saturday Lifeboat movement*, Charleston SC, Nabu Press, 2010, p. 23.

16 'PoW charity flags and flag days' [web page], Prisoners of War 1914–1918, 2012, www.prisonersofwar1914-1918documents.com/charity-flags-and-flag-days-copy.php, accessed 13 March 2018

17 Beth Breeze, *The New Fundraisers: Who organises charitable giving in contemporary society?*, Bristol, Policy Press, 2017, p. 43 citing George Behlmer, *Child Abuse and Moral Reform in England, 1870–1908*, Stanford, CA, Stanford University Press, 1982, p. 144.

18 Louise Daintry, 'British Red Cross: The £7.7 billion appeal that changed British fundraising for ever' [web article], SOFII, http://sofii.org/case-study/british-red-cross-the-7.7-billion-appeal-that-changed-british-fundraising-forever, 29 September 2010.

19 Aline Reed, 'The Absent-Minded Beggar: Bigger than Band Aid' [web article], SOFII, http://sofii.org/article/the-absent-minded-beggar-bigger-than-band-aid, 18 June 2014.

20 'History of Oxfam' [web page], Oxfam, 2018, www.oxfam.org.uk/what-we-do/about-us/history-of-oxfam, accessed 13 August 2018.

21 'Our history' [web page], Macmillan Cancer Support, 2018, www.macmillan.org.uk/about-us/who-we-are/organisation-history.html, accessed 13 August 2018.

22 Paul de Gregorio, 'Cancer Research UK: The race for life' [web article], SOFII, http://sofii.org/case-study/cancer-research-uks-race-for-life, 6 June 2013.

23 'History' [web page], BBC, 2007, www.bbc.co.uk/programmes/articles/5ZBrwt3l3Q9JdstzshblqM6/history, accessed 5 September 2018.

24 *Friends with Money* [PDF], Social Misfits Media and Just Giving, 2014, https://pages.justgiving.com/rs/justgiving1/images/Friends%20with%20Money%20-%20a%20guide%20to%20%23fundraising%20on%20%23socialmedia.pdf, p. 5, accessed 14 August 2018.

25 Howard Lake, '£2.3million donated on JustGiving over London Marathon weekend' [web article], UK Fundraising, https://fundraising.co.uk/2017/06/05/2-3m-donated-justgiving-london-marathon-weekend, 5 June 2017.

26 'Five of the best charity online campaigns of 2014' [blog post], https://blog.justgiving.com/five-of-the-best-charity-online-campaigns-of-2014, JustGiving, 12 December 2014.

27 Elizabeth Kessick, 'How MOB events are changing the event fundraising landscape' [web article], JustGiving, https://blog.justgiving.com/how-mob-events-are-changing-the-event-fundraising-landscape, 8 July 2015.

28 'Knickers model's own: A testament to solo fundraising' [web article], *The Guardian*, www.theguardian.com/voluntary-sector-network/2015/dec/21/fundraising-charities-cancer-tips-knickers-models-own, 21 December 2015.

29 David Lumb, 'Stephen's story: What's the secret to teens' fundraising success?' [web article], BBC News, www.bbc.co.uk/news/uk-england-27192089, 1 May 2014.

30 'Jack draws anything' [web page], 2014, https://jackdrawsanything.com, accessed 5 September 2018.

31 Harry Brown, *Community Fundraising*, London, DSC, 2002, p. 15.

32 Adrian Sargeant and Elaine Jay, *Fundraising Management: Analysis, planning and practice*, Abingdon, Routledge, 2014, p. 234.

33 Robert Paton, 'Fundraising as marketing: Half a truth is better than none', in *Thoughtful Fundraising*, edited by Jill Mordaunt and Robert Paton, Oxford, Routledge, 2007, p. 31.

34 Barış Yörük, 'How Responsive are Charitable Donors to Requests to Give?', *Journal of Public Economics*, vol. 93, nos 9–10, 2009, pp. 1111–17.

35 Jonathan Meer, '"Brother, can you spare a dime?" Peer pressure in charitable solicitation', *Journal of Public Economics*, vol. 95, no. 7, 2011, pp. 926–41.

36 *Money for Good: Donor segmentation research* [PDF], Ipsos MORI, 2012, www.thinknpc.org/wp-content/uploads/2013/03/Money-for-Good-UK-Ipsos-Mori-data-report.pdf, p. 59, accessed 14 August 2018.

37 Abigail Payne, Kimberley Scharf and Sarah Smith, *Online Fundraising: The perfect ask?* [working paper], University of Warwick Department of Economics, no. 194, 2014, https://warwick.ac.uk/fac/soc/economics/research/centres/cage/manage/publications/194-2014_scharf.pdf, p. 6, accessed 3 August 2018. (Note that all page numbers noted in Payne *et al.* 2014 references correspond to the PDF numbering in the particular version of the file that this URL leads to. The pages of the report itself are unnumbered.)

38 *Ibid.*

39 *2018 M+R Benchmarks Study* [PDF], M&R, 2018, https://mrbenchmarks.com, p. 12, accessed 7 September 2018; figures are derived from research on non-profit organisations in the USA and Canada.

40 *2016 Blackbaud Peer-to-Peer Fundraising Study* [PDF], Blackbaud, 2017, http://hi.blackbaud.com/p2p, p. 22, accessed 7 September 2018. These figures are derived from research on event-organising non-profits in the USA and Canada. The numbers of emails it takes for a peer-to-peer fundraiser to get a donation are as follows: 5Ks – seven emails; cycling events – seven emails; walks – six emails; endurance events – four emails.

41 James Isaacs, T. O'Sullivan and Robert Paton, *Resources from Individuals*, Milton Keynes, Open University, 2007, pp. 11–39.

42 *Ibid.*

43 *Ibid.*

44 *Ibid.*

45 Kevin Filo, Daniel Funk and Danny O'Brien, 'Examining Motivation for Charity Sport Event Participation: A comparison of recreation-based and charity-based motives', *Journal of Leisure Research*, vol. 43, no. 4, 2011, pp. 491–518.

46 *Just the Ticket* [PDF], New Philanthropy Capital, 2003, www.thinknpc.org/publications/just-the-ticket, p. 6, accessed 14 August 2018.

47 James Andreoni, 'Impure Altruism and Donations to Public Goods: A theory of warm-glow giving', *Economic Journal*, vol. 100, no. 401, 1990, pp. 464–47.

48 Kimberley Scharf and Sarah Smith, *Relational Warm Glow: Giving in social groups* [working paper], University of Warwick and CEPR, 2014, www.bristol.ac.uk/media-library/sites/cmpo/migrated/documents/wp327.pdf, p. 8, accessed 6 September 2018.

49 *Ibid.*, p. 13.

50 Abigail Payne, Kimberley Scharf and Sarah Smith, *Online Fundraising: The perfect ask?* [working paper], University of Warwick Department of Economics, no. 194, 2014, https://warwick.ac.uk/fac/soc/economics/research/centres/cage/manage/publications/194-2014_scharf.pdf, pp. 13–14, accessed 14 August 2018.

51 *Ibid.*, p. 15.

52 Tracy Griffin, *Making the Connection: Bring donors into your own community* [PDF], Commission on the Donor Experience, 2017, http://sofii.org/images/Articles/The-Commission-on-the-Donor-Experience/P11d-Community-FULL-PDF.pdf, p. 9, accessed 14 August.

53 *Marie Curie Annual Report and Accounts 2017/18* [PDF], Marie Curie, 2018, www.mariecurie.org.uk/globalassets/media/documents/who-we-are/plans-reports-and-policies/previous-reports/annual-reports/marie_curie_annual_report_2017-18.pdf, p. 36 and *Cancer Research UK Annual Report and Accounts 2017/18* [PDF], Cancer Research UK, 2018, www.cancerresearchuk.org/sites/default/files/cruk_annual_report_2017_18_final.pdf, p. 28, accessed 19 March 2019.

54 Abigail Payne, Kimberley Scharf and Sarah Smith, *Online Fundraising: The perfect ask?* [working paper], University of Warwick Department of Economics, no. 194, 2014, https://warwick.ac.uk/fac/soc/economics/research/centres/cage/manage/publications/194-2014_scharf.pdf, p. 8, accessed 14 August 2018.

55 *The Status of UK Fundraising: 2018 benchmark report*, Blackbaud, 2018, https://hub.blackbaud.co.uk/npinsights/the-status-of-uk-fundraising-2018-benchmark-report, p. 13, accessed 19 March 2019.

56 *Sports Fundraising Market Snapshot* [PDF], massive, 2019, www.wearemassive.co.uk/insight/sports-fundraising-market-snapshot, p. 1, accessed 8 July 2019.

57 'Fundratios 2014' [web page], Centre for Interfirm Comparisons, 2015, www.cifc.co.uk/Fundratios14.html, accessed 13 August 2018.
58 Joe Saxton and Rei Kanemura, *Hospice Fundraising Benchmark 2015: Core report*, London, nfpSynergy, 2016, p. 17.
59 'Community fundraising benchmarking 2018' [web page], THINK Consulting, 2018, www.thinkcs.org/community-fundraising-benchmarking-2018, accessed 17 September 2018.
60 Research commissioned by St Catherine's Hospice and conducted by Crossbow Research in 2013.
61 See, for example, Renne Bekkers and Pamela Wiepking, 'A Literature Review of Empirical Studies of Philanthropy: Eight mechanisms that drive charitable giving', *Nonprofit and Voluntary Sector Quarterly*, vol. 40, no. 5, 2011, pp. 924–73; Arminda do Paço, Ricardo Gouveia Rodrigues and Luís Rodrigues, 'Branding in NGOs: Its influence on the intention to donate', *Economics and Sociology*, vol. 7, no. 3, 2014, pp. 11–21.
62 Roger Bennett and Helen Gabriel, 'Image and Reputational Characteristics of UK Charitable Organizations: An empirical study', *Corporate Reputation Review*, vol. 6, no. 3, 2003, pp. 276–89.
63 Data from a peer-to-peer US DIY fundraising campaign in 2013; presentation by Blackbaud at the Association of Fundraising Professionals conference, 27 March 2014.
64 Daniel Webber, 'Understanding Charity Fundraising Events', *International Journal of Nonprofit and Voluntary Sector Marketing*, vol. 9, no. 2, 2004, pp. 122–34.
65 'Unlocking the value of peer-to-peer fundraising' [web article], JustGiving, http://blog.justgiving.com/unlocking-the-value-of-peer-to-peer-fundraising, 6 March 2015.
66 Adrian Sargeant and Harriet Day, *Great Fundraising Events: From experience to transformation*, Plymouth, Hartsook Centre for Sustainable Philanthropy, Plymouth University, 2017.
67 *Closing the Loop* [PDF], Institute of Fundraising and Blackbaud, 2015, www.institute-of-fundraising.org.uk/library/closing-the-loop, p. 14, accessed 14 August 2018.
68 Adam Goodwin, Ryan Snelgrove, Laura Wood and Marijke Taks, 'Leveraging Charity Sport Events to Develop a Connection to a Cause', *Event Management*, vol. 21, no. 2, 2017, pp. 175–84.
69 Becky Hamlyn, Alice Fitzpatrick, Emma Coleman and Keith Bolling, *Giving of Time and Money: Findings from the 2012–13 Community Life Survey* [PDF], Cabinet Office, 2013, www.gov.uk/government/uploads/system/uploads/attachment_data/file/314432/2012-2013-giving-time-and-money-report.pdf, accessed 23 April 2018.
70 Sally Bagwell, Lucy de Las Casas, Matt van Poortvliet and Rob Abercrombie, *Money for Good UK: Understanding donor motivation and behaviour*, London, New Philanthropy Capital, 2013, p. 19.
71 'Macmillan World's Biggest Coffee Morning' [web page], Homepride, 2019, https://homeprideflour.co.uk/macmillan-coffee-morning, accessed 17 May 2019.
72 'UK Civil Society Almanac 2015: Income from government' [web page], https://data.ncvo.org.uk/a/almanac15/government, NCVO, 2015, accessed 6 September 2018; note that NCVO almanacs from 2016 to 2018 did not contain more up-to-date findings.

73 *Local Government Funding: Moving the conversation on* [PDF], Local Government Association, 2018, www.local.gov.uk/moving-the-conversation-on/funding, pp. 6–7, accessed 6 September 2018.
74 *Commissioning in Crisis: How current contracting and procurement processes threaten the survival of small charities* [PDF], Lloyds Bank Foundation for England and Wales, 2016, www.lloydsbankfoundation.org.uk/Commissioning%20in%20Crisis%202016%20Full%20Report.pdf, p. 6, accessed 14 August 2018.
75 *Local Charities Day: Exploring attitudes towards charity* [PDF], CAF, 2016, www.cafonline.org/docs/default-source/about-us-publications/local-charities-day-2016.pdf, p. 4, accessed 26 September 2018.
76 'Smaller charities top the list for consumer trust' [web page], Open University Business School, 2018, www.open.ac.uk/business-school-research/centre-voluntary-sector-leadership/news/smaller-charities-top-list-consumer-trust, accessed 4 September 2018.
77 'The cost of living alone' [web article], Office for National Statistics, www.ons.gov.uk/peoplepopulationandcommunity/birthsdeathsandmarriages/families/articles/thecostoflivingalone/2019–04-04, 4 April 2019.
78 *Impactful Volunteering: Understanding the impact of volunteering on volunteers* [PDF], NCVO, 2018, www.ncvo.org.uk/images/documents/policy_and_research/Impactful-volunteering-understanding-the-impact-of-volunteering-on-volunteers.pdf, pp. 2–3, accessed 9 May 2019.
79 Mark A. Musick and John Wilson, 'Volunteering and Depression: The role of psychological and social resources in different age groups', *Social Science and Medicine*, vol. 56, no. 2, 2003, pp. 259–269.
80 James Nazroo and Katey Matthews, *The Impact of Volunteering on Well-being in Later Life: A report to WRVS* [PDF], Royal Voluntary Service, www.royalvoluntaryservice.org.uk/Uploads/Documents/Reports%20and%20Reviews/the_impact_of_volunteering_on_wellbeing_in_later_life.pdf, 2012, p. 21, accessed 8 May 2019.
81 *Ibid.*, p. 22.
82 Dawn C. Carr, Ben Lennox Kail, Christina Matz-Costa, Yochai Z. Shavit, 'Does Becoming A Volunteer Attenuate Loneliness Among Recently Widowed Older Adults?', *The Journals of Gerontology: Series B*, vol. 73, no. 3, 2018, pp. 501–510.
83 Jinho Kim and Kerem Morgül, 'Long-term Consequences of Youth Volunteering: Voluntary versus involuntary service', *Social Science Research*, vol. 67, 2017, pp. 160–175.
84 Sally Panayiotou, Sarah Newton, Peter Matthews, Hannah Webster, David Andersson, Gavan Conlon and Viktoriya Peycheva, *National Citizen Service 2016 Evaluation: Main report* [PDF], Department for Digital, Culture, Media & Sport, https://assets.publishing.service.gov.uk/government/uploads/system/uploads/attachment_data/file/678057/NCS_2016_EvaluationReport_FINAL.pdf, 2017, p. 5, accessed 9 May 2019.
85 *Ibid.*, pp. 50–52.
86 *Ibid.*, pp. 54–55.

87 Peter Taylor, Larissa Davies, Peter Wells, Jan Gilbertson and William Tayleur, *A Review of the Social Impacts of Culture and Sport* [PDF], Sport Industry Research Centre and Centre for Regional Economic and Social Research (Sheffield Hallam University) and Business of Culture, 2015, https://assets.publishing.service.gov.uk/government/uploads/system/uploads/attachment_data/file/416279/A_review_of_the_Social_Impacts_of_Culture_and_Sport.pdf, p. 52, accessed 14 May 2019.
88 Tess Kay and Steven Bradbury, 'Youth Sport Volunteering: Developing social capital?', *Sport, Education and Society*, vol. 14, no. 1, 2009, pp. 121–140.
89 Claire Daniels and Sam Rider, 'Community Fundraising Snapshot', manuscript in preparation, 2017.
90 *Community Life Survey 2017–2018: Statistical bulletin* [PDF], Department for Digital, Culture, Media and Sport, 2018, www.gov.uk/government/statistics/community-life-survey-2017-18, p. 15, accessed 5 March 2019.
91 Joni Brown, Veronique Jochum and Jonathan Paylor, *The Value of Giving a Little Time: Understanding the potential of micro-volunteering* [PDF], Institute for Volunteering Research and NCVO, 2013, https://www.wcva.org.uk/media/739801/micro_volunteering_full_report_071113.pdf, p. 25, accessed 14 August 2018.
92 *Ibid*., p. 35.
93 Claire Daniels and Sam Rider, 'Community Fundraising Snapshot', manuscript in preparation, 2017.
94 *Harris Hill Salary Survey 2017* [PDF], Harris Hill, 2017, www.harrishill.co.uk/cms-uploaded/Harris_Hill_2017_Salary_Survey.pdf, 2017, p. 6, accessed 14 August 2018.
95 *The UK Small Charities Skills Gap survey 2014/15* [PDF], Foundation for Social Improvement, 2016, www.thefsi.org/wp-content/uploads/2015/06/UK-Small-Charity-Sector-Skills-Survey-2014%EF%80%A215.pdf, p. 2, accessed 14 August 2018.
96 *Fundraising Salary Survey 2019* [PDF], Kage Partnership, 2019, www.kagep.com/download_file/view/1620, p. 2, accessed 23 April 2019.
97 Percentage calculated from *The Massive Top 25* [PDF], massive, 2019, www.wearemassive.co.uk/insight/mass-participation-top-25-2, p. 1, accessed 30 July 2019.
98 Claire Daniels and Sam Rider, 'Community Fundraising Snapshot', manuscript in preparation, 2017.
99 'Is the public getting tired of sponsoring fundraising events?' [web article], nfpSynergy, https://nfpsynergy.net/blog/public-getting-tired-sponsoring-fundraising-events, 15 January 2018.
100 'Trends in mass participation events fundraising' [web page], massive, 2017, www.wearemassive.co.uk/insight/trends-in-mass-participation-events-fundraising, accessed 23 April 2018.
101 Zoe Amar and David Evans, *The Charity Digital Skills Report* [PDF], Skills Platform, 2018, http://report.skillsplatform.org/charitydigitalreportdetail-2018, p. 4, accessed 23 April 2018.
102 Salesforce, *Nonprofit Trends Report: Insights from over 450 nonprofit leaders into the trends shaping the social sector* [PDF], 2018, p. 10, accessed 24 May 2019.
103 *The Status of UK Fundraising 2019 Benchmark Report* [PDF], Blackbaud and Institute of Fundraising, 2019, https://hub.blackbaud.co.uk/npinsights/the-status-of-uk-fundraising-2019-report, p. 6, accessed 18 July 2019.

CHAPTER TWO

Undertaking a fundraising audit

Sam Rider

Introduction

Community fundraising can deliver considerable benefits, but it also brings risks and challenges. It is a people-intensive form of fundraising, reliant on multiple low-value gifts, so it needs to be carefully and deliberately planned if returns are to be maximised.

Community fundraising operates within the context of an ever-changing external environment, and success depends upon understanding and responding to the opportunities and threats this presents. Crucially, it is also a major source of income to charities, with an estimated total value in the UK of £4.4 billion, which in 2014 represented 42% of the total donated to charity by UK adults.[1] As chapter 1 highlights, charities are embracing the potential of community fundraising, witnessing its popularity and growth and making commitments to increase investment. This recognition of the value of community fundraising implies more competition for participants and volunteers across an array of events and activities. To compete, a charity must:

- continually explore supporters' needs and motivations;
- understand which experiences compel different communities, networks and demographics;
- innovate and test new methods to engage and retain support;
- ensure the highest possible standards of supporter care.

All this requires organisational commitment and understanding of the timescales involved in achieving success, clarity on what that success looks like, the best opportunities for growth and the requisite resources for fundraising activities, support, relationship building, data management and insight, and staffing. So, to gain this understanding before embarking on a community fundraising programme, you need to carry out a structured process of analysis and evaluation. This will help to ensure that you select the *right* actions and activities for your strategic plan (see chapter 3), which should comprise what needs to be done, by whom and by when.

After considering the factors underlining the importance of strategic planning, this chapter outlines the first stage of any strategic planning process, including how to:

- place community fundraising planning in the context of your organisation's vision, mission, strategic aims and organisational objectives;
- undertake an audit of the wider external environment in which you carry out your community fundraising;
- assess your organisation's internal capacity to deliver community fundraising competitively within that environment;
- pull these external and internal audits together using a SWOT (strengths, weaknesses, opportunities and threats) analysis (see page 61).

The importance of strategic planning

The need to plan may seem obvious, as a plan identifies what you want to do and how you want to do it. However, there are at least six further good reasons to have a strategy in place.

1. To align with your organisation's top-level direction

Every charity is driven by its vision and mission. Any strategic aims that a charity sets and the strategies it outlines to achieve them should always be in pursuit of its vision and mission. Placing strategic planning at a fundraising departmental level within this big picture allows your department to contribute most effectively towards realising the impact your organisation is seeking to achieve. (See 'Top-level direction' on page 30 for details.)

2. To enhance public trust

Planning can help to enhance the public trust upon which fundraising depends. In order to help build the public's confidence in your organisation, be clear about how you fundraise and what the funds are for, and highlight that a process is in place to identify the most efficient, effective and sustainable methods of fundraising.

3. To ensure trustees' duties are fulfilled

The Charity Commission expects charities to fundraise in a way which protects their reputation and inspires public trust. Having a fundraising plan is part of the six principles which the Charity Commission requires trustees to follow:[2]

- planning effectively by agreeing or setting and monitoring (alongside fundraisers) the charity's fundraising approach, including by considering risks, income needs, the charity's values and its relationship with stakeholders;
- supervising fundraisers to ensure they are acting in the charity's best interests;
- protecting the charity's reputation and assets by ensuring the impact of fundraising on donors, supporters and the public is adequately considered, also making sure the charity receives all the money it is entitled to and reducing the risk of loss or fraud;
- ensuring the charity complies with the laws and regulations that apply to fundraising;
- ensuring that fundraising adheres to the Fundraising Regulator's Code of Fundraising Practice;
- being open and accountable by complying with statutory accounting and reporting requirements, demonstrating that the charity is well run and effective, and explaining the charity's fundraising to the public, donors and supporters.

4. To promote a cohesive approach

A strategic fundraising plan gives everyone involved clarity of expectation in terms of income, resources required, responsibilities and measures of success and performance. This enhances internal relationships and builds efficiency and effectiveness across teams.

5. To reduce risk

Creating a strategy requires you to:

- review all the external factors that could have an impact on your fundraising;
- assess the various options for a community fundraising programme and evaluate your charity's capacity to carry each one out;

- analyse all options and select the best ones;
- have a costed and adequate budget.

In this way, strategic planning helps to future-proof an organisation by looking usually three to five years ahead, so as to ensure that activities and expectations are realistic.

6. To provide continuity

With fundraising departments experiencing relatively high turnover rates (see chapter 13), having a written plan provides a common focus that gives a sense of continuity in periods of staff change.

The planning process

There are four elements that are common to any strategic planning process. You need to know:

- where you are now (the fundraising audit);
- where you want to be (fundraising objectives);
- how you will get there (fundraising strategy);
- what you will do to get there (fundraising tactics).

Various planning frameworks have been suggested to help fundraisers answer these questions. One particularly useful model, which is used in the Institute of Fundraising's professional training programmes, is Adrian Sargeant and Elaine Jay's generic planning framework (see figure 2.1).[3] The hierarchy illustrated in this figure forms the basis of the structure in this chapter and in chapter 3.

Strategic planning theories

Methods of planning fall into two categories. There are those who see it as a rational, top-down process, which tends to work well when a charity is operating in a stable environment (the rational analytic strategy). The alternative view is that strategies must be driven from the bottom of the organisation and emerge and evolve continually over time (the emergent strategy).[4]

In fact, the two approaches are not mutually exclusive; while structure has its benefits, organisations also need to continually review and adjust plans in light of external and internal changes that emerge.

FIGURE 2.1 THE FUNDRAISING PLANNING PROCESS

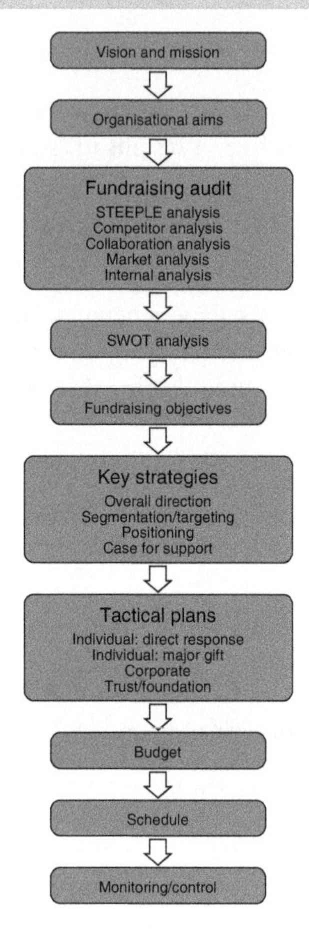

Where you are now

As highlighted in the introduction, you first need to place community fundraising planning in the context of your organisation's vision, mission and strategic aims, and the top-level strategies that your organisation has set to achieve those aims.[5]

Top-level direction

Vision and mission

The vision is the desired future the charity is seeking to achieve. For example, the vision of a homelessness charity might be:

> A society where everyone has a safe place to call home.

The mission outlines what a charity is doing to achieve its vision and clearly differentiates it from others working in the same field. For example, the same homelessness charity's mission might be:

> To provide emergency shelter for homeless people.
>
> To advocate for and advise people facing a housing crisis.
>
> To campaign for more affordable homes.

To clarify the purpose of any fundraising plan, it is necessary to have a clear and common understanding of your charity's vision and mission and the strategic aims the organisation has set to achieve these.

Figure 2.2 illustrates a typical strategic structure within an organisation. The objectives and strategies of a community fundraising department sit within the intermediate level of an organisation. The intermediate level of an organisation includes fundraising and other divisional, departmental, regional, service and campaign functions (which vary depending on the size and/or complexity of the organisation).

FIGURE 2.2 HOW THE ELEMENTS OF STRATEGIC DIRECTION FIT TOGETHER[6]

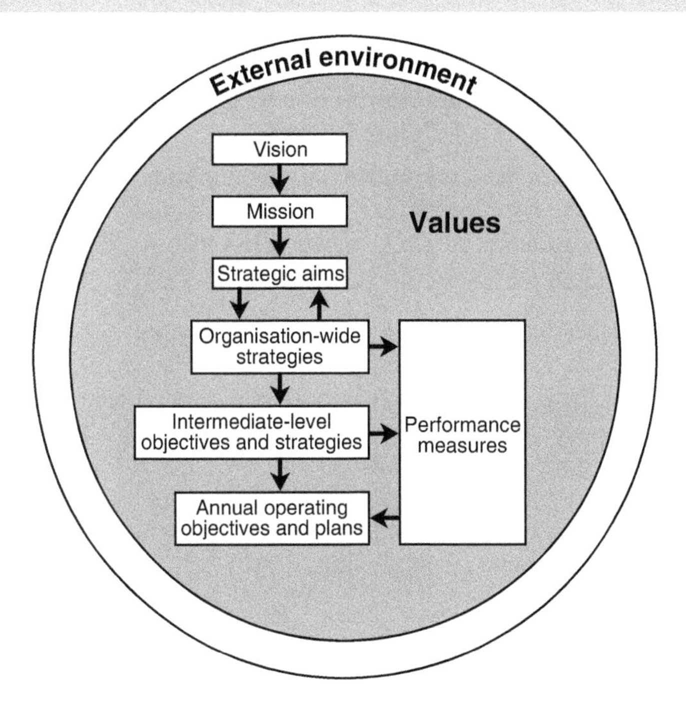

Strategic aims

The main aim of any fundraising strategy will be to facilitate the achievement of the organisation's strategic aims. The strategic aims specify the organisation's intended outcomes (and the timeframes within which they are to be achieved). For example, these might be around:

- improving the quality and impact of the organisation's current services and programmes for its beneficiaries;
- expanding the organisation's services into new areas of work;
- influencing the public and/or policymakers on issues related to the cause.

There should be performance measures (for example, key performance indicators (KPIs)) at this level of the strategy. (See also page 91 for details on using KPIs for programme-level objectives.)

Intermediate objectives

As well as strategic aims, an organisation has intermediate objectives, i.e. its corresponding divisional, departmental, regional, service-level and/or campaign objectives. Intermediate objectives are the means to achieve the strategic aims and are set around:

- **developing organisational capabilities:** for example, investing in research and development or investing in infrastructure, such as new buildings or equipment;
- **differentiating the organisation from others:** for example, investing in branding or changing the marketing strategy;
- **increasing independence and improving sustainability:** for example, decreasing dependency on particular funders (or reducing over-reliance on a single source of income), growing unrestricted income, building up reserves or raising more regular long-term funding.

Some organisations combine their strategic aims and the means of achieving them (i.e. their intermediate objectives). However, it is important to recognise that the ultimate goal is not raising money, increasing capacity and so on; instead, it is what you are trying to achieve by raising those funds and making those improvements.

The strategic aims and top-level objectives are the context within which you can determine what type of income your fundraising programme needs to generate, including:

- **unrestricted income:** funds that can be spent on any activities that further your organisation's mission;
- **restricted income:** funds that have been raised and must be used for a specific purpose – these could be towards either capital or revenue costs.

Once these wider organisational objectives are clear, both the overall fundraising objectives and then your specific community fundraising objectives can start to be formulated. These, however, must be informed by an audit of the external and internal environments in which your community fundraising is operating. This chapter focuses on carrying out an audit through the lens of community fundraising, but the same process should be undertaken for all strands of your organisation's fundraising programme.

The fundraising audit

The fundraising audit helps you to understand how well your community fundraising is currently performing and all the factors that might impinge upon your future fundraising success. As such, this is arguably the most important stage of the planning process. The process of auditing requires that you research, analyse and evaluate the trends and issues that have an impact on the capacity of your organisation to develop and deliver community fundraising both now and in the medium-term and long-term future.

The fundraising audit process

The audit involves analysing the external environment you are operating in and the previous and current performance of your community fundraising. This allows you to evaluate the appropriateness and effectiveness of your community fundraising in relation to the external environment and your internal capacity. (See figure 2.3 for a breakdown of the elements of the external and internal audits.) The following sections outline this process which mainly involves undertaking secondary research and analysis of internal data and practice. It may also require additional primary research to fill in some information gaps you might identify about supporters' needs, interests and motivations.

FIGURE 2.3 THE INTERNAL AND EXTERNAL AUDIT PROCESSES

Types of research

Before considering what research you need to carry out for your fundraising audit, it is useful to review the types of research methodology.

Secondary research

Research based on secondary sources is research based on existing data that has not been collected specifically for your current purposes. This includes both internal and external sources, such as:

- previous analyses of the data you hold on your database;
- any previous analyses of data from your website and social media presence (including Google Ads trends and influencer research sources such as Traackr.com and BuzzSumo.com);
- internal management reports;
- academic or sector sources;
- competitor data;
- government research sources (including census data).

Owing to the cost of carrying out primary research (see below) and the amount of time it takes, most of the research that you carry out in your fundraising audit will be secondary research.

Primary research

Primary market research is original research that doesn't use any existing data either from outside or inside your organisation. Primary research is conducted to answer specific questions that you weren't able to answer in the secondary research phase. For instance, you can carry out primary market research on your supporters to gain additional information on their demographics, event experience, motivations to volunteer, etc.

With permission from supporters you have communicated with, information from primary research may be integrated into your database and, when used at a later date, becomes internal secondary research.

If you carry out primary research, you will need to consider whether your charity or a third party will collect the data and how it will be collected (i.e. which channels you will use). Note that under the Code of Fundraising Practice you are responsible for ensuring any third parties you use comply with data-protection legislation (see chapter 5).

Qualitative research

Qualitative research explores people's ideas, preferences, feelings, emotions and motivations. You can use this method to ask why people support your organisation, to elicit ideas for new initiatives or to gain views and opinions on artwork, messages and creative content. By its nature, qualitative research is not statistically valid generalised data, but rather data on the subjective perspectives and attitudes of those interviewed. Qualitative research can also generate hypotheses to test on the wider population of supporters to see what proportion of that population share such views. You can conduct qualitative research by using open-ended questions in face-to-face situations, such as in-depth interviews or focus groups with small groups of individuals, or via telephone interview. You can also conduct ongoing qualitative research by following up unsolicited feedback from supporters.

Quantitative research

Quantitative research measures the incidence of opinions or supporter characteristics. It seeks 'yes or no' answers to questions, or records a person's judgement of their own preferences on a given scale (for instance, how much they agree with a given statement on a scale of 1 to 10). You can use quantitative methods to find out your supporters' demographic characteristics (age, gender, occupation, income, family size, etc.), communication preferences, preferred event location, views on the affordability of different events, etc. This data is collected via surveys that use structured, closed questions. The surveys can be carried out online, by post, face to face or on the telephone. Low-cost quantitative email survey tools, such as SurveyMonkey, enable fast and easy analysis.

Some common methods of regularly gaining new quantitative data from your supporters might include:

- offering well-timed online surveys at different stages of an event experience – for instance, pre-event surveys (to find out where the supporter heard about the event, or rate how easy they found the registration process, etc.) and post-event surveys (to find out how the supporter would score the quality of support, on-the-day logistics, etc.);
- sending annual surveys to identify supporters' interest in the charity's work and satisfaction with their relationship with it.

The external audit

1. Research into the macro environment

Macro environmental factors are major external forces which are beyond your organisation's control. They are the socio-cultural, technological, economic, environmental, political, legal and ethical influences and trends which, although not specific to the fundraising market, affect and shape the context in which fundraising operates. They may influence your community fundraising either positively or negatively, posing both opportunities for and threats to your future success. For example, an economic downturn is out of your control, but you will need to consider the potential impact of lower levels of disposable income among the public when, for example, setting event fees, anticipating average sponsorship levels, and predicting merchandise sales and collection returns.

Your charity will need to assess the potential impact of these macro factors, which together are abbreviated as STEEPLE (as shown in table 2.1).

TABLE 2.1 STEEPLE FACTORS

Socio-cultural	Changes in: • demographics; • social attitudes and values; • people's behaviour; • civic participation; • the shape of communities; • the formation of families; • patterns of working.
Technological	The influence of technological developments on behaviours and fundraising techniques, including: • contactless payments; • live streaming; • virtual reality; • wearable technology; • AI and mobile technology.

Economic	Trends in: • wealth; • disposable income; • employment; • consumer spending; • taxes; • inflation; • wage rises; • insurance costs; • investment returns; • new or declining industries.
Environmental	Changes in: • weather patterns (for instance, climate change may have an impact on outdoor events programmes); • renewable energy sources; • use of the countryside (such as access rights); • recycling and infrastructure (such as transport systems, leisure and park facilities).
Political	Developments in: • political make-up of national or international governments; • local and national government funding priorities; • leaving the European Union. Changes of mayors, county and parish councillors, etc.

Legal	Changes to fundraising regulation and to legislation that affects fundraising practice, such as: • data protection and privacy; • Gift Aid; • event licence requirements; • health and safety laws (see 'Legislation and regulations governing community fundraising' on page 54 for a summary of the legal and regulatory environment in which community fundraising operates).
Ethical	The concerns and moral values that affect how charities and fundraising are perceived and judged, such as how charities are seen to: • depict their beneficiaries (do they portray them with dignity, for instance?); • use funds; • depict event participants; • treat volunteers; • balance participant benefit with beneficiary benefit; • apply fundraising tactics (are they seen to excessively pressure donors, for example?); • use third-party suppliers (are they paying overly high fees?).

When conducting your STEEPLE analysis, you should use secondary research findings (research that has already been undertaken) rather than just opinion or assumptions to identify trends that are relevant to your organisation. Once you have done that, the likely impacts of these trends can be evaluated based on your judgement and experience.

Macro trend research

Some examples of useful sources of secondary research on macro trends include:

- Office of National Statistics data (www.ons.gov.uk)
- YouGov polls (https://yougov.co.uk/results)

- British Chambers of Commerce economic surveys (www.britishchambers.org.uk/page/policy-and-media-centre/policy-reports-publications)
- NatCen research (http://natcen.ac.uk), including the British Social Attitudes surveys (www.bsa.natcen.ac.uk) and NHS health surveys for England, Scotland and Wales (https://digital.nhs.uk/data-and-information); the Northern Ireland health surveys are produced by the Northern Irish Department of Health (www.health-ni.gov.uk)
- Academic studies, such as research into public attitudes and social trends
- Local council surveys – check the relevant borough's website for details on what is available, such as annual surveys of residents

To help you keep track of the various trends, impacts and research sources, and the priority or importance of each trend, it is helpful to put STEEPLE results into a table format. Under each STEEPLE heading, list all the trends you have identified as having a potential impact and the nature of the impact. While some trends might be common to all charities undertaking community fundraising, others will be unique to your organisation and type of community fundraising. Table 2.2 features just one example trend and one reference (which has been fictionalised) under each heading and focuses on the example of a local hospice's community events programme. Your own STEEPLE analysis should include as many trends as are relevant to your community fundraising under each heading. You can then prioritise these trends based upon which you think are likely to have the greatest impact on your future success.

To confidently base your decisions on the results of research, it is wise to have at least two (preferably more) credible research sources that separately replicate the same findings. Avoid intermediaries such as newspaper articles or blog posts – it is safer and more accurate to go to the source of the research, such as a report by an official association or an article in a professional or scientific journal. You can also take into account the opinions of experts regarding the likely impact of governmental or other changes (for example, the opinions of people from think tanks or from official national bodies, which in the case of our hospice example might include Hospice UK).

TABLE 2.2 EXAMPLE STEEPLE RESULTS

STEEPLE heading	Trend (fictionalised)	Impact	Reference (fictionalised)	Priority of trend: ranked from 1 (high) to 5 (low)
Socio-cultural	56% of people say they have become more health-conscious in the past year.	Potential of greater interest in health-promoting mass participation events and activities. An opportunity to engage more participants.	healthinsights journal.com	3
Technological	There was a 90% increase in contactless transactions in 2019; 65% of all transactions are now made contactlessly.	More people will be looking to give contactlessly at events. Currently the charity does not have contactless collecting tins and is therefore missing out on some potential donations.	UKpayments association.com	1
Economic	Young people are spending ever-higher proportions of their income on rent or saving for deposits in the future.	Ongoing pressure on disposable income for the charity's core group of event participants may negatively affect both ticket sales and sponsorship income.	government statistics.gov	4
Environmental	Climate change researchers predict that the capacity for floods in the UK in the next 100 years (from 2018) is approximately 40% higher than it was in the previous 100 years.	Increased flooding could disrupt outdoor fundraising events, leading to cancellation.	climatechange journal.co.uk	4
Political	Changes to NHS staff pay bands are predicted to result in a 10% rise in nurses' salaries over the next six years.	There may be additional pressure to meet this shortfall through fundraising from the community. Funding higher pay for nurses may not be appealing to our supporters, whose own wages may be stagnant.	healthcare.org	2
Legal	Changes to the Licensing Act will affect temporary event notices.	This may reduce the number of events the charity is able to hold on unlicensed premises.	legal commission. org.uk	1
Ethical	The public has significant concerns about trusting charities with their data.	We may have increasing difficulty gathering sufficient data to tailor event opportunities to participants' interests.	trustedsurveys.gov	2

2. Research into competitors

In the UK there are hundreds of thousands of charities and local organisations, all competing for fundraising participants and volunteers. While you cannot do anything about the presence of competitors, by understanding their modus operandi you can learn from their successes and failures and start to identify how you might differentiate your fundraising activities and proposition from theirs. Conversely, you might notice ways in which your charity might usefully collaborate with another organisation.

The first step is to define who your competitors are and which types of competitor are most relevant to your organisation:

- **Geographic:** other charities competing for participants from the same communities as your charity. These might be local charities or national charities with a local presence.
- **Size:** your charity's performance as it compares to organisations of a similar size and stature that run similar events and activities.
- **Cause:** your charity's presentation of its cause to attract participants versus how other organisations serving the same cause present their cause and their effectiveness in doing so.
- **Size and cause:** some sectors, such as hospices and air ambulances, can benchmark themselves against organisations in the same field that are both of a similar size and address a similar cause. As these organisations tend to operate within defined catchment areas, they may not be competing locally but will be using similar fundraising methods, resources and core propositions. Organisations such as hospices often work co-operatively to share best practice and learning.
- **Sector leaders:** how your charity measures up to leading organisations in the sector. These organisations often provide a source of learning due to the depth of their experience or the quality and originality of their ideas. Usually, but not exclusively, these are larger organisations which have the resources to innovate and test new ideas – smaller charities might then adapt their ideas or learn from them.
- **Commercial organisations:** how private organisations running local events and activities compete with your events and activities. Depending on the range of community fundraising activities you undertake, this could include music festivals, outdoor cinemas and sports events without a fundraising element.

Once you have selected the criteria by which you define your competition, you will need to gather and analyse information about your competitors. Ask yourself the following three questions.

How well is their community fundraising performing?

Each income stream should be considered separately – for example, local events, fundraising groups, schools, collections, centrally run mass participation activities, DIY initiatives, and third-party groups.

- How has each organisation's income performed over the past three to five years?
- Are they investing in particular activities, more staff or improved infrastructure?
- What expenditure and ROI (return on investment) are they achieving? (See page 85 for details on how to calculate ROI.)
- Are participant numbers or volunteers rising or falling, and what is the trend in average sponsorship values?

What are your competitors' ambitions?

Which areas of fundraising are targets for growth? A competitor may be willing to share this information in discussion articles and presentations. When this is not the case, you need to ascertain what can be inferred from changes in their activity, such as increased staff recruitment, a drive for more volunteers or a shift in activities being promoted. Once these ambitions are understood, how might they impact on your own future plans?

What strategies and tactics are they engaged in now, and what have they committed to for the future?

For example:

- What recruitment methods, engagement techniques, types of support and ways of recognising supporters are your competitors using?
- Who are their audiences?
- How distinctive is their fundraising?
- What types of events and activities do they promote and how?
- How are your competitors using social media (Twitter, Facebook, Pinterest, etc.) to promote their fundraising?
- What range and quality of online and physical resources do they have available to support their fundraising?
- What online and mobile giving methods are they using?

- How do they recruit and support volunteers?
- What can you learn from their successes and failures?

Sources of competitor (and collaborator) information include competitors' own websites; annual reports; benchmarking studies by organisations such as the Institute of Fundraising and other umbrella charities; conferences; the trade press; and networking and professional groups, such as the Institute of Fundraising's Community Fundraising and Event Managers' Forum special interest groups.

Becoming a charity version of a mystery shopper is another useful way of understanding your competitors' tactics. You can do this by requesting information from them, signing up to their email newsletters, joining their Facebook pages, tracking their Twitter feeds, reading their blogs, requesting information, or even directly experiencing their activities by participating in an event or volunteering.

Examining competitors in this way enables you to consider your own organisation's relative strengths and weaknesses, the threats competitors might pose and the opportunities that emerge from investigating your competitors' successes and failures.

3. External market research

To understand the opportunities and threats in your area of fundraising, it is vital to get to know the trends across the fundraising markets in which you operate. The internal audit (see page 46) looks at the behaviour of those in the market who have already supported you, while this section analyses the overall behaviour of the market.

What is a market?

In a fundraising context, a market is a group of supporters you are seeking to recruit or retain. In community fundraising, you may have multiple markets (schools, young people, small businesses, membership groups, volunteers, charity events, hobby groups, etc.). You will need to understand each of these markets before you are able to determine which activities (or further activities) and approaches might be the most appropriate and appealing to them.

External market research can help you to identify:

- whether the market is growing;
- the value of the events and activities within the market;

- the different segments in the market and whether they are performing differently;
- what activities these different segments prefer;
- what the characteristics, motivations, preferences and interests of each market segment are;
- where and when the different segments participate;
- what methods they use to fundraise.

Having a well-documented story of a market's activities:

- uncovers the market trends that inform which activities and relationships to invest in;
- helps you to predict who is likely to support particular organisations and activities and therefore identify potential new markets;
- equips you with the information needed to identify the right people to target and tailor communications to meet their motivations, needs and levels of engagement.

Once you have gained an understanding of the trends, you can evaluate the best way to respond to them. For example, research shows that one of the biggest challenges fundraising event participants face is not knowing how to fundraise towards their target.[7] This information would indicate an opportunity to improve the materials and advice your charity might provide to help participants to raise funds more effectively.

This understanding is crucial because organisations with a supporter-centric approach to event planning – that is, they design their events based on insight into participants' motivations and expectations – tend to run the most successful events.[8]

Market trend research

There are a number of secondary sources of information on market trends. The following are some examples.

Websites and blogs

- *Blackbaud Europe Resource Hub* (http://hub.blackbaud.co.uk)
- *Charity Digital News* (www.charitydigitalnews.co.uk)
- *Civil Society* (www.civilsociety.co.uk)
- *Eventbrite* (www.eventbrite.co.uk/blog)

- *The Guardian* voluntary sector network (www.theguardian.com/voluntary-sector-network)
- *International Journal of Nonprofit and Voluntary Sector Marketing*
- *JustGiving* (http://blog.justgiving.com)
- *Third Sector* (www.thirdsector.co.uk)
- *UK Fundraising* (www.fundraising.co.uk)

Organisations

- Charities Aid Foundation (www.cafonline.org)
- Directory of Social Change (www.dsc.org.uk)
- Institute of Fundraising (www.institute-of-fundraising.org.uk)
- NCVO (www.ncvo.org.uk)
- nfpSynergy (https://nfpsynergy.net)
- SOFII (www.sofii.org)
- Event agencies, such as massive (www.wearemassive.co.uk) and Burnett Works (http://burnettworks.co.uk)
- Universities, such as the University of Kent's Centre for Philanthropy (www.kent.ac.uk/sspssr/philanthropy) and the University of Plymouth's Hartsook Centre for Sustainable Philanthropy (www.plymouth.ac.uk/schools/plymouth-business-school/centre-for-sustainable-philanthropy)

Academic research publications

- *Chronicle of Philanthropy* (www.philanthropy.com)
- *International Journal of Nonprofit and Voluntary Sector Marketing* (https://onlinelibrary.wiley.com/journal/1479103X)
- *Journal of Nonprofit & Public Sector Marketing* (www.tandfonline.com/loi/wnon20)
- *Nonprofit Quarterly* (https://nonprofitquarterly.org)

The internal audit

While the external audit identifies the opportunities for and threats to your community fundraising activities, the internal audit examines and analyses the performance of all the elements of your community fundraising activities and your organisation's capacity to effectively respond to the opportunities and threats identified. This will help you to then set your objectives (as outlined in chapter 3) and determine which products and experiences are most appropriate for which supporters and how you will need to present and communicate these.

Broadly speaking, there are five elements to the internal audit (see figure 2.3).

1. Assessing your fundraising performance

Two factors are necessary for evaluating fundraising performance:

- direct comparison between how much each fundraising method is generating and the cost of achieving each result (i.e. the ROI of your fundraising activities);
- comparison of current performance with prior years' results to determine whether or not results are being matched or improved.

To gather information on your department's fundraising performance, you will need historical management accounts and finance reports, and you will also need to generate reports from your database.

Understanding the past performance of each fundraising activity will indicate what has previously worked well (or not so well). Each fundraising activity, campaign or product needs to be evaluated using appropriate metrics to plot key trends and the type of insight they might provide. Table 2.3 lists some of the metrics you can use.

TABLE 2.3 METRICS FOR EVALUATING COMMUNITY FUNDRAISING PRODUCTS

Metric	**Insight** **Allows you to evaluate whether the activity is:**
Gross income	In growth or decline *How much are people prepared to give or how much can they raise (whether through ticket sales, sponsorship, purchases, etc.)? You can analyse this by trialling different pricing or target levels.*
Net income	Profitable

Metric	**Insight** **Allows you to evaluate whether the activity is:**
Cost	Becoming more or less expensive
ROI (net and gross)	Efficient *Could this be improved? How does it compare with competition and industry benchmarks? (See page 85 for details on how to calculate ROI.)*
Number of participants	Attracting enough people and meeting participants' needs *If numbers are increasing, this implies the activity meets with approval. Also, understanding who participants are lets you know whom to ask again.*
Average gift/sponsorship values	Appealing enough *If average values are falling, this could suggest that the event is becoming less appealing. Do supporters need more information and help to raise funds? Do people understand your charity's case for support? (See page 77.) Do you give them a suggested target? Is it clear how the funds raised will benefit the cause?*
Number of new participants/donors	Effective at widening the supporter base *Are new supporters the same or different from existing supporters?*
Number of repeat participants	Effective at engaging and retaining support *Do some activities encourage repeat support more than others? Does loyalty vary across supporter groups? For instance, do some types of supporter give higher-than-average contributions of time and money? What might be the reasons for this? How does your supporters' level of commitment reflect on the quality of your stewardship, thanking and volunteer retention programmes?*
Other types of support	Encouraging supporters to move on to other types of support *Do some activities inspire supporters to engage in further support more than other activities? Who is most likely to volunteer, organise or lead an event or activity?*

Metric	Insight Allows you to evaluate whether the activity is:
Response rates of different segments (including new and repeat supporters)	Appealing to different types of participant or volunteer *How many non-responses, attending or not attending responses, etc., have you received for different groups? How do teams behave differently from individuals?*
Response rates from different communication methods	Appropriate to the target audience *Do your communication methods achieve the desired impact? Which messages generate the best response? How do supporters react to different forms of communication? Are some types of supporter more or less responsive to communications than others? What digital content do supporters tend to share? Do supporters understand your communications and do they have an easy way to respond? (For more detail on insight into supporters' response to communications, see page 52.)*
Average cost per gift (new and repeat)	Effective and efficient *How do your various recruitment methods perform against one another?*
Average cost per new supporter	Effective and efficient *Are some supporters more expensive to recruit than others?*
Number of Gift Aid sign-ups	Maximising tax-effective income *How well are you explaining the value of Gift Aid and ease of sign-up?*
Lifetime value (see also page 85)	Generating long-term supporters *How well are you retaining and developing the community fundraisers you are recruiting?*
Incremental permission value (the value over time of each supporter's consent)	Encouraging consent for future communications *How many supporters can you contact again? How much trust do they have in how you will use their data? What is your level of compliance in respecting supporters' wishes?*

If your charity has not captured the information it needs for this analysis or does not have the means of extracting it from its database, you will need to identify this in itself as a weakness, as an inability to track and evaluate performance is a barrier to informed decision-making.

These metrics can then be compared to data from competitors and market trends. However, when making comparisons, bear in mind that a charity's performance will differ depending on how established the fundraising activity is, the nature of the cause, and the location, size and awareness of your charity – you need to consider whether you are comparing like for like. For instance, while ROI is a particularly helpful and common benchmarking metric, it is also imperfect because different organisations might include different costs in their data.

Increasingly, charities also measure the longer-term and more holistic nature of their relationships with supporters – for example, supporter satisfaction, lifetime value, percentage of opt-ins by channel and loyalty scores.

> 'Our lifetime value work feeds in non-financial actions as well as financial contributions to include campaigning, volunteering and networked contributions, so that we are considering the total value of our supporter's engagement.'
>
> Joe Jenkins, Director of Fundraising and Supporter Engagement, The Children's Society[9]

For details on how to calculate ROI and LTV, see page 85.

2. Understanding your supporters

Who supports you and how?

Understanding your current fundraising performance requires insight into who currently supports your community fundraising and how.

Your starting point will be to analyse the data you already hold in your database as a result of supporters' previous engagement. The breadth of your data will depend on what you have judged is necessary for your organisation to collect and on the permissions you have sought and received. (See chapter 5 for details on how to gather, seek permission for and store this data.)

It is helpful to analyse this information using the following categorisations:

- **Demographics:** Who takes part in your activities? What is their age, gender, socio-economic group, family size, income, religion, ethnicity, occupation, education level and so on?
- **Geography:** Do your supporters live or work in particular areas?
- **Psychographics:** What are your supporters' values, lifestyles, hobbies, beliefs, and social, political and cultural attitudes?

- **Attitudes to your organisation:** What motivated your supporters to take part in one of your activities? What experiences are they seeking? Do they have a personal link to your cause? What benefits are they seeking from participation? What part or which aspects of your organisation's work do they value the most?

- **Behaviour:** One of the most important aspects of supporters' behaviour is how engaged they are. Does loyalty vary? In other words, how do your supporters' average contributions of time and money differ and what might be the reasons for this? Understanding supporter behaviour in terms of the **recency** (time elapsed since last gift or activity), **frequency** (how often they fundraise in a given period) and **value** (donation or sponsorship amount) of their gifts – known as RFV analysis – can help you to identify which supporters are most engaged with your organisation. (For details on RFV analysis, see page 72.) To thoroughly understand supporters' behaviour you also need to consider the following questions:

  – Which types of activity have they undertaken?

  – How do they sign up for events? When do they sign up?

  – How much do they raise? How do they raise it?

  – Do demographic differences influence their behaviour? For example, do more young supporters sign up to your online events than older supporters?

  – What kinds of supporter introduce new supporters?

  – Who is most likely to volunteer, organise or lead an event or activity?

  – Do they fundraise alone or with family or friends in teams?

  – How do teams behave differently from individuals?

  – Do some groups raise more funds than others?

  – What do supporters share or like on social media?

  – How many participants drop out of events or volunteering and why?

  – How many achieve their fundraising target and, for those who don't, why not?

  – What other types of activity do they engage in?

Finding the answers to these types of question allows you to understand and describe your supporters by identifying your most engaged supporters, where they are located, which of your activities appeal to them the most, and (depending on the level of data you hold) what their motivations are for taking part. This in turn will help you to start to consider how well you are aligning with their motivations and meeting their needs. It will also raise questions about which other groups or types of people you are not yet engaging. Evaluating this data will help to inform how you might adapt existing products or develop new ones.

To gain a more complete picture of your most engaged supporters, you can combine RFV analysis (see page 72) with behavioural, geodemographic, psychographic and attitudinal data.

Consumer classification organisations

You can supplement this type of internal data on your supporters with information from external sources, which classify people based upon where they live. Geodemographic classifications are based on the principle that people living near each other, in a particular postcode area, are likely to share similar demographic, socio-economic and lifestyle factors. For example, similarities such as marital status, wealth indicators (including income and home type/location), number and age of any children, age of the adults in the household, and so on.

There are two commonly used consumer classification systems that offer geodemographic data: Acorn and Mosaic. Both these systems classify the entire population in the UK into different groups or types of people who share attributes based on key demographic variables and lifestyle characteristics. These systems' classification codes can be added to your supporter records and, by giving insights into people's demographic and lifestyle characteristics, can help you to analyse the types of activity that best fit a supporter's profile.[10]

In addition to these broader consumer classification companies, the Audience Agency is a charity that has a culture-specific segmentation system called Audience Spectrum, which can tell you how culturally engaged the people in your catchment area are on a scale of most engaged to least engaged and what types of cultural interest they have. The Audience Agency also has a free national audience data and development tool called Audience Finder, which helps organisations to find opportunities for audiences by building and exploring a picture of their audiences locally and nationally.[11]

When using third-party data, you will need to ensure that you have collected appropriate consent from supporters and carried out any necessary due diligence on the third parties themselves. (See 'Consent for collecting data for profiling and analytics' on page 166 for details.)

Gaining insight into supporters' response to communications

As well as understanding existing supporters' characteristics, you will need to assess how effectively you are communicating with them. Collecting data about your campaigns and about each of the communications you use to promote an activity will help you to identify how your supporters respond to different communications. This will help you to understand whether you are using the right channels to reach them and how effective your messages are (for details on how to develop effective communications, see chapter 4). For example:

- What response rates are different communications generating and what type of response (enquiry, sign-up, attendance, gift, etc.)?
- Are some supporters more or less responsive than others?
- How do they react to different forms of communication? That is, which channels and combination of channels (emails, social media, paid search, magazine inserts, etc.) do they respond to the most? (See page 108 for details on media channels.)
- Which online or offline channels create the most conversions and provide you with the most participants?
- Which messages generate the best response? That is, what type of content works best with which groups?
- What digital content do supporters currently tend to share and what other opportunities for social sharing might they seek?
- What are their preferred social media sites?
- Which online giving platforms do supporters prefer?
- Do demographic differences influence behaviour? For example, are women more likely to respond to email and men to text messages?
- What materials and support do they need? Do they prefer to receive information electronically (whether by email or downloading) or by post?
- What recognition do they want?

Whenever you send out a communication, you should allocate it a unique code. These codes will allow you to track responses on your database, and this will allow you to run reports to analyse who is responding to which communications and in what ways.

Additionally, as more communications and interactions are taking place in digital platforms such as social media, feeds from these are becoming ever more important. For example, Google Analytics is a free tool that you can use to analyse and monitor how people find and use your website. It records how many visitors you draw to your website, the number of page views and how long visitors spend on each page. It provides insights into visitors' demographics and geographical location, albeit at an overall level rather than an individual level. Review your website's Google Analytics to check for any trends – in particular your goal completions, if this function is set up.[12] Google's goals tool enables you to see, for example, how many people reached your event sign up page or where they might be dropping out (see 'Google Analytics' on page 146 for details).

You can also look at visitors by which channel they arrived on your site; for example, you can identify who clicked through via Twitter versus who clicked through from the emails you sent. As Google Analytics continually updates, it enables you to reconsider and potentially change your tactics depending on the results and trends you are seeing.

You can learn more about your audiences using social media sites' own analytics. These include Facebook Audience Insights, Instagram Insights (which is only available to accounts with business profiles and with high levels of engagement), Pinterest Analytics and Twitter Analytics. These all allow you to learn more about your followers' activities on those sites, including which of your pages, posts or tweets they like most, and also about their demographics and wider interests. (See 'Consent for collecting data for profiling and analytics' on page 166 for information on how you can do this lawfully.) The data you collect at this stage will later inform the communications tactics that you use (see chapter 4).

After completing this element of the internal audit, you may find you have gaps in your data and questions about your supporters and their behaviour that you are unable to answer. This may require you to undertake some additional primary research – either quantitative research (to track behaviours or find out more about your supporters' characteristics) or qualitative research (to better understand your supporters' motivations and feelings about your activities).

If, having reviewed your data, you aren't able to make any impactful decisions or take actions, ask yourself whether you are recording and reporting the right information.

3. Assessing your fundraising processes

All the processes that support community fundraising activities need to be assessed for efficiency, effectiveness and whether or not they are supporter-centric. Examples of which processes to evaluate include:

- data collection, processing and management;
- donation processing;
- cash handling;
- thanking procedures;
- fulfilment of materials;
- query handling;
- complaints procedures;
- event logistics;
- internal co-ordination with other departments.

You will also need to scrutinise whether each process is compliant with relevant legislation and the Code of Fundraising Practice.

Legislation and regulations governing community fundraising

Given the breadth of the activities undertaken within the portfolio of community fundraising, fundraisers need to be aware of the range of legislation and regulations that apply to their work. Fundraisers should ensure that they are familiar with both legal requirements and best practice, and these should form part of all community fundraisers' training programmes.

Fundraising in England, Wales and Northern Ireland is self-regulated but is overseen by the Fundraising Regulator. Fundraising self-regulation in Scotland is different from the system in place within England, Wales and Northern Ireland.

Fundraising by charities only registered in Scotland is subject to Scottish charity law and the Scottish system of self-regulated fundraising through the Scottish Fundraising Standards Panel. Fundraising undertaken by charities registered in England and Wales and in Scotland, but where the lead regulator for the charity is the Charity Commission in England and Wales, is regulated by the Fundraising Regulator. However, the Code of Fundraising Practice also applies in Scotland. As the Code of Fundraising Practice is reviewed and legislation updated, fundraisers should ensure they stay abreast of changes by signing up to the Fundraising Regulator's newsfeeds (www.fundraisingregulator.org.uk) and updates from the Institute of Fundraising (www.institute-of-fundraising.org.uk).

Each code also identifies the key legislation that applies to the different countries that comprise the UK.

The sections in the Code of Fundraising Practice which are particularly relevant to community fundraisers are:

1. Behaviour when fundraising
2. Responsibilities of charitable institutions and those who govern them
3. Processing personal date
4. Processing donations
5. Volunteers
6. Fundraising involving children
7. Professional fundraisers, commercial participators and partners
8. Collecting money or other property
9. Fundraising communications and advertisements
10. Digital
11. Events
12. Lotteries, prize competitions and free draws

4. Evaluating your organisation's characteristics

Research has found that charities which deliver 'great fundraising', defined as achieving transformational growth, are characterised by having the right teams, the right structure and the right culture.

To evaluate the effectiveness of your team, explore the answers to the following questions:[13]

- Do staff have the right skills?
- Are staff passionate about the cause and open to new ideas?
- Is the team well supported by the chief executive and senior management?
- Does the team have good relationships with any agencies it uses?
- Is there high staff turnover?

Similarly, for your organisational structure, consider:

- What is the balance between staff and volunteers?
- Are staff based in the right locations?
- Should community and events fundraising be integrated?
- Is there good communication between local and national teams?
- Is talent fostered through training and development?

And, for your organisation's culture:

- Is the organisation supportive of community fundraising?
- How well is community fundraising understood by the trustees and senior management?
- Is there a culture of learning and continual improvement?
- Do staff feel free (and are they encouraged) to problem-solve, ask for help and share learning?

5. Analysing your portfolio of products

The internal audit can generate a substantial amount of information, which can be used to help you assess which community fundraising products your charity should continue to invest in and what each activity's future performance might look like. Each product needs to be evaluated on an individual basis and in comparison to the whole portfolio of community fundraising activities to understand where its strengths and weaknesses may lie.

Product life-cycle analysis

Product life-cycle analysis is an established marketing concept[14] that illustrates the idea that products typically have a predictable life cycle. This relies on the idea that a product's existence is finite (i.e. it will stop being offered after it has served its purpose or is no longer viable) and that, as the product goes through stages of development, its profitability changes, as shown in figure 2.4.

The main function of life-cycle analysis is to help you plan ahead by highlighting how a product needs to be managed differently depending on which stage in the life cycle it is at. Each stage requires different strategies and tactics.

> A 'product' in the context of community fundraising can be defined as any distinct activity or campaign marketed to a specific group of supporters. This could be a form of collection (e.g. static), a particular event (e.g. annual fun run), a type of DIY fundraising activity (e.g. bake sales) or a specific mass participation campaign.

- At the **launch** stage, both income and profits are low owing to high set-up costs. During this period, marketing focuses on the need to raise awareness of the new product and to gain supporters or participants.
- At the **growth** stage, the number of people signing up increases and income grows. Profits start to grow but costs may still be high, particularly if other charities introduce similar products. At this stage it is

helpful to invest in ways of differentiating your products from others to target your supporters better.

- During the **maturity** phase, growth slows but costs drop and profit is stable. At this stage, marketing support may be reduced in order to cut costs or a charity may aim to cause the product to enter a **renewal** stage. This can be done by, for example, conducting market research to find new groups of people to target, redesigning the product or adding new features to it, or taking a fresh approach to positioning the product.
- Over time, as tastes and technology change and new products emerge, income and profits move into **decline**.

FIGURE 2.4 THE GENERIC PRODUCT LIFE CYCLE

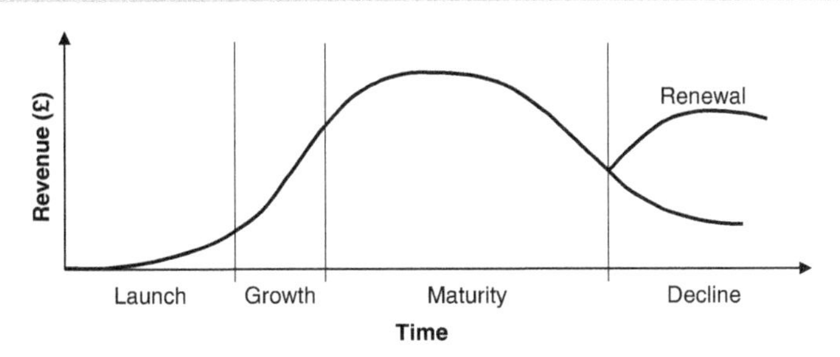

Product portfolio analysis: External attractiveness and internal appropriateness

To analyse the relative health of the community fundraising products in your portfolio you can evaluate each product by its attractiveness to participants (external attractiveness) and by how appropriate it is for the organisation to deliver (internal appropriateness).[15] This approach, created by Adrian Sargeant and Elaine Jay, adapts corporate portfolio analysis models, such as the Boston Consulting Group's classic growth-share matrix and the McKinsey matrix, for the charity sector.[16]

The factors against which you measure **external attractiveness** will depend on the nature of the activity and the insights you have gathered about your potential participants. You could include:

- relevance of the experience to participants;
- numbers of potential participants;
- perception of the cause and of your charity;
- ease of participation and uniqueness of the activity.

Internal appropriateness is determined by your organisation's capacity to deliver the product. Does it have the skills, resources, structure, contacts, profile, volunteers, budget and appetite to achieve the likely return?

Table 2.4 shows an example of the factors a charity might score to assess the external attractiveness and internal appropriateness of a local fun run. Once you have identified the relevant external and internal factors that determine your product's attractiveness and appropriateness, these can be scored. For example you might decide that a score of 10 would be where a product measures very well against an attractiveness/appropriateness factor, with a score of 1 being very poor.

Additionally, if some factors are considered to be more important than others as determinants of attractiveness/appropriateness, then they can be weighted accordingly. For example, if you have a total of three external factors and one is much more important than the other two, you might assign it a weighting of 50% and the other two weightings of 25% each. The weightings of your external and internal factors must each add up to 100% (as shown in the example in table 2.4).

Finally, if you are using weightings, you will need to calculate a total for each factor. This is done by applying the weighting to the attractiveness/appropriateness scores. For example, 25% of an attractiveness/appropriateness rating of 9 gives a final score of 2.25.

TABLE 2.4 EXTERNAL ATTRACTIVENESS AND INTERNAL APPROPRIATENESS OF ORGANISING A LOCAL FUN RUN

External factor	**Attractiveness score (1 = low; 10 = high)**	**Weighting**	**Final score**
Uniqueness	4	20%	0.8
Existing supporters' likely interest	8	40%	3.2
Potential supporters' interest	7	20%	1.4
Available routes	7	20%	1.4
Total score		**100%**	**6.80**
Internal factor	**Appropriateness score (1 = low; 10 = high)**	**Weighting**	**Final score**
Staff expertise	9	25%	2.25
Budget	8	25%	2
Marketing capacity	7	25%	1.75
Volunteer support	6	25%	1.5
Total score		**100%**	**7.50**

Once you have completed the scoring process, you can map each activity or product onto a matrix to determine whether it should:

- receive investment;
- receive further adaptation to improve its score;
- be divested due to lack of attractiveness and/or appropriateness.

The fun run scores 6.8 for external attractiveness and 7.5 for internal appropriateness, so it falls into the category of investment (shown as activity A in figure 2.5).

FIGURE 2.5 INTERNAL APPROPRIATENESS VERSUS EXTERNAL ATTRACTIVENESS MATRIX[17]

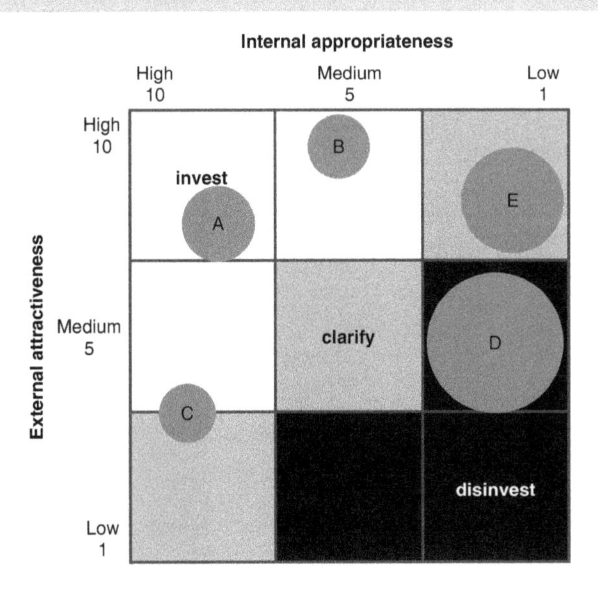

The level of risk within a portfolio of community fundraising products is associated not only with each product's attractiveness/ appropriateness but also with the relative value of each community fundraising product. Figure 2.5 shows a set of activities depicted using circles, where the size of each circle is proportional to the percentage of total fundraising income it generates. In this example, activity D generates a large percentage of income but is in fact both internally and externally unattractive. This model indicates the need to replace this product by focusing on the activities nearer to the top left-hand corner (A, B and C) as well as revisiting activity E to assess whether it might be tweaked to improve its internal appropriateness or external attractiveness, or otherwise whether it should be discontinued if it is not feasible for it to be improved.

Pulling the external and internal audits together

After completing all of this research and analysis, you need to filter the information gathered in order to focus on the most crucial and relevant elements that will affect your future fundraising. It is this analysis that will help to inform realistic objective setting.

Summarising the fundraising audit

Before identifying strengths, weaknesses, opportunities and threats (as outlined in the following section), it is useful to list the most salient findings from your fundraising audit broken up by the sections of your research. This will help you to filter your initial research results. It will also help to ensure that you don't overly focus on one area at the expense of any others that may contain equally important factors. Table 2.5 illustrates some examples for a fictional hospice.

TABLE 2.5 FILTERING YOUR FUNDRAISING AUDIT RESEARCH RESULTS

		Positives	Negatives
External audit	Macro environment	• A catchment area with some affluent and active communities with disposable income • A new trading estate due to open in 12 months' time (potential additional corporate partners) • Ageing population and need for hospice care creating greater awareness of funding needs and widening impact on the community	• GDPR (General Data Protection Regulation) may result in reduction in contactable supporters • Uncertainty over the economic impact of Brexit and disposable income • Local schools are fundraising for their own needs
	Competitors	• Option to collaborate on joint events	• Highly popular local children's charity recruiting similar DIY fundraisers
	Market trends	• Ongoing popularity of lower-value community fundraising events and activities • Growth in popularity of peer-to-peer fundraising over the past three years	• Fundraising participants report finding that their fundraising targets are set too high and they don't know how to start fundraising • Sector-wide drops in average sponsorship values

Internal audit	Fundraising performance	• Growth of community ambassador scheme by 30%, which has increased engagement within individuals' social networks and within schools	• Declining membership among friends group • Average sponsorship values have declined by 5% over the past two years
	Supporters	• Strong email list – produces 80% of our overall conversions • 20% of our audience who convert come from peer recommendations	• Low levels of social media engagement
	Fundraising processes	• Database of over 50,000 participants with compliant data management	• Limited database functionality for segmentation and automation • Collection tins do not facilitate cashless giving • Lack of integration of in-memory giving into community and events programme
	Organisational characteristics	• Trustee commitment to investment in innovation and digital marketing • Over 200 regular volunteers and a volunteer retention rate of 70% • An experienced events team and high retention of local community fundraising staff • Brand awareness at an all-time high	• Limited investment in the training of fundraising staff
	Portfolio of products	• Three newer products with medium or high external attractiveness	• Overdependence on one mature flagship event

SWOT analysis

SWOT analysis provides a simple tool for pulling together the findings of your audits to prioritise the opportunities you might exploit, the threats you need to account for, the weaknesses that you need to address and the strengths you can build on.

Strengths and weaknesses are identified from your internal audit and opportunities and threats are identified from your external audit. Once you have identified your strengths, weaknesses, opportunities and threats, you will need to decide how to prioritise their relative importance to your future planning. To help with this, ask yourself the following questions:

- **For each strength:** Based on your knowledge of the macro environment, your competitors and the market, how much competitive advantage does this strength give you?
- **For each weakness:** How much does this hinder your fundraising?
- **For each opportunity:** Is this an opportunity you have the strength or potential to exploit?
- **For each threat:** How seriously might this affect your ability to fundraise?

Consider how these factors will influence your future plan and number each factor to help you identify the most salient. Figure 2.6 offers an example of a SWOT analysis for a fictional hospice.

FIGURE 2.6 AN EXAMPLE SWOT PRIORITISATION MATRIX, WITH FACTORS NUMBERED IN ORDER OF IMPORTANCE TO THE CHARITY

Strengths (internal)	Weaknesses (internal)
1. Effective email communications that produce high levels of conversions. 2. Brand awareness at all-time high. 3. Over 200 regular volunteers and a volunteer retention rate of 70%. 4. Large database of over 50,000 supporters. 5. Experienced events team and high retention of local community fundraising staff 6. Trustee commitment to investment in innovation and digital marketing. 7. Growth of community ambassador scheme by 30%. 8. Good number of strongly performing products.	1. Limited database functionality for segmentation and automation. 2. Overdependence on one mature flagship event. 3. Declining membership among friends groups. 4. Lack of integration of in-memory giving into community and events programme. 5. Collection tins do not facilitate cashless giving. 6. Average sponsorship values have declined by 5% over the past two years. 7. Low levels of social media engagement. 8. Limited investment in fundraising training.
Opportunities (external)	**Threats (external)**
1. Ongoing popularity of lower-value community fundraising events and activities. 2. A catchment area with some affluent and engaged communities. 3. New trading estate due to open in 12 months' time. 4. Growth in popularity of peer-to-peer fundraising over the past three years. 5. Ageing population and need for hospice care creating greater awareness of funding needs and widening impact on the community. 6. Option to collaborate on joint events.	1. GDPR may result in reduction in contactable supporters. 2. Uncertainty over economic impact of Brexit and disposable income. 3. Sector-wide drop in average sponsorship values. 4. Local schools fundraising for their own needs. 5. Fundraisers report finding that their fundraising targets are set too high and they don't know how to start fundraising. 6. Highly popular local children's charity recruiting similar DIY fundraisers.

Conclusion

To develop a realistic and sustainable strategic plan for your community fundraising programme, you need to place it within the context of your organisation's overall strategy. It will then be informed by detailed research into the external environment that you are operating in and into your organisation's capacity to respond to potential opportunities and threats. Auditing your fundraising in this way will allow you to choose the right objectives, strategies and tactics to inspire the communities you are seeking to engage. As plans also need to be dynamic to be future-proofed, you need to continually monitor the trends and changes in the internal and external environments.

Notes

1 Estimated by THINK's Community Forum 2015 benchmarking survey, as reported by Tracy Griffin, *Making the Connection: Bring donors into your own community* [PDF], Commission on the Donor Experience, 2017, sofii.org/images/Articles/The-Commission-on-the-Donor-Experience/P11d-Community-FULL-PDF.pdf, p. 9, accessed 14 August 2018.
2 Paraphrased from *Charity Fundraising: A guide to trustee duties (CC20)* [PDF], Charity Commission, 7 June 2016, www.gov.uk/government/publications/charities-and-fundraising-cc20, p. 6.
3 Adrian Sargeant and Elaine Jay, *Fundraising Management: Analysis, planning and practice*, Abingdon, Routledge, 2014, p. 18, figure 2.1.
4 Gerry Johnson, Kevin Scholls and Richard Whittington, *Fundamentals of Strategy*, Harlow, Pearson Education, 2012, p. 13.
5 For more on setting an organisation-wide strategy, see Mike Hudson, *Managing Without Profit*, London, DSC, 2017, in particular chapters 3–6.
6 Mike Hudson, *Managing Without Profit*, London, DSC, 2017, p. 47.
7 *Closing the Loop* [PDF], Institute of Fundraising, 2015, www.institute-of-fundraising.org.uk/library/closing-the-loop/closing-the-loop-report-final.pdf, p. 18, accessed 10 September 2018.
8 Adrian Sargeant and Harriet Day, *Great Fundraising Events: From experience to transformation*, Plymouth, Hartsook Centre for Sustainable Philanthropy, Plymouth University, 2017.
9 *Consent Case Studies* [PDF], Fundraising Regulator, 2018, www.fundraisingregulator.org.uk/sites/default/files/2018-07/personal-info-guidance-case-studies.pdf, p. 32, accessed 29 June 2017.
10 For more information visit acorn.caci.co.uk and www.experian.co.uk/marketing-services/products/mosaic-uk.html.
11 See www.theaudienceagency.org/audience-spectrum and www.theaudienceagency.org/audience-finder for details.
12 See www.google.com/analytics/analytics/features.
13 Based on Adrian Sargeant and Jen Shang, *Great Fundraising: What makes fundraising truly great?* [PDF], Clayton Burnett, 2013, http://studyfundraising.com/wp-content/uploads/2016/07/Great-Fundraising.pdf, accessed 23 October 2018.

14 Gregory E. Osland, 'Origins and Development of the Product Life Cycle Concept', *Scholarship and Professional Work – Business*, no. 237, 1991, pp. 68–84, http://digitalcommons.butler.edu/cob_papers/237, accessed 23 October 2018.
15 Adrian Sargeant and Elaine Jay, *Fundraising Management: Analysis, planning and practice*, Abingdon, Routledge, 2014, p. 30.
16 For more details on corporate portfolio analysis models, see 'Strategic portfolio analysis' [web page], CEOpedia Management Online, 2018, https://ceopedia.org/index.php/Strategic_portfolio_analysis, accessed 25 October 2018.
17 Model adapted from Adrian Sargeant and Elaine Jay, *Fundraising Management: Analysis, planning and practice*, Abingdon, Routledge, 2014, p. 30.

CHAPTER THREE

Developing a community fundraising plan

Sam Rider

Introduction

Chapter 2 looked at the importance of researching the impact of external and internal environments on your community fundraising. It also examined how this research needs to inform the basis of any fundraising plan. This chapter discusses how to start using these findings to develop a strategic fundraising plan.

The basic purpose of a strategic plan is to clearly identify what you want to achieve, by when, with what supporters and activities, using what tactics and resources. The sections cover how to:

- set SMART (specific, measurable, achievable, relevant and timetabled) objectives;
- analyse which markets to target with which fundraising products;
- segment those markets;
- position your organisation and activities as distinct from your competition;
- create the elements of a tactical plan;
- present the investment case and develop budgets;
- schedule the plan;
- monitor performance and control activities and risk.

While there are clear stages to devising a plan, working through the planning process may raise additional questions about internal capacities, supporters or markets. Answering these may require additional secondary or primary research to add to the audit findings. You will need to review plans continually while you test your strategies and each element of your tactics. Tactics may need to be tweaked as you go along to ensure you are giving your supporters the most inspiring fundraising experience.

What do you want to achieve?

Setting community fundraising objectives

Having established as a result of your audit where you are now, it is possible to start setting objectives for what you want to achieve with each strand of your community fundraising programme. Objectives are the means by which success can be measured, and they articulate what will be achieved and at what cost. Fundraising objectives should address the following three issues:[1]

- the amount of funds raised (and type of funds);
- the categories of supporters or participants who will supply these funds;
- the acceptable costs or ROI for raising these funds.

The risk in writing objectives is that they can be too vague and therefore unmeasurable. Phrases such as 'increasing event income', 'growing numbers of DIY fundraisers', 'maximising volunteer support' and 'expanding collections' are all imprecise.

Objectives therefore need to be SMART (specific, measurable, achievable, relevant and timetabled):

- **Specific:** Each objective should focus on one group of supporters or type of activity. It is worth having separate objectives for new or repeat supporters, as the communication methods, acceptable response rates and average values may differ for these audiences.
- **Measurable:** Each objective should only use terminology that is quantifiable – for example, 'to increase fun run income by 10%', 'to recruit 1,000 new DIY fundraisers' or 'to establish three new friends groups'.
- **Achievable:** Objectives are only achievable if they are rooted in an understanding of the external environment that impacts on community fundraising and are matched to your organisation's capacity to deliver them.
- **Relevant:** Each objective should support the overall organisational objectives (such as a focus on growing unrestricted income) and the overall fundraising strategy (such as increasing support in particular locations or engaging younger supporters).
- **Timetabled:** The period over which the objectives should be achieved must also be included.

Any community fundraising objectives that you choose must be linked to an overall fundraising objective. An example of an overall fundraising objective, using the results from your overall fundraising audit, might be:

> To attract £5 million in unrestricted voluntary income by the end of the financial year at an ROI of 8:1.

Based on this overall fundraising objective, you would then know that the focus of your community fundraising objectives should be to maximise unrestricted income. Drawing on your audit findings your overall community fundraising objective might then be as follows:

> To raise £1 million in unrestricted income from community fundraising activities by the end of the financial year at an ROI of 5:1.

This objective would then be supported by specific objectives for each form of community fundraising activity your organisation is involved with. For example, a DIY fundraising objective might be:

> To raise £250,000 from DIY fundraising by signing up 420 participants at an ROI of 3:1 by [date].

For each objective you set, you will then need to decide on the strategies and tactics you will use to deliver it.

How you will get there

Setting strategies

Strategies are the broad means by which the objectives will be achieved. A fundraising plan usually requires decisions to be made on four key areas: the overall direction, segmentation, positioning and the case for support.[2] Under each of these headings is a tool or process you can use to help set the most appropriate strategies.

1. The overall direction: selecting products and audiences

A core strategic decision is how to grow income by optimising the range and reach of your community fundraising activities. Ansoff's matrix, as shown in figure 3.1, is a tool for brainstorming and evaluating which of your existing or new fundraising products you might offer to which markets to achieve each fundraising objective.

FIGURE 3.1 ANSOFF'S MATRIX

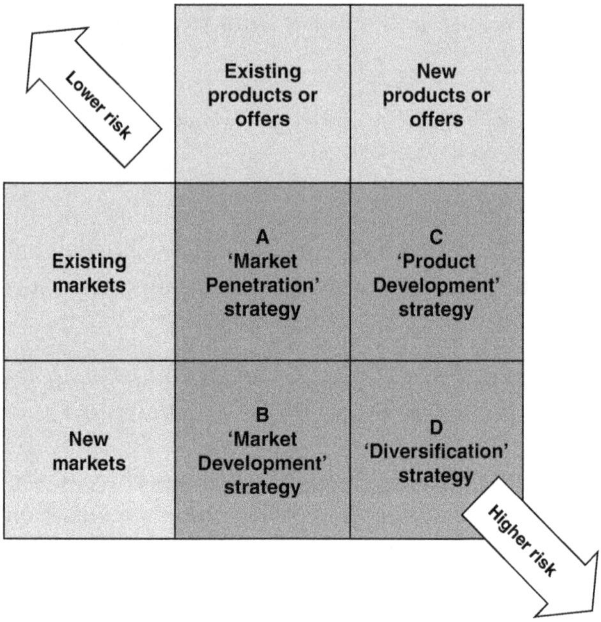

Lower risk

	Existing products or offers	New products or offers
Existing markets	A 'Market Penetration' strategy	C 'Product Development' strategy
New markets	B 'Market Development' strategy	D 'Diversification' strategy

Higher risk

Adapted and reprinted with permission from 'Strategies for Diversification' by H. Igor Ansoff, *Harvard Business Review*, September 1957.

Market penetration

In this first quadrant, market penetration, list all the products you currently offer to existing markets (or existing types of supporter) and consider how you might reach and sign up more people or organisations in those markets with these existing products. For example, you might already promote a specific fundraising product to primary schools and want to increase the number of primary schools signing up to that product. This is the least risky option as you already have experience of fundraising with primary schools as your existing market and delivering this product. However, it is not without risk, as relying only on this option would mean that you would not be looking for innovation to draw on should this market become saturated.

Product development

Product development involves creating or adopting new products to solicit funds from a market you already fundraise from. For example, you may already organise a night-time walk, marketed to women aged 25 to 45. Attendance is dropping so, based upon your audit research, you decide to introduce your first mud run to this group. This is a new product because it is new to this group of supporters and you have not promoted it to this particular existing market before. It is more risky than a market penetration strategy, as response to a new product cannot be guaranteed, but the choice is informed by the insight you have gathered on these supporters through your audit and research.

Market development

Within the market development quadrant, you assess whether to target markets new to your fundraising programme with a product or activity you already offer to existing supporters. This may be a new market geographically speaking (a new city or region) or new organisations or groups of people you have not previously fundraised from. For example, you might hold Santa runs in one town and decide to roll these out to three new towns. Alternatively, you might decide to offer your schools fundraising product (which you currently offer to primary schools) to a new market of secondary schools. Here the risk lies in not knowing how well your tried-and-tested product will work in a new area or with a new group of supporters.

Diversification

Diversification is the most risky option. This is where a new product is designed for a previously untargeted group of supporters. Sometimes, this may be the only option available for growth. It is possible that all your current markets are saturated with a wide portfolio of your existing fundraising products. Therefore, diversification is the only logical route forward to achieve new income.

Putting them all together

The risks associated with each of these four strategic directions need to be balanced against the potential benefits and informed by the full range of your audit findings. For example:

- If your market research identified that certain products are dropping in popularity and your internal audit found that the income you are generating from these products is falling, you might select a product development strategy.
- If you face significant competition within a particular market you are currently targeting and your internal analysis found weaknesses in your capacity to address this, you might consider new markets for your product through a market development strategy.

- If your portfolio analysis found that one of your products has low scores for external and internal attractiveness, you might consider diversification.

Usually charities pursue a mixture of options within their community fundraising programme to balance their risk.

2. Market segmentation strategies

Once you have selected, using Ansoff's matrix, the combination of markets and products you will use to achieve an objective, you need to ensure that each product is designed and promoted in a way that appeals to existing and potential supporters on a personal level.

As explored in chapter 1, within a chain of contributors, different people may have different motivations and different corresponding roles (see 'Motivations for participating in community fundraising' on page 9). Even when they have the same role, their needs might still differ. Being supporter-centric means identifying these motivations and needs by paying attention to how your supporters behave, why they participate, how they like to be communicated with, how much they raise, what support they need, when they want to hear from you, which communication channels they prefer, what recognition they want and so on. This is the type of data you will have already gathered during the information collection phase of your internal audit process, as well as from secondary research undertaken to understand the particular community fundraising market you are focusing on (see chapter 2).

The information you have gathered will allow you to identify the types of experience different groups of supporters are seeking and the communication messages and methods that they will find most appealing. By ensuring that the way you engage with your supporters matches their motivations and needs, you can build more meaningful relationships that can improve response rates, loyalty, peer recruitment, and average sponsorship or donation values.

Market segmentation is the process of breaking your markets down into groups of people where each group shares common properties. These properties represent the characteristics, needs and interests that are most likely to influence participation and active profitable fundraising. Segmentation therefore enables you to tailor your communications and activities to maximise the relevance of your activities and messages for a specific group of supporter.

Segmentation is only necessary where groups of supporters are distinct enough to require a discrete communications approach. For example, you may find that your audience has such similar needs and motivations that you can approach everybody in the same way. (For details on how to verify your segments' validity, see number 6 in 'The six-step segmentation process' below.)

Don't forget, as explained in chapter 5, the collection and use of data about your supporters must comply with the legal rules and regulation in this area, including GDPR, PECR and the Code of Fundraising Practice. This includes segmentation and similar work.

By returning to the results of your internal and external audit, you can identify the characteristics that are most likely to influence people's participation in the product or activity you selected to achieve your fundraising objective. These characteristics are the variables by which you might segment, which are as follows:

- **Behaviour:** You might segment by whether or not someone has already supported your activity – existing supporters need their previous support to be acknowledged whereas new supporters require more education about the activity they have signed up for. Alternatively, you might segment by how people sign up for events (for instance, those who sign up online will likely prefer online communications methods and those who sign up offline may prefer offline methods). Other behaviours to consider might include when people sign up (for instance, when a participant signs up for a sporting event will determine how much time they have to train and what support and advice you might provide), which activities they prefer, and whether they fundraise alone or in teams.

- **Geography:** You can group participants by their location. This can be useful if, for example, you are offering an activity in a certain location.

- **Demographics:** You can segment your supporters by, for instance, age, gender, socio-economic group, family size, income, religion, occupation and education. If, for example, your audit shows that your highest-value mass participation event fundraisers are women aged 35 to 45, you might segment this group in order to suggest higher sponsorship targets in your communications to them.

- **Geodemographics:** If you have sourced or purchased geodemographic information (see 'Consent for collecting data for profiling and analytics' on page 166 for details on the legal conditions for doing so), you can segment by whichever groupings the classification organisation uses. For example, if you use Mosaic data, your analysis might find that those with a Mosaic classification of 'Professional Rewards' are more likely to attend cultural events and so you might focus on this group when promoting a music concert.[3]

- **Psychographics:** This type of segmentation groups people by their attitudes, motivations and values. For example, perhaps a group of your supporters has a strong affiliation with your organisation because someone they know and care about has been directly affected by a particular project or service you run. Making this aspect of your organisation's work a focus of your communications can link a fundraising activity with this segment's motivations, making participation more meaningful for them.

- **Lifestyle:** Factors relating to supporters' lifestyles, such as their interests, hobbies, sporting activities and preferred social media sites, can help you to identify the experiences people might seek from participation and some of the channels through which you might reach them. For instance, you might segment supporters who like cultural events and propose a fundraising concert or art exhibition to appeal to that segment.

Recency, frequency, value

Recency, frequency, value (RFV) analysis is another form of behavioural analysis that can help you to identify your warmest and potentially most profitable supporters. This analysis is based on the following assumptions:

- those who raise more funds are more attractive to you than those that do not;
- those who fundraise or give more frequently are more likely to repeat their support;
- those who have fundraised or given most recently are more likely to support you than those who have not supported you for the last two years.

In this context, those supporters who raise the most funds, support you frequently and have supported you most recently are the most valuable to you. You can use RFV to segment your supporters depending on:

- when they last fundraised (recency);
- how many times they have fundraised (frequency) in a given period;
- the average value of their donations to your organisation to date (value).

You can then grade each supporter based upon how recent their support has been, how many times they have given and the value of their support. For example, you could allocate a score of 1 to 5:

- For **recency**, you rank your supporters from the most recently active to the longest-lapsed, assigning the 20% who gave most recently (0–6 months) a score of 5, then the next 20% (6–12 months) a score of 4, and so on.

- With **frequency**, you calculate the total number of times a supporter has given to your organisation over a period of time of your choice. The frequency of support could include a wide range of types of support, such as event participation, purchasing merchandise, buying a raffle ticket and even volunteering. You might choose to score all of those who have supported you more than 6 times a year a score of 5, those who have supported you more than 4 times but less than 6 times a score of 4, and so on.
- For **value**, you rank your supporters from highest-value fundraiser on average to lowest-value fundraiser on average. You would then set 5 bands of average value, scoring those in the highest band a 5 down to those in the lowest band a score of 1.

You can then just add the three RFV scores together to get the overall score or total RFV value. You can also vary the score weight for each of the RFV variables depending on their importance to you and so, if you consider the value band to be of most importance, then you might, for example, allocate double points to that part of the analysis. For more details on RFV, see Blackbaud's *RFM: A Formula for Greater Direct Mail Success.*[4]

The five-step segmentation process

It is common to use behavioural variables to segment existing supporters and to use demographic and lifestyle variables to segment prospective supporters.

While reviewing which variables might have the greatest impact on someone's support, you may find that you require more insight into your existing or potential supporters and might undertake further research at this point.

The process of segmenting your target audience broadly involves five steps:

1. Once you have identified your market, **the first step** is to determine the range of variables that influence participation. Using the example of a local sponsored bike ride in London, these variables might include previous participation (behavioural), membership of cycling clubs (lifestyle), location (geographical) and the age group a cyclist is most likely to fall into (demographic).

2. **The second step** is to select from these four variables the one that is most predictive of profitable participation. This can be referred to as the universal variable – the variable that is common to all of your audience. For the bike ride, as it is a local event, this is likely to be whether or not people live in London.

3. **The third step** is to determine the next most predictive variable. In this case, it might be whether or not a person has participated in the event previously (the behavioural variable). Previous supporters are more cost-effective to contact than prospective supporters: previous participants understand the cause and, if they had a great experience last year, they may repeat their support. As your communications need to recognise this previous support, your communications with these supporters should be distinct from those with your new supporters. You now have two segments comprising new and previous supporters, but your audit might show that there are further variables that will influence profitable participation. You may know from your market research that people who fundraise as a team raise more funds, so you might want to communicate differently with previous supporters who fundraised as a team last year, with a focus on higher targets than those who participate individually. With your prospective new supporters, your market research might show that those most likely to participate in cycling events are salaried professionals aged 30 to 55 (the demographic variable). It might also show that more serious cyclists in clubs are seeking reassurance that longer routes will be available, whereas less serious cyclists may be looking for an event that has more of a fun element (the lifestyle variable).

4. **The fourth step** is to map out your segmentation. In this example, you end up with four segments, as shown in figure 3.2. Once the segments have been mapped in this theoretical way, you can calculate from your database how many of your previous participants fall into each segment. For your potential participants you would, for example, research cycling clubs to quantify the total number of people in the cycling club member segment. (See chapter 4 for details on how to plan communications campaigns.)

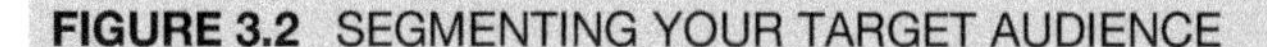

FIGURE 3.2 SEGMENTING YOUR TARGET AUDIENCE

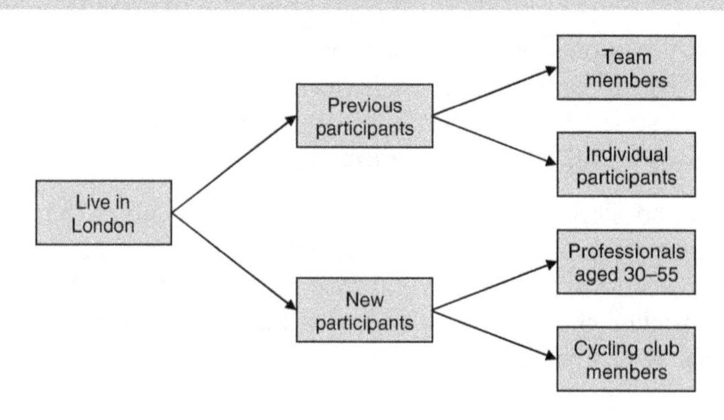

5. **The fifth step** is to consider which segments you are going to target. First you need to check all of the segments you have identified for validity. To be valid, a segment must meet seven criteria. It must be:[5]

   – **Measurable:** will it be easy and inexpensive to get hold of the information you need to define the segment's size and characteristics?

   – **Accessible:** can you identify and afford the appropriate media to reach these supporters and do you have permission to contact them?

   – **Substantial:** is the segment large enough to be cost-effective to target? Consider likely response rates – how many people do you expect to sign up and what is the average value you could expect to receive per person?

   – **Stable:** are the future behaviour and characteristics of the segment predictable?

   – **Appropriate:** is it appropriate for you to approach this segment, given your organisation's mission and the nature of your relationship with the people in the segment? For example, if you have a segment of local companies, do their values match your organisation's values?

   – **Unique:** are the segment's characteristics distinct enough to justify a tailored approach? For example, you may find that your audience has such similar needs and motivations that you can approach all its members in the same way.

   – **Sustainable:** is a relationship with this group of supporters likely to be successful and can it be sustained?

If all of your segments meet these criteria, you then need to decide whether or not you are going to target all of them and how you might prioritise them. For example, you might prioritise those segments that your research suggests will yield the highest response rates and will be easiest to contact. Using our bike ride example, the cold segment of professionals aged 30 to 55 might be less attractive, as you may not have sufficient internal resources to undertake the level of multi-channel promotional activities required to reach such a large audience. In this scenario, you might revisit your budget or break this segment down further to see whether you could prioritise smaller sub-segments. There may be circumstances where it is appropriate to focus on just one segment for an activity. While the benefit of this is that over time you may gain in-depth knowledge and understanding of this segment, the risk of this approach lies in overreliance on just one group of potential supporters.

At the end of the segmentation process, you will have a clear image of your audience and its characteristics and needs. Chapter 4 looks at how you might start to describe and plan your communications with each segment.

3. Positioning strategies

Once you have identified the segments for each of your products, you need to consider how you will 'position' your organisation and products. This relates to how you want your organisation and products to be perceived by the audience you are targeting in relation to other similar charities and their fundraising products or offerings. You are seeking to identify how your fundraising offer is unique and different from those of other organisations. Figure 3.3 shows an example of how a local hospice might position itself in relation to other similar local and national charities to help inform its marketing of a local community event.

FIGURE 3.3 EXAMPLE POSITIONING MAP FOR A LOCAL HOSPICE

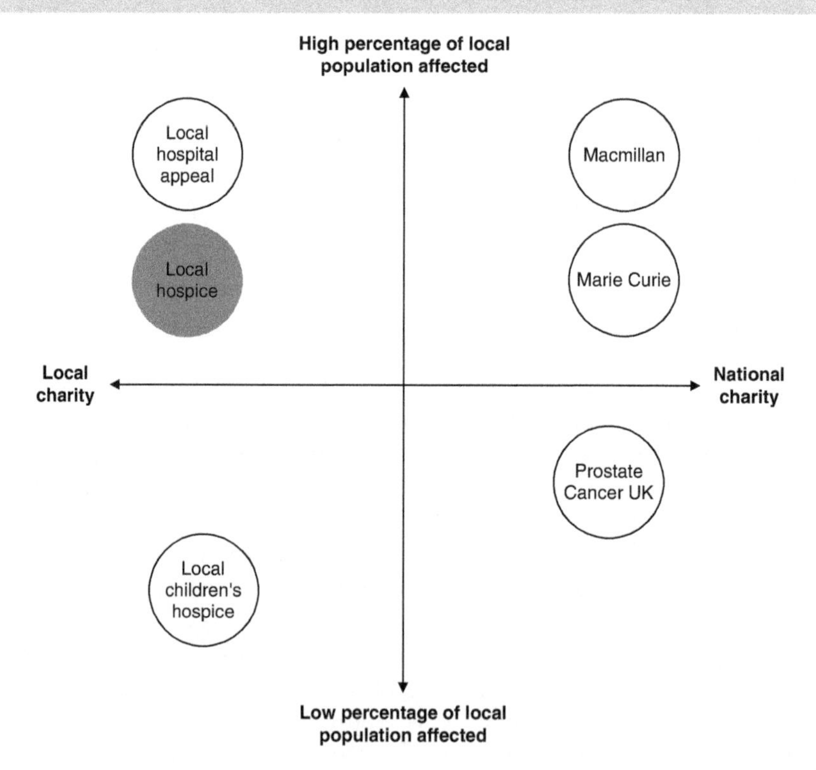

In this example, the hospice is positioned as local and benefiting a large proportion of the community. However, this positioning is similar to that of the local hospital, so the charity may need to distinguish itself further in the minds of potential supporters. For example, it could do this by communicating its holistic approach to providing care: its support of people with terminal illnesses by helping them to live their lives fully and by supporting their family members too.

4. The case for support

The case for support presents the basic argument for support and the rationale upon which all fundraising messages are built. This is a generic internal document that contains the core information needed for fundraising. It specifically covers:

- the need the organisation is seeking to meet;
- the evidence for that need;
- the scale and urgency of that need;
- what would happen if the need was not met;
- who the beneficiaries are;
- why the solutions proposed by the charity are the right ones;
- why the charity is the right organisation to deliver those solutions;
- what the charity's work involves (i.e. its projects);
- the impact it makes;
- its budgets;
- how the charity communicates.

This consistency of core message is vital in building understanding of the charity and trust among supporters. (For details on how to develop effective communications, see chapter 4.)

Case statements

For each product and target audience, you can create internal case statements, adapted from the case for support. These focus on those features of your organisation and its work that are most motivating to the specific audience being targeted, given the activity in question. For example, the features of a running event that would motivate an individual to run for your charity will be different to the features of the same event that would motivate a company to sponsor it. For example, what would motivate an individual to run a marathon for your charity (as opposed to what would motivate a company to do so)?

A good case statement is written in a way that is easy to understand, and it should focus on how you will make supporters feel a sense of immediacy, excitement and importance about the activity. The case statement can then be used to develop the fundraising proposition, which will be the crux of your communications with specific groups of supporters.

The fundraising proposition

The fundraising proposition, a concept developed by Stephen Pidgeon,[6] is the idea that the case statement can be distilled into a single succinct proposition which is expressed through the use of images and language. It is a short, powerful answer to the key question: *why should I fundraise for you?* It is about highlighting the benefits of participation and creating a feeling that taps into an emotion that your research has identified will drive action (whether this is stimulating empathy or a feeling of being part of a social experience). (See 'Creating great content' on page 126.)

It is constructed from four pillars:

- **the vision:** what the world would look like if the organisation achieved its mission;
- **the enemy:** the main factors that prevent the vision from being achieved;
- **the hero:** the person, action or thing that defeats the enemy, which could be the participant or donor, or someone they are uniting with to share the battle;
- **the recipient:** the beneficiary, who is often personalised (for example, as 'someone I know' or 'people like me') to create a connection with the donor.

To maximise impact, the proposition must also clearly express:

- the **need**;
- the **solution**;
- a focus on the **now**.

Alzheimer's Research UK's promotion of its Running Down Dementia event provides an example of how this model can be applied:[7]

Sign up to Running Down Dementia and join the thousands taking part in the fightback against dementia (**enemy**). We can do this together (**heroes**).

Your support powers research

Right now there are 850,000 people with dementia (**need**) in the UK alone, and every three minutes (**now**) another person develops the condition.

Around every one of those people are friends and family (**recipient**), often struggling themselves to keep life on track. But by participating in Running Down Dementia you (**hero**) give everyone (**recipient**) hope by helping to fund vital research (**solution**).

While you smash your running goal, the money you raise will get us closer to the goal of defeating dementia (**vision**).

Reproduced with permission from Alzheimer's Research UK

What you will do to get there

Developing tactics

Once you have selected your strategies for each objective, you can develop the tactics you will need to employ to implement those strategies. These tactics will of course be specific to the type of community fundraising activity you are undertaking and are discussed in detail in the following chapters. Selecting the most appropriate tactics will also be informed by what you have learned from your fundraising audit and these findings will form the rationale for the tactical decisions you now need to make.

Broadly, the tactical plan comprises:

- what needs to be done;
- by whom;
- how;
- where;
- by when.

Tactics relate not only to the recruitment of the participants and their experience during the activity but also to how you will manage all of the stages of the fundraising cycle (see figure 3.4). The stages are:

1. identifying potential supporters and qualifying the likelihood of their support;

2. cultivating your relationship with them;
3. crafting the means of asking for support;
4. thanking and rewarding them;
5. stewarding the relationship towards further support of the organisation.

FIGURE 3.4 THE FUNDRAISING CYCLE

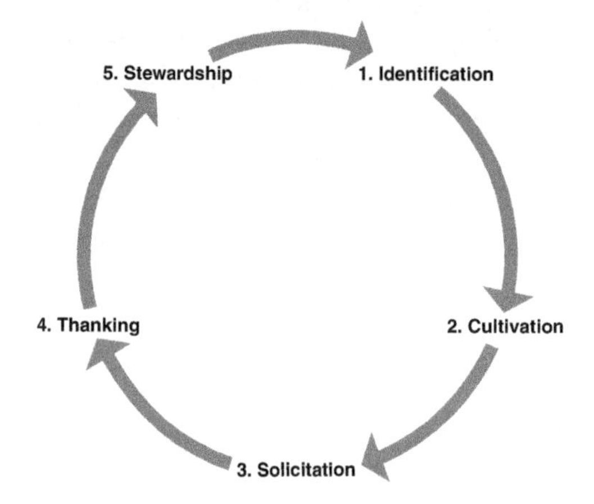

Figure 3.5 offers a model for thinking through all the detailed elements and tasks you need to deliver.

FIGURE 3.5 TACTICAL CONSIDERATIONS MODEL

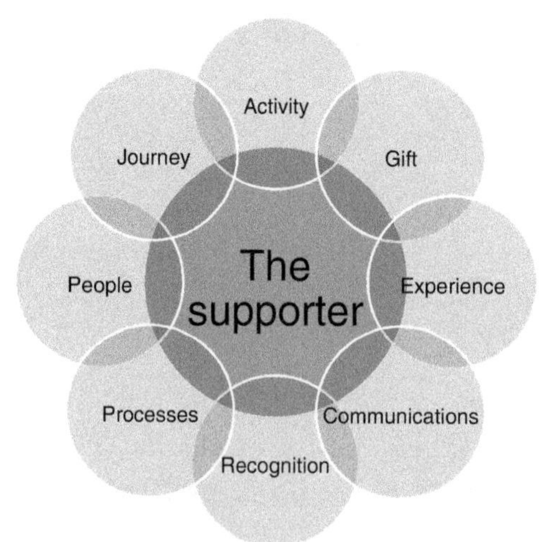

The supporter

When you start to develop your tactics, make sure you are very clear about the specific group of supporters you are developing them around. The supporter's needs will shape the detail of each of the other elements of the tactics. In your tactical plan, you need to clearly identify and describe who you are targeting and any segmentation you might undertake to tailor your communications and activities to the needs and motivations of your various audiences.

The activity

You will already have used Ansoff's matrix (see figure 3.1) to select which products or activities (for example, a bake sale, colour run, trek, collection or quiz) to offer to your selected group of supporters in order to achieve your objective. You will be able to explain the details of the activity, how it has been designed to meet the needs of the supporters, and why it is appropriate in light of what your competitors might be doing and the trends in the market.

The gift

How much will you be asking your supporters to contribute and through what method (for example, ticket sales, sponsorship or merchandise sales)? (For more about pricing and income sources, see 'Maximising event income' on page 192.)

The experience

You need to consider all the different ways a participant might experience an activity and what the nature of that experience needs to be. For example, how are you going to ensure that your street collectors feel confident in their role, feel appreciated and supported, have fun and know how their time is making a difference? The quality of this experience needs to be consistent throughout every element of their participation. In the case of events, what are all the logistical elements that must be in place to ensure a seamless and satisfying experience? And, afterwards, how might you gain feedback on the quality of participants' experience?

The communications

Consider how you are going to promote the activity. What response rates will you need to reach your targets? What are all the different communication stages and what are your objectives for each stage (raising awareness of the activity, providing more information, encouraging sign-up, and providing information before, during and after the event)? What are the key messages and how will you communicate the proposition? Consider also which channels you will select and how you will integrate your communications across multiple channels. For example, you might use an advert to raise awareness, ask participants to sign up through a website, and offer materials to download. How will you maintain your core messages and work across all the teams involved in these touchpoints? (See chapter 4 for more on communicating your activities.)

The recognition

How are you going to show your appreciation of your supporters' time, efforts and donations through each stage of their participation in the activity? For instance, will you send an email as soon as they sign up, followed by a welcome pack and invitations to attend meet-ups? Will you send any certificates or medals or offer opportunities to visit projects so that supporters can see the difference they are helping to make? (To help with planning the thanking see 'Thanking DIY fundraisers' on page 238.)

The processes

Consider all the steps you need to follow to ensure the activity runs smoothly. The steps might include briefing staff and volunteers, processing data and donations, carrying out the registration processes, collecting Gift Aid, doing risk assessments, booking and managing suppliers, and reporting. (See chapter 5 for details on data management processes.)

The people

Who is responsible for delivering the various tactics? This might include, for example, those who are the agents in the chain of contributors (see page 8), community fundraising and other staff, agencies and partners, or the volunteers you will need to recruit and manage. (See chapter 9 for volunteer management and chapter 13 for developing and managing community fundraising staff.)

The journey

What will happen with this group of supporters once they have completed the activity and you have thanked them? How will you develop your relationship with them in the longer term? You need to decide what their supporter journey will be. (For details, see 'Planning supporter journeys' on page 137.)

Legal and ethical considerations

When developing tactics you must be mindful of ensuring that every element of your plan is compliant with relevant legislation and the Fundraising Code of Practice. You should also consider whether the tactics are ethical and in line with your organisation's fundraising ethics. (For more information on fundraising ethics see *Rights Stuff* by Ian MacQuillin.)[8]

Reviewing your tactics

Once you have written your tactics, review them by asking the following questions:

- Will the tactics help you to achieve the objectives?
- Are they relevant to your strategic decisions?
- Do they reflect your audit results?
- Do they reflect the main trends in community fundraising?
- Are they realistic given the available resources and targets?

Setting the budget

After determining the tactics, you will need to identify the costs of undertaking each task. This is known as the 'task method' of budgeting. It can be based on looking at last year's costs and adding an internally agreed level of inflation, or you can seek competitive quotes and base your budget on those. Each objective for each activity should have its own separate budget line – different techniques are employed to achieve different objectives and the techniques you choose will have various cost and return implications. For example, your internal and external research might show that you would expect a higher return from your DIY fundraising than from a mass participation event that is managed in house. Having separate lines also enables you to assess where investment is generating the greatest return. The costs of each activity, within each strand of your community fundraising programme (events, friends groups, schools, third-party groups, volunteers, DIY fundraisers, etc.) can then be aggregated to provide an overall budget.

Direct costs

The costs of delivering each activity are defined as the direct costs. These are the actual costs of implementing the tactics required to deliver each stage of the fundraising cycle. They include things like print, postage, advertising, meeting costs, venues, equipment hire and refreshments.

Indirect costs

Indirect costs are the costs that cannot be allocated in their entirety to a single activity and are instead incurred by a combination of activities. These include, for example, staff (salaries, overtime, training, national insurance, pensions and benefits), database management and licences, website hosting, data processing, thanking and gift processing, online giving platform commissions, newsletters, banners, consultants, office supplies, collection buckets, general merchandise, research, and volunteer recruitment and management. These costs might also include allocations of costs from other departments, such as support from a communications team.

Overhead costs

Overhead costs are costs that the organisation is committed to regardless of whether its activities take place, such as electricity, heat, insurance, rent and depreciation. A relative proportion of these costs might be charged to your budget, depending on your organisational policy.

It is important to ensure that the hidden costs of the indirect and overhead expenses are not ignored, as they may have an impact on the profitability of your fundraising. For example, a major new mass participation campaign that requires significant input from your communications team and IT upgrades, when fully allocated against the campaign's income, may make you think twice about the campaign's viability. (See chapter 6 for more detail on event costing and pricing.)

Managing costs

While all activities should be fully costed, it is advisable to build in an expenditure contingency, which would normally represent 10% of the total costs. This provides for any corrective actions you might need to undertake and any other unexpected costs. To manage cash flow, income and expenditure need to be split out according to the months in which they will be spent and received (respectively). This might be particularly important in small organisations, which tend to have limited funds and may not receive the income from a fundraising activity for several months. Often budgets are drawn up indicating the worst-case and best-case scenarios within tolerances acceptable to an organisation (see 'Forecasting scenarios' on page 200). This can be particularly helpful when running pilot projects or launching new campaigns.

The process of developing a budget can be iterative – plans may change over time when the balance of costs and income are discussed with other fundraising teams and senior management.

Short- and long-term return on investment

To be able to justify your budget, it is important to develop an investment case which, at a basic level, includes both a short- and a long-term ROI. Fundraising activities can take a while to build momentum, profile and understanding and may only start to show a desirable ROI after two to three years.[9] Therefore, it is advisable to present a budget over a number of years, as investment on annual cycles fails to recognise the longer-term value of investing in innovation and nurturing ongoing supporter relationships.

Return on investment

Return on investment (ROI) is the ratio of income to cost (income ÷ cost). For example:

£100,000/£25,000 = 4

An ROI of 4 is a gross ROI. It means that for every £1 spent, £4 was raised. This can be expressed as a ratio of 4:1.

The net ROI would be the profit generated per £1 spent, which would be a ratio of 3:1.

Some organisations include only direct costs in calculating fundraising ROI, whereas others include indirect costs and overheads.

Lifetime value

Community fundraising can be a means of recruiting new supporters who continue to support your community fundraising activities or support your charity in other ways as donors. Justifying the cost of recruiting these individuals can therefore be expressed in terms of the value of their support over the lifetime of their support, i.e. their lifetime value (LTV).

LTV is a predictive measure used to analyse the contribution (donations and other contributions) a supporter makes to a charity over their giving lifetime. It can be used to compare groups that are recruited through the same channels, groups that have similar demographics and groups that are participating in the same types of event. It is a model widely used in business for budgeting, investment planning and deriving the real value of sales projections, and it is known in that sector as net present value (NPV). The assumption made in the LTV or NPV calculation is that money in the hand is worth more than anticipated income in the future – so, £100 today is worth more than £100 in a year's time and *much* more than £100 in, say, five years' time. The example that follows shows how the calculation is made.

Consider a group of event participants who support your charity for an average of three years. During that time they might (again on average) participate in three events at a value of £200, purchase Christmas cards at £25 per year and participate in your annual raffle at £15 per year. The gross value to your organisation of each of these supporters is therefore £720, or £240 per year. They may also become volunteers, in which case the value of this time to your organisation would also be added in the calculation (this value is not included in this example).

The costs of raising these funds over the three-year period then need to be subtracted to identify the total net value of this supporter type. This would include the costs of all communications, such as newsletters, fundraising packs, merchandise and each solicitation. The cost of these activities might be £90 per year, making the annual net value of the supporter £150. However, it becomes more difficult to predict costs and revenue the further ahead you look, because of factors such as inflation, risk and estimating accuracy. The value of £150 in three years' time may be less in real terms than it is today, so you need to apply a discount to the projected future income. In order for your comparisons to be valid, you must use the same discount rate for all supporters. The formula for this calculation is as follows:

$$LTV = \sum_{i=1}^{n} C_i(1+d)^{-i}$$

Some fundraising databases can automatically calculate this for you (as can Microsoft Excel, which includes an NPV function). You can, however, use this complicated-looking formula yourself – it is quite straightforward when it is broken down, as shown in table 3.3 and in the illustration of the formula that follows the table.

The formula calculates the net value (C, which stands for revenue minus cost) of each future year's fundraising activities and then applies a discount rate (d) that increases the further away you are from the present day (i represents the number of years into the future up to n, which stands for the expected duration of the relationship in years).

In table 3.3, a discount rate of 10% is applied to an event participant in every future year, which enables the calculation of a more realistic LTV for new participants. (To make the calculation simple, this example uses 10% as the discount rate. In reality, the discount rate applied would be based on the interest rates at the time of doing the calculation. When comparing projects, it is essential that the same discount rate is used.) You never discount year 1, as that is your base point. You are aiming to compare potential future income with how you might alternatively invest that money if you had it in your hands today (for instance, if you took the £150 net value from year 2 and invested it at a 10% interest rate, you would have £165 in a year's time). To translate each future year's value into today's monetary value, you divide the net value in year 2 by 1.1 and in year 3 by 1.1 squared. (You would continue to divide the value by an additional 1.1 for each extra year if you had more years in your table.) In year 2, the calculation gives you the figure 0.909 and in year 3 it is 0.826. You then multiply these discount rate figures by the net value (£150) to get the real annual values (£136.36 in year 2 and £123.97 in year 3).

TABLE 3.3 LIFETIME VALUE OF AN EVENT PARTICIPANT

	Year 1	**Year 2**	**Year 3**	**Total over three years**
Income				
Event sponsorship (including Gift Aid)	£200	£200	£200	£600
Raffle	£15	£15	£15	£45
Christmas cards	£25	£25	£25	£75
Total income	**£240**	**£240**	**£240**	**£720**
Costs				
Event recruitment and support	£75	£75	£75	£225
Raffle mailing and fulfilment	£2	£2	£2	£6
Christmas card mailing and fulfilment	£4	£4	£4	£12
Annual newsletter	£2	£2	£2	£6
Annual thank-you phone calls	£5	£5	£5	£15
Email updates	£2	£2	£2	£6
Total costs	**£90**	**£90**	**£90**	**£270**
Net value	**£150**	**£150**	**£150**	**£450**

	Year 1	Year 2	Year 3	Total over three years
Discount rate formula[i] (This shows how the discount factor in the row below is derived, based on a 10% discount.)	n/a	=1/(1.1)^1	=1/(1.1)^2	
Discount factor	1.00	0.909	0.826	
Discounted value of 10% per year (net value × discount factor)	**£150**	**£136.36**	**£123.97**	**£410.33**

[i]The number in the formula in brackets is the discount rate (in this case 10%) applied to each year. The carat symbol (^) is the power function and that relates to the number of years you are projecting ahead. Year 1 is not discounted because it is your baseline starting point, year 2's discount rate is to the power of 1 because it is one year on from that starting point and year 3's discount rate is to the power of 2 because it is two years on from that starting point.

Using the example in table 3.3, the formula shown earlier would look like this:

$$LTV = \sum_{i=1}^{2} £150 \times 1(1+0.1)^{-i}$$

And this would break down as follows:

$$LTV = £150 + \frac{£150}{(1+0.1)^1} + \frac{£150}{(1+0.1)^2}$$

$$= £150 + £136.36 + £123.97 = £410.33$$

The LTV over three years, therefore, is £39.67 less than the £450 total net value.

Keeping the plan on track

Once you start implementing the plan, you will need to ensure that progress is monitored effectively.

Scheduling

With multiple tactics being actioned by various team members, co-ordination and timetabling are essential.

Critical path analysis

A critical path analysis identifies all key tasks, their duration and which other tasks their completion is dependent upon. Table 3.4 shows an example of some of the elements requiring scheduling for a series of local pub fundraising quizzes. Each task is allocated a letter in column 1, with column 3 showing which other tasks its completion is dependent upon. For example, developing a campaign brief (A) might take 5 days and requires management approval (B), which might require a window of 2 days to receive. Task B cannot be started without task A being completed.

TABLE 3.4 CRITICAL PATH ANALYSIS FOR A LOCAL PUB QUIZ CAMPAIGN

Task identifier	Task	Dependent on	Duration of task/window for approval
A	Write campaign brief	–	5 days
B	Approve campaign brief	A	Window of 2 days
C	Analyse data to identify previous participants	B	5 days
D	Research new pub participants in target areas	B	5 days
E	Select data for email recruitment campaign	C, D	1 day
F	Write brief for fundraising materials and pack	E	1 day
G	Approve fundraising materials and pack brief	F	Window of 2 days
H	Launch email campaign and record responses	E, N	3 weeks
I	Email shareable social media graphic to pubs	E, N	3 weeks
J	Brief copywriter for print and digital copy	G	2 days

Task identifier	Task	Dependent on	Duration of task/window for approval
K	[Copy being written]	J	4 days
L	Copy delivered	K	Milestone
M	Design artwork for print and digital material	G	4 days
N	Approve copy and artwork	L, M	Window of 2 days
O	Launch web page and place Facebook adverts	N	2 days
P	Oversee print and delivery of pack materials	N	5 days
Q	Pack delivered	P	Milestone
R	Mail packs and collecting tins to pubs	Q	1 day
S	Define thanking methods and messages	B	2 days
T	Email quiz questions to quizmaster	H	1 day
U	Completion of quizzes and monies received	R, T	2 weeks
V	Receipt pub participant payments	U	2 weeks
W	Thank participants and process their data	S, U	6 weeks

Gantt charts

Once the task dependencies are clear, each task can be plotted in a Gantt chart to identify who is responsible for each task and the start and completion dates for each task. Once you see how the tasks all link together, they may end up in a different order from the one in your tabulated list. Any scheduling should consider staff holidays, the length of time it takes for approvals and a contingency. See figure 3.6 overleaf for a condensed example of how the pub quiz campaign could be scheduled.[10]

You can lay out your Gantt chart using an Excel sheet, but free programs such as GanttProject offer better functionality.[11] With a program such as this, if you need to change a date, the rest of the activities automatically update, which can save a considerable amount of time and avoid errors slipping into your chart. Furthermore, you can allocate tasks to individuals, allowing you to see within the resources chart whether anyone working on the project is overloaded and enabling you to update the plan accordingly.

Key performance indicators

Key performance indicators (KPIs) are quantifiable measures that can help you to track your progress against key achievements that are necessary to meet your objective. For example, an objective could be:

> To raise £50,000 from a regional schools fundraising programme at a cost of £12,500 to achieve a gross ROI of 4:1 over the next 12 months.

The KPIs for this objective might be:

- achieve a response rate of 10% from 2,000 primary schools, resulting in the recruitment of 200 school participants;
- receive an average income from each school of £250;
- have 50% of schools signed up by October half-term and 50% by February half-term;
- gain the participation of two classes per school (averaging 50 children per school);
- have an average sponsorship per child of £5.

By monitoring KPIs, you can track whether or not you need to take any corrective action. For example, if the response rate were only 8%, to receive the same total income you would have to increase the average income objective to £312.50 per school. Alternatively, a reduced average income might be accepted but with costs cut to £10,000 to maintain the target ROI. (See also table 2.3 for details on some of the metrics you might use to set and track your KPIs.)

FIGURE 3.6 GANTT CHART FOR A LOCAL PUB QUIZ CAMPAIGN

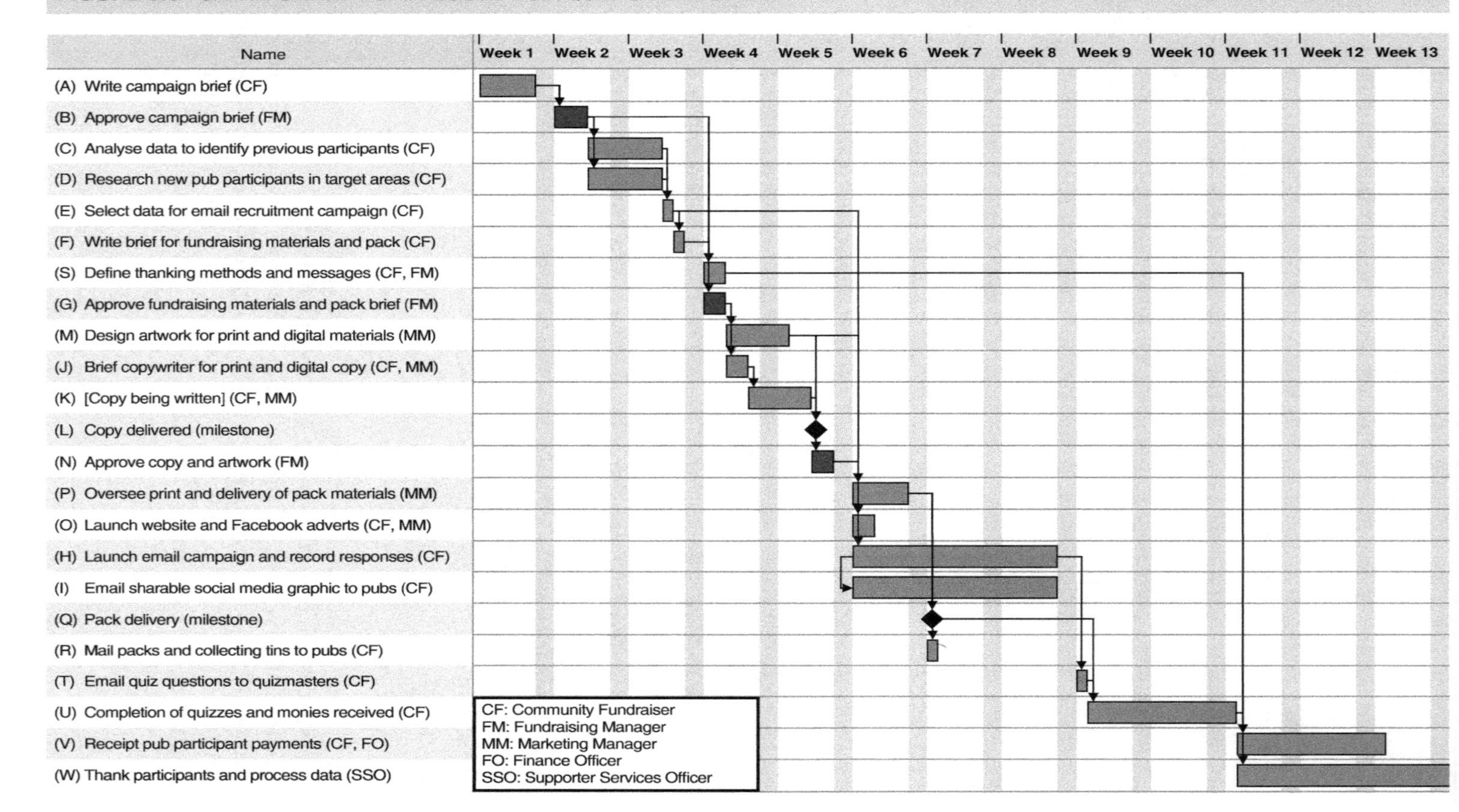

Identifying and managing risks

Within any community fundraising programme there are potential risks. You will need to identify these and put in place controls and contingencies to mitigate them. The most common risks to a community fundraising plan's success can be categorised as:

- **compliance:** for instance, dealing with the effects of legislative changes or failing to meet legal requirements or best practice, such as contacting supporters without a legal basis for doing so; for example, where they have not given permission to be contacted and there is no legitimate interest or other lawful basis for doing so;
- **financial:** for example, not achieving income due to lower response rates, lower average sponsorship values, increased costs, etc.;
- **logistical (or operational):** an inability to deliver an activity (or difficulties in doing so), for example caused by failure of processes, suppliers or equipment;
- **relational:** for example, failing to meet donor needs, resulting in lost support;
- **reputational:** for example, where an activity brings the charity into disrepute or where a community or public group is upset, irritated or offended; this category also includes changes in wider public trust of charities which could damage participation and donations.

Ways in which these examples might be controlled include:

- setting sponsorship targets (**financial**);
- conducting market research into needs (**relational**);
- undertaking community consultation and putting complaints procedures in place (**reputational**);
- ensuring there are contracts with all suppliers (**logistical**);
- carrying out health and safety risk assessments and creating checklists (**compliance**);
- ensuring an effective system to make certain that legislation and the Code of Fundraising Practice are complied with when collecting and using personal data (**compliance**).

Any risk management process should measure the effectiveness of the controls and include these in regular team reporting. Table 3.5 illustrates an example plan for logging, managing and monitoring risks and includes examples of just two potential risks (in reality you may identify multiple risks). For details on determining the priority level of the risk, see 'Risk assessments and health and safety' on page 208. Following that section, see also the example risk assessment form which you can use specifically for evaluating risk at an individual event level.

TABLE 3.5 SAMPLE PLAN FOR LOGGING, MANAGING AND MONITORING RISKS[12]

Type	Date identified	Date of last update	Description	Notes	Priority	Action	Monitoring activity	Lead	Timing
Financial	12 Nov. 2019	10 Apr. 2020	Not enough participants	There aren't enough participants to make activities viable; risk of reduced income	High	• Conduct market research into needs • Create marketing strategy to target groups • Tailor marketing messages to each group	• Keep daily attendance figures • Monitor weekly attendance trends • Monitor monthly attendance trends	Activity leader	Review quarterly
Compliance, logistical, reputational	12 Nov. 2019	21 Sep. 2020	Venue is potentially unsafe	Some equipment and elements of venue environment not up to quality standards; risk of non-delivery of activity – potential compliance, finance and reputation risks	Medium	• Ensure daily checks of equipment • Ensure equipment is regularly maintained • Establish health safety checklist and complete prior to each event • Create alternative venue register	• Monitor maintenance schedules monthly • Check safety checklists	Centre manager	Review monthly

Monitoring and reporting

All elements of the plan need to be monitored and reported on, so as to identify whether KPIs and objectives are being met, activities are within budget and on schedule, and the focus on your charity's relationship with its supporters and the public is being maintained.

To monitor progress you need to identify:

- the metrics you are measuring (e.g. target number of new members and target attrition rates);
- who is responsible for which metrics;
- the schedule and budget against which performance is being judged;
- where the data will be drawn from;
- by when and with what frequency the metrics need to be reported against;
- who is responsible for undertaking the reporting, how they should report and when they need to report by;
- who receives and evaluates the results.

And, at a basic level, income and expenditure reporting includes:

- monthly and cumulative actual income against the budgeted income;
- actual costs incurred against those budgeted;
- actual versus projected ROI;
- performance against financial KPIs.

The plan will also need to be monitored against the schedule to ensure all activities are on track and to determine how any slippages can be rectified.

Table 3.6 provides a monitoring framework, using a simple example of monitoring recruitment of friends group members, that can be used for each community fundraising objective.

TABLE 3.6 A MONITORING FRAMEWORK

What to monitor	Metrics	Variance to target	Where	When	Who	To whom
Recruitment of new friends group members	Number of new members Attrition rates	+2% −3%	Reports from database	Monthly	Regional community fundraising manager	Community fundraising manager

If there are any variances against budgets and KPIs, reports should explain these variances and recommend corrective actions to put the plan back on track. Having already identified risks, controls and potential contingencies, you can more easily and quickly determine and implement corrective actions.

You will also need to evaluate your activities to judge their overall success against the original objectives. How appropriate and effective were the strategic decisions and the range of tactics selected? How well were the tactics implemented?

Part of your evaluation should include information on participants' experiences. This will help you to identify which elements of an activity met their expectations and where you could make improvements. (See 'Primary research' on page 34 for details on how you can gather this data.) The results of your evaluation can then be developed into recommendations which explain what changes are needed, their impact and who and how they will be implemented. These will then feed into your future plans.

Conclusion

Effective strategic planning is critical to future-proofing your fundraising, mitigating risks and exploiting your best opportunities for sustainable growth. By building on a robust audit to set objectives, you will make your community fundraising targets realistic and therefore more achievable. Analysing and evaluating all the options by which objectives can be met helps to drive innovation and ensure that the activities you select are those most appropriate for both your supporters and your organisation. Community fundraising is undoubtedly highly competitive but good planning will mean you can tailor your activities to your supporters' needs and differentiate your offer based on insight and understanding of your audiences. Reviewing each element of your tactics in light of this insight will help you to focus the delivery of your plans on the supporters' experience. Finally, you should ensure that all planning is carefully controlled and monitored, and you should continually test, learn from and adapt your approach to better enable you to inspire communities to help you deliver your charity's mission.

Notes

1 Adrian Sargeant and Elaine Jay, *Fundraising Management: Analysis, planning and practice*, Abingdon, Routledge, 2014, p. 96.
2 *Ibid.*, pp. 98–117.
3 For more information visit www.experian.co.uk/marketing-services/products/mosaic-uk.html.

4 *RFM: A Formula for Greater Direct Mail Success* [PDF], Blackbaud, 2004, www.blackbaud.com/files/resources/downloads/WhitePaper_RFM.pdf, accessed 11 June 2019.

5 Adrian Sargeant and Elaine Jay, *Fundraising Management: Analysis, planning and practice*, Abingdon, Routledge, 2014, p. 109.

6 Presentation by Stephen Pidgeon, 'Why should I give you my money?', ICAWC workshop, 2014, www.slideshare.net/dogstrust/icawc-2014-workshop-why-should-i-give-you-my-money-stephen-pidgeon, slide 24, accessed 26 October 2018.

7 Alzheimer's Research UK used this wording for its website marketing campaign in 2017.

8 Ian MacQuillin, *Rights Stuff: Fundraising's ethics gap and a new theory of fundraising ethics v1.1* [PDF], Rogare, 2016, www.plymouth.ac.uk/uploads/production/document/path/7/7407/Rogare_Fundraising_Ethics_White_Paper_v1.1.pdf, accessed 19 March 2019.

9 James Greenfield, 'Hardwiring for Maximum Fundraising Return on Investment', *New Directions for Philanthropic Fundraising*, no. 49, 2005, pp. 61–85.

10 Holidays and contingencies are not included in this example because of space limitations in displaying the figure.

11 GanttProject is free to download from www.ganttproject.biz. To learn how to use the program, search for 'GanttProject' in YouTube – there are various tutorials available. Note, however, that GanttProject is not a cloud-based program, so any charts you create are stored on your own computer (unless you export them to a PDF or other format to send to others). If you would like the ability to collaborate with team members on your charts, you will need cloud-based software. There are a range of both free and paid options online, some of which are integrated into wider project management programs. See Agannty, for example, at www.agantty.com/en.

12 Reproduced with adaptations from Elizabeth Gray-King, *Risk Management*, London, DSC, 2009, p. 14.

CHAPTER FOUR

Developing a communications plan

Debbie Warren and Sam Rider

Communicating your cause and opportunities to make a difference is a fine art and essential to community fundraising's success. Good communications can inspire support and are the foundations for building a relationship with supporters. While great content, powerful visuals, effective use of emotion, channel selection and personalisation are all important ingredients, communication is also a process. It involves considering every point of contact (or touch point) a supporter might have with your organisation, from prompting awareness to encouraging participation, providing support and advice, shaping the supporter experience, thanking and demonstrating the impact of their support, and maintaining an ongoing relationship. These multiple messages must each stand alone while also combining to form a conversation that builds a supporter's sense of being a valued part of achieving your charity's vision and facilitating the delivery of its mission.

This chapter looks at how to plan effective communications by:

- understanding the communications process;
- setting communications objectives;
- developing supporter personas to describe audience segments;
- selecting the right combination of media to target each segment;
- shaping messages and considering the power of emotion and effective design;
- building relationships;
- planning supporter journeys;
- monitoring and evaluating results.

You will also need to ensure your communications plan complies with data management law and regulation (see chapter 5).

Understanding the communications process

Strong supporter communications are the basis of relationship-building. Good communications are about creating and sustaining a conversation with a supporter – a conversation that grows over time and involves multiple points of contact that build mutual understanding and trust. Communication is therefore a process.

Technology is continually evolving and enabling ever-greater opportunities for two-way communications between charities and their supporters, as well as between supporters, their peers and influencers. You can better navigate this complexity by understanding some of the basic principles of the communications process.

Communications models and concepts

How communication works

There are various communications models put forward by theorists, but Wilbur Schramm's theory of how communication works has some particularly helpful practical implications.

Schramm likens communication to a radio or phone circuit, where there is:[1]

- **a source:** a person speaking, writing, etc., either individually or on behalf of an organisation;
- **an encoded message:** the person puts the information and feelings they want to share into a format that can be transmitted (e.g. video, spoken words, or the text of an email);
- **a signal:** the transmission of the message through a particular medium or channel (e.g. posting a video on a website or sending an email);
- **a destination or receiver:** the individual or group of people who is listening, reading or watching the message;
- **decoding:** the process by which the person or group receiving the message understands the message (e.g. the person's experience of watching a video or reading an email);
- **feedback:** communication from the person or group receiving the message back to the source (e.g. any response to the video or email).

Schramm notes that there are multiple levels to a message: if you are communicating in spoken words, in addition to the words you use, the message will be influenced by how the tone and intonation of your voice and your facial expressions convey your message. Similarly for a written message: headlines, pictures and italics, for example, all express meaning. He also highlights the importance of gaining feedback from the receiver. This enables the sender to understand how the intended audience has received the message, whether it has reached who it was intended to reach, whether the receivers understand what the message was meant to convey, and whether they will respond in the way that is desired.[2]

Feedback may come in many forms. For a speech, this would be communicated through the level of applause you would receive. For an email with a call to action, this would be conveyed by the number of sign-ups you achieve. Schramm also notes that you can give yourself feedback by reviewing your messages and correcting spelling in your writing or fixing mispronunciations in what you're saying.

Today, people can interact with one another more easily than when Schramm formulated this model in 1955, thanks to the speed at which technology allows us to respond to messages. This means that people have ample opportunity to provide feedback and this can turn into a conversation. In Schramm's terms, nowadays once a message has been decoded by the receiver, the roles can be reversed where the receiver may encode and send a response to the initial sender. The success of these potentially ongoing exchanges by phone, email, social media and text (and, in time, using AI) relies on senders and receivers building understanding of one another quickly by listening and adapting their behaviours.

Your audiences may also put messages from you in their own words (encode them) and share these with others in their network. The likelihood of your audience encoding these messages in a way that is consistent with your original meaning will be influenced by how well you have conveyed your message and also by how much the receiver trusts, understands and feels positively towards your organisation as the original sender. (For details on building trust, see 'Building relationships' on page 134.)

Indeed, the main point of Schramm's model is to help you consider how you can improve your messages so that people receive them with a minimal amount of distortion (like a radio signal being transmitted clearly) and have the highest chance of understanding them as you intend. This distortion is often referred to as 'noise',[3] where the receiver is prevented from receiving all or part of a message in full. This could be physical noise, such as the receiver being interrupted by someone when they are trying to read something, or cognitive noise, where extraneous information detracts from the intended message. To address this distortion, Schramm's model focuses on the elements of communication you can control – i.e. composing your messages and deciding on how, when and where to send them. To do this, he suggests:

- gaining the attention of your receivers – as well as making a message engaging in terms of its content, it is helpful to time when you send messages (e.g. at the right point in the supporter journey – see 'Planning supporter journeys' on page 137);
- conveying points of common ground and shared experiences between you and the receivers (e.g. by understanding your audience well – see 'Creating supporter personas' on page 107);

- stirring feelings of needs or wants in receivers and suggesting ways to fulfil those needs or desires (e.g. by eliciting emotions in your audience – see 'Creating great content' on page 126);
- taking account of who might influence an individual's decision-making (e.g. by engaging those who have the most influence in their communities – see 'Word of mouth' and 'Adopters and the diffusion of innovations model' below).

Word of mouth

Word of mouth (known as WOM) consists of informal conversations and exchanges of ideas between friends, families and peers. When people interact in this way, the exchanges influence each person involved in the conversation. This sharing of ideas and opinions is powerful because supporters are more likely to believe the impartial views of others than what they are told by an organisation that is marketing directly to them. It is important to keep this principle in mind in your communications. For example, it can be very effective for existing supporters to share their positive experience of fundraising for your charity via word of mouth, as this can lead to them recruiting members of their networks to fundraise for you.

Adopters and the diffusion of innovations model

In 1962, Everett M. Rogers gave the name 'diffusion of innovations' to the process by which networks of people communicate new ideas.[4] According to this process, after a new idea has been put into the world, as time goes on, distinct groups of people will adopt it and spread it to new groups. Rogers labelled these groups 'adopters' and divided them into five categories (as also shown in figure 4.1):[5]

- **Innovators** are people who like new ideas, understand complex technical information and have plenty of disposable income. They love taking risks by trying new ideas. They form cliques with other innovators and do not connect with their local community. The average member of a community would perceive an innovator to be too divergent from societal norms and, as such, would not be persuaded by an innovator's adoption of an idea.
- **Early adopters** principally include opinion leaders (see next section), who themselves spread information about new ideas. They are more a part of their community than innovators and have the respect of their peers, so they can effectively influence others. They do so by reducing uncertainty around a new idea. Nowadays, this category includes bloggers and vloggers.
- **The early majority** follow the early adopters and may deliberate for a while before fully adopting a new idea. They often communicate with

their peers but rarely lead them. They are nevertheless an important part in the process of spreading an idea by increasing the overall number of adopters.

- **The late majority** are more sceptical than the early majority and are likely to have limited resources. They adopt new ideas or products for economic necessity or because almost everyone they know already has. Peer-pressure is key for the late majority to adopt an idea.

- **Laggards** are suspicious of new ideas and products, and are the last people in society to adopt them. They are traditionalists, are cautious and are likely to have limited resources.

As shown in figure 4.1, as each group (represented by approximate percentages) starts to adopt the idea, the market share of the idea (represented by the grey line) increases and eventually reaches saturation. The model is important for recognising that some people become interested in and convert to a new activity early on in its lifespan, while others get involved much later. It can also help you to think through how to plan your communications for the different categories of adopter. The model suggests that when you are introducing a new event (for example), you should promote it to those who are most likely to be early adopters. These people will speed up the adoption of the activity by sharing and discussing it.

FIGURE 4.1 THE DIFFUSION OF IDEAS

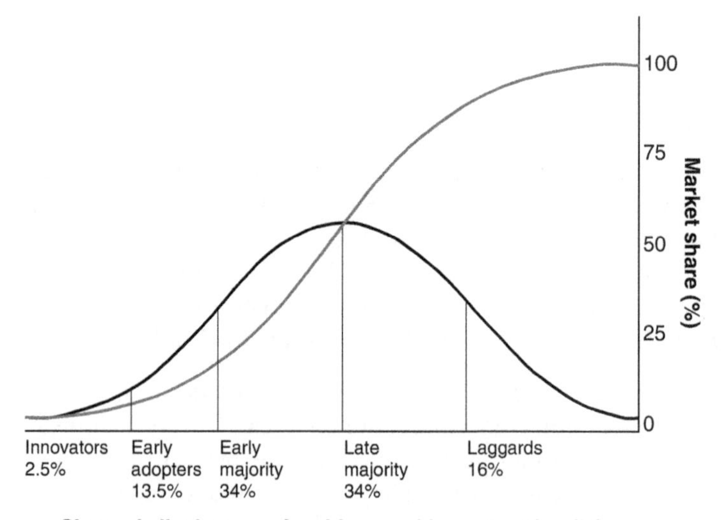

Reproduced and adapted under the Creative Commons licence[6]

Opinion leaders

An **opinion leader** is someone who is able to informally influence other people's attitudes or behaviour.[7] In today's terms, opinion leaders are often called influencers. Opinion leaders are most likely to be early adopters because, as outlined above, early adopters have greater respect from their peers than innovators do and can sway others' opinions as a result. They are the individuals to whom the intended receiver of your messages is likely to turn for further information, guidance or advice and their views may positively reinforce or negatively disrupt your messages. In a community fundraising context, an influencer could be someone who comments to their peer group positively or negatively about participating in an event.

In contrast to opinion leaders, who are not seen as experts in their field, **opinion formers** are those who have authority in a subject area because of their knowledge, which may be as a result of their occupation, qualifications or experience.[8] In a community fundraising context, this could be one of your volunteers sharing positive or negative information on volunteering based upon examples of their own positive or negative experience.

There is a potential problem with the influencing power of technically competent professionals – if people perceive them be too different from themselves (in the same way as they view innovators), they are less likely to adopt their ideas. Ideally, an influencer is most effective when they are similar to their peers in most aspects (socially, educationally, etc.) and only different with regard to their specialist knowledge on the subject they are influencing others on.[9] Similarly, if an influencer is seen to be trying to persuade others too often, they may begin to lose credibility with peers.[10] In a fundraising situation, if a volunteer were seen by others as an official influencer for your organisation, this may impair how credible they appear to others when recommending one of your activities.

A planning framework

To ensure that the purpose of all your messaging is clear and its execution is effective, you will need to plan your communications systematically. The stages of a planning process are shown in figure 4.2. The first stage, 'Research supporters' needs and behaviours during the fundraising audit', is explored in chapter 2. The rest are explored in the remainder of this chapter.

FIGURE 4.2 A SUGGESTED PLANNING PROCESS

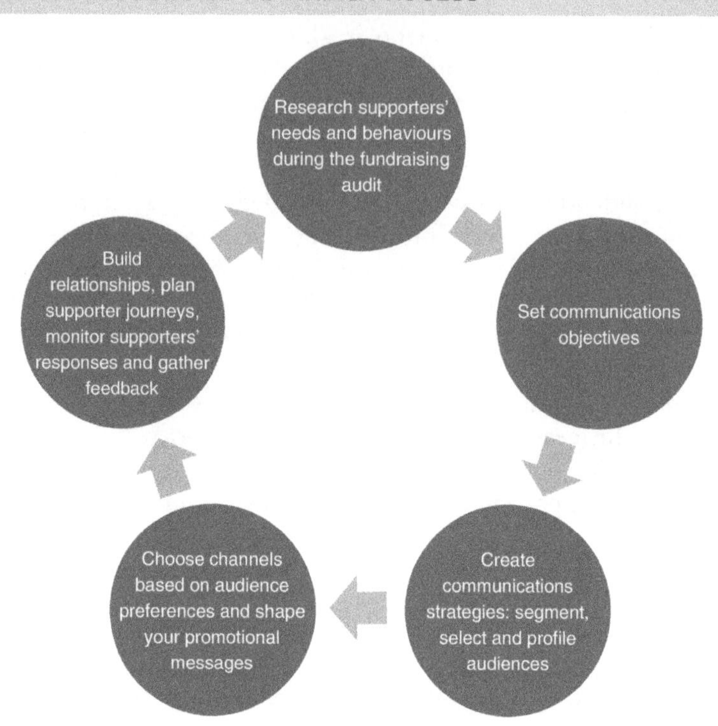

Setting communications objectives

Any communications objective should directly support the delivery of your fundraising objectives, which should in turn support the fulfilment of your charity's legal objects or purposes (see 'Setting community fundraising objectives' on page 66). However, while the focus of a fundraising objective is how much is to be raised, from whom and by when, the focus of a communications objective is creating the awareness, knowledge, understanding, changed attitudes, perceptions or behaviours that will help to deliver the fundraising objective. Writing a communications objective involves defining the audience, the desired outcome and acceptable cost, and ensuring, like any objective, it is SMART (specific, measurable, achievable, relevant and timetabled) to allow you to assess later on whether or not it has been achieved.

RACE

One useful model for identifying the outcome within a communication objective is RACE, which stands for reach, act, convert and engage. This model can help you to clarify the nature of the behaviours you are seeking to cause – i.e. what you want to influence your supporters to do at different stages of the communications process.

It was created by Smart Insights for setting a digital communications plan but is expanded here to integrate offline channels:

- **Reach:** this stage focuses on attracting potential supporters. The idea is to gain awareness and interest to draw people in so they want to find out more about your activity or organisation. For example, you might want to attract people to your website events page. You can do this using tactical campaigns such as email (see page 111) and influencer outreach (see page 113) or by using display adverts (i.e. advertising on websites, apps or social media) or direct mail targeted at a chosen audience. You can also drive traffic more organically through searches by improving your search engine optimisation (see page 112). You can gauge your reach by measuring traffic on your channels using, for example, Google Analytics, the Facebook pixel and Twitter Analytics (for details see 'Monitoring tools and what they show you' on page 146).

- **Act:** this stage, where 'act' is short for 'interact' or 'action', is about engaging potential supporters online or offline. The idea is to encourage prospects to act upon the information you provided via your communications in the 'reach' stage. An action could be sharing one of your Facebook posts, clicking through to your website from an email or looking up your web address after seeing a press advert and then reading a blog post, or browsing your event options.

- **Convert:** conversion occurs when prospects take the action you are seeking, such as requesting an information pack or signing up to an event. You can track conversions using Google Analytics or via your email deployment system; services such as MailChimp and Adestra can measure the number of responses to an email or direct mail campaign.

- **Engage:** this stage involves developing long-term relationships with supporters. You might encourage further engagement with your organisation via, for example, thanking supporters, showing how their support has made an impact, and encouraging them to take part in another event or to give a donation to an appeal.

Communications objectives will also be developed out of the understanding you have gained through your audit and research of your audiences' needs, interests, values, motivations, behaviours and use of different media (see chapter 2).

Using the example of the sponsored bike ride in London in chapter 3, and having segmented your audience (see the 'The five-step segmentation process' on page 73), you can set targets for how many participants you want to retain (i.e. repeat participants) and how many you want to recruit (i.e. new participants). For example:

> Retain 450 existing participants at a cost of £10 per supporter, each raising £100.
>
> Recruit 250 new participants at a cost of £15 per supporter, each raising £100.

You might then break this down further:

> Retain 250 team members and 200 individual participants at a cost of £10 per supporter, each raising £100.
>
> Recruit 150 cycle club members and 100 non-cycle club members aged 30–55 at a cost of £15 per supporter, each raising £100.

Focusing on those you are aiming to retain, you might set the following communications objective:

> To convert 250 previous participants to sign up online for our next cycling event by [date], each raising £100 at a cost per sign-up of £10.

Defining your audience

Determining your communications plan involves reviewing the segments you have decided to target and defining these segments by illustrating them as supporter personas.

Reviewing your segments

At this point in the planning process, you know which segments you are going to target and understand the characteristics that are most likely to influence people's participation in your selected product or activity (see 'Market segmentation strategies' on page 70). The next step is to create supporter personas. This process will help you to create the right messages for these supporters and identify the right channels through which to deliver them to ensure that your communications are relevant, engaging and motivating.

Creating supporter personas

Supporter personas (also known as 'pen portraits') describe your segments using amalgamations of each segment's most common characteristics. They help you to describe the audience segments you want to market your activities to, identify ways of attracting more people like them, and do a better job of communicating with and serving them.

Personas are built from the information you have already gathered about your existing supporters, particularly where you are trying to recruit more of the same type of supporter. For segments that constitute a completely new audience, personas are likely to be developed from research into external markets (see page 43) and some educated assumptions that can help to fill in any gaps in your knowledge. However, personas are only helpful if their key features are based on robust data and research; beware of making assumptions based on anecdotal knowledge. Be careful, too, not to hide large differences within a segment. For example, if the gender split of a segment is close to 50:50, it will be unhelpful to represent this whole group as a male or female persona. Similarly, it is wise not to base the age of your supporter personas on the average age within a segment; for example, you could end up with a single persona based on 30-year-olds when you really need two separate personas of people who are mostly in their early twenties and early forties.[11] Therefore, to help ensure that your personas are representative of real segments of your audience, avoid mean averages and instead look for groupings in age (or mode averages).

The following examples explore how two of the segments identified in chapter 3 (see figure 3.2) might be represented as personas, called 'Alice' and 'Andrew', for the purposes of marketing a cycle ride. Alice's profile might be based primarily on internal database findings that show the typical profile of a segment of a charity's existing supporters who took part in the same event last year as individuals. Andrew's profile represents cycle club members the charity could aim to recruit; this information might be more reliant on external market research. In both cases, the data is fleshed out with reasonable assumptions about the lifestyles of these kinds of people.

Alice

Alice lives in Wimbledon, London, is 28 and works for a publisher on Kensington High Street. She cycles to work and most weeks she buys a *Big Issue* from outside Wimbledon station. She has a busy job but stops to eat lunch at her desk while catching up on Facebook. Sometimes she uses Google to research different book genres. After work she often heads to the gym. Once she is home, she eats her dinner while watching television and scans through her personal emails. She notices an email from the cancer charity she supports asking her to take part in their bike ride again this year. This is close to her heart, as her mother died from breast cancer.

Andrew

Andrew lives in High Wycombe with his wife and children, is 46 and is a business development manager in a blue-chip company. He usually commutes into Marylebone and then gets the Tube into work. He has been known to cycle the 30 or so miles into work, as he's a keen long-distance cyclist and likes to test himself. He enjoys raising money for charity by doing challenge events, especially with his mates from his cycling club and also with colleagues as part of their team-building and his company's corporate social responsibility programme. On the Tube and train home, he uses the free Wi-Fi to research on Google, check Twitter, prepare for the next work day and check his cycling group's web page to find out when its next trip is scheduled.

Alice and Andrew's personas give insights into their lifestyles and media choices, alongside their motivations. Personas like this can help you to determine the best channels to reach your segments and which messages to send to encourage participation.

Selecting media

To determine your communication tactics for each of the segments, you will need to select the most appropriate online and offline media channels through which to reach them.

Media types

Media types can be categorised into three core groups: paid media (advertising and promotions), owned media (digital presence and printed materials) and earned media (PR, influencer networks and word of mouth). The following sections outline these media types in the context of community fundraising.

Paid media

Paid media is anything that costs you to access it, such as paid search (rather than organic search), display adverts (i.e. advertising on websites, apps, social media, outdoor signage or print media) and affiliate marketing (i.e. advertising on a third-party website, blog or portal). A digital example of affiliate marketing is gateway sites, such as MSN and Yahoo, that lead people elsewhere on the internet. An example of using affiliate marketing offline is including a flyer within a third party's mailing. Paid media advertising provides access to wider audiences, but it can be costly and difficult to track.

Owned media

Owned media includes any media owned by your brand – websites, blogs, apps and social media presence, printed materials (e.g. newsletters and annual reviews), notice boards, etc. It is important to remember that you do not own social media channels, which contain both positive and negative user content and, as such, are not under your control. You will need to monitor any such content and respond to people's complaints and queries.

Earned media

Earned media is coverage of your brand or activity that is created by other people and published in channels you do not own and in which you have not purchased space. It may be generated as a result of your communications through paid and owned media, where these messages are picked up by other publications, sites or social media users. Earned media therefore includes reviews, shares of your content, retweets, social media mentions, press and broadcast coverage, blogs authored by those independent of you and word of mouth. You can encourage the growth of your earned media by developing engaging and useful content that people may want to share, for example:

- sharing content that provides people with useful information while also making them more aware of your brand (often called 'content marketing');
- monitoring social media conversations that mention your charity or cause and getting involved by 'liking' or commenting;
- looking out for whole online communities that are relevant to your charity or cause and getting involved in discussions on online community boards;
- developing relationships with key journalists to facilitate stories being developed within print and broadcast media;
- tweeting or sharing events and stories to be picked up by news sites, the press and broadcast media.

Each of these media types can work together to raise awareness, reach different audiences and ultimately persuade people to take action. Which you use will depend on your objectives – for example, you may use paid media to reach a specific new audience to gain awareness of an event, which in turn may also generate earned media through word of mouth or positive reviews from previous participants.

Digital channels

The pace of change in digital communication can seem overwhelming: as soon as fundraisers master one thing, something new gains traction. Fundraisers need to keep on top of such innovations to ensure they are meeting people's preferences for how they want to engage.

Without doubt, digital communications can facilitate charities' access to wider audiences. This is particularly the case for smaller charities, which are able to reach broad audiences cost-effectively. These technologies have given people unprecedented freedom in how they choose causes, determine how they fundraise, and integrate these experiences into their personal social media stories. Moreover, the array of digital tools available means you can target audiences at a granular level – for example, by demographics, interests and life stage. Unlike in offline communications, you can track prospects' actions even if they do not respond, such as by monitoring click-through rates or social media content sharing. This tracking can provide detailed insights into why campaigns are working or not working.

Your own website and blog content

Your own website is a critical component of your digital strategy, as it is where the vast majority of new and existing supporters will gain further information about your fundraising activities. All digital channels – email, social media, organic search, paid search, display advertising and blogs – should include a direct click-through button to relevant pages on your website. Merely directing prospects to your website's homepage may result in them clicking onto other pages, being distracted by other content or clicking out of your site.

Ensure your website can receive large volumes of traffic during big events. Around 1.4 million people visited the JustGiving website on the 2017 London Marathon weekend, with three donations being given every second.[12] Consider using a third-party website to facilitate participant sign-up if you are expecting peaks of traffic or if your website lacks a certain functionality (such as mobile responsiveness – see box below).

Mobile-responsive sites

Given people's increased use of mobile devices, your website needs to be mobile responsive, i.e. your web pages should change their size and format according to the device they are being accessed on. As Google increasingly focuses on making the user experience as smooth as possible, websites which are not mobile responsive are likely to be penalised on Google's algorithms, resulting in lower search rankings.

Blogs provide additional content to supporters, and they can focus on telling stories from a personal perspective. You can include peer-to-peer messaging on your blog – for example, a marathon runner giving an overview of how their training is going or of the marathon day itself. This personal content may inspire others by giving a sense of the true experience of an event. Blogging also keeps your website content fresh, which is an important aspect of search engine optimisation (see page 112). A blog can engage potential supporters who click through from other sources, such as social media. As a rule of thumb, a blog post should be at least 300 words long (approximately a screen of copy) with images and/or video, and links to longer posts.

Email

Email is an important channel through which charities can talk to their existing supporters. According to research on people's preferred ways of being reached by charities, among all the communication channels available, people are most willing to consent to receive email.[13] (For details on ensuring you have opt-in consent to contact your email list, see 'Consent for sending marketing communications' on page 161.) This finding was the same regardless of people's gender, age and amount donated.[14] Email is also event participants' preferred method of being contacted by charities.[15]

Email is convenient as well as easy to respond to and share, but to use it effectively you need to create compelling messages and present them in an appealing way that gains attention and is memorable. This includes writing a captivating subject line that encourages supporters to open and read your email. Deliver information in bite-sized chunks and provide click-through buttons to your website for more information.

Supporters will engage with a mixture of text, images and video. These can be tailored to different segments' online consumption preferences. To encourage peer recommendation and sign-ups to your activity, include a prominent call to action – i.e. a button to click through to your website. Methodically test each email element (subject headings, images, click-through buttons, etc.) to evaluate what works best with which audience segments.

Mobile devices and text messaging

As smartphones are the most popular devices in the UK for accessing the internet,[16] 24/7 access to digital media is widespread. Mobile phones and tablets have not necessarily cannibalised people's use of their desktop computers, laptops and notebooks but rather added to the total time they spend online.[17] Different demographics prefer different types of technology; for instance, people aged 55 or over prefer using a tablet compared to a smartphone, whereas younger age groups are more likely to use smartphones than tablets.[18] Different demographics also use mobile devices for different reasons; for example, in the UK women aged 16 to 24 are the most frequent users of text messaging whereas men aged 25 to 44 is the group most likely to spend time browsing online.[19] These demographic variances highlight the importance of understanding your charity's different audiences' digital consumption preferences when thinking about the best ways of reaching and engaging them.

Mobile devices can provide a convenient means of staying in touch with supporters through text messaging and can enable convenient peer-to-peer fundraising. In 2017, for example, London Marathon runners who chose to include a text-to-give option (where sponsors could use text messaging to donate) on their fundraising page raised an average of £200 more than runners who did not use this option.[20] Text messaging is also a shareable form of communication. It can be used either to generate a response or to provide information, and it can be personalised to welcome supporters to an event, wish them luck or thank them immediately afterwards.

Search

As well as having a well-constructed and accessible website, you need to ensure that people who are not currently linked to your charity are able to easily find it. One of the key ways that people seek information online is through searching for information via websites such as Google. This process and the mechanisms surrounding it are often collectively referred to as 'search'.

Any activity which increases the visibility of a website is known as search engine optimisation, or SEO. BrightEdge Research reports that 65% of websites' traffic is from search:[21] 51% comes from 'organic search' (i.e. unpaid-for search results from Google or other search engines) and 14% is from paid search. (Of the remaining 35%, 5% is from social media and 30% derives from display advertising, email, and referred traffic.)

To ensure potential supporters can easily find your website and campaign pages, use keywords or phrases (i.e. terms that potential supporters are likely to search for) across your website; this will help to optimise your SEO so that your website is more likely to appear higher up in organic search listings. Search engines use algorithms to determine which websites will appear within their search results and in which order, based upon each website's content and how well it links to other sites, such as national press and social media. Links can be crucial for improving your SEO and reaching out to influencers (see below) to ask them to cite your web links in their articles is an effective strategy for increasing the number of links to your site.[22] It is also helpful to enlist the support of an SEO specialist, if that is an affordable option for your organisation.

Paid search results (such as Google Ads results) are paid adverts that are placed onto digital platforms by ad servers (software that places the adverts) when a person carries out an online search within a search engine. Despite paid search's relatively low traffic figure (as mentioned, only 14% of website traffic comes from this channel), it has the advantage of enabling your web page to appear on the first page of search results without the extensive work it can take to do this organically. This will provide potential supporters with particular pages to click through to, making it easier for you to determine which pages a supporter sees when they arrive on your website.

Influencer outreach

Identifying influencers who can help to deliver content to your target audience (whether as opinion leaders or opinion formers; see also 'Opinion leaders' on page 103) can be a low-cost means of engaging supporters. Influencers may be bloggers, journalists or celebrities and the process is usually mutually beneficial, allowing you to grow your reach organically while providing the influencer with something in return – be it financial remuneration, web traffic for their own online articles or simply affiliation with a good cause. A number of tools are available (such as Traackr.com and BuzzSumo.com) to help you identify key influencers; these tools provide detailed insights by topic and identify the influencers with the largest number of fans. You can also proactively join conversations – for example, by posting on blogs, forums, chatrooms or social media group pages – to help promote your community activities (see 'Earned media' on page 109 for more ideas).

Social media

Social media is a useful means for charities to engage with supporters. For example, community fundraisers might help to motivate supporters as an event draws nearer, or supporters might interact with other members of the event group community. Social media can also be used to share updates and messages with others. However, research has shown that charities tend to overestimate the extent to which people share charities' content with others and, as such, it is important not to focus on social media to the neglect of other media. The nature of sharing can also vary by age group; for example, over-55s are more likely to share a charity's update about a cause or campaign than people aged 18 to 34. So, while members of this age group may be less likely to use social media than others, they can be more responsive when they do.[23]

Facebook

While some types of social media have distinct audiences in terms of demographics, use of Facebook is so widespread that its users are largely representative of the UK population. Facebook's algorithms automatically sort and prioritise the content it believes will be of most interest to individual users, based on what or who the person has interacted with in their newsfeed. This means that, in order for your Facebook posts to reach your target audience organically, users need to have expressed an interest in your content – whether through sharing, liking or clicking on a post.

Alternatively, rather than relying on organic delivery, you can pay Facebook to promote a post to ensure you reach a specific audience or use Facebook Ads. Facebook Ads Manager (a tool that allows you to create and manage adverts on the site) provides you with a wide range of data to help you monitor how effective your ads and promoted posts have been, for example by measuring impressions, audience reach, clicks and video views. You can target audiences by selecting who you want to see the ad, based on demographics, geographical location, behaviour (for instance, the person gives to charity) and interests, as indicated on Facebook through a person's engagement with other content. You can also retarget people – that is, deliver ads in Facebook to people who have visited your website – and use Lookalike Audiences. Using Lookalike Audiences involves instructing Facebook Ads or Google Ads to target audiences based on your Facebook page fans or on people who have taken a certain action, such as viewing one of your videos. Facebook can then target ads at people who are similar to these specified audiences. Facebook is becoming increasingly sophisticated, with the introduction of lead-generation tools, such as pre-filled forms containing the respondent's name and email address.

Historically, supporters have only been able to donate on Facebook by clicking through to third-party platforms, such as JustGiving. However, Facebook's Donate button has now made the giving process seamless, enabling donations to be made without leaving the app or website. At the time of writing, the impact on community fundraising is unclear but, combined with Facebook Live (which allows users to broadcast videos of themselves live), it could enable fundraisers to encourage peer donations while they are completing their event or challenge. A glimpse of this future may be seen in Ariana Grande's 'One Love Manchester' concert (in June 2017) in aid of victims of the Manchester Arena bombing, which raised $450,000 (around £350,000) using donate buttons within Facebook Live.[24]

Twitter

Twitter allows users to post updates (tweets) of any information they like – often content that is interesting, funny or useful – to their followers. Posts are essentially like micro-blogs and can contain up to 280 characters (at the time of writing). Twitter is a great place to make connections to facilitate community fundraising outreach (for example, through celebrities, businesses or individuals such as journalists). It can also be used to direct people to online giving platforms, and Twitter has its own Donate buttons.

Pinterest

Pinterest has around 13 million unique visitors in the UK every month.[25] Unlike other social media platforms, which focus on recording events or actions, Pinterest is used creatively for planning and inspiration. For example, someone undertaking a sponsored event might look for 'pins' (information, articles or photos) to gain motivation or tips to help with their event.

Pins are found through users' feeds (i.e. pins recommended to them) or through search (i.e. keywords). Content therefore needs to be visually appealing and useful and to have a clear call to action. Figure 4.3 shows an example of a Pinterest board for Mind's Crafternoon. It is visually interesting and includes useful instructions and a call to action to visit Mind's website to download its Crafternoon pack.

FIGURE 4.3 A PINTEREST BOARD FOR MIND'S CRAFTERNOON

YouTube

Video brings a cause to life by featuring beneficiaries or projects. Although YouTube is a social network in its own right, it is best deployed alongside other digital activities, such as by promoting YouTube videos through social media or on your website.

Offline channels

Traditional media

Don't overlook the traditional media that may be appropriate for your target audience. Posters, leaflets, outdoor advertising (including the less traditional offline digital billboards), direct mail, telephone, radio, television, magazines and newspapers reach large audiences, help to build brand identity and can be paired with more responsive, personalised and flexible online tactics.

Direct mail

Before planning any direct mail campaign, you must verify and record your legal basis for contacting supporters. (See 'The lawful bases' on page 157 for details.)

Writing to supporters is usually more costly than online forms of communication but can provide an opportunity for an intimate and personalised approach. Mail provides a means of getting tailored messages out to large numbers of people at the same time, and it is targeted and scalable. Some supporters prefer to receive printed fundraising packs rather than downloading materials themselves, and the tangibility of information and materials can provide an ongoing reminder of the need to sign up to an activity or take action. Mail also provides more room to be creative with imagery and can be helpful when you need to include a longer message or where you need to provide a lot of detail about an activity.

Over-55s have a particularly high level of engagement with mail and have experience of responding to mail appeals over the years.[26] Mail can also be popular with younger supporters, with some research showing that in events fundraising the 25 to 34 age group identified direct mail as their preferred communication method.[27] Overall, mail follows email as the second most likely channel through which people will consent to further communications. Mail is trusted by supporters, and people retain materials which they may then refer to or respond to later.[28]

Given this potential for supporters to hold on to materials, you should aim to design mail packs in a way that maximises their retainability and to ensure that distinct elements within a pack can work on their own. Whenever you develop direct marketing materials, ensure that you are clear about what response you are seeking from recipients and that any reply device is easy to use. Include other options for response, such as via email or your website or by phone or text message.

You can also send mail unaddressed but targeted by postcode. In such cases the response rates may be considerably lower due to the approach being less sophisticated, in that you are not personally targeting supporter groups and tailoring messages to them, but the costs are lower and this may provide access to new audiences.

Telephone

When planning any telephone campaign, you must also verify whether you have a legal basis on which to make the calls (see 'The lawful bases' on page 157). Ensure you are clear as to whether the calls are for fundraising or marketing or administrative purposes.

The telephone can be a highly versatile channel for finding out more about supporters' needs and building a connection through a conversation. It can be relatively low cost (depending on whether the campaign is run in-house or by an agency) and provides a flexible means of quickly contacting supporters in a very personalised way. It can provide a powerful means of personally thanking and welcoming people, gauging their level of connectedness, gaining feedback, finding out more about their communication preferences and discussing further ways in which they might be interested in providing support. By calling supporters before they participate in an event or to congratulate them on completing it, you can help them to feel valued by your charity. Conversations of this sort can also help you to determine their motivation for participating, which you can record (with their permission) to help tailor future communications. In community fundraising, it is best to use the telephone when you have an existing relationship with a supporter.

Provide supporters with an inbound telephone number – this will enable you to encourage and respond to their questions, and it will allow them to find out more about taking part in fundraising activities, request information or guidance, and change their communication preferences. Having dedicated community fundraising inbound numbers also helps to reassure participants that you are available to assist them throughout the time that they are participating.

When planning inbound calls, prepare for:

- how you will train the people who will be making or receiving calls;
- various likely scenarios and responses for different types of request and caller;
- what scripts you might use;
- how you will capture information;

- how you will fulfil requests for further information, resource any data capture from the call, and handle questions and queries.

For more information on using the telephone in fundraising, see the Institute of Fundraising's publication *A Good Call: Using the telephone for successful fundraising*.[29]

Print advertising

Print advertising through newspapers, magazines, outdoor advertising, flyers and so on still plays a valuable role in reaching potential participants. Advertising in local newspapers can be effective in raising awareness of local events, and niche publications can provide a means of reaching new supporters you are targeting on the basis of lifestyle interests. Those aged over 55 are the most likely to engage with a charity's press advertising.[30]

Distractions, such as hypertext, when reading on-screen mean that people's concentration when reading print publications is often deeper than when they read digital text.[31] Thanks to readers of print publications not being distracted by the various notifications, images and videos that online advertising has to compete with on digital devices, it is reasonable to infer that print advertising may have a greater impact on readers than online advertising does.

The cost of press and magazine advertising varies by the size of a publication's circulation. Inserts, such as postcards, can be low cost and you can target them at particular audiences. For example, to recruit people to take part in a mass participation team sports event, you might distribute flyers or postcards in gyms or in cafes that are used by office workers. These materials can be kept and not immediately discarded in the way that many forms of digital promotion can be.

In contrast, outdoor advertising can be much more expensive but provide a means of reaching large audiences, such as people using train stations, buses and the Tube or shopping in retail centres. Although it is generally harder to target specific audiences using this channel, you can use creative and powerful images and language to make a significant impact, particularly when your objective is to raise awareness. There are many examples of charities using creative site-specific print advertising to both raise awareness and generate a response, such as organisations involved in sanitation and women's health advertising on the doors of public toilets.

If your objective in using print is to generate action, then consider the most appropriate range of response mechanisms to offer (for example, by text message or telephone, via your website, or via response sections in direct mailings, perhaps offering a Freepost service). Your choice will depend on your target audience and the type of response you are seeking.

For example, if you are seeking a donation, you may want to provide multiple ways to do this; alternatively, if you want people to send off for an information pack, it might be appropriate to limit the options to the telephone and your website.

Television and radio

TV advertising is usually associated with individual giving, but a number of national charities, including Cancer Research UK, Oxfam and Alzheimer's Society, have used it to recruit for mass participation events as part of campaigns using multiple channels. TV advertising can be regional or national and is a means of reaching a mass market. However, it is costly in terms of both airtime and production, and it is more difficult to target particular groups via TV advertising than via many other channels. Nevertheless, like print advertising, it can be effective for raising awareness of your cause and activities.

When considering direct response TV (DRTV), the costs may be prohibitive for all but the biggest budgets. However, DRTV's mass appeal is evidenced by the very high engagement levels it achieves across all demographic profiles. It is particularly powerful at commanding attention – it is memorable, trusted and can bring to life the kinds of emotions that can generate engagement and response.[32]

Radio provides a less expensive means of reaching large audiences and you can target local populations using regional stations. As a very personal medium, in that people listen to radio at home or when driving, it is well suited to telling your charity's story. 'Drive-time' slots (which are the time of day when live radio broadcasters reach the highest numbers of people who listen to car radios while driving)[33] can catch people at times of focused listening.

Door-to-door and face-to-face methods

Chapter 11 looks at house-to-house and street collections, which are the main door-to-door and face-to-face fundraising methods in the context of community fundraising. However, many charities successfully recruit lottery players via door-to-door canvassing, and some smaller charities' volunteer groups approach people door to door to promote a local event.

The strength of both methods is their interpersonal nature, which enables people to ask questions about the aspects of a charity's work that interest them most. Furthermore, these channels can reach those who are time-poor and can provide a means of determining future communication preferences. People can instantly respond or sign up rather than doing so in a delayed fashion, in the way they would in response to a broadcast or print advertisement. The quality of a face-to-face interaction will, of course, rely upon how well informed and trained your canvassers or collectors are.

Guerrilla marketing

Guerrilla marketing can work well for events and includes low-cost tactics such as advertising in unusual places that reach people in their everyday surroundings without the use of additional media (flash mobs, temporary graffiti, dressing of buildings, stickers, stunts, etc.). These tactics can help your organisation to stand out from the crowd and create good word of mouth, but they do need relevant permissions (for example, permission from a landlord if you plan to conduct any of these activities in a shopping centre).

Securing media coverage

When budgets are tight, charities' options may be limited to securing editorial coverage through print, online or broadcast media. To gain editorial coverage, always ensure that, whatever media outlets you are approaching, you are building relationships with journalists and producers. Run your story by them first by phone or email, and demonstrate that you understand the nature of their programming and audience and are aware of the deadlines they are working to. As most community fundraising activities are of local relevance, be sure to follow your local press and radio contacts on Twitter – they will be picking up stories from social media so, when appropriate, mention them when posting your content.

When writing press releases:

- know what coverage you are seeking and what you are aiming to achieve;
- boil your story down to one key point so that it passes the 'so what?' test – i.e. asking why it is of interest to the audience;
- focus on the local angle of your cause or activity and provide compelling stories featuring real fundraisers or beneficiaries;
- decide in advance how you will handle responses to a call to action;
- make sure you can guarantee the availability of spokespeople, photos or video – all of which have to be relevant to the audience.

For more guidance on writing press releases, see the National Council for Voluntary Organisations' article 'How to Write a Brilliant Press Release'.[34]

Rather than using their own reporters, more and more stations are looking to use others' audio or video content, both on air and through their own online channels. If you are planning new content, liaise with local media first to see how they might want to work with you.

There are also many hyperlocal or community news sites and printed publications, such as village and parish magazines. These publications are usually well trusted and those who produce them are likely to be keen to receive content that is specific to their local community. This makes them perfect for promoting many community events.

Finally, make the most of access to the relevant audiences your ready-made partners can offer – corporate supporters, friends groups, your retail operation, relevant service users, your organisation's suppliers, etc.

Integration of online and offline channels

In practice, there is no strict separation between online and offline channels. For example, you can integrate offline channels with digital channels by including a website address in a Tube or press advert. Or you might offer potential supporters an option to respond to an offline advert by text message to make the sign-up process quick and easy. This multi-channel approach can integrate a message across the various media to build momentum and harness what each channel does best. By examining where channels share common ground, as well as their uniqueness, you can evaluate their potential to work together. Additionally, knowing how and why different people interact differently with channels will help you to plan and test your approach in such a way as to optimise supporters' experience.

The importance of this multi-channel approach is that it reflects the nature of a target audience's media consumption. Furthermore, donors reached through multiple channels give nearly double the amount donors reached by online-only channels do, and four times the amount that donors reached by offline-only channels give.[35] Whatever combination of channels you use, remember that not all recipients will see all the communication pieces you are using across different channels. Therefore, each piece must be able to stand alone in terms of its relevance to the recipient.

The range of channels and touchpoints available to reach consumers, and the technologies those consumers use, are evolving rapidly (see table 4.1). You will need to continually monitor your channel use and development needs so as to ensure you are selecting the most appropriate channels to target messages effectively to specific audiences.

TABLE 4.1 CURRENT AND EMERGING CHANNELS AND TECHNOLOGIES

Current	Emerging
Building features and design (e.g. a charity's offices can be designed to showcase its cause and messages)	Digital coupons
Outdoor advertising	Digital signage
POS (point of sale) systems	Gesture recognition
Print	In-store navigation
Products (e.g. products related to the charity's cause, or ads placed on products as part of a charity–company partnership)	Mobile payment systems
QR (quick response) codes	Motion trackers
Radio	Store checkouts
Social media	Video and facial recognition
Telephone	Wearable technology
Television	

To understand where to invest your budget most effectively, you need to evaluate your return on investment from both online and offline channels, comparing response rates and gift values. Also consider how different media channels might interrelate. For instance, outdoor ads within Tube stations may create awareness of your campaign, while Google Ads may encourage supporters to actually respond. The integration of different channels is crucial, as supporters will have multiple touchpoints with your campaign. They may open an email from you in the morning, read an article about your campaign in a newspaper in the afternoon, and click on paid or organic search results to access your website in the evening. It is important to consider how your touchpoints vary by your different target audiences, depending on factors such as age and the audience's level of digital savviness.

Developing multi-channel tactics for each segment

At this point, you will have explored your segments' personas and considered the range of channels available to reach them. Using the bike ride example above, you might identify the following channels for targeting the Alice and Andrew segments.

Offline channels

- Alice watches television, so she will see TV adverts.
- Alice buys the *Big Issue* every week, so she will see its press adverts and inserts.
- Andrew travels to work by Tube, so he will see advertising in carriages, on platforms and on escalators.

Online channels

- Alice uses Facebook.
- Both Alice and Andrew check their emails regularly.
- Andrew uses Twitter, and Google as a research tool.

Table 4.2 illustrates an example of a plan for each segment defined as a result of the segmentation process (see page 73). The plan details what you might aim to achieve for each segment and which channels you might choose. Having clearly documented plans with quantifiable targets for each segment provides a basis against which marketing activities can be monitored and success measured.

TABLE 4.2 EXAMPLE TACTICS FOR REACHING SEGMENTS FOR A SPONSORED BIKE RIDE

Audience segment	Channels to reach audience segments	Target reach	Target percentage of visitors to the page (action)	Target percentage of visitors signing up (conversion)
Previous participants: team members	Facebook posts Email Press adverts (e.g. *Big Issue*)	2,400	25% (600)	35% (210)
Previous participants: individuals	Facebook posts Email	1,500	40% (600)	40% (240)

Audience segment	Channels to reach audience segments	Target reach	Target percentage of visitors to the page (action)	Target percentage of visitors signing up (conversion)
New participants: aged 30–55	Facebook Ads and posts Email from previous participants to friends (recommend-a-friend strategy) Tube adverts	4,500	10% (450)	20% (90)
New participants: bike club members	Digital display adverts on club websites Influencers Google Ads	8,000	10% (800)	20% (160)

Tactics for re-engaging team members and individuals

These two groups can be reached through the same channels – email and Facebook posts. However, as you identified during your segmentation process (see 'Market segmentation strategies' on page 70), they require different messaging to acknowledge their different motivations for supporting your cause. Your messaging will also need to take into account that some of these people will be taking part in teams and some will be participating on their own. These segments will therefore require different materials.

Tactics for targeting new participants aged 30–55

You might use Facebook Ads Manager to target your audience by selecting the location, gender, age and other demographics (such as job title) of the people you wish to target. Once you have selected these characteristics, Ads Manager tells you the size of the resulting audience, which allows you to expand it if necessary by, for example, extending the age range.

You might choose the technique of approaching friends of your existing supporters by instructing Ads Manager to target friends of people who like your Facebook page (either your brand page or a specific event page). The theory is that these people will have similar interests and a similar mindset to those of their friends. Furthermore, they may be more likely to take part because of the phenomenon of 'social proofing' – i.e. because another person they know has already taken part. You might also choose to target new participants by creating a Lookalike Audience (see page 114 for details).

When supporters sign up to the event, you could request that they contact friends and family who might also be interested in taking part. To make it easy for them, include the wording that they could use or adapt to make that request, for example via email or social media.

Tactics for targeting new participants from bike clubs

Your tactics for this target group might be to place adverts on club websites, approach influencers and use Google Ads. This might involve:

- asking bike clubs in your target area to put adverts on their websites (these could be pro forma adverts provided by your charity);
- using Google Ad Manager to target your Andrew audience using the keywords this segment is likely to search for;
- identifying relevant influencers by looking at who is listed as having the top cycling blogs in the UK and reaching out to them with compelling content that is tailored to the persona of this segment.

Shaping the message

Choosing the right channels to reach the right people at the right time needs to be paired with content that is impactful, engaging and appropriate to the purpose of the communication.

How you shape your message will be influenced by where the members of your audience are in the process of adopting a new idea, where you want to take them and what behaviour you want to achieve. The process by which people adopt information (known as the innovation-decision process) requires a number of stages, as shown in figure 4.4.[36] The message you seek to communicate will be determined by which stages in this process you are seeking to move your audience to. Depending on your audience and the nature of the existing relationship you have with them, you may seek to move them through just one of these stages or through all of the first four. Once the purpose of the message has been established, it then needs to be constructed.

FIGURE 4.4 THE PROCESS BY WHICH AUDIENCES ADOPT NEW ACTIVITIES[37]

Knowledge
The activity becomes known to the audience but they have very little knowledge or awareness of it – information needs to be provided through direct or indirect advertising.

Persuasion
The audience becomes aware of how an activity will meet a need; e.g. a desire to meet new people by joining a fundraising group. The influence of others can help to persuade people.

Decision
A positive or negative attitude may be developed that leads to a decision. At this stage, continual prompts towards a positive decision are needed.

Implementation
To adopt the activity, the audience needs to know how and where to sign up or join in, and needs to be reassured of the ease and convenience of doing so.

Confirmation
The activity is accepted or rejected. If it is accepted, continual communication is needed to reinforce this adoption through engagement.

Creating great content

To create great content for both traditional and online media, you need to draw on your understanding of both your audiences and the different channels they use. With traditional media, you will be seeking to interrupt an audience's engagement with someone else's channel (for example, a magazine publisher) so that they pay attention to your message. In the case of digital media, you will continually be aiming to build and retain an audience by developing content that provides some value to them. This distinction is particularly important in the case of social media, as this should be content that people will want to share – and people share material that not only interests them but also reflects well on them when they share it with their social networks.

You also need to know what will inspire them to act. This includes understanding how emotions affect actions and giving behaviour, and how to use this knowledge to increase the chances of your communications persuading people to decide to support you. (See also 'Motivations for participating in community fundraising' on page 9).

The following sections explore how to engage people's emotions and suggest some of the ways you might ensure your supporters are at the heart of the way you communicate.

Engaging emotional decision-making processes

Communicating with your audience in a way that moves them to take action involves using both facts and emotions – with the emphasis on emotions.

Researchers have shown that people have two ways of thinking: emotionally and intuitively (which is fast and easy to do) or rationally and logically (which is a slower and more difficult process).[38] The effect of these two ways of thinking on generosity clearly reveals that it is the triggering of emotion that positively influences the act of giving.

This can be seen in studies which show that when potential donors are presented with larger groups of people in need, they are less generous. For example, when participants in a study read an appeal letter which focused on one little girl in need, they gave more than twice as much as when they read statistics about millions of children in need ($2.38 versus $1.14).[39] The researchers also offered a third option – both the statistics and the story about the little girl – with the theory that reading both of these would make participants more generous. In fact, they choose to give less money ($1.43) than they did when reading about the little girl's story alone.

The researchers' theory about why this occurred was that engaging people's analytical minds with facts and statistics blocked their ability to feel an emotional response to the little girl's story. To test this theory, in a second study they primed one group to think analytically (giving them some mental arithmetic) and another group to think emotionally (by asking them how they feel when hearing the word 'baby'). Afterwards, they gave each group the letter about the little girl in need. Confirming their theory, the group that was primed to feel gave $2.34, whereas the group primed to think analytically gave $1.26.

The reduction in compassion and generosity that occurs when individuals are faced with groups or populations of other people actually begins with a startlingly low number of people. The results of one group of studies showed that seeing an image of just two people in need reduced participants' emotional response, and their level of giving, in comparison to when they were shown an image of one person in need.[40] Participants became even less generous when presented with larger groups of people in need. Why did this happen? The researchers found that people felt more distressed and less compassionate when presented with larger groups, and became less generous as a result. By contrast, seeing one person in need made them feel relatively more compassionate and less distressed, making them more generous. The following sections examine the influences of different types of emotion and explore the delicate balance of eliciting the right emotions at the right levels.

The power of evoking emotions through storytelling

While the potential motivations for participating in community fundraising vary greatly from having fun to social contact or gaining new skills (see chapter 1), we also know that the cause itself is a key driver for both those participating in activities[41] and those giving through sponsorship and donations.[42] Developing content requires the fundraiser to know how to trigger the right emotions in the right context, for all those in the chain of contribution. These include the emotions that will lead to participation in a meaningful event experience, the desire to make a difference for a particular cause and the engagement of peer support.

Charities commonly aim to elicit emotions in potential supporters using story-based appeals. Every story is about something, someone or a situation that has undergone some sort of change. A good fundraising story should focus on an individual beneficiary, their needs and desires, and the obstacles they face. It should also be written in active language that draws upon the very real life drama and challenges the story's protagonist faces.

In fundraising, a story will include a 'problem statement' which describes the situation of a potential beneficiary who is suffering. The potential supporter is then offered a way of helping that individual to make a positive and even life-saving change. Researchers who have studied these stories came to the following conclusions after testing their own story-based appeals:[43]

- Eliciting emotions through stories is an effective way of increasing donations.
- Problem statements provoke negative feelings in potential supporters.
- Taking action to donate to solve the problem both increases positive emotions and reduces negative feelings in supporters.
- Receiving feedback from the charity relieves any residual negative feelings and increases the supporter's likelihood of donating again.
- No feedback from the charity increases the supporter's level of negative feelings.

These results suggest that charities should aim, through their storytelling, to take a potential supporter through various emotional stages. First, they should cause the supporter to feel emotions that compel them to act. This action, in turn, should help to relieve the supporter's negative feelings and increase the positive emotions they feel. But the narrative shouldn't end there. The charity should let the supporter know that they have helped to bring about a happy ending to the story. The feedback and thanking should continue to be about the particular story that caused the person to give or participate and, as a result of this feedback, the supporter should feel the impact that they have made. This should relieve the negative emotions the supporter feels and increase their likelihood of donating again.

This process of triggering emotions and then relieving negative feelings is explored further in the following sections.

Triggering the right emotions at the right intensity

Researchers have proposed that emotions fall into different categories, with the number of categories ranging from 6 to 27.[44] Given that emotions are often not felt in isolation (guilt, for example, might provoke feelings of anger and irritation), studies have looked at a broad spectrum of both positive and negative groups of emotion in relation to charitable appeals. They have found that appeals which initially elicit negative emotions are more effective in causing an intention to make a donation or support a charity in some other way.[45] However, the following studies, which attempted to isolate and examine particular emotions in relation to appeals to the public, show that striking a balance between eliciting a negative emotion and offering a solution is the key to causing people to take action:

- **Fear:** A study tested the theory that the same processes that cause us to want to protect ourselves when we feel fear are triggered in appeals where others need protection. It found that two components are needed to successfully compel people to help others (including animals): you must show the awfulness of the situation of those in danger and the effectiveness of the solution. For example, an environmental charity might show images of an endangered species being hunted but then the activists from the charity saving the animals from the hunters.[46]

- **Anger:** Both anger and feelings of disgust at injustice and suffering can be powerful emotions and are often used by charities. One experimental study[47] found that when participants were made to feel angry, they gave more to a charity whose activities aimed to *repair* the lives of the people in need than to another charity which aimed to lessen suffering and prevent people's suffering. Therefore, if anger is elicited it is important to demonstrate that the money raised or donated will be for a solution that fixes a problem by curing, rescuing or saving the lives of those in need (or that re-establishes justice or restores the environment) rather than helping to improve a situation or prevent or reduce suffering.

- **Guilt:** Some research has found that communicating in a way that causes people to feel guilt makes the message less persuasive[48] and causes people to feel anger towards the charity behind the message.[49] A study of guilt-provoking charitable appeals found that requests which aimed to induce a high level of guilt caused people to perceive that they were being manipulated, making them feel irritated and the appeals more repellent than persuasive as a result.[50] Other research has found that eliciting guilt in appeals increases supporters' intention to take action,[51] even in cases when they don't believe the solution presented to them to be effective.[52] While, overall, the research indicates that guilt is a powerful way of both inducing people to act and causing anger and resentment towards the charity,[53] experience suggests that triggering guilt may be best be avoided. If a goal of fundraising is to make supporters feel good about their efforts, their actions and themselves, any appeal should avoid being heavy handed and causing negative emotions in themselves or towards the charity, which in turn can result in making people turn away from the problem.

- **Sadness:** Researchers looking into which emotions are most likely to stimulate action found that when they caused study participants to feel sad, the participants were more likely to feel like doing nothing than taking action.[54] However, other researchers found that when they induced participants to feel sad and when the participants believed that carrying out a task to help a charity would help to improve their mood, they were more likely to take action than people who thought that helping would not relieve their sadness.[55] Another study that looked into the effect of images of young girls with happy, sad or neutral expressions found that images showing sad expressions caused a higher level of giving than images showing the other expressions. This is likely to occur because people initially feel someone else's pain when they see them suffering (i.e. they feel empathy), which triggers feelings of concern for that person (i.e. sympathy) and, as a result, makes people more likely to help.[56] Sadness can also trigger other emotions, such as nostalgia.

- **Nostalgia:** When a person's feelings of nostalgia are linked to their past experiences with a charitable organisation, this influences their motivation to support that organisation.[57] For example, a person might have felt a connection with a cancer charity ever since their mother died of cancer; they may therefore fundraise for that charity every year with the hope of helping others who are experiencing what their mother experienced.

- **Surprise, compassion and interest:** In one study,[58] researchers analysed people's responses to three types of charity advert (neutral, positive and shocking), for the same cause. They looked at the adverts' effects on participants' intentions to engage with the charity (by donating, volunteering, etc.) and found that the shocking advert created the biggest emotional impact overall. The neutral advert had the lowest overall emotional impact. It was not feelings of shock, however, that were effective at causing people to take action – it was feelings of surprise, compassion and interest, caused by the shocking and positive adverts, that made people act. Compassionate feelings caused by the adverts also made people to want to engage with the charity more. However, compassion was provoked more by the positive advert and less by the shocking advert.

- **Happiness, joy, hope and regret:** In the same study, feelings of happiness, joy and hope caused by the adverts each made people less likely to intend to engage with the charity presented. The researchers propose that this is because when people feel happy, joyful or hopeful, they perceive less of a need and as a result do not take action to help. Regret was the only other emotion that acted as a deterrent, perhaps because it causes people to avoid taking action.[59]

Overall, these studies show that campaigns which initially elicit negative emotions generate a stronger response than those that initially generate positive responses. This negative approach tends to be most successful, however, when it is balanced by showing the positive outcome of that response – in other words, how the problem has been solved. This positive outcome in turn generates positive feelings, such as relief, happiness or a sense of justice, in supporters (a process which follows the pattern in the research on the power of storytelling outlined above).

The last study mentioned, however, advises charities not to assume that inducing a particular number of emotions in appeals will consistently cause the same behavioural responses from supporters. They emphasise instead the importance of testing your appeals on different audiences.[60]

It is also important to remember that these studies mostly focus on people's intention to donate rather than their intention to take part in an event. When thinking about what might stimulate event participation, positive emotions such as happiness and fun may predominate in many cases. For example, some groups of people will expect to have a good time during events, and this expectation will be a strong determinant of whether they take part. This will particularly be the case for social events such as coffee mornings and fun runs. Those taking part in more gruelling challenge events may be motivated by an expectation of feeling a sense of great achievement after the event.

Making it personal

A basic principle of fundraising is that when communications are personal to the supporter, relationships can be more easily built. The stronger the relationship, the greater the chance of securing and retaining support.

There are four broad considerations in making communications personal: show you know the supporter, a sense of connection, demonstrating similarity between supporters and beneficiaries, and ensuring that communications are sent from a person, not an entity.

Show you know the supporter

A communication should feel like it's been sent from a person to a person, and it should therefore reflect what you know about the supporter and what they know or might want to know about you. No word is more powerful than our own name, and supporters should be addressed in person, whether by letter, by email, on the phone, face to face or on social media. When you further craft your communications to reflect what you know about a supporter's interest in your cause, motivations, preferred activities, previous support and communication preferences, your messages will start to look and feel unique and authentic to the recipient.

Sense of connection

People feel connected to an organisation or a brand when its values reflect their own (see 'Identification' on page 135 for details). Communications can therefore feel more personal if they reflect these values. For example, if you know that someone identifies as being caring, or a leader, or a fun personality, or sporty, etc., consider how your content can mirror and reinforce this.

Similarity to recipient

Research has shown that individuals are more likely to give to recipients who are similar to themselves than to those with whom they do not identify.[61] Finding commonality between your supporters and your beneficiaries is important in stimulating feelings of empathy, which allows people to feel for others by putting themselves in those others' situation. Storytelling can feel more personal and relevant when the reader can connect with your beneficiaries. While all of our experiences differ, common points of connection can be around the experience of being a parent and wanting the best for our children, needing food and shelter, or the relief of pain.

From a person, not an entity

For a communication to be part of a conversation, it needs to clearly come from an individual person. Consistency of contact with a community fundraiser who is dedicated to looking after specific supporters can help to build a high-quality relationship. However, also consider when it is relevant for personal notes of thanks to come from a beneficiary, your chief executive, a member of your service team, etc. (For further details, see 'Thanking DIY fundraisers' on page 238.)

Demonstrating impact

Supporters care about the impact a charity has and three in five donors pay close attention to what their donation will achieve.[62] When people are choosing between charities that all serve a single cause that they feel passionate about, they will choose the one that appears to be the most effective.[63] Although individuals who sponsor friends and family are motivated by how much they care about that person, that person's concern for the cause and the nature of the event (see page 11), the general interest the public have in how charities spend their funds means that both the individual fundraiser and their sponsors need to be reassured that supporting your charity will deliver the impacts and changes they are passionate about.

Different aspects of a charity's work will inspire different supporters. Conversations with supporters about what motivated them to become a supporter and the changes they are passionate about will help you to tailor how you give feedback to them on what your charity has achieved. This will ensure that you are connecting with their emotions throughout their experience of supporting you, not just at the point of solicitation. People's desire to know what donations are spent on should be linked to the impacts they care about the most.

There are many ways of communicating impact, and ongoing research into which methods work best will enable you to fine tune your approach. For example, you could:

- Create videos and stories about individual beneficiaries.
- Arrange for supporters to visit your projects.
- Supply DIY fundraisers with shareable content on the positive changes your charity has delivered. They can then engage potential sponsors by demonstrating how the money they donate will be used. Use stories about real beneficiaries to bring to life the tangible impact supporters' fundraising will make on an individual.

Minding your language and making your design shine

Fundraising communications are about having a conversation with supporters and so the language you use should reflect this. For example:

- Write how you would speak by using shorter and simpler words and phrases (for example, 'take part' and 'set up' rather than 'participate' and 'establish').
- Putting the supporter at the heart of your content means using the language of 'you'. This means writing in the first person, referring to 'your support' or 'your help', saying 'thank you' and including phrases such as 'because of you'.
- Use short sentences and paragraphs.
- Avoid jargon or sector-specific terms such as biodiversity, community development and empowerment, and scrap tautologies, such as 'first invented', 'mutual agreement' and 'fatal death'.
- The most powerful verbs are active and direct because they communicate both action and emotion. Think about *beating* cancer versus finding a *cure for* cancer, *crave* safety versus *need safety from conflict* or *saving* the environment versus *caring about* it.

• Most adverbs can be replaced with a stronger verb. For example, instead of 'the child walked unsteadily', consider 'the child staggered'. Or, instead of 'the floodwaters rose quickly', choose 'the floodwaters surged'.

• Stick to adjectives that are evocative and specific and don't use any that are unnecessary. Too many adjectives – such as 'astonishing', 'agonising' or 'groundbreaking' – can feel overwhelming, whereas a good story told well, coupled with powerful imagery, should evoke the emotions you are seeking to stimulate.

• Bring a story and situation alive by involving the senses to activate the reader's imagination. What did it look like? What sounds do you hear? What does something smell like or taste like?

• Attention spans are short – don't lose the reader in too much context. Sometimes you just need to get to the point.

• Keep it simple and avoid distracting metaphors and cleverness. Humour can be very effective but it must be used carefully.

• Make sure your copy applauds your supporters. Use descriptors that reflect their innermost perceptions of who they are as individuals (see page 135) – for example if they perceive themselves to be kind, caring and compassionate, describe them as being so.

Many smaller charities do not have the luxury of design teams and therefore have to put packs and newsletters together themselves. Here are some simple tips to avoid common design errors:

• Avoid putting words entirely in uppercase.

• Ensure that your headlines sum up a story – people skim-read.

• Avoid reversing text out of a solid background or using light coloured text – it's too difficult to read.

• Avoid photographs of cheque presentations – focus on your beneficiaries thanking supporters and on the difference your supporters make.

• Be easy on the eye: make your publications visually appealing and dominated by photos and not text.

• Ensure that your photographs reflect the emotions you are aiming to stimulate and are consistent with the stories you are telling.

Building relationships

To sustain the long-term support of community fundraising participants, your communications need to focus on building a relationship. In a review of the fundraising and marketing literature on building customer and donor loyalty, Adrian Sargeant considered four main factors that determine loyalty: trust, identification, satisfaction and commitment.[64]

The following sections outline the practical steps Sargeant recommends and our own observations on how to promote these four elements.

Trust

Trust is the most significant factor in developing long-lasting relationships with supporters.[65] You can increase this sense of trust by:

- communicating to supporters the impact their fundraising is making on your organisation's beneficiaries;
- communicating how your organisation's values and good judgement inform its overall direction and the services it provides to its beneficiaries;
- honouring any promises you make to supporters (this could include a huge range of promises, from assurances regarding the nature of an event experience to guarantees about how much volunteering support you will provide and expectations about how quickly you will provide materials and thank supporters);
- ensuring that staff are trained to have the knowledge and demeanour to offer excellent supporter care;
- engaging in two-way communication with supporters by providing plenty of feedback opportunities and having teams that are available and trained to answer queries.

Another part of building trust involves developing a dialogue with supporters, using for example supporter surveys, to find out more about their interests and experiences of engaging with your organisation. These dialogues will help to build your understanding of how supporters want you to connect with them differently over time and, if acted upon, can in turn build their confidence in your organisation.

Identification

Identification is a term that describes people's experience of feeling a sense of connection with an organisation. This connection occurs when people's own values – and how they see themselves – fit with the values and brand of the organisation.[66] For instance, someone might support the Canal & River Trust because they see themselves as a responsible person who cares about the preservation and enjoyment of the environment both now and for future generations. They may have seen those values reflected in the charity's literature and when they have encountered its fundraisers in person, which will have reinforced their feeling of connection with the organisation.

In this way, if you are seeking to build a relationship with your supporters, consider the various ways in which they see themselves and aim to communicate with them in a manner that reinforces their self-identities and values. Help them to build this positive view of themselves by showing them how their contribution will reinforce the type of people they are or want to be.

Satisfaction

The more satisfied a supporter is with the interactions they have with an organisation, the more loyal they become.[67] In a community fundraising context, a supporter's initial sense of satisfaction might be related to how well your organisation assisted their participation in an event and how much fun they had during the experience (if having fun was their main motivation for taking part).

To measure supporters' levels of satisfaction, carry out surveys following your fundraising activities. Bear in mind that the nature of satisfaction can change over time, so you will want to know any given supporter's level and type of satisfaction when they first participate in your community fundraising programme and again at later points of participation. Doing this can help you to identify further ways of achieving supporter satisfaction and building relationships. For example, if an event participant valued the social element of the experience the most, you could offer more ways of satisfying this motivation. If their motivation then changed at a later stage, you could tailor what you offered them to fit accordingly.

At an organisational level, by measuring levels of satisfaction, you can evaluate whether you are getting better at satisfying your supporters' needs over time and report on these findings.

Commitment

Commitment is about a supporter's intention to continue their relationship with an organisation. Active commitment is where a supporter genuinely believes in a charity's cause, whereas passive commitment is where a supporter will continue to support an organisation regardless of how satisfied they are with it.[68]

You can increase levels of active commitment among supporters by building trust (as outlined above) and by demonstrating to your supporters that your charity shares their beliefs and can provide effective solutions.[69] This involves providing multiple two-way engagement opportunities, such as project visits, thank-you events, social get-togethers with other volunteers, opportunities to offer ideas for new events and opportunities to give feedback on how to improve existing activities.

Another way to build active commitment is to emphasise to supporters the difference that their support makes to your organisation and its beneficiaries. If you explain how much of an impact their contributions are making, supporters are more likely to maintain their support because of a sense that withdrawing it would have a negative impact on your beneficiaries.[70] This aspect of commitment is linked to supporters having trust that your organisation will have a positive impact on its beneficiaries.

Lastly, the more supporters learn and know about your organisation from the communications you send, the more committed they will be. To deepen supporters' sense of commitment, it is crucial to plan supporter journeys that allow supporters to continually learn and expand their knowledge about your organisation's work, as opposed to offering them a succession of one-off activities to participate in.[71]

Planning supporter journeys

The supporter journey is a conceptual framework that can help you to think through all of the interactions, or touchpoints, your charity has with supporters to build a relationship with them. This extends from the first point of contact with your charity (such as signing up to an event) to the end of the first period of engagement (completing the event) and onwards into encouraging further support.

Understanding the journey your supporters are likely to take when they engage with your charity can help you to identify how best to communicate with them to encourage the actions you are seeking at each point of contact you have with them. These different actions might include enquiring, signing up, participation, peer-to-peer recommendation, repeat participation and other forms of support. Of course, supporters may not follow a set path in their engagement, so you will need to continually review your expectations and perhaps outline multiple potential supporter journeys, segmented by audience (see 'Market segmentation strategies' on page 70).

Whatever path your supporters follow, you will need to ensure it matches the experience they are seeking. A supporter journey should be personalised to meet the individual's preferences and the nature of their responses and engagement with your organisation. Identifying these supporter preferences, characteristics and stages of support needs to be matched with robust and manageable processes for responding to and recognising them. For example, as outlined in chapters 2 and 3, it is important to capture information on why people are participating in your event (for example, in memory of someone, to get fit, to find a cure for cancer or to support a friend), segment them according to these reasons, and then acknowledge these reasons in your welcome email, letter or phone call. (See, however, chapter 5 regarding seeking consent for capturing this information, particularly 'Special category data' on page 161. You will also generally need to ensure that you comply with data protection regulations throughout the supporter journey.)

You need to provide choices about how and when participants can hear from you and through which channels, by gathering data at the point of sign-up and at key milestones (see chapter 5). Continually offer your supporters choices, as their preferences may change over the course of their journey. For example, they might start out preferring to be contacted by email but then want to receive text messages just before and during an event.

Understanding how participants might feel at any point in time means providing opportunities for two-way communication, such as via social media and emails. For example, you might encourage them to give feedback on their preparation for an event (for instance, if the event is a physical one, you might try to find out about their training). This can trigger opportunities for you to thank and encourage supporters and to focus on highlighting the impact their efforts will have on your charity's beneficiaries.

Make your communications as personal as possible by, for instance, including messages from beneficiaries or recognising how much the fundraiser has raised. Provide plenty of thank-you messages and updates that do not ask for anything in return. Chapter 7 provides further examples of some common ways of supporting participants (see 'Enabling DIY fundraisers' success' on page 228).

Ultimately, supporter journeys should help you to create a regular pattern of communication and events that you use to develop your relationships with supporters. Remember that to shape the tone and content of these communications, you need to understand your audience and consider the importance of emotion and how relationships are built, which are covered earlier in this chapter.

Using our cycle event, figure 4.5 shows an example of what a supporter journey could look like over a 12-month period. This includes all the communications for the event, ongoing stewardship, cross-selling of additional forms of support, and thanking and recognising. Individual supporters will always vary in the exact journey they take, depending on the nature of the relationship they want with your charity, but creating a plan of the most likely pathways can help you to determine how a supporter's behaviour and interests trigger the next most appropriate communication.

FIGURE 4.5 EXAMPLE SUPPORTER JOURNEY

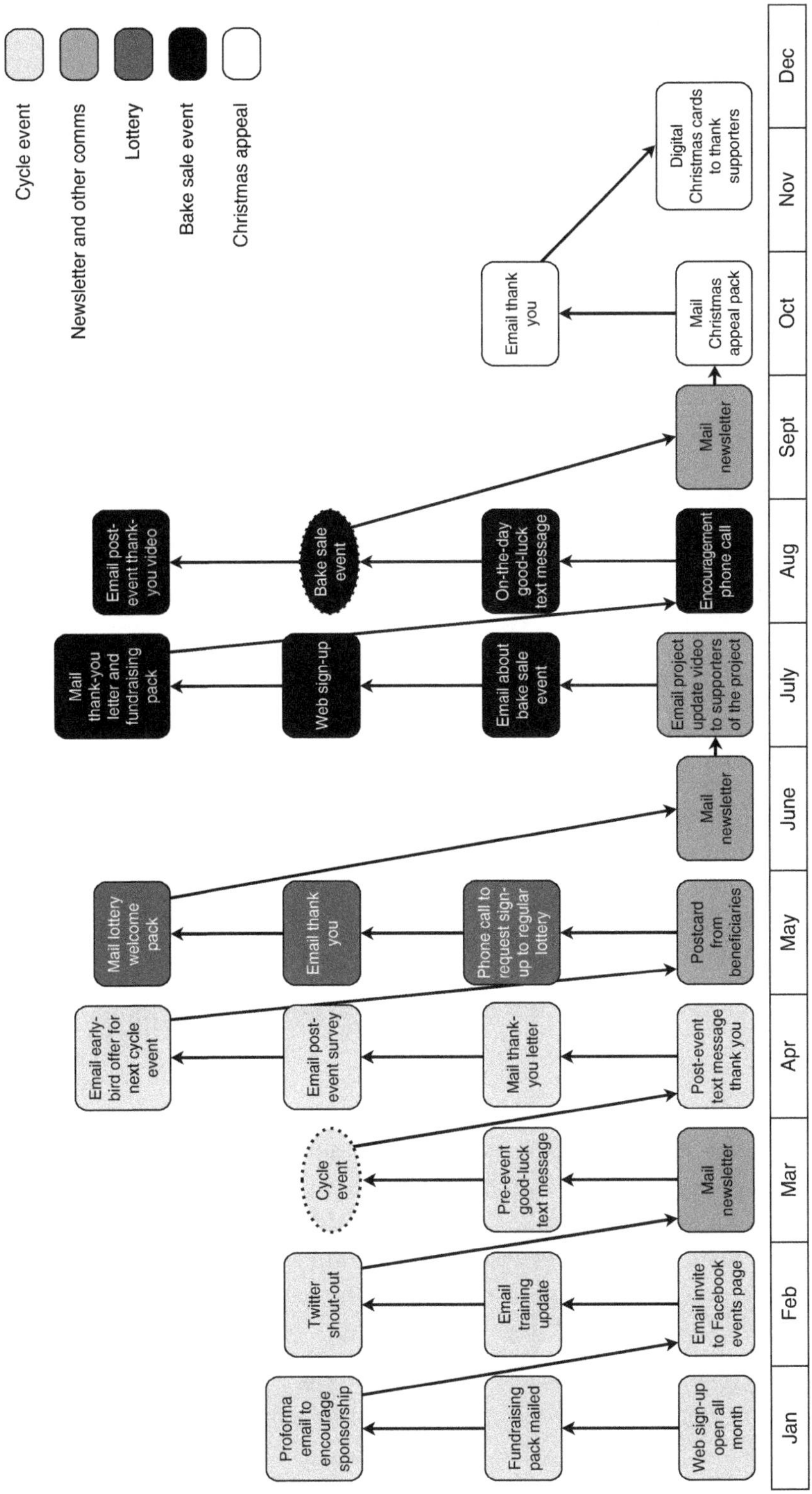

Case study: JDRF UK – tweaking the supporter journey

At JDRF UK – 'the type 1 diabetes charity' – we have been organising London-based 5K and 10K sponsored walks, aimed at families and adults who have a connection to type 1 diabetes, since the year 2000. However, as time went on, it became more and more difficult to increase both participation and average sponsorship values. Based on feedback, our community fundraising team tested a few simple tweaks to the supporter journey:

- To create a greater sense of community, the team introduced a 'face of the walk', which was a participating family raising funds for their son with type 1 diabetes.
- The story of the family was featured across all marketing materials. This allowed us to emphasise our supporters' shared passion for realising the best possible treatment and care for family members and others with type 1 diabetes.
- The team sent personalised emails to former participants thanking them for the amounts they had previously raised and giving examples of the difference this had made to families and people with type 1 diabetes.
- People signing up for the first time were emailed a message from existing participants with whom they might identify. For example, if a supporter was a grandparent, they received a message from another grandparent who was taking part with an explanation of the impact their fundraising would achieve.
- The team called all individuals who had signed up for the event to thank them and wish them luck.

To deepen the sense of family participation, families could use a photo booth on the day and their photographs were sent to them after the event as part of our thank you. The mailing also included an option to sign up for the next year's walk.

By changing the supporter journey, enhancing personalisation and strengthening the case for support, we increased the average gift value to our charity from £94 to £212.

Hannah Roberts, Development Manager (South, East and London), JDRF UK

Scheduling and resourcing

You will need to assign responsibility for the delivery of each element of your communications plan, decide by when the responsible people must complete the key actions, and allocate the required costs. You should also identify which tasks can be managed in-house versus by agencies. Table 4.3 shows an example of a planning tool. (For more information on budgeting see 'Setting the budget' on page 83, and for further planning tools see 'Scheduling' on page 88.)

TABLE 4.3 SCHEDULING PLANNING TOOL

Project area	**Activity**	**Who manages this function?**	**Written brief required?**	**Budget**	**Deadline for brief**	**Go-live date(s)**
Owned media						
Your website	New website sections or pages	☐ In-house ☐ Agency ☐ Freelancer	Y/N	£	E.g. 1 January 2020	E.g. 31 March 2020
	Updating existing website pages (copy, images, content)	☐ In-house ☐ Agency ☐ Freelancer	Y/N	£	E.g. 1 January 2020	E.g. 31 March 2020
	Functionality updates (new payment gateways, forms, etc.)	☐ In-house ☐ Agency ☐ Freelancer	Y/N	£	E.g. 1 January 2020	E.g. 31 March 2020
	Blog	☐ In-house ☐ Agency ☐ Freelancer	Y/N	£		
Your social media content	Facebook posts	☐ In-house ☐ Agency ☐ Freelancer	Y/N	£		
	Tweets	☐ In-house ☐ Agency ☐ Freelancer	Y/N	£		
	Pinterest	☐ In-house ☐ Agency ☐ Freelancer	Y/N	£		
	Instagram	☐ In-house ☐ Agency ☐ Freelancer	Y/N	£		
	YouTube	☐ In-house ☐ Agency ☐ Freelancer	Y/N	£		
	Other					

Project area	Activity	Who manages this function?	Written brief required?	Budget	Deadline for brief	Go-live date(s)
Emails (to warm supporters and prospects)	Copy	☐ In-house ☐ Agency ☐ Freelancer	Y/N	£		
	Design	☐ In-house ☐ Agency ☐ Freelancer	Y/N	£		
	Build	☐ In-house ☐ Agency ☐ Freelancer	Y/N	£		
Printed materials	'Take one' leaflets	☐ In-house ☐ Agency ☐ Freelancer	Y/N	£		
	Mail packs	☐ In-house ☐ Agency ☐ Freelancer	Y/N	£		
	Other	☐ In-house ☐ Agency ☐ Freelancer	Y/N	£		
Earned media						
Editorial copy for local/ national media	Radio	☐ In-house ☐ Agency ☐ Freelancer	Y/N	£		
	TV	☐ In-house ☐ Agency ☐ Freelancer	Y/N	£		
	Print	☐ In-house ☐ Agency ☐ Freelancer	Y/N	£		
Online outreach	Websites	☐ In-house ☐ Agency ☐ Freelancer	Y/N	£		
	Newspapers and magazines	☐ In-house ☐ Agency ☐ Freelancer	Y/N	£		
	Influencers and blogs	☐ In-house ☐ Agency ☐ Freelancer	Y/N	£		

Project area	Activity	Who manages this function?	Written brief required?	Budget	Deadline for brief	Go-live date(s)
Guerrilla marketing	Ambient	☐ In-house ☐ Agency ☐ Freelancer	Y/N	£		
	Online viral marketing	☐ In-house ☐ Agency ☐ Freelancer	Y/N	£		
SEO	n/a	☐ In-house ☐ Agency ☐ Freelancer	Y/N	£		
Paid media						
Social media adverts	Facebook	☐ In-house ☐ Agency ☐ Freelancer	Y/N	£		
	Twitter	☐ In-house ☐ Agency ☐ Freelancer	Y/N	£		
	YouTube	☐ In-house ☐ Agency ☐ Freelancer	Y/N	£		
	Other	☐ In-house ☐ Agency ☐ Freelancer	Y/N	£		
Google Ads	Grant	☐ In-house ☐ Agency ☐ Freelancer	Y/N	£		
	Paid	☐ In-house ☐ Agency ☐ Freelancer	Y/N	£		
Display ads	Digital display	☐ In-house ☐ Agency ☐ Freelancer	Y/N	£		
	Print media	☐ In-house ☐ Agency ☐ Freelancer	Y/N	£		
	Broadcast media	☐ In-house ☐ Agency ☐ Freelancer	Y/N	£		

Project area	Activity	Who manages this function?	Written brief required?	Budget	Deadline for brief	Go-live date(s)
Affiliates	Digital	☐ In-house ☐ Agency ☐ Freelancer	Y/N	£		
	Print	☐ In-house ☐ Agency ☐ Freelancer	Y/N	£		
Outdoor ads	Billboards, posters, etc.	☐ In-house ☐ Agency ☐ Freelancer	Y/N	£		
Direct dialogue	Telemarketing (outbound)	☐ In-house ☐ Agency ☐ Freelancer	Y/N	£		
	Door-to-door	☐ In-house ☐ Agency ☐ Freelancer	Y/N	£		
	Face-to-face	☐ In-house ☐ Agency ☐ Freelancer	Y/N	£		
Response handling						
Supporter care	Responding to email replies and queries, social media comments, website enquiries, etc.	☐ In-house ☐ Agency ☐ Freelancer	Y/N	£		

Monitoring: how to know whether you've succeeded

To measure how successful you have been with your communications, both for specific activities and for specific segments, you will need to start with your communications objectives. Using the example at the start of this chapter, the communications objective was:

> To convert 250 previous participants to sign up online for our next cycling event by [date], each raising £100 at a cost per sign-up of £10.

One of the tactics used to achieve this objective (see table 4.2) was to email the previous participants. To determine how close you are to achieving this objective via the tactic of emailing, you would need to set key performance indicators (KPIs) for how many of those who were emailed went on to click through to your website and how many actually signed up. For example, your KPIs could be:

> 40% of those emailed click through to website.
>
> 40% of these sign up.

If you emailed 1,500 previous participants and 600 of these clicked through to your website's sign-up page, you would meet this 40% click-through rate KPI, and, if 240 of those people signed up, you would achieve your desired target of a 40% conversion rate from click-throughs. A low number of sign-ups – say, a conversion rate of only 20% – would fail to achieve your target sign-up rate. In this case, you would need to gather feedback from those who didn't re-register to analyse what the barriers were to signing up. For example, did you ask for too much information? Were the design and messaging uninspiring? Did the links work? And so on.

For more information on KPIs, see page 91, and for details on monitoring and reporting at the level of your overall community fundraising strategic plan, see page 95.

Examples of metrics to monitor

For each channel that you use, you will need to develop a set of KPIs that allow you to compare the performance of different segments against one another and your previous year's results against your current year's results. Table 4.4 provides example KPIs for various channels and what each KPI indicates.

TABLE 4.4 EXAMPLE OF CHANNEL-SPECIFIC METRICS

KPI	Media channel(s) being measured	What it tells you
Open rate	• Email	How many people opened your email, usually shown as a percentage
Click-through rate	• Email • Social media (paid and organic) • Paid search	How many people clicked through to your website to seek more information
Conversion rate	• Email • Social media (paid and organic) • Paid search	How many people converted to take an action as a result of receiving a digital communication

KPI	Media channel(s) being measured	What it tells you
Cost per acquisition	Any paid media, such as: • Facebook Ads • Google Ads (although not-for-profit Google Ads grants are also available so this is not necessarily a paid channel) • Display adverts	How much you paid to acquire a new supporter or event participant
Mailing response rate	• Direct mail	How many people converted to take an action as a result of receiving a direct mail message

Monitoring tools and what they show you

The following tools provide you with some of the key data you need to measure the success of your online communications.

Google Analytics

Google Analytics is a free tool that can be used to analyse and monitor the results of digital campaigns. Examples of what it records include how many visitors you draw to your website, the number of page views you receive and the amount of time visitors spend on pages. It provides insights into visitor demographics alongside geographical location, albeit at an aggregated level rather than an individual level. It can also tell you how many people visited your site and from what source – for example, social media, referral, direct, paid search (such as Google Ads) or organic search.

Google Analytics enables you to see how many people completed a particular 'goal'.[72] For instance, if a person visits a particular page you want them to visit or moves through a series of pages to complete an action, such as signing up for your e-newsletter or downloading a DIY event pack, these would count as completed goals (i.e. conversions). This can help you to see, for example, how many people reached your thank-you page and signed up to an event, or where they might be dropping out. In this way, tracking goals allows you to see how well your website is helping or hindering the achievement of your objectives. You can also look at visitors by segment – for example, to identify which segments of people clicked through via Twitter, via your emails or via other pages on your site. As Google Analytics continually updates, it enables you to reconsider and potentially change your tactics depending upon the results and trends you are seeing.

You can also set up Google goals to more closely monitor specific actions you want prospects or supporters to take on your website. You will find free tutorials online to help guide you through set-up.

The Facebook pixel

The Facebook pixel is a piece of code you can add to your website that allows you to track conversions from Facebook Ads. It collects data about the actions people have taken on your website, such as donating, signing up to a newsletter or downloading a fundraising pack. Again, there are various guides online that you can use to get started.

Your database

Your customer relationship management system will allow you to generate the reports needed to analyse, for example, your cost per acquisition and which custom landing pages or bespoke email addresses were used most often as a result of an offline campaign.

Social media monitoring tools

There are many different social media monitoring tools that provide reporting functions that can help you to demonstrate the impact of your social platforms. Which tool you should use will depend on what metrics you would like to measure. Many offer free trials so that you can try before you buy and others have free versions that are more limited than their full paid offerings. Hootsuite, for example, is a social media management tool which can help you to measure the impact of your social media communications, including levels of brand reach and engagement. It offers a free plan and a non-profit discount.[73] There are also more focused analytics tools on offer; for example, TweetReach helps you to measure the impact of your tweets, and Twitter has its own Analytics dashboard that tells you about your followers and how many people are engaging with your tweets.

Email monitoring tools

The performance of emails can be monitored to track how different segments respond to emails and assess the most effective types of content, headers and calls to action. Using a good email deployment system, such as MailChimp or Adestra, will enable you to analyse results, such as open rates, when and where an email has been read, click-through rates and actions (such as signing up to an event, subscribing to your e-newsletter, or sharing a post). This helps you to continually improve your email's responsiveness through design and content, and also know when and how to follow up. For example, if someone has not opened an email from you, then follow-up is likely to be inappropriate, whereas if they open and click through to a link giving more information but do not respond, follow-up could help to prompt a response. You should also define proper use of email tracking tools in your privacy policy and disclose when people sign up for email subscriptions that email tracking notifications are in use.

How Mind used digital to grow Crafternoon

In 2014, Mind analysed the types of activity its community fundraisers were undertaking and noticed a trend towards DIY fundraisers arranging craft sessions to produce decorations and cards. The concept of social craft sessions, called 'crafternoons', was already big in the USA and it appeared to be growing organically in the UK.

We did a launch of Crafternoon in December 2014, with some limited paid-for Facebook marketing resulting in 1,500 enquiries with a conversion rate of 3%. We wanted to find out why this initial interest didn't translate to registrations and undertook quantitative research to identify participant demographics.

Subsequently, we created audience segments and ran focus groups to identify how participants wished to be engaged and supported. This informed the testing of new Crafternoon collateral, including the Crafternoon kit and templates, and resulted in our extending the life of Crafternoon from a Christmas fundraiser to a year-round theme.

As Crafternoon grew, so did the marketing activities to support it – we used an automated email system to send out bespoke communications based on the fundraiser's registration and event dates. So, for example, following registration, communications concentrated on encouraging the fundraiser's support until their Crafternoon event date was confirmed. After this point, our communications then focused on stewardship and included countdown timers, wishes of good luck and follow-up communications after the event concluded to thank the fundraiser. These communications helped to boost the number of registrations by 187% and led to a growth in income from £12,000 in 2015 to £40,000 in 2016, £40,000 in 2017 and £100,000 in 2018.

We created a closed Facebook group specifically for people who registered for Crafternoon. This was designed to engage participants in the activity and the charity by posting stories that linked to the cause, and to offer tips and advice on how to hold a Crafternoon. The purpose of the group was also to foster a sense of community and excitement within the Crafternoon participants through peer-to-peer interaction. In addition, we found that Facebook advertising particularly well as a platform to encourage registrations. This was because Facebook allowed us to focus on users who expressed or had shown an interest in crafting ideas (by sharing or liking crafting posts) and subsequently targeted them with an advert on Crafternoon in their newsfeeds.

We also experimented with Pinterest by creating some Crafternoon boards to test whether this would attract a younger audience and identify those people with an active interest in crafting.

Having gained more detailed insights into our Crafternoon audiences, we were able to make more informed decisions about where we might reach them. After looking at the media pack for Sainsbury's magazine, we identified that its audience was comparable to our insights into our own audience. As such, we ran a series of online adverts through the Sainsbury's magazine online platforms, which allowed us to reach their customers.

Maria Khosla, Community Fundraising Manager, Mind

Conclusion

However well researched, designed and managed your community fundraising activities are, their success will also be dependent upon your ability to win people's hearts. This requires carefully constructed communication plans that will attract, excite and engage supporters. Understanding your supporters and continually learning about them will help you to personalise the conversations you are having with them throughout their supporter journey. Recognising the power of emotion and stimulating the right emotions can help to inspire your fundraisers to feel that your cause is theirs and that the solutions are within their power.

Digital media will continue to have a significant impact on the evolution of community fundraising. Ways in which we use digital channels will inevitably continue to develop as technology advances and new digital fundraising events and activities become more commonplace. However, the principles that underpin the use of digital channels are the same as those that make for effective offline recruitment, engagement and retention – the difference is in the methods and means of communication. Success will lie in reaching the right people, through the right channels, with the right messages at the right time.

Notes

1 Wilbur Schramm, 'How Communication Works', in *The Process and Effects of Mass Communications*, edited by Wilbur Schramm, Illinois, University of Illinois Press, 1955, pp. 3–26 at p. 4.
2 *Ibid.*, p. 9.
3 Claude E. Shannon and Warren Weaver, *The Mathematical Theory of Communication*, Urbana, University of Illinois Press, 1963, p. 8.
4 Everett M. Rogers, *Diffusion of Innovations*, New York, Free Press, 2003 (the first edition of this book was published in 1962).
5 *Ibid.*, see chapter 7, 'Innovativeness and adopter categories', pp. 267–99.
6 Everett Rogers, 'File:Diffusion of ideas.svg' [Wikimedia Commons file], https://commons.wikimedia.org/wiki/File:Diffusion_of_ideas.svg, 28 February 2012. Based on Everett M. Rogers, *Diffusion of Innovations*, New York, Free Press, 1962.
7 Everett M. Rogers, *Diffusion of Innovations*, New York, Free Press, 2003, p. 27.
8 The term 'opinion former' is not mentioned in Everett M. Rogers' *Diffusion of Innovations*. It appears to have been coined by marketers after the popularisation of the term 'opinion former' and is defined in, for example, Chris Fill, *Essentials of Marketing Communications*, Harlow, Pearson Education, 2011, p. 46.
9 Everett M. Rogers, *Diffusion of Innovations*, New York, Free Press, 2003, p. 19.
10 *Ibid.* p. 27.
11 Nick Mason, 'Donor profiling: Busting the myths' [web article], www.charitychoice.co.uk/the-fundraiser/donor-profiling-busting-the-myths/108, 21 August 2012.
12 Presentation by Keith Williams for JustGiving, 'Big trends from the biggest fundraising event in the world', London, Institute of Fundraising Community Fundraising Conference, 5 June 2017.
13 *Fundraising Media DNA 2016/17: The engagement of donors with different fundraising channels* [PDF], Institute of Fundraising and fastmap, 2017, www.fastmap.com/fundraising-campaigns, p. 10, accessed 13 April 2019.
14 *Ibid.*, p 44.
15 *Closing the Loop* [PDF], Blackbaud and the Institute of Fundraising, 2015, www.everydayhero.com/uk/closing-the-loop, p. 10, accessed 13 April 2019.
16 'Internet access – households and individuals, Great Britain: 2018' [statistical bulletin], Office for National Statistics, 2018, https://www.ons.gov.uk/peoplepopulationandcommunity/householdcharacteristics/homeinternetandsocialmediausage/bulletins/internetaccesshouseholdsandindividuals/2018, accessed 13 April 2019.
17 *UKOM Insights: UK digital market overview June 2017* [PDF], Comscore, 2017, www.comscore.com/Insights/Presentations-and-Whitepapers/2017/UKOM-Insights-UK-Digital-Market-Overview-June-2017, p. 4, accessed 13 April 2019.
18 *Ibid.*, p. 8.

19 *Mobile Consumer Behaviour Report: Evolution of the digital swiss-army knife* [PDF], Textlocal, 2018, www.textlocal.com/mobile-consumer-behaviour-report, p. 9, accessed 15 April 2019.
20 Presentation by Keith Williams for JustGiving, 'Big trends from the biggest fundraising event in the world', London, Institute of Fundraising Community Fundraising Conference, 1 June 2017.
21 *65% of all trackable website traffic comes from search* [PDF], https://videos.brightedge.com/assets/documents/channel-report-2017.pdf, BrightEdge Research, p. 2, accessed31 May 2019.
22 Marcela De Vivo, 'How influencer marketing can benefit your SEO strategy' [web article], Search Engine Watch, https://searchenginewatch.com/2017/03/08/how-influencer-marketing-can-benefit-your-seo-strategy, 8 March 2017.
23 *Fundraising Media DNA 2016/17: The engagement of donors with different fundraising channels* [PDF], Institute of Fundraising and fastmap, 2017, www.fastmap.com/fundraising-campaigns, pp. 47–49, accessed 13 April 2019.
24 Jane Dudman, 'Facebook to roll out donate buttons to UK and Europe' [web article], *The Guardian*, www.theguardian.com/voluntary-sector-network/2017/sep/12/facebook-donate-buttons-uk-charities, 12 September 2017.
25 *UK Digital Market Overview: March 2018* [PDF], UKOM, 2018, http://ukom.uk.net/digital-market-overview/56-q1-2018-uk-digital-market-overview-report.php, p. 42, accessed 13 April 2019.
26 *Fundraising Media DNA 2016/17: The engagement of donors with different fundraising channels* [PDF], Institute of Fundraising and fastmap, 2017, www.fastmap.com/fundraising-campaigns, p. 19, accessed 13 April 2019.
27 *Closing the Loop* [PDF], Blackbaud and the Institute of Fundraising, 2015, www.everydayhero.com/uk/closing-the-loop, p. 10, accessed 13 April 2019.
28 *Fundraising Media DNA 2016/17: The engagement of donors with different fundraising channels* [PDF], Institute of Fundraising and fastmap, 2017, www.fastmap.com/fundraising-campaigns, p. 20, accessed 13 April 2019.
29 *A Good Call: Using the telephone for successful fundraising* [PDF], Institute of Fundraising, 2019, www.institute-of-fundraising.org.uk/library/a-good-call-using-the-telephone-for-successful-fundraising, accessed 13 April 2019.
30 *Fundraising Media DNA 2016/17: The engagement of donors with different fundraising channels* [PDF], Institute of Fundraising and fastmap, 2017, www.fastmap.com/fundraising-campaigns, p. 52, accessed 13 April 2019.
31 For example, see Elizabeth Dobler, 'E-textbooks: A personalized learning experience or a digital distraction?', *Journal of Adolescent and Adult Literacy*, vol. 58, no. 6, 2015, pp. 482–91.
32 *Fundraising Media DNA 2016/17: The engagement of donors with different fundraising channels* [PDF], Institute of Fundraising and fastmap, 2017, www.fastmap.com/fundraising-campaigns, pp. 14–17, accessed 13 April 2019.
33 *RAJAR Midas Audio Survey* [PDF], RAJAR, 2018, p. 12, accessed 25 April 2019.
34 'How to write a brilliant press release' [web article], National Council for Voluntary Organisations, https://knowhow.ncvo.org.uk/how-to/how-to-write-an-effective-press-release, 23 January 2018.
35 *Multi-channel Fundraising* [PDF], Blackbaud, 2014, www.blackbaud.com/files/resources/downloads/2014/CRM_Insert_MultiChannel_v2.pdf, p. 1, accessed 2 July 2019.
36 This image is loosely based on figure 5.1 in Everett M. Rogers, *Diffusion of Innovations*, New York, Free Press, 1983, p. 165.

37 Based on Everett M. Rogers, *Diffusion of Innovations*, New York, Free Press, 1983, p. 165, figure 5.1.
38 Daniel Kahneman, *Thinking, Fast and Slow*, New York, Farrar, Straus and Giroux, 2011.
39 Deborah A. Small, George Loewenstein and Paul Slovic, 'Sympathy and Callousness: The impact of deliberative thought on donations to identifiable and statistical victims', *Organizational Behavior and Human Decision Processes*, vol. 102, no. 2, 2007, pp. 143–53.
40 Daniel Västfjäll, Paul Slovic, Marcus Mayorga and Ellen Peters, 'Compassion Fade: Affect and charity are greatest for a single child in need', *PLOS ONE*, vol. 9, no. 6, 2014, doi:10.1371/journal.pone.0100115.
41 *Closing the Loop* [PDF], Blackbaud and the Institute of Fundraising, 2015, p. 14, accessed 13 April 2019.
42 *Insights into Charity Fundraising: Why people give and their experience of donating* [PDF], Institute of Fundraising, 2017, www.institute-of-fundraising.org.uk/library/insights-into-charity-fundraising-final-report, p. 8, accessed 9 July 2019.
43 Altaf Merchant, John B. Ford and Adrian Sargeant, 'Charitable Organizations' Storytelling Influence on Donors' Emotions and Intentions', *Journal of Business Research*, vol. 63, no. 7, 2010, pp. 754–62.
44 See Paul Ekman, 'An argument for basic emotions', *Cognition and Emotion*, vol. 6, nos. 3–4, 1992, pp. 169–200 and Alan S. Cowen and Dacher Keltner, 'Self-Report Captures 27 Distinct Categories of Emotion Bridged by Continuous Gradients', *PNAS*, vol. 114, no. 38, 2017, doi:10.1073/pnas.1702247114.
45 See, for example, C. D. B. Burt and K. Strongman, 'Use of Images in Charity Advertising: Improving donations and compliance rates', *International Journal of Organisational Behaviour*, vol. 8., no. 8, 2005, pp. 571–80 and R. P. Bagozzi and D. J. Moore, 'Public Service Advertisements: Emotions and empathy guide prosocial behavior', *Journal of Marketing*, vol. 58, no. 1, 1994, pp. 56–70.
46 M. L. Shelton and R. W. Rogers, 'Fear-Arousing and Empathy-Arousing Appeals to Help: The pathos of persuasion', *Journal of Applied Social Psychology*, vol. 11, no. 4, 1981, pp. 366–78.
47 Janne van Doorn, Marcel Zeelenberg and Seger M. Breugelmans, 'The Impact of Anger on Donations to Victims', *International Review of Victimology*, vol. 23, no. 3, pp. 303–12. Note that the study caused the participants to feel anger by asking them to recall incidences that made them angry, rather than by using examples of people in need. There was no difference in donation intentions between the two charities when people were not feeling angry. The researchers also highlight that this was a preliminary study that needs to be replicated using other charitable examples.
48 Lorne Bozinoff and Morry Ghingold, 'Evaluating Guilt Arousing Marketing Communications', *Journal of Business Research*, vol. 11, no. 2, 1983, pp. 243–55.
49 Arvid Erlandsson, Artur Nilsson and Daniel Västfjäll, 'Attitudes and Donation Behavior When Reading Positive and Negative Charity Appeals', *Journal of Nonprofit and Public Sector Marketing*, vol. 30, no. 4, pp. 444–74.
50 C. Chédotal, B. Berthe, B. de Peyrelongue and M. Le Gall-Ely, 'Using Guilt Appeals in Communication', *Recherche et Applications en Marketing* (English edition), vol. 32, no. 4, 2017, pp. 91–110.

51 D. Z. Basil, N. M. Ridgway and M. D. Basil, 'Guilt and Giving: A process model of empathy and efficacy', *Psychology & Marketing*, vol. 25, no. 1, 2008, pp. 1–23; S. Hibbert, A. Smith, A. Davies and F. Ireland, 'Guilt Appeals: Persuasion knowledge and charitable giving', *Psychology and Marketing*, vol. 24, no. 8, 2007, pp. 723–42.

52 J. Albouy, 'Emotions and Prosocial Behaviours: A study of the effectiveness of shocking charity campaigns', *Recherche et Applications en Marketing* (English edition), vol. 32, no. 2, 2017, pp. 4–25.

53 Daniel J. O'Keefe, 'Guilt and Social Influence', *Annals of the International Communication Association*, vol. 23, no. 1, 2000, pp. 67–101.

54 Ira J. Roseman, Cynthia Wiest and Tamara S. Swartz, 'Phenomenology, Behaviors, and Goals Differentiate Discrete Emotions', *Journal of Personality and Social Psychology*, vol. 67, no. 2, 1994, pp. 206–21.

55 Gloria K. Manucia, Donald J. Baumann and Robert B. Cialdini, 'Mood Influences on Helping: Direct effects or side effects?', *Journal of Personality and Social Psychology*, vol. 46, no. 2, 1984, pp. 357–364.

56 Deborah A. Small and N. M. Verrochi, 'The Face of Need: Facial emotion expression on charity advertisements', *Journal of Marketing Research*, vol. 46, no. 6, 2009, pp. 777–87.

57 A. Merchant, J. B. Ford and G. Rose, 'How Personal Nostalgia Influences Giving to Charity', *Journal of Business Research*, vol. 64, no. 6., 2011, pp. 610–16.

58 Antje Cockrill and Isobel Parsonage, 'Shocking People into Action: Does it still work? An empirical analysis of emotional appeals In charity advertising', *Journal of Advertising Research*, vol. 56, no. 4, pp. 401–13.

59 *Ibid.*

60 *Ibid.*

61 Avner Ben-Ner, Brian P. McCall, Massoud Stephane and Hua Wang, 'Identity and In-Group/Outgroup Differentiation in Work and Giving Behaviors: Experimental evidence', *Journal of Economic Behavior and Organization*, vol. 72, no. 1, 2009, pp. 153–170.

62 Sally Bagwell, Lucy de Las Casas, Matt van Poortvliet and Rob Abercrombie, *Money for Good UK: Understanding donor motivation and behaviour* [PDF], New Philanthropy Capital, 2013, www.thinknpc.org/wp-content/uploads/2018/07/MONEY-FOR-GOOD-UK.pdf, p. 3, accessed 9 July 2019.

63 Jonathan Z. Berman, Alixandra Barasch, Emma E. Levine and Deborah A. Small, 'Impediments to Effective Altruism: The role of subjective preferences in charitable giving', *Psychological Science*, vol. 29, no. 5, 2018, pp. 834–44; 'Hearts, Minds and Money: Maximizing charitable giving' [web article], Wharton School of the University of Pennsylvania, http://knowledge.wharton.upenn.edu/article/maximizing-charitable-giving, 1 June 2018.

64 Adrian Sargeant, *Donor Retention: What do we know and what can we do about it?* [PDF], Indiana University, 2013, http://studyfundraising.info/wp-content/uploads/2016/03/Donor-retention-what-do-we-know-abd-what-can-we-do-about-it.pdf, pp. 3–8, accessed 13 April 2019.

65 *Ibid.*, pp. 7–8.

66 *Ibid.*, pp. 4–6.

67 *Ibid.*, pp. 3–4.

68 Adrian Sargeant and Lucy Woodliffe, *Building Donor Loyalty: The antecedents and role of commitment in the context of charity giving* [PDF], 2007, https://scholarworks.iupui.edu/bitstream/handle/1805/5743/building_donor_loyalty_-_the_antecedents_and_role_of_commitment_in_the_context_of_charity_giving.pdf?sequence=1, pp. 7–8, accessed 13 April 2019.
69 Adrian Sargeant, *Donor Retention: What do we know and what can we do about it?* [PDF], Indiana University, 2013, http://studyfundraising.info/wp-content/uploads/2016/03/Donor-retention-what-do-we-know-abd-what-can-we-do-about-it.pdf, pp. 6–7, accessed 13 April 2019.
70 *Ibid.*, pp. 6–7.
71 *Ibid.*, p. 7.
72 For details on how to create goals, see 'Create, edit, and share goals' [web page], Google Analytics, 2019, https://support.google.com/analytics/answer/1032415, accessed 13 April 2019.
73 For details about Hootsuite's non-profit discount see https://hootsuite.com/pages/landing/non-profit-discount-application2.

CHAPTER FIVE

Managing community fundraising data

Michelle Martin

Introduction

With increased scrutiny from the media and high public expectations of charities, it is essential for organisations to make the best use of their resources and to ensure they are compliant with legislation and regulations. It is also crucial for charities to visibly demonstrate the effectiveness of their fundraising to their supporters and the wider public. Lawful data management and appropriate data-driven fundraising help to ensure the best use of resources and are vital factors in maintaining the reputation of charities. After all, a poorly executed fundraising activity wastes the money given or raised by previous supporters. It also risks a loss of trust among supporters and a dent in the charity's reputation. All of this can ultimately affect the chances of the organisation's future fundraising success.

By using accurate data to lawfully carry out research on fundraising participants, their motivations, and the messages and activities that resonate with them, charities can help to future-proof their fundraising by making better decisions about their relationships with supporters. However, many charities struggle to use data in this way – in 2015, only 24% of charities collected, analysed and used data as part of their strategic planning and decision-making processes.[1]

This chapter provides guidance on:

- the foundations for recording and using data lawfully;
- what data you can collect to describe your supporters and their behaviour, in relation to both fundraising performance and day-to-day fundraising management;
- how to ensure you get the appropriate consents;
- how to judge legitimate interests;
- where to find information to stay up to date on legislation and regulations;
- how to store your data appropriately and ensure it is joined up, clean and secure;
- how to configure the right database.

Data protection legislation and fundraising regulations

When considering what data you can legitimately collect and record, and what you can use it for, in order to deliver your community fundraising objectives, it is crucial to do so through a data protection lens.

The foundations for lawfully recording and using data

In May 2018, the General Data Protection Regulation (GDPR) came into force. The GDPR regulates the processing of personal data and privacy for all individual citizens in the EU. It also addresses the export of personal data outside the EU and, as part of its wide-ranging guidance, sets out the rules governing direct marketing.

The GDPR legislation places greater importance on respecting individual privacy than the Data Protection Act 1998 did. For example, in a fundraising context, it helps to reassure donors that their information will not be used without their express permission and, in a workplace context, it helps ensure that employee data is protected. Alongside the GDPR, the Privacy and Electronic Communications Regulations, or PECR (which this chapter will generally refer to as the ePrivacy rules), set out marketing rules that cover the sending of electronic messages, whether by phone, email, text or fax, and the use of cookies on websites.[2] The PECR is based on the 2002 ePrivacy Directive, which will be replaced by the ePrivacy Regulation (at the time of writing, it is unclear when the ePrivacy Regulation will come into force), so it is wise to keep abreast of any changes in the law and potentially to take legal advice on this complex area.

Types of communication defined as direct marketing

Direct marketing includes any communication which promotes the aims and objectives of a charity, not just the promotion of fundraising activities. The GDPR and the ePrivacy rules apply whenever you collect and use an individual's personal data (names, contact details and any other information about them, even if you are just holding this on your database and not using it).

Types of communication not defined as direct marketing

The types of message that are often unofficially referred to as 'operational communications' and not defined as direct marketing (and so the GDPR and the ePrivacy rules do not apply) include when:

- you send supporters routine messages containing information that they *need* to know about – for example, if a supporter has signed up for an event, this could include travel directions, instructions on timings, a training guide and any briefing on kit they need to wear;

- you contact your supporters to carry out market research in order to make better decisions on your future fundraising activities – for example, to improve the quality of your events (but not for future marketing purposes – this falls under the heading of direct marketing, so you would need consent to use market research findings in this way).

These types of message may include standard branding (logos, straplines, etc.) but must not include any promotional communications that are sent with the aim of getting supporters to sign up for services or events, to donate or to buy products. Any market research enquiries, therefore, must be purely for that purpose: they must not be used in an indirect way to do any sort of promotional activity or to collect data for future promotional activities. So, if you are carrying out market research to inform your future marketing campaigns, you must inform the people you are communicating with that this is your purpose and you must comply with GDPR and the ePrivacy rules. The key is to be clear about the purpose of communications and let that guide how you comply.

The GDPR also does not apply if the information you use is not personal – for example, sending material to the 'homeowner' rather than a named individual. The ePrivacy rules, however, apply even if you do not know the name of the person you are contacting or you are not processing any personal data.[3]

The lawful bases

There are six lawful bases for processing a supporter's data (as set out in Article 6 of the GDPR) and at least one basis must apply. The bases all have equal standing – none is superior to any other. The two most relevant for community fundraising marketing are:

> (a) Consent: the individual has given clear consent for you to process their personal data for a specific purpose. . . .
>
> (f) Legitimate interests: the processing is necessary for your legitimate interests or the legitimate interests of a third party, unless there is a good reason to protect the individual's personal data which overrides those legitimate interests.

Information Commissioner's Office, 2019,
reproduced under the Open Government Licence v3.0[4]

(Both of these lawful bases are explained in detail in this chapter. See 'Consent for sending marketing communications' on page 161 and 'Legitimate interests for sending marketing communications' on page 168.) To show that you are complying with the GDPR, you should be able to:

- demonstrate that you have fully considered which lawful basis applies to each reason you have for processing the data (the 'processing purpose');
- justify your decision for choosing the lawful basis for the processing purpose in question;
- show that you have the correct associated policies and procedures in place (such as a privacy statement and policy, a consent policy, a cookie policy and a data management policy).

This means that you should keep records of your considered justifications for each processing purpose. (See also 'Recording and storing data' on page 170 and 'Privacy notices' on page 163.)

The seven GDPR principles

This chapter will refer to various GDPR principles, as set out by Article 5(1), which you need to comply with when processing personal data. These principles state that personal data must be:

1. processed lawfully, fairly and in a transparent manner in relation to individuals ('lawfulness, fairness and transparency');
2. collected for specified, explicit and legitimate purposes and not further processed in a manner that is incompatible with those purposes; further processing for archiving purposes in the public interest, scientific or historical research purposes or statistical purposes shall not be considered to be incompatible with the initial purposes ('purpose limitation');
3. adequate, relevant and limited to what is necessary in relation to the purposes for which they are processed ('data minimisation');
4. accurate and, where necessary, kept up to date; every reasonable step must be taken to ensure that personal data that are inaccurate, having regard to the purposes for which they are processed, are erased or rectified without delay ('accuracy');
5. kept in a form which permits identification of data subjects for no longer than is necessary for the purposes for which the personal data are processed; personal data may be stored for longer periods insofar as the personal data will be processed solely for archiving purposes in the public interest, scientific or historical research purposes or statistical purposes subject to implementation of the appropriate technical and organisational measures required by the GDPR in order to safeguard the rights and freedoms of individuals ('storage limitation');

6. processed in a manner that ensures appropriate security of the personal data, including protection against unauthorised or unlawful processing and against accidental loss, destruction or damage, using appropriate technical or organisational measures ('integrity and confidentiality').

Information Commissioner's Office, 2019,
reproduced under the Open Government Licence v3.0[5]

And article 5(2) outlines the seventh principle, as follows:

7. The controller shall be responsible for, and be able to demonstrate compliance with, paragraph 1 [the other data protection principles] ('accountability').[6]

What you can collect

Status of your current data

If you have collected data before considering data protection compliance, you will need to run an initial consent audit to evaluate the following:

- What data have you collected?
- Is any of it 'special category data'? (See page 161.)
- Why are you collecting the data and what is its purpose?
- Who is using or has access to the data?
- Did the supporter grant permission? If so, when? And specifically what for? If you don't know, you must undertake an exercise to go back to people and clarify.
- Where did the supporter grant permission (for example, when signing up for an event, at the time of making a donation or face to face)?
- Where are you storing the data and do you have any paper copies?

When collecting fresh data, you need to think carefully about:

- what you really need to collect;
- why you need it;
- how you will use it now and in the future;
- how you will gain consent or justify legitimate interest for collecting and using the data;

- how you will record consent, your lawful bases and any separate conditions (see 'Special category data' on page 161);
- how you will ensure that the data is accurate and secure;
- how long you can keep it.

If you are planning to process data that may result in a high level of risk to individuals or to start a major project that will involve using personal data, you must carry out a data protection impact assessment (DPIA).[7] For example, given your charity is legally responsible for assessing the GDPR-compliance capability of any third parties carrying out data processing on its behalf, it would be advisable to carry out a DPIA when you are considering working with a new supplier or if you intend to buy data from third parties for profiling purposes.[8]

Evaluating what to ask for

It is wise to strip back what data you aim to collect to a minimum. This will help to ensure that you comply with an important principle in the GDPR, which is to keep no more data than you need (the data minimisation principle – see page 158). In addition, by keeping the amount of information you ask new supporters to supply to a manageable minimum, you avoid putting them off from signing up to your newsletter, event and so on. Consider the following:

- How easy will it be for supporters to provide you with the data you are requesting?
- Is it appropriate to ask for this information?
- Assess when it would be most appropriate in the supporter's journey to request the data: at what points in the supporter journey will having the data help you to provide a more personalised experience for the supporter and to make better decisions about supporting them? (For details on the supporter journey, see page 137.)

In this way, you should only be collecting personal information that is relevant to the purposes for which you are collecting and processing it. If it seems strange to ask a supporter at any given point to supply and to give consent to use certain data – for example, if the supporter would think, 'Why would you need to know that?' – then either you don't need to collect that information or you need to explain why you are asking the supporter to provide it. For example, if someone is signing up for an event, it would be appropriate to ask for their contact details and address, information on health and safety (in the case of someone signing up for a challenge event, this might be regarding medical conditions and their emergency contact details), and whether they will be taking part on their own, as part of a team, with their colleagues or with someone else. It would also be legally valid, in order to better tailor communications to reflect why supporters have chosen to help your charity, to ask what the supporter's motivation is. However, you must pay special attention to capturing this sort of information because it may constitute 'special category data'.

Special category data

Special category data is broadly similar to what constitutes 'sensitive personal data' under the Data Protection Act 1998. It includes a person's politics, religious beliefs and ethnicity, and any physical or mental health issues. For this reason, if you were to collect this data to carry out the common practice of segmenting people by personal motivation, you would be contravening the regulations if you did so without identifying:

- a lawful basis;
- another condition (there are a total of ten) for processing special category data under Article 9.[9]

For the purpose of our event example, the lawful basis is consent and the supporter would need to give 'explicit consent', which is one of the ten conditions. The supporter might raise money for your charity because they have direct experience of the illness that is the subject of your cause. If you wanted to record their motivation for fundraising, the supporter would have to give explicit consent for your organisation to process this special category data for the particular purpose or purposes you specify. This would include the purpose of segmentation. In effect, this is not much different from obtaining consent, but you must record that you have identified both a lawful basis (under Article 6) and a separate condition (under Article 9) for processing the special category data. (So, as noted in the example above, under Article 6 the lawful basis would be consent and under Article 9 the condition would be explicit consent.) You must also keep a record of the consent given and when and how it was given.

Consent for sending marketing communications

To gain consent to contact a supporter with direct marketing communications using email or SMS, you will need to ask supporters to actively opt in to receive these messages. Consent is needed under the ePrivacy rules for this type of communication, even if you would otherwise conclude you could rely on the legitimate interests basis under Article 6. They must give this consent freely and be able to change their minds at any time – the option to withdraw consent must therefore be clear in all your communications and the process of doing so must be straightforward and easy. You must also be specific about what your supporters are consenting to. That is, you need to think through what else you might want to use their data for in the future – just because they have consented to receive information about an event does not mean that they have consented to receive a fundraising appeal. So, if you want to contact them (using the same lawful basis of consent) about further donations, events, volunteering and campaigns they need to consent to these uses separately (see 'The lawful bases' on page 157).

Consent must be 'unambiguous', which means that neither silence nor inaction imply consent and so opt-out systems (where a charity sends marketing communications to someone unless they specifically opt out) are in fact ambiguous. Ensuring that supporters actively opt in, therefore, is the best way of ensuring that you are within the law. Under the ePrivacy rules, the law is clear that your organisation must not make automated calls or phone people who are signed up to the Telephone Preference Service (TPS) unless the people you are contacting have actively opted in to receive these calls.

While there is no legal time limit for consent, how long it lasts depends upon the context in which it was given. So, if a supporter gives consent for a time-limited campaign, it must end with that campaign, unless you have asked the supporter to consent to a longer-term relationship. If a supporter has given consent for a longer-term relationship, the ICO and the Fundraising Regulator suggest that you should renew this consent within 24 months of the supporter initially granting permission.

When judging whether your supporters have granted consent to receive marketing communications, you also need to take account of the Fundraising Preference Service. Launched in 2017, this web-based service enables supporters to register that they want to stop email, telephone calls, addressed post and/or text messages directed to them personally from a selected charity or charities. You will therefore need to check your data against any notifications you receive from the Fundraising Preference Service and update your data within the deadline given.

As asking for consent is in itself classified as a marketing activity, under the ePrivacy rules it is not lawful to email someone or to send an SMS to ask for their consent. However, it can be permissible to do so by post or telephone (although not by automatic telephone) if you have consent to contact them in this way or you have a legitimate interest.

Multiple data collection points and channels

Given the multiple potential data collection points and channels (including websites, email, mobile devices, face-to-face interactions and phone calls) and potential variations in your lawful bases for processing a supporter's data across these points and channels, you will need to provide different privacy notices and consent requests to cater for each situation. Rather than attempting to outline all scenarios, the following sections will cover privacy notices and consent requests for tracking technologies (cookies) and face-to-face interactions.

Privacy notices

A privacy notice is a public notification that an organisation supplies to individuals at the point of collecting their personal data. Privacy notices are required in order to comply with the GDPR's 'right to be informed' condition, which states that you must ensure people are fully informed about how and why you are collecting and using their personal data. The GDPR also requires you to record your processing activities, including by documenting privacy notices and consent (outlined in the following section). These records are vital for proving that you have complied with the law, should you be required to in the case of any complaints.[10] Privacy notices are distinct from consent requests and should be provided even if you are not asking for consent.

Although it is unlikely that you will be personally required to write privacy notices for your organisation, it is important to be aware of what these notices should include and why they are important. Armed with this knowledge, you can raise any red flags or suggest edits to any privacy notices that may fall short of the requirements.

Your privacy notice cannot be a one-size-fits-all policy because an organisation will use data from different audiences, for different purposes, with different legal bases for doing so. Therefore, in any given situation, you will need separate privacy notices, which include:

- your lawful basis (or bases) for processing a supporter's data (e.g. consent);
- any separate conditions (under Article 9) regarding special category data (e.g. explicit consent);
- why you are processing this data.

The ICO provides comprehensive information, including checklists, about what to provide in your privacy notices to comply with the requirement. Although it doesn't specifically refer to these privacy notices being digital, they will in practice appear on your website and any other digital means (such as apps) and can be referred to in offline communications.

The guidance covers the following points:

- **What information you need to provide,** including (among many other points) the name and contact details of your organisation and the lawful basis for the data you are processing.

- **When you should provide privacy information to your supporters.** For example, when you communicate with someone and use their personal data to do so, you must provide privacy information the first time you contact them.
- **How you should put together your privacy information.** This includes making sure that you put yourself in the shoes of the people who will be reading the notice and convey information that is easily understandable, clear and succinct.
- **How you should provide your privacy information to your supporters.** The guidance states:

> There are a number of techniques you can use to provide people with privacy information. You can use:
>
> - A layered approach – typically, short notices containing key privacy information that have additional layers of more detailed information. [Editor's note: 'additional layers' might include, for example, links within the short notice that expand to reveal more detailed information. That information may, in turn, include links to further explanatory material.]
> - Dashboards – preference management tools that inform people how you use their data and allow them to manage what happens with it.
> - Just-in-time notices – relevant and focused privacy information delivered at the time you collect individual pieces of information about people.
> - Icons – small, meaningful symbols that indicate the existence of a particular type of data processing.
> - Mobile and smart device functionalities – including pop-ups, voice alerts and mobile device gestures.
>
> Information Commissioner's Office, 2019,
> reproduced under the Open Government Licence v3.0[11]

See also 'Consent for collecting data for profiling and analytics' on page 166 for information on what you need to inform supporters of if you buy personal data from other organisations or obtain it from publicly accessible sources.

Consent requests

If you have determined that consent is the right lawful basis for processing a person's data, the same principles apply in all cases when seeking consent (but this does not mean that you can use one non-specific request template for all scenarios). These principles include ensuring that:[12]

- your request for consent is obvious and is distinct from other information, such as your privacy notice and your terms and conditions;

- you ask supporters to positively opt in rather than using any sort of default consent options (such as using pre-ticked boxes);
- your request is concise and phrased in easily understandable language;
- you make clear why you want the data and what you intend to do with it;
- you tailor the request message based on the types of processing you will be doing and for what purpose you'll be doing it;
- you name your organisation and any third parties that will rely on the consent;
- supporters know that they can withdraw their consent or refuse to give it without any consequences (for example, not allowing the supporter to use a service as a result of refusing to give consent);
- you keep records of consent given.

The following sections suggest how these principles might be applied in the case of tracking technologies and face-to-face interactions.

Cookies

Cookies (and other tracking technologies) help you to track how your supporters are interacting with your services by viewing which pages they visit on your website.

The ePrivacy rules require you to ask users to agree to your site's use of cookies. For consent to be valid, the ICO states that:

- The user must understand that they are giving your organisation consent to use cookies.
- The user must take an 'unambiguous positive action', such as ticking a box or clicking on a link.
- The user must understand that by clicking on a link or ticking a box, they are agreeing to cookies being set, rather than just agreeing to continue to use the website.

Given these stipulations, you must not offer pre-ticked boxes or assume that no response means that the person has given their consent. Therefore, on a user's first visit to your website, you need to include a consent banner on that website explaining in an easily understandable way:

- what your tracking technologies do;
- what your site uses cookies to track;
- what you will use the information for and why.

The ICO notes that since more than one person may use a device, it is wise to ask again for consent after a certain amount of time has passed (although the guidance does not suggest what a suitable period would be).[13]

Face-to-face interactions

If you are gathering information face to face – for example, if you are collecting case studies and photos in order to raise awareness of your cause or your activities – you will need to be clear to any given supporter about your intentions. Supporters must give explicit consent for the case study and/or photo(s) to be used in the way you have stated you will use them and within a certain specified timeframe. They must also understand that they can withdraw the consent they are giving. It is also prudent to have an expiry period for using photos (within the timeframe already agreed with supporters), after which they are no longer used.

A standard way of recording consent is by using a consent form that details these agreed points in plain language and is signed by the individual. Signing a form, however, is not sufficient: the person needs to fully understand what they are agreeing to, so ensure you explain the details to them in easily intelligible language and ask them questions to test that they understand what they are agreeing to.

Consent for collecting data for profiling and analytics

If you want to collect supporters' data for profiling and analytics for the purpose of direct marketing, consent needs to be specific – that is, they need to consent to these uses separately from consenting to be contacted for marketing purposes (which is outlined in the following section). It also needs to be informed, meaning that the person must properly understand how your charity is going to use their data. If they do not, then the consent is not valid.

Your privacy notices (see page 163) must specify the use of data that people are consenting to, including for:

- data analysis, including profiling;
- segmentation;
- website tracking (see 'Cookies' on page 165);
- social media tracking;
- combining any of this data with data from other sources.

If you are obtaining data from publicly accessible sources or buying supporter data to add to your own for profiling and segmentation (see 'Consumer classification organisations' on page 51), the GDPR makes it clear that people must understand how exactly you are doing so and agree to this use. You must also ensure that appropriate due diligence has been carried out to verify that the seller of the database has consent from those listed to sell their details.

For example, you might combine data from different sources to create profiles of supporters' interests and preferences so that you can contact them with information that is relevant to them. This research could include observations on how your supporters interact with your services, such as calling your support line or visiting particular pages on your website. It might also incorporate publicly available or bought demographic and geodemographic information, including analytics from social media sites (such as Facebook Audience Insights, Instagram Insights, Pinterest Audience Insights and Twitter Analytics). When seeking consent you would need to explain in the relevant privacy notice that you are adding external data to your database, specify all the places you are gathering data from, and explain for what reasons you are adding this data and combining it.

See 'Privacy notices' on page 163 for details on how to communicate to supporters the ways in which you are using data.

Consent for selling or sharing data

Selling data

While selling data, or sharing it freely, is not necessarily illegal, the transfer of personal data to a third party is tightly regulated. To do so in relation to a database would require the explicit consent of each person on that database. There have been a number of high-profile cases involving large fines to charities for unlawfully selling databases.[14] Even if a charity had consent to sell a database, and could provide evidence of consent were there to be a legal challenge, the reputational risks of either owning up to the practice or being found to have sold a database without being open about it should discourage most organisations from considering it.

Sharing data with third parties

You can only share supporters' data with another organisation if all of the following are true:

- your charity states in its privacy notices the organisations (or the types of organisation) with which you will be sharing the information;
- the individual provides 'freely given, specific, informed and unambiguous' consent[15] for this use of their data;
- you can give evidence that they have consented in this way.

For example, you will need to make it clear to your supporters in your privacy notices if you share your data with third-party data services (such as Experian) or third-party advertisers (such as Facebook or Google). You will need to state why you are sharing the data. Potential reasons are to understand your audience better, to identify supporters who are similar to your existing audience or to offer relevant advertising to your supporters on third-party websites. It is also a requirement of the

GPDR that you will need to implement a third-party data sharing agreement to ensure appropriate technical and organisational security measures are in place to protect the data and data management by that third party which is compliant and supports your own compliance.

To identify supporters who are similar to your existing audience using the Facebook Audience Insights tool, you would need to use existing supporters' email addresses. However, this personal data would be 'pseudonymised', i.e. the email address itself would not be shared because pseudonymisation replaces personal identifiers with anonymous data. Stating that their personal data will be protected in this way and also that they may opt out of your use of their email address at any time (you must give them an easy way to do this) will help your audience to make an informed choice. Note that the Information Commissioner's Office highlights pseudonymisation is a security measure and, like all security measures, it is not infallible. This is why pseudonymised data is still personal data – there is always a small risk that the anonymised data could be linked, with the use of additional information, to identifiable people.[16]

Legitimate interests for sending marketing communications

Legitimate interests (as outlined on page 157) is one of the lawful bases that can be used for processing a supporter's data. According to the ICO, this basis can be the correct choice for processing a person's data when:[17]

- the processing is not legally required but it would be clearly beneficial to you or other people;
- the individual would reasonably expect the processing;
- the processing would cause minimal impact on the person's privacy;
- you cannot seek consent or when the individual would be unlikely to object to the processing and so asking for consent would be unnecessarily disruptive.

Nevertheless, in a practical sense for fundraising, legitimate interests can only be used in narrow circumstances. For example, this chapter does not include a section on using legitimate interests as a lawful basis for data collection and analysis because you will always need consent from supporters to collect their data and to analyse it. Furthermore, according to the ePrivacy rules, you may not use legitimate interests as the basis for communicating with supporters via email, SMS or automatic telephone, or to those who are signed up to the TPS – in these cases you would also need consent.

Legitimate interests may be a valid lawful basis, however, for processing an existing supporter's data without their renewed consent for the purpose of communicating with them by post or telephone. So you may, given certain conditions (outlined below), send direct marketing appeals by mail to existing supporters or ask them by mail or phone whether you may contact them by email or other means.

If you choose legitimate interests as a lawful basis in this way, the onus is on you to make a compelling case that your data processing is necessary for the purpose you are proposing. Furthermore, the GDPR also requires you to consider whether the individual's rights and freedoms to have their data protected override your legitimate interest to contact them.[18]

This is a balancing act that essentially involves determining whether contacting a supporter would be within their reasonable expectations. Guidance from the Institute of Fundraising[19] offers examples of how you might judge this. The examples given of scenarios that would pass the legitimate interests test have the following characteristics in common:

- At the time you collected any data, you supplied clear information on your privacy notice regarding how the supporter's data would be used.
- The privacy notice highlighted that future marketing communications would be sent to the supporter.
- Your last communication with the supporter was sufficiently recent – perhaps within 24 months (depending on the context).
- Your charity is confident that the supporter would not be surprised to receive the mailing or phone call and would not object to receiving it.

Under the GDPR's accountability principle (see page 159), you must record any decisions you make regarding legitimate interests in order to show that you are compliant with the GDPR.

Keeping up to date

As legislation and regulations continue to evolve, it is essential to stay abreast of developments. The following organisations provide up-to-date information on how to ensure you remain compliant:

- **The Directory of Social Change** (www.dsc.org.uk) runs training on data protection legislation.
- **The Institute of Fundraising** (www.institute-of-fundraising.org.uk) provides guidelines, information and a data protection checklist for fundraisers.
- **The Information Commissioner's Office** (www.ico.org.uk) is the UK's independent authority set up to uphold information rights in the public interest. Its website contains guidance on legal obligations, including how to comply with the GDPR and ePrivacy requirements.

- **The Fundraising Regulator** (www.fundraisingregulator.org.uk) is the independent regulator of charitable and philanthropic fundraising. Guidance on the GDPR and ePrivacy requirements can be found on its website.

If your charity operates outside the UK, you should seek advice on data protection from relevant national or regional bodies.

Recording and storing data

When you are planning what data to capture, it is helpful to understand how this data might be stored in a database. Each single piece of data is known as a data field. Data fields can be collated to describe individual supporters in the form of a supporter record, which can then be segmented into data files or groups of donors (see figure 5.1). (For details on segmentation, see page 70.)

FIGURE 5.1 THE DATA STORED WITHIN A DATABASE

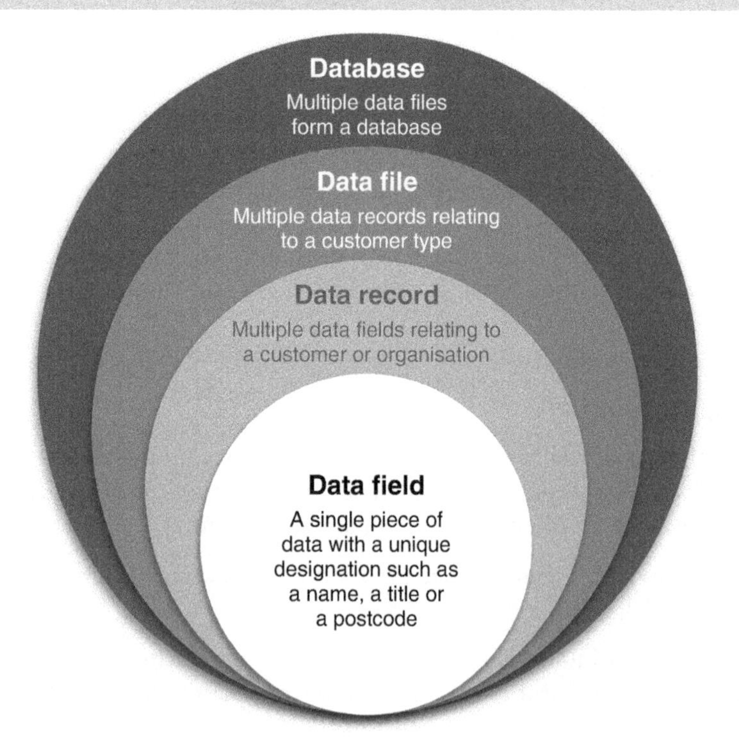

Data options for market research, segmentation and targeting

The information in a database is stored in a series of tables. All database systems have a large number of tables in which you can enter and modify standard data (titles, honours, job titles, marital status, etc. – the list is almost endless). Some databases will have standard tables that come as part of the software package provided by the supplier, other tables can be tailored slightly to suit your organisation, and others might be entirely bespoke to your organisation's needs.

Of course, as outlined in the earlier sections of this chapter, what you can include will depend on what information you have requested from supporters, what you have stated you will be tracking (such as their habits on your website or on social media), and whether they have consented for you to record their information and/or tracking observations.

Table 5.1 includes some examples of the typical data fields in a supporter record. This table also illustrates the scale of the types of data that can be included in a database and shows the potentially onerous nature of data management that may be necessary in a large and complex charity. But not every charity has complex data to manage or high levels of data processing requirements – if you are a community fundraiser in a smaller charity, your data may be limited to some newsletter recipients and a few donors. No matter the size of your data processing requirements, however, GDPR always applies.

In addition to knowing whether and how you can use your data for marketing you also need to consider the capacity of your database to apply GDPR rules to this data in a sophisticated way (see page 158 for details on the GDPR principles mentioned):

- Does the database record consent for each purpose the data is to be used?
- Does the database record any decision regarding legitimate interests, what type of data processing that decision relates to, and when the decision was made?
- Is the data segregated so that users of the system only have access to the information they need in order to carry out their tasks? This applies particularly to special category data, but would also include financial details, for example (the GDPR security principle).
- Does the database support use of the data only for purposes it has been obtained? (The GDPR limited purposes principle.) That is, does it ensure that you know what you can and can't use data for and warn you if you stray?
- Does the database enable a decision to be made on a category of individuals and then that decision applied and automatically marked in the database for all such individuals?

• Does the system allow for selective deletion according to criteria that you can set? (The GDPR retention principle.)

• Does the system allow you to record a timescale for the consent with reminders for consent to be reviewed and refreshed?

If your database can select individuals on a wide range of criteria, then the fields have to support those criteria, as well as recording the accountability data (such as when and how they gave consent). When recording any information in data fields (see table 5.1), always be conscious of whether the data should be classed as special category data (see page 161 for details).

TABLE 5.1 POTENTIAL DATA FIELDS IN A SUPPORTER RECORD

Database table	*Data fields*
Personal information	• Unique reference number • Salutation • First name • Surname • Address lines 1 and 2 • Town/city • Postcode • Age (if no date of birth is available but a date band is, such as 40–45, most databases will estimate the year by picking the mid-point of the date band) • Email address • Telephone number • Social media user name(s)
Lawful bases for purpose and date of decision	• Consent • Contract • Legitimate interest • Legal obligation • Vital interests[20] • Public interest

Database table	*Data fields*
Special category data	• Race • Ethnic origin • Politics • Religion • Trade union membership • Genetics • Biometrics (where used for ID purposes) • Health • Sex life • Sexual orientation For details on special category data, see page 161.
Supporter consent to contact, and means and date of consent	**Opted in to receive communications:** • By post • By telephone • By email • By text **Means and date of opting in or out:** • By post • By telephone • By email • By text • In person **Opted in to hear about:** • Raffles • Events • Volunteering • Merchandise • Appeals **Opted in to receive our newsletter**
Communications and campaign/ response history	• Which communications the supporter has been sent and when • The supporter's response to each (non-response, attending, not attending, etc.)

Database table	*Data fields*
Campaign and content coding	Ensure every form of communication you send to donors has a unique code to track how your supporters respond to your communications and activities
Events	**Any information relating to events; for example:** • Registration or enquiry about an event • Whether a T-shirt was requested • Whether the supporter attended and completed the event, with information split out by type of event
Financial information	**Detailed breakdown of transactions and giving history; for example:** • Date • Amount • Payment method • Gift details • Gift Aid generated • Event entry fees paid • Sponsorship values • Tickets bought • Merchandise bought • Total donation history
Supporter roles	**Other roles they have in relation to your charity; for example:** • Legacy pledger • Event attendee • Speaker • Received support from our charity • Collector: checks completed, permit issued, tins allocated and numbers, tins returned, amount per tin **Volunteer details; for example:** • When recruited • How recruited • Role • Supervision details • Reward and recognition details • DBS checks

Database table	*Data fields*
Interpersonal relationships or connections to your organisation	**Links to other records and specific fields showing any relationships between the supporter and other supporters or the supporter and your organisation; for example:** • whether they are an existing major donor • other supporters they are related to • where there are two records at one address, whether they are husband and wife, father and son, etc. • names of people they have fundraised with as part of a team • names of anybody they have raised money in memory of (Note: by recording relationships between individuals, you can potentially understand something of their motivation. For example, a supporter may be related to a service user or to another supporter. Understanding relationships between individuals will help you to understand the complex networks that link supporters with your organisation. By recording that a supporter fundraised in memory of someone, you will have an indication of how engaged and active a fundraiser and ambassador they might be.)
External interpersonal links	**Other organisations they have access to (employers, clubs, schools, etc.);** for example, they may be a member of a local group or association (a captain of a golf club could be linked to the golf club record in your database) an employee of a company where you have a charity partnership (their record could be linked to the company record) • Next of kin • Employer details (Note: how connected someone is in terms of the people and networks they can access is an indicator of their fundraising potential.)
Supporter journey stage	**Current status in their fundraising journey using any internal classifications** (such as 'current active supporter') (Note: different organisations, and even different departments within the same organisation, use different terminology, such as 'prospect', 'enquirer', 'new supporter', 'active participator' and 'repeat participator'.)
Geodemographic information	• Any additional supporter information, such as their wealth indicators • Profile of supporter based on their consumer classification organisation grouping (Note: see 'Consumer classification organisations' on page 51 for details.)

Database table	*Data fields*
Attitudes and questionnaire results	• What their motivation is for supporting your charity (beware this information may be special category data) • Which aspects of your charitable activities appeal to them • Which projects they would like to support • What they hope to achieve by supporting your organisation • Any other organisations that they support (Note: recording motivations will indicate how affiliated a person is with your cause or charity. Someone with personal experience of your cause or charity and knowledge of your work is likely to be an active and passionate fundraiser with a strong story to tell. Furthermore, past fundraising experience, either for your cause or for other organisations, can indicate how much support an individual may need and their level of knowledge of how to plan and implement a fundraising activity. If someone has organised a regular event which is established in their social network's calendar, they are likely to require less guidance than someone learning how to run a profitable event for the first time. Likewise, if someone has had a positive experience of fundraising, they may feel more confident about fundraising again.)

Data to track for assessing fundraising performance

To evaluate your fundraising performance (see 'Monitoring and reporting' on page 95), you will need to calculate and/or track key performance and relationship data, such as:

- gross income;
- net income;
- ROI (net and gross);
- number of participants;
- average gift and sponsorship values;
- number of new participants and donors;
- number of repeat participants;
- other types of support;
- response rates of different segments (including new and repeat supporters);
- response rates from all of your communication methods;
- average cost per gift (new and repeat);

- number of Gift Aid sign-ups;
- incremental permission value (the value over time of each supporter's consent – similar to lifetime value, which is explained on page 85).

Data to track for day-to-day fundraising activities

Think about what data you need in terms of its level of detail and why you need it, and consider how frequently you will require it. You might need some information on a daily basis to allow you to respond to requests, welcome new supporters and thank existing supporters. How quickly are you notified if a supporter starts fundraising for you on an online platform? If a fundraiser decides to carry out their own DIY event, can you capture this information to support them before and during their event? Do you need reports to help you monitor workloads and prevent backlogs in supporting and servicing fundraisers? (For example, you might want to see reports on how many people you need to send event registration packs to and by when or reports on how much fundraisers have raised via their online giving page.) Other indicators may only need to be assessed on a quarterly or annual basis. (See 'Monitoring and reporting' on page 95 for details on reporting against the fundraising plan.)

Data to report back to individual fundraisers

In addition to the data you use for internal reporting and evaluation, what data do you need to extract in order to report back to individual fundraisers? For example, you might report the number of people who attended an event that a fundraiser took part in, how much money the event raised, and any cumulative amount the event has raised over its lifetime. This allows your organisation's volunteer fundraisers to recognise the people who supported their fundraising efforts and inform how they thank their supporters on your charity's behalf. You therefore need to consider how you will help fundraising participants and organisers capture information that they can use in this way.

The following letter is an example of how one volunteer fundraiser used the information that Macmillan provided to show her coffee morning supporters the impact of their efforts.

World's Biggest Coffee Morning

Thank you very much for supporting my coffee morning with my family at Park Road. The World's Biggest Coffee Morning is a national event. The first coffee morning, held by 2,600 supporters in 1991, raised £208,000; this year, Macmillan is hoping to pass the £200 million mark raised by the event since it began. Our coffee mornings at Park Road have raised almost **£42,000** since we began in 2001. Macmillan uses this money to provide much needed support to people affected by cancer.

This year over 130 people attended and I would like to thank you all so much for making it such a memorable 16th coffee morning for us. We managed to raise **£2,934**, with more money promised. Thank you all so much for your help in raising this fantastic sum, which now takes the total to date that we have raised for Macmillan to over **£96,700**.

I would like to say a big thank you to everyone who made such generous donations to the raffle – such lovely gifts. We were overwhelmed by your generosity again this year. Thank you to all who donated home-made cakes and savouries; the cake table was positively straining under the weight. They were very well received. The 'Copper Pot' raised over **£201** this year, so keep saving those pennies for next year please or you can donate them at any time.

I would also like to say thank you to all my helpers, who worked tirelessly on and before the day to make it such a great success. It was lovely to see everyone. Thank you to all those who were unable to come but made generous donations – I'm just sorry you missed out on all the cake and friendship that abounded.

Just well done to everyone – I couldn't do it without you all. Macmillan has made such an impact on my quality of life for nearly 18 years and I am passionate that the charity will be there for all those that sadly will follow and will require their help. Over 1,000 people every day in the UK are given a cancer diagnosis!

Many thanks again to everyone.

Best regards

Elizabeth and David Waite

Elizabeth lost her battle to cancer in September 2018. Elizabeth channelled her energy into a cause she loved and brought the whole community along with her to help others. She often said that her fundraising helped keep her going. Her passion and enthusiasm were infectious and her efforts to help others unstoppable, resulting in her raising over £100,000 for Macmillan. Elizabeth's legacy continues to inspire me and many others to fundraise in her memory.

Ensuring your data is joined up, clean and secure

Consider how you want to categorise different types of activity and income and how you might code these against fields in your database. The activity and income types need to correspond to codes used for banking monies and budget lines. Work with colleagues responsible for finance, supporter care and data management to understand how you can use your data fields, naming conventions and coding structures to track and report on different types of event, audience, marketing campaign, fundraising activity and payment method. Does the way you code activities and income enable you to report and plan effectively? Or are there too many codes, naming conventions and business rules that are open to misinterpretation or error?

Ensure you have clear and well-understood definitions of your various data fields, as inconsistency will undermine the integrity of your reporting and results. Furthermore, the GDPR accuracy principle (see page 158) requires you to take proactive steps to correct inaccurate personal data or to delete it. Document your processes, have clear and easy-to-follow business rules, and give inductions for and training on how people in your organisation should capture, enter, update and use data. For example, your database might have a 'J. Smith' and a 'John Smith' at the same address and both are male – the business rules could allow these two records to be consolidated into one, or the rules might dictate that further information needs to be gathered to determine whether these are, in fact, different people. To encourage personal responsibility for data integrity, carry out regular checks on accuracy and set objectives to reduce the number of errors. Different database users can be given different access rights that determine what they can input, change, merge, delete or export.

Any data you collect must also be stored securely. You need to evaluate whether:

- you are using strong passwords (including upper-case and lower-case letters, numbers and symbols);
- you are encrypting portable devices (laptops, mobiles, tablets and memory sticks);
- you really need printed copies of personal information (if you need to print out personal details, store them securely and shred them when no longer needed).

Configuring the right database

A good customer relationship management (CRM) database should facilitate the data capture, storage and analysis necessary to achieve the best possible supporter experience. It should be:

- easy and intuitive to use;
- easy to report from;
- stable and reliable;
- secure;
- logically structured;
- well supported by the software supplier;
- designed to support the needs of fundraising;
- affordable and cost-effective.

Having already looked at what you are seeking to achieve, you can clarify your CRM database requirements. Summarise the information you need the database to deliver to do this, including:

- what data you need in order to identify who your supporters are, what they do, what information they need, and how, when and by whom they wish to be contacted;
- how the database can automate some of the information-gathering you currently do manually, saving you time and reducing the risk of human error;
- how the system can improve the quality of data capture – for example, via prompts for missing data or drop-down menus;
- which other systems the database needs to interface with internally or externally – for example:
  - How are you capturing online gifts?
  - What information do you and your finance team need to share?
  - How might you identify whether someone is a service user or volunteer for a different part of the organisation?
- how well the software interfaces with other web-based fundraising platforms and your own website;

- how your system can better facilitate supporter journeys – for example, whether it can provide prompts to highlight when someone makes an enquiry, signs up to an activity, makes progress towards their fundraising target, or participates in an event;
- how it can help you monitor performance against targets – for example, by having the facility to represent your data as dashboards.

The data analysis which may be required as part of your fundraising audit (see chapter 2), segmentation process (see page 70) and reporting (see page 95) cannot be done on a traditional operational CRM database. To do the simplest of data analysis, except for basic analysis such as RFV, you need a separate analytical CRM database, more commonly known simply as a 'marketing database'.

If your organisation does not have a marketing database, you can install a basic system in-house (even if your organisation has a minimal budget). For example, there are a small number of cloud-based systems that have significant UK-specialised functionality, such as CiviCRM (an open-source system) and Salesforce.com.

Audit all databases to check there is no duplication of effort, breach of data protection, or conflicting messaging or engagement with supporters. For example, are there duplicate spreadsheets, contact books or attendee lists or has data been generated by volunteer groups which never made its way into the central system? Finally, work with your software supplier to ensure the system meets your requirements and complies with new and evolving data protection legislation and fundraising regulations.

Conclusion

Managing community fundraising data effectively underpins future fundraising success. A data-driven approach to fundraising and evidence-based decision-making has helped many fundraising teams to save time, reduce costs and increase income.

Good data management helps fundraisers to build great supporter relationships and develop new fundraising opportunities. Poor data management could undo years of hard work in an instant and cause irreparable damage to your charity's reputation and reduce public trust in your organisation. By effectively managing risks to your community fundraising data, you are managing risk to income and ensuring your supporters can make the biggest impact on your cause.

Notes

1 'What's data got to do with it?' [blog post], JustGiving, https://blog.justgiving.com/free-data-and-fundraising-guide-whats-data-got-to-do-with-it, 7 July 2015.
2 The PECR implement the ePrivacy Directive (officially known as European Directive 2002/58/EC). See 'Guide to the Privacy and Electronic Communications Regulations, Information Commissioner's Office' [web page], Information Commissioner's Office, 2019, https://ico.org.uk/for-organisations/guide-to-pecr, accessed 19 March 2019. At the time of writing, the latest version of the PECR came into effect on 9 January 2019.
3 *Ibid.* and *Direct Marketing* [PDF], Information Commissioner's Office, 2018, https://ico.org.uk/media/1555/direct-marketing-guidance.pdf, accessed 19 March 2019.
4 'Lawful basis for processing' [web page], Information Commissioner's Office, 2019, https://ico.org.uk/for-organisations/guide-to-data-protection/guide-to-the-general-data-protection-regulation-gdpr/lawful-basis-for-processing, accessed 19 March 2019. (See www.nationalarchives.gov.uk/doc/open-government-licence/version/3 for details on the Open Government Licence v3.0.)
5 'The principles' [web page], Information Commissioner's Office, 2019, https://ico.org.uk/for-organisations/guide-to-data-protection/guide-to-the-general-data-protection-regulation-gdpr/principles, accessed 19 March 2019. (See www.nationalarchives.gov.uk/doc/open-government-licence/version/3 for details on the Open Government Licence v3.0.)
6 *Ibid.*
7 For more details on DPIAs and to download a DPIA template, see 'Data protection impact assessments' [web page], https://ico.org.uk/for-organisations/guide-to-data-protection/guide-to-the-general-data-protection-regulation-gdpr/accountability-and-governance/data-protection-impact-assessments, Information Commissioner's Office, 2018, accessed 23 May 2019.
8 For details on the legalities of using third parties see 'What responsibilities and liabilities do controllers have when using a processor?' [web page], Information Commissioner's Office, 2019, https://ico.org.uk/for-organisations/guide-to-data-protection/guide-to-the-general-data-protection-regulation-gdpr/contracts-and-liabilities-between-controllers-and-processors-multi/responsibilities-and-liabilities-for-controllers-using-a-processor, accessed 28 June 2019.
9 For details on what constitutes special category data and for the full list of conditions, see 'Special category data' [web page], Information Commissioner's Office, 2019, https://ico.org.uk/for-organisations/guide-to-data-protection/guide-to-the-general-data-protection-regulation-gdpr/lawful-basis-for-processing/special-category-data, accessed 11 February 2019.
10 See 'Accountability and governance' [web page], Information Commissioner's Office, 2019, https://ico.org.uk/for-organisations/guide-to-data-protection/guide-to-the-general-data-protection-regulation-gdpr/accountability-and-governance, accessed 26 June 2019 – and 'Documentation' within that section of the Information Commissioner's Office website.
11 'Right to be informed' [web page], Information Commissioner's Office, 2019, https://ico.org.uk/for-organisations/guide-to-data-protection/guide-to-the-general-data-protection-regulation-gdpr/individual-rights/right-to-be-informed, accessed 12 February 2019.

12 'Consent' [web page], Information Commissioner's Office, 2019, https://ico.org.uk/for-organisations/guide-to-data-protection/guide-to-the-general-data-protection-regulation-gdpr/lawful-basis-for-processing/consent, accessed 28 March 2019.

13 'Cookies and similar technologies' [web page], Information Commissioner's Office, 2019, https://ico.org.uk/for-organisations/guide-to-pecr/cookies-and-similar-technologies, accessed 11 February 2019.

14 'ICO fines eleven more charities' [web article], Information Commissioner's Office, https://ico.org.uk/about-the-ico/news-and-events/news-and-blogs/2017/04/ico-fines-eleven-more-charities, 5 April 2017.

15 '5.0 Personal information and fundraising' [web page], Fundraising Regulator, 2019, www.fundraisingregulator.org.uk/code/personal-information, accessed 12 February 2019.

16 'What is personal data?' [web page], Information Commissioner's Office, 2019, https://ico.org.uk/for-organisations/guide-to-data-protection/guide-to-the-general-data-protection-regulation-gdpr/what-is-personal-data/what-is-personal-data, accessed 28 March 2019.

17 'When can we rely on legitimate interests?' [web page], Information Commissioner's Office, 2019, https://ico.org.uk/for-organisations/guide-to-data-protection/guide-to-the-general-data-protection-regulation-gdpr/legitimate-interests/when-can-we-rely-on-legitimate-interests, accessed 28 June 2019.

18 'Legitimate interests' [web page], Information Commissioner's Office, 2019, https://ico.org.uk/for-organisations/guide-to-data-protection/guide-to-the-general-data-protection-regulation-gdpr/lawful-basis-for-processing/legitimate-interests, accessed 12 February 2019.

19 *GDPR: The essentials for fundraising organisations* [PDF], Institute of Fundraising, 2017, www.institute-of-fundraising.org.uk/guidance/key-iof-guidance/understanding-gdpr, accessed 12 February 2019.

20 Vital interests is used as a lawful basis in cases of needing to process personal data to protect someone's life. This is would occur, for example, in a life-threatening medical situation where someone's medical history needed to be disclosed to a hospital in order to save their life. Vital interests might also apply if you are processing data for humanitarian reasons to, for example, monitor epidemics, or in cases of humanitarian emergency, particularly caused by natural or man-made disasters. For further details, see 'Vital interests' [web page], https://ico.org.uk/for-organisations/guide-to-data-protection/guide-to-the-general-data-protection-regulation-gdpr/lawful-basis-for-processing/vital-interests Information Commissioner's Office, 2019, accessed 6 June 2019.

CHAPTER SIX

Planning and managing community fundraising events

Susannah Forland

Introduction

In recent years we have witnessed a boom across the whole of the fundraising events market – JustGiving reported a 106% growth in money raised via event fundraising between 2012 and 2017.[1] As well as growth in mass participation events and bucket list challenges, charities have seen greater interest in smaller, more traditional community events such as coffee mornings, walks, runs, bike rides and swimming, with bake-offs cited as more appealing than challenging experience-based activities.[2]

However, behind these top-line facts and figures is a more complex picture and a maturing market. For instance, not all forms of sporting event are growing;[3] different events appeal to different demographics – men are more likely to participate in cycling events and women in running events;[4] younger fundraisers (aged 30 to 49) are more responsive to virtual events[5] (where supporters raise money for a charity from wherever they live, usually within a particular month or other period of time, rather than in the same place at the same time); and 25- to 34-year-olds are most likely to bake for charity.[6] Also, different types of activities achieve vastly different average incomes per participant (runs £395, cycling £770, triathlons £749[7] and bake sales £12[8]). Fundraisers must therefore carefully consider which events are right for which audiences, where growth can be achieved and what levels of income are realistic.

Events have inherent risks, particularly their upfront organisational and recruitment costs and the opportunity cost of their relatively low return on investment (ROI) in comparison to other sources of voluntary income.[9] They can be at the mercy of uncertain weather conditions, celebrities turning up, participants honouring sponsorship pledges and the reliability of suppliers. To compete in a saturated market, events need to be distinctive, harness the technology that facilitates a personalised participant experience, and work harder than ever to grab attention as people increasingly self-select their media content.

Yet, well-conceived and well-executed events can provide both intrinsic and associated benefits for charities of all sizes. Events can provide an engaging means of cultivating, acknowledging and rewarding supporters;

building on social motivations; and identifying potential major donors. They create memories that can last a lifetime, thereby strengthening participants' relationship with a charity or cause. They raise additional funds and, to some extent, awareness, and they help charities to access new supporters who may convert to other forms of giving. Indeed, research by the Institute of Fundraising asked whether event participants would support the same charity in other ways. It found that 92% of them would do so and, among these people, over a quarter of people would consider giving one-off donations to specific appeals, about a fifth would consider becoming a regular supporter, and the same proportion would consider becoming a volunteer.[10]

There are endless forms of fundraising event. This chapter provides a short guide to some common events and then focuses on how to plan events effectively.

Events within a community fundraising portfolio

To evaluate which events to include in your community fundraising portfolio, you need to consider the different types of fundraising event.

In-house events

In-house events are organised by charity staff, usually community or event fundraisers. To help select the types of event that are most likely to prove successful, shape your activities by using feedback from existing event participants and consider what makes your competitors' most popular activities successful (but also how you can distinguish your event from theirs).

A varied calendar of events might range from muddy-trainer events (for example, sponsored walks, runs, rides and Santa dashes) to special events (for example, dinners, golf days and concerts) and community-focused events (for example, fetes, fairs, family days, pub quizzes and open gardens). While in-house events provide more control over the audiences you can reach, the methods of engagement you can use and how your charity is presented, they require internal skills and can be restrictive if suitable locations are unavailable or too expensive.

Supporter-led events

Referred to in a variety of ways (for example, DIY fundraising, third-party events, grassroots fundraising, supporter-led fundraising and in-aid-of fundraising), these events are designed and run by non-staff and the types of activity carried out are decided by supporters themselves.

Even though these activities are led by supporters, to ensure that they generate income and that supporters have an optimum experience, your charity should take a proactive approach to stewardship. While you will have less control over how these events are presented, they tend to have a higher ROI and appeal to those seeking personal determination over how, when and where they fundraise. (For more information on DIY fundraising, see chapter 7.)

Third-party challenge events

Challenge events can be run by third-party event organisers or in-house, and they involve participants achieving a significant physical goal for which they seek sponsorship. Some of the major UK challenge events include the London Marathon, RideLondon and the Great North Run. Charities can purchase places from third-party organisers to offer to supporters for a minimum suggested level of sponsorship. Supporters can also secure their own places through ballots and fundraise for a charity of their choice. Alternatively, charities can run their own challenge events in house, independently of third-party organisers.

If you hold places in a third-party event, you will need to develop a recruitment campaign to fill the places by a set deadline. This will require a range of recruitment methods, and there is also the option of buying data packages from companies such as Realbuzz for events such as the London Marathon. These provide the contact details of people who initially selected your charity when applying for a ballot place. You can then encourage unsuccessful ballot applicants to apply for one of your own places.

UK and overseas treks usually involve a third-party provider who sets the itinerary and organises the logistics. A charity can then form a 'closed' group of participants or become part of an 'open' group. A closed group comprises supporters of one specific charity, which will need to recruit a minimum number of people for the trek to go ahead. An open group's participants can choose a charity for which to fundraise (sometimes from a pre-selected list of charities and sometimes from among all charities). While being chosen from an open group removes the risk of your charity not filling enough places, you lose the sense of community that can evolve from a closed group's collective focus on your cause.

On the downside, challenge events have received criticism that participants are just funding a holiday or sporting hobby; in addition, it is becoming increasingly difficult to fill places for smaller third-party challenge events.[11] However, by attracting highly committed individuals these can be profitable events which can also foster participants' bond with your cause through the transformational nature of once-in-a-lifetime physical and emotional challenges. These events also provide popular team-building exercises for corporates, often raising substantial sums.

Mass participation events

Mass participation events are fundraising events that involve a large group of people undertaking the same activity, at the same time and/or in the same place, for the same cause. Some charities develop mass participation events targeting specific demographics with a specific activity (for example, Movember) or particular groups (such as Save the Children's Den Day for schools). Others have events for a broader range of supporters (for example, Macmillan's World's Biggest Coffee Morning).

Developing a mass participation campaign requires a match between a relatively easy activity and target audience; it also requires the resources to reach and support large numbers of people. Given the need to cut through the noise of social, terrestrial and printed media, it is hardly surprising that the larger charities dominate this form of fundraising (see figure 8.1 in chapter 8 for a list of the top 25 mass participation events).

Planning your event

> There are no second chances at a great event so the best one can do is to plan, prepare and most importantly be ready for the unexpected.[12]
>
> Adrian Sargeant and Harriet Day, 2017

To mitigate the risks of running events, planning is essential. Some of the common causes of event failure include:

- lack of understanding of supporter motivation;
- lack of appropriate or competent staff members;
- lack of an appropriate or competent event partner;
- undefined objectives;
- unrealistic budgets;
- no clarity on roles and responsibilities;
- staff overwhelmed due to poor scheduling or resourcing;
- event licence refused or not sought;
- major or serious incident (e.g. participant injuries or loss of life) due to lack of planning.

Selecting appropriate objectives for your event

All events need SMART (specific, measurable, achievable, realistic and timetabled) objectives. To start developing these, consider:

- How will your events meet the needs of the participants?
- How will your events programme benefit your charity in the long term?
- How will your events programme boost your charity's brand within its communities?

• What is the primary goal of your event? To fundraise, to recruit new supporters, to retain existing supporters or to thank supporters?[13]

• What levels of participation and retention will be considered successful?

• What overall level of income and ROI are acceptable?

• How might your events support wider cultivation and/or stewardship of supporters?

• What competitive advantages could your events achieve (for example, lower costs, access to new audiences, increased profile, or greater loyalty)?

Table 6.1 outlines a format you can use for planning your event once you have decided on your high-level objectives. (See also section 11.0 of the Code of Fundraising Practice, 'Events'.)

TABLE 6.1 EXAMPLE OF AN EVENT PLANNING DOCUMENT

Category	**Information to be completed and topics to consider**
Event commissioner(s)	Who is leading on this?
Proposed event type	What type of event are we looking to organise: dinner, briefing, drinks reception, etc.?
Proposed event theme	For example, launch of a national appeal.
Event unique selling point	Why is this event unique? What are the key event unique selling points we should be communicating to participants?
Target audience	Who is the event aimed at (e.g. top participants, top prospects, corporates, trusts)?
Target number of attendees	How many people do we want to attend?
Event goals	What are we aiming to achieve? For example: • raise money on the night; • update on appeal; • launch new research; • engage new prospects; • access supporter networks; • meet supporters face to face.

Category	Information to be completed and topics to consider
Event KPIs (key performance indicators)	Target response rate: Target no. of attendees: Target no. of participants: Average donation, ticket or sponsorship value per participant: Target no. of volunteers needed to help with the event: Target no. of participants to convert to donors, participants in a second event, etc.:
Risk analysis	Identify potential risks. What would be the key risks if this event were to be delivered? Consider both internal and external factors. Explore solutions and assess whether or not the risks are too big for the event to take place. How can we minimise these risks? Do senior management and/or trustees need to be consulted on making a decision about any of the risks? Has a risk assessment form been completed?
Budget outlined in plan	How much budget would we like to deliver this event?
Preferred date(s)	When would we ideally like the event to take place? Are there any specific days of the week to aim for or avoid?
Preferred location	Where would we ideally like the event to take place?
Preferred venue type	What type of venue are we looking for?
Ideal event timings	What are the ideal event timings (start and finish)?
Food and catering	Will food be served – if so, what type?
Speaker requirements	Will there be presentations and/or speakers? Are we seeking celebrity participation? If so, who are we looking for and who is approaching them? Do we have any requirements requested by celebrities?

Category	Information to be completed and topics to consider
Technical requirements	What technical requirements will we need (projector, sound system, stage, microphones, Wi-Fi, etc.)?
Invitation process	What will be the method of invitation? Who is sending out invitations? When do they need to be sent (how far in advance of the event)? Who is drafting the text? What are the arrangements for ensuring actions take place and dealing with queries?
CRM system	What appeal code would you like to set up? Attached to which department? Who will set it up?
Staff attendance	Which members of staff would you like to attend – senior staff, chief executive, trustees? Who is approaching them?
Sponsorship	Whom could we approach? Who will approach them? How much will we ask them for? What will we offer in return – e.g. attendance, speeches, branding? What is the deadline for securing sponsorship?
Post-event follow-up	How will this be done (e.g. email, letter)? Who will send the communication? What will we invite participants to next? What follow-up will there be for declines and non-attendees? Is it appropriate to send hand-written letters? Think about your participants' journey and cultivation process.

Understanding motivation

Research has found that organisations with a detailed understanding of supporter expectations and motivation tend to have better-performing events.[14] Therefore, to increase your organisation's likelihood of running a successful event that delivers an excellent experience for your supporters, you need to understand your audience and what will motivate them to participate. This will vary by audience type: a corporate may want networking opportunities, whereas an individual who is personally affected by your charity's work may want to raise funds for a very specific element of that work.

Reading secondary research is a good way of staying on top of wider event trends and keeping apprised of which events people are becoming more, or less, motivated to take part in. To understand how your own events might relate to participants' motivations, you should build a research and feedback phase into your planning process. (For details on how to do this, see 'The fundraising audit process' on page 33.) This will allow you to confirm who currently participates in your organisation's events, determine whether you are meeting their needs and find out how you might change your events to make them more relevant and appealing.

Participants might be motivated by internal drivers (such as values, beliefs or sense of self) or by external drivers (such as status, who they were asked by, or opportunities to gain advancement in a personal or professional sense – such as by gaining friends or establishing themselves as part of a team). How well do the different elements of your event help your participants meet these needs? How do these needs differ by type of participant? The challenge is to build into your events features that will tap into motivations and emotions that are strong enough to result in an action. As noted in chapter 1 (see page 9), event participants usually have more than one motivation; the key is to understand which is the strongest and what combination of participants' motivations your event can be designed to meet. (See also 'Multiple income sources' on page 194.)

Hygiene factors

As well as personal motivations, you also need to understand 'hygiene factors' – these are the basics that need to be in place for people to feel confident in your event. Frederick Herzberg first came up with the concept in relation to employee satisfaction; he argued that, however exciting or satisfying a job, we expect basic hygiene factors such as a contract, holidays, a desk and a salary before our personal motivations, such as personal achievement or recognition, can be met.[15] Hygiene factors for events could include ensuring that supporters (whether they are participants or volunteers):

- feel confident in the charity's use of funds raised from the event (and overall);
- find it easy and quick to sign up;
- are thanked;
- receive speedy responses to queries and questions;
- receive high-quality fundraising and training advice that is appropriate to the activity;
- receive easily shareable content;
- can download or order any fundraising packs or other materials quickly and easily;
- receive free merchandise;
- experience appropriate facilities on the day;
- are provided with refreshments.

Maximising event income

Events can comprise a mixture of income sources. Choosing the right ticket price, registration fees, sponsorship targets, pricing enhancement strategy (such as early-bird discounts) and ancillary purchase options will determine your event's profitability.

Registration fees and sponsorship targets

Some events have a combination of registration fees and minimum sponsorship levels. If you have challenge event places, ideally the registration fee should cover the cost to the charity of purchasing the event places. The sponsorship raised is then profit. For in-house events, registration fees should fully cover your costs. Some charities waive a registration fee for certain supporters (such as corporate partners or teams that raise more money) or if they are struggling to fill places. However, sponsorship income will still need to cover costs and generate a surplus. Providing free places may fill your event but may result in less committed participants with higher drop-out rates and lower engagement in fundraising.

Price points

The event prices you set will be influenced by several factors:

- **What is your primary event objective?** Is it to grow income, awareness or participation?
- **How established is your event?** A popular event can be priced higher than a new event, which may need to be priced very competitively to become established.
- **What is your event's capacity?** If limited, then demand may allow for an increased price.
- **Did you meet your targets for last year's event?** Were you oversubscribed? Could you increase prices?
- **How do your prices compare to those of other events?** Look at local events beyond your event category which appeal to the same audience (for example, a potential participant might choose between a mud run and a concert).
- **How do you want your event to be perceived?** A premium event needs a premium price.
- **Where are you drawing your audience from?** Are you competing with national events? How are these priced?
- **Who are your participants and how loyal are they?** Pricing for a one-off bucket list event might be lower than pricing for an event with a loyal following.
- **What age are your participants?** Will their demographic have an impact on their likely disposable income and fundraising capacity?
- **What are the ancillary costs of attending?** Can you decrease the costs of travel or accommodation through supplier donations and/or discounts?

Pricing will also be determined by what costs you need to cover, how much you need to charge to break even, and how much you need to generate to create an acceptable surplus and ROI.

Pricing enhancements

Pricing promotions and limited capacity create incentives and a sense of urgency, driving people to register early. Early registration helps with cash flow and provides participants with longer to train, raise funds and encourage peer participation. It gives a reason not to put off registration to the extent that it is too late to prepare or recover from injuries.

Eventbrite suggests three tactics for creating urgency, based on time, number and rewards:[16]

- **Time:** Early-bird pricing within a restricted amount of time can encourage people to buy their tickets early. It also gives them an opportunity to share the offer on social media. Bear in mind the risk of selling too many or too few tickets at this lower price.
- **Number:** Offering a discount on a particular number of tickets, such as 20% off the first 50 tickets sold, can also encourage people to take action early. This method is easier to align with your budget than offering time-restricted discounts but the end date of the promotion is not within your control.
- **Reward:** Offering discounts to loyal supporters by giving them an exclusive opportunity to purchase early (before the rest of the tickets go on sale) rewards them for their support and encourages them to promote your event to their friends and colleagues. You could also provide shareable discount codes for previous participants to offer to people in their social networks.

Some participants might pay a premium for items such as:

- VIP packages with additional benefits (free parking, meeting a celebrity, no-queue Portaloos, etc.);
- reserved seating near the action;
- merchandise and backstage passes provided in the form of bundling (i.e. adding additional promotional items to the price of the ticket).

Incentive schemes can recruit more participants and reward performance before, during and after the event. Rewarding performance can be as simple as inviting participants to a closed Facebook group to chat about their training or sending an extra running vest when minimum sponsorship targets are met.

Multiple income sources

Some participants may be able to give more than the value of the ticket price, so it is worth offering people further opportunities to give. Daniel Webber argues that the maximum that can be raised from each individual is determined by their financial capacity (wealthier people having more disposable income) and their motivation.[17] Motivation determines the most appropriate form of secondary income over and above the ticket price. So, if someone is motivated by participating in a fun and unique event but they have little philanthropic interest in your cause, a raffle that provides further private benefit may be most relevant. Someone who is philanthropically motivated, on the other hand, might prefer to make a personal donation using a donation envelope provided at the event. Consider the full range of income sources in relation to motivations, including:

- participant ancillary purchases, such as refreshments, merchandise and sports massage;
- spectator participation through mini-challenges, collections, refreshments, merchandise, face painting and stalls;
- matched funding from participants' employers;
- raffles, auctions, tombolas and lucky dips;
- corporate sponsorship, in-kind donations, media sponsorship and cause-related marketing promotions;
- additional donations from participants on the day;
- Gift Aid income.

Tax-effective giving

In addition to ensuring that your charity maximises income via fees, pricing enhancements and so on, you should take care not to lose money by paying tax unnecessarily (or, indeed, by falling foul of the rules) or by failing to maximise Gift Aid opportunities.

VAT

Fundraising is, in general, exempt from the payment of VAT, and the majority of fundraising events fall under the one-off events exemption. This exemption means that each year a charity can hold up to 15 events, of the same kind, in the same location, without them becoming liable for VAT. Charities are permitted to hold unlimited small-scale events in the same location, such as coffee mornings, as long as the income from them does not exceed £1,000 per week.

Setting a minimum level of sponsorship as a condition of event participation makes this income liable for VAT, although sponsorship above this minimum is not liable. However, rather than asking for a conditional minimum, participants can be asked to pledge a certain amount of money in total, which is collected after the event.

Be careful not to give away any individual benefits that might jeopardise the classification of sponsorship money as a donation. HMRC does not consider T-shirts, training advice, massages and support during an event, or pre- or post-race meetings as benefits. However, free travel, accommodation and gifts (such as a Fitbit) will be thought of as benefits.

The majority of overseas challenge events will be liable for VAT in some way – for example, when travel and accommodation are supplied as part of the package. However, the way that you put the package together will alter the amount of VAT that is payable. If your charity acts as an agent for a tour operator, any commission your organisation receives is payable at the standard rate. However, if you buy the package and sell it on to the participants, VAT is due on the whole profit margin. As with challenge events, in order to avoid paying VAT on sponsorship income, you should collect funds after the event has taken place. For more information on VAT and charities, visit www.gov.uk/government/publications and search for 'VAT Notice 701/1'.

In the case of auctions, donated items are zero-rated for VAT, but income from this kind of event cannot be treated as donations for Gift Aid purposes due to the 'benefit rules' (see next section).

Gift Aid

Gift Aid allows UK charities to claim back the basic rate of tax that donors have already paid on any donations they make. So, if someone donates £10, this money is net of the tax they would have paid on their earnings. Therefore, the value of £10 prior to having paid tax would be £12.50. The tax they paid on this at 20% was £2.50. It is this £2.50 that the charity can claim from HMRC. This is the equivalent of 25% on every £1 donated. You can reclaim Gift Aid only on donations made by individuals who pay UK income or capital gains tax at a rate at least equal to the amount reclaimed on their donations in the current tax year. Higher-rate taxpayers can claim the difference between the higher 40% rate and the basic 20% on their annual tax return. In some circumstances, even if a fundraiser and those sponsoring them have not made a Gift Aid declaration, you may still be able to claim on cash donations of £20 or less under GASDS (the Gift Aid Small Donations Scheme).

Online giving platforms automatically process Gift Aid claims made through their pages and send the resulting income to the beneficiary charities. As reported by JustGiving in 2015, over 85% of donations through JustGiving are eligible for Gift Aid.[18]

Gift Aid can be reclaimed on fundraising income when it meets the 'benefit rules'. This means that if a supporter receives a benefit in return for a payment, the income does not qualify for Gift Aid. So, ticket sales, purchases (such as merchandise and refreshments) and minimum sponsorship that is a condition of participation do not qualify for Gift Aid. One way to maximise Gift Aid is to consider separating donations from event costs. If you were selling tickets to a cinema night for £10 and the cost per head of showing the film was £5, you could ask for this as a ticket price and another £5 as a donation. The donation would then be eligible for Gift Aid. For more information on Gift Aid visit www.gov.uk/claim-gift-aid.

Setting your budget

Each individual event should have its own budget. To be able to calculate how many participants, based on a certain average sponsorship or ticket price, are needed to cover costs and achieve an acceptable ROI, you will need to know your event's break-even point.

Calculating break-even points

Events have two forms of cost:

- **Fixed costs:** Overhead costs that do not vary regardless of the number of attendees (core staff, venue, marketing, insurance, suppliers, etc.).
- **Variable costs:** Costs that change depending on the number of participants (cost per head for refreshments, free merchandise, etc.).

For example, the costs of a venue, entertainment, marketing and staff might be £10,000.

Let's say that 250 guests are expected and the variable cost of food, drink and fulfilment is £60 per head.

The total event cost is therefore:

£10,000 + (250 × £60 = £15,000) = £25,000

If there are no alternative sources of income, such as a sponsor, the ticket price needs to be:

£25,000 ÷ 250 = £100 to break even (but this would not make a profit)

An alternative method for this calculation is:

Fixed costs ÷ (ticket price – variable costs per head) = break-even point in units (i.e. number of tickets in this case)

So in this example:

£10,000 ÷ (£100 – £60) = 250 tickets to break even

Some of the items to consider in an events budget

When building your budget, consider whether you may need to hire or arrange any of the following items:

Venue

- Hire
- Staff
- Equipment
- Deposit
- Security
- Audiovisual equipment, Wi-Fi, lights, etc.
- Parking charges

Dressing

- Flowers, banners and balloons
- Tables
- Signage
- Branding
- Sets

Suppliers

- Performers and/or celebrities
- Walkie talkies and/or phones
- Equipment (electrical, seating, structures, flooring, recording equipment, screens, IT, etc.)
- Portaloos
- First Aid
- Catering (for participants, spectators, staff, volunteers and suppliers)
- Cleaning and waste disposal
- Set-up costs
- Photographer

Marketing and communications

- Internal staff time
- Posters, ad space, flyers and broadcast time (space, design and production costs)
- Web design, online content, hosting costs and online advertising (space, design and production costs)
- Merchandise and fulfilment costs
- Postage, courier and delivery costs

Supporter experience

- Design and printing of packs, certificates, instructions, passes, programmes and race chips
- Accommodation, storage, transport and prizes

Staff costs

- Event organiser
- Additional staff on the day – time and expenses
- Volunteer costs
- Support services staff
- IT support
- Marketing

Financial and administration costs

- Online donation platform charges
- Gift Aid
- Banking
- Software upgrades and purchase of apps
- Insurance and licence fees

Calculating staff costs

As well as considering the direct fixed costs of running an event, you need to take staff time into account. Monitor staff time by logging hours spent on each event, calculating the cost per hour and aggregating this into the expenditure budget. Consider which staff should be included in these costs (such as event staff, supporter services, the marketing team and the volunteer manager). It is possible to reduce staff costs by using volunteers and streamlining processes.

Using technology to save time and money

There is a plethora of time- and money-saving technology, such as:

- apps that monitor attendee check-in and send welcome text messages;
- silent auction online bidding apps;
- apps that monitor online donation collection during an event;
- apps that automate the sending of bulk personalised emails;
- online registration and payment systems that processes participant details straight into your database.

Forecasting scenarios

When setting your budget, forecast your best-case, medium-case and worst-case scenarios based on different participant and sponsorship/ticket levels. Table 6.2 offers an example of the different scenarios for a charity pre-purchasing 50 challenge event places from a third-party event organiser and then promoting the event to potential participants.

TABLE 6.2 EXAMPLE OF CHALLENGE EVENT BUDGET SCENARIOS BASED ON VARIANCE OF PARTICIPATION NUMBERS AND AVERAGE SPONSORSHIP VALUES

	Best case			Medium case			Worst case		
Income	**Amount**	**Participant number**	**Total**	**Amount**	**Participant number**	**Total**	**Amount**	**Participant number**	**Total**
Minimum participant sponsorship	£400	50	£20,000	£400	50	£20,000	£400	40	£16,000
Registration fee	£100	50	£5,000	£100	50	£5,000	£100	40	£4,000
Additional best-case income if 20% of participants achieve 50% additional sponsorship	£200	10	£2,000	n/a	n/a	n/a	n/a	n/a	n/a
Total gross income			**£27,000**			**£25,000**			**£20,000**
Charity place (£100 each)	£100	50	£5,000	£100	50	£5,000	£100	50*	£5,000
Marketing costs: paid social media ads and print ads	£500	n/a	£500	£500	n/a	£500	£500	n/a	£500
Running vests (£10 each)	£10	50	£500	£10	50	£500	£10	40	£400
Registration packs (£1.50 to mail each)	£1.50	50	£75	£1.50	50	£75	£1.50	40	£60
Total expenditure			**£6,075**			**£6,075**			**£5,960**
Total net income			**£20,925**			**£18,925**			**£15,040**
ROI			4.44			4.11			3.35

*Note: the participant number is 50 because all the places will be purchased/the expenditure made, regardless of how many places have not been sold.

Looking beyond the budget

While it is important to continually try to minimise costs, there is a fine balance to be achieved in ensuring that you do not strip out too much expenditure at the expense of participants' experience. Also remember that assessing the ROI of fundraising activities only looks at the financial costs and gains – it does not take into account any non-financial benefits of awareness (if you are able to realistically measure this), brand-building among existing or new supporters, supporter experience and so on.

Working with suppliers

Events can involve multiple suppliers, from venues, performers and photographers to suppliers of catering, equipment and Portaloos. Suppliers should be selected based on value for money and reliability. Always get quotes from suppliers and examine why some are cheaper than others. Cheaper options may save money but may not provide the reliability and quality you need.

All supplier relationships should have binding written agreements signed by both parties. At a minimum they should outline:

- the cost of the services or items;
- whether VAT is included;
- the responsibilities of both parties;
- the timings for delivery and/or set-up;
- cancellation clauses;
- insurance and compliance requirements.

When working with third parties, the Fundraising Regulator requires that charities adhere to section 7.0 of the Code of Fundraising Practice, 'Professional fundraisers, commercial participators and partners', which can be accessed at www.fundraisingregulator.org.uk.

Working with celebrities

Celebrities are generally considered valuable in helping charities to reach new audiences, achieve credibility, and position events or organisations distinctively in relation to their competitors. However, research suggests that the public is indifferent to celebrity recommendations.[19] Furthermore, celebrities can be expensive to secure and manage and it can be difficult to measure the impact of this investment. They can also bring the risks of unreliability and any negative publicity if they fall from grace or misrepresent your charity. They can quickly lose popularity or change their image in a way that no longer fits your brand. Bear in mind that celebrities' motivations are often a combination of the altruistic and egotistic, making it important to manage their expectations.

If your charity intends to seek celebrity involvement, you should start with some clarity around the outcomes their association is designed to achieve. Would you like them to:

- Reach particular audiences through their fan base?
- Promote a particular call to action?
- Share the impact of your work?
- Endorse your event or cause?
- Attend an event to add uniqueness to it?

Any celebrities you approach should be attractive to your target audience, have personality and expertise which are credible, and be compatible with your brand in terms of identity, personality, positioning, and lifestyle. Identify how your cause aligns with the celebrity's professional and personal life and whether they already have an interest in the issue or type of event. It is common for well-known celebrities to charge for endorsements and appearances, as well as expenses (and even tweets), so don't limit yourself to the most famous. Consider local celebrities such as newsreaders and sportspeople, or celebrities who happen to live locally and are concerned about local issues. Niche celebrities may be easier to access – for example, a well-known scientist, businessperson, designer or chef. People are more likely to support organisations whose celebrities show a sincere commitment to and knowledge of the cause.[20]

The most usual route for contacting a celebrity is through their agent, but research any connections your charity, colleagues, supporters and contacts might have with them. Track on social media those whom you have identified as providing the right fit, and follow up any shares and uses of hashtags or likes that might help you to open a dialogue with them.

Once you have secured a celebrity's support, ensure you have the agreement – with regard to fees, the type of support you are seeking and so on – in writing. Ensure the celebrity has a point of contact and is stewarded as you would a major donor, building their knowledge and understanding of your organisation and demonstrating your appreciation of their support.

Selecting a venue

The right venue will meet the needs and expectations of your target audience, fit with your event's objectives and be within your budget. It may also be the key differentiator of your event. Other factors to consider include:

- **Capacity:** How much space do you need for participants and spectators, storage, staging, parking, etc.? A venue's licensed capacity may vary by whether you are holding a stand-up or sit-down event.
- **Functionality:**
  - Can the venue facilitate all of your requirements, such as audiovisual equipment, catering facilities, security staff, disabled access, and heating or air conditioning?
  - If the event is held outdoors, does the venue have secure storage? Does it have dry areas in case of bad weather?
  - What do your suppliers need in terms of facilities and time to set up and clear down? Venues that include all of the equipment you and your suppliers need may work out less expensive than having to hire equipment.
  - Does the venue require that you use its suppliers? Who has responsibility for cleaning, waste disposal, lifting and handling, etc.?
  - How good are the acoustics and lines of vision?
  - Are there enough toilets?
  - Are there any areas that cause bottlenecks?
  - Does the venue have free Wi-Fi to facilitate supporters sharing selfies and other content on social media or any interactive technology or apps that you intend to use?
- **Location:** Is it convenient for participants and spectators – i.e. near public transport, with local accommodation and so on?
- **Payments and cancellations:**
  - What is included in the hire charge?
  - What deposits are required?
  - When is final payment due?
  - What are the cancellation arrangements?

Scheduling

Scheduling will differ for every event, depending on its size and format.

Develop a Gantt chart for each event to identify who is responsible for each task, and then combine the schedules for all of your events to check for bottlenecks in workloads. Will you need temporary staff or more volunteers in your busiest periods, and how long will you need to recruit and train them? As with all scheduling, build in contingency for unforeseen delays, staff holidays and sickness. Ensure that you include post-event activities in your schedules. (For details on using Gantt charts, see page 90.)

Each event should also have an on-the-day running order which clearly indicates the roles of all those involved in its delivery. Table 6.3 gives an example of a running order.

TABLE 6.3 EXAMPLE OF AN EVENT RUNNING ORDER FOR A HOSPICE FUNDRAISING CONCERT

Time	Action
Morning	**Stage delivered and assembled**
	Car park area coned off
	Signage put up
	Loos delivered
13.00	**PA, crew and lights arrive to set up**
14.00	Refreshments available for band and crew
16.00–17.30	**Sound check and band arrive**
	Waste bins set up in grounds
16.45	**Volunteers and helpers arrive**
17.00	**Stewards and volunteers arrive for briefing**
	St John Ambulance crew arrive and set up
	Merchandise stall and ticket office set up
17.30	**All volunteers and staff in position**
18.00	**Gates open**

Time	Action
	Stalls open
	Supper served to the band and crew (10 people)
19.45	Stalls close and merchandise stall packed away
19.55	Intro and welcome by charity representative
20.00	**Event begins**
21.30	**Event ends**
	Audience leave with bucket collections at exits
22.00	**Stage and grounds cleared**
22.30	St John Ambulance team leave
24.00	Stage is dismantled and cleared
Post-event clear-up	
Morning	Loos collected
	All signage removed
	Staff debriefed
	Volunteer thank-you letters drafted
	Income from stalls and bucket collection counted, coded and banked
	Social media thank-you messages and pictures posted
	Equipment unpacked

Promoting your event

Every event will need its own promotional plan that includes measurable objectives and methods of monitoring progress. This requires you to clearly define which audience segments you are marketing the event to and the most appropriate channels and messages for reaching them. (For more information on how to plan your communications, see chapter 4.) In addition, you will need to devise a supporter journey for everyone you recruit to the event, defining the purpose and nature of every point of contact they have with your organisation. (See page 137 for more on supporter journeys.) The following section describes gamification, which can be used in the supporter journey to deepen engagement with participants and help to build a sense of community between participants.

Gamifying fundraising activities

To 'gamify' an activity is to take typical elements of what people find fun and engrossing about games and put them into a (non-gaming) activity with the aim of getting people more involved and absorbed in it.[21] In the context of fundraising, gamification involves motivating people towards achieving their fundraising targets by offering them opportunities both to express themselves (via, for instance, social media or an online platform created by your organisation) and to build social status through their achievements (by providing forms of public recognition, such as featuring top fundraisers on leader boards). It also involves using rewards. Psychologically speaking, rewards evoke repeated behaviour, so opportunities to earn points towards prizes for key steps towards a fundraising target (such as for each £100 raised) or training goal (such as for each training run) can keep people motivated. You can apply the principles of gamification to any type of community fundraising event.

Case study: Gamification of Diabetes UK's virtual event Swim22

At Diabetes UK, we used to organise a Channel swim where swimmers braved the sea between Kent and Calais. While this event generated a lot of income, its costs were high and it required intensive staff support. To mitigate these issues, we set about trying to find a way to make Channel swimming more accessible, where swimmers could do the same distance but in a pool.

As a result, we launched a virtual fundraising event called Swim22 to run between 22 February and 22 May – long enough to complete the challenge and avoiding January, which had become crowded with fitness challenges. In 2014, to address the limited sense of community that is characteristic of any individual sport and to motivate participants throughout their training and fundraising, our UK digital agency, Manifesto, developed an online platform for participants to track their progress and set up their online fundraising. Swimmers could log their training miles to unlock achievement badges at crucial training stages (first distance entered, halfway mark, etc.). Their individual fundraising pages showed how close they were to both their fundraising and their training targets. Participants could then share these milestones with friends and families to encourage them to lend their support via JustGiving.

The activity feed updates every time a participant enters a distance or unlocks a milestone, encouraging swimmers to check out other swimmers' profiles, and helping to build a sense of community and friendly competition. In 2017, the event raised £300,000.

Jess D'Arcy, Mass Participation Manager, Diabetes UK

Gamification is not limited to the online environment, as the principle of rewarding bite-sized chunks of achievement is well established (from stickers for small gifts to certificates for top fundraisers). Online platforms, however, can make recognition and reward instant, social and shareable.

Handling supporter responses

Resources and plans for response-handling need to be in place before a promotional campaign starts. Make sure that your preparations consider all of the following:

- Decide who is responsible for response-handling at each point in the supporter journey (see 'Planning supporter journeys' on page 137). Will you use agencies, staff or volunteers?
- Set your required service levels: deadlines for fulfilment and thanking, speed of response to enquiries and social media posts, etc.
- Test phone lines, online systems and databases.
- Include event details and Q&As on websites to ensure relevant information is easily accessible.
- Consider when responses might peak to ensure adequate staffing.
- Include your response-handling in your budget.

Staying legally compliant

The following advice covers England and Wales; details of the law vary in Scotland and Northern Ireland. For instance:

- the Food Safety Act covers England, Wales and Scotland but Northern Ireland has a different Act (see The Food Safety (Northern Ireland) Order 1991 at www.legislation.gov.uk/nisi/1991/762 for details);
- Scotland has different fire legislation from England, Wales and Northern Ireland;
- the Health and Safety at Work Act 1974 covers England, Wales and Scotland but Norther Ireland has a different order (see www.health-ni.gov.uk for more details).

In any case, ensure that you are informed of and compliant with all the legislation relevant to your event and region, and gain professional advice where necessary.

Risk assessments and health and safety

Charities have a legal duty to protect everyone involved in the events they run – staff, volunteers, participants, spectators, the public and suppliers. Every in-house event requires a health and safety risk assessment, and you should ensure that adequate risk assessments are being carried out by any third-party organiser with which your charity is connected. The person in charge of organising the event should carry it out at the site where the event will be held. You should ensure that all staff, volunteers and suppliers involved in the event have a copy of the assessment and that you revisit and update it regularly both during the event and whenever the event is repeated.

Risk assessments involve:

- identifying risks;
- evaluating the likelihood and severity of each risk;
- putting in place actions and controls to mitigate and monitor the risks.

As shown in the following section, a common means of determining a scale of risk is to score the likelihood and severity of each risk and multiply their value.

How to determine scale of risk

Scale of risk can be calculated by assigning scores (on a scale of 1 to 5) to likelihood (i.e. how likely a risk is to happen) and severity (i.e. how bad it would be if the risk happened). These are then multiplied together:

likelihood score (1–5) × severity score (1–5)

For example, a risk of trips and falls might score:

- 4 for likelihood;
- 5 for severity.

Multiplying these together gives a score of 20 out of 25.

Scoring can be banded by level of importance to help you prioritise your efforts towards mitigating the greatest risks:

- 1–10: low;
- 11–15: medium;
- 16–25 high.

So, the risk of trips and falls can be categorised as a high risk.

The following box shows a sample risk assessment form that could be used for a local event.

Example risk assessment form

Date and event:

Location of event:

Name, position and department of assessor(s):

Location of risk assessment:

There are five steps to successful risk assessment:

- *Identify the hazards.*
- *Establish the risk – who might be harmed and how?*
- *Evaluate the risks (assessment) and put in place controls (safety measures).*
- *Record the findings.*
- *Review the assessment.*

Risk area	Risk identified (type of harm)	Risk (severity × likelihood score)	Person at risk	Person responsible	Solution and safety measures to reduce risk
Weather (please specify)		☐ Low (1–10) ☐ Medium (11–15) ☐ High (16–25)	☐ Staff ☐ Volunteers ☐ Attendees ☐ Other [specify]		
Noise and visual distraction		☐ Low (1–10) ☐ Medium (11–15) ☐ High (16–25)	☐ Staff ☐ Volunteers ☐ Attendees ☐ Other [specify]		
Venue space (please specify type of venue)		☐ Low (1–10) ☐ Medium (11–15) ☐ High (16–25)	☐ Staff ☐ Volunteers ☐ Attendees ☐ Other [specify]		
Transporting equipment		☐ Low (1–10) ☐ Medium (11–15) ☐ High (16–25)	☐ Staff ☐ Volunteers ☐ Attendees ☐ Other [specify]		

Risk area	Risk identified (type of harm)	Risk (severity × likelihood score)	Person at risk	Person responsible	Solution and safety measures to reduce risk
Uninvited guests		☐ Low (1–10) ☐ Medium (11–15) ☐ High (16–25)	☐ Staff ☐ Volunteers ☐ Attendees ☐ Other [specify]		
Poor lighting		☐ Low (1–10) ☐ Medium (11–15) ☐ High (16–25)	☐ Staff ☐ Volunteers ☐ Attendees ☐ Other [specify]		
Overcrowding		☐ Low (1–10) ☐ Medium (11–15) ☐ High (16–25)	☐ Staff ☐ Volunteers ☐ Attendees ☐ Other [specify]		
Set-up takes longer than anticipated		☐ Low (1–10) ☐ Medium (11–15) ☐ High (16–25)	☐ Staff ☐ Volunteers ☐ Attendees ☐ Other [specify]		
Fire		☐ Low (1–10) ☐ Medium (11–15) ☐ High (16–25)	☐ Staff ☐ Volunteers ☐ Attendees ☐ Other [specify]		
Audiovisual problems		☐ Low (1–10) ☐ Medium (11–15) ☐ High (16–25)	☐ Staff ☐ Volunteers ☐ Attendees ☐ Other [specify]		
Food-handling		☐ Low (1–10) ☐ Medium (11–15) ☐ High (16–25)	☐ Staff ☐ Volunteers ☐ Attendees ☐ Other [specify]		

Risk area	Risk identified (type of harm)	Risk (severity × likelihood score)	Person at risk	Person responsible	Solution and safety measures to reduce risk
Cancellation/ no-show by event speakers		☐ Low (1–10) ☐ Medium (11–15) ☐ High (16–25)	☐ Staff ☐ Volunteers ☐ Attendees ☐ Other [specify]		
Other		☐ Low (1–10) ☐ Medium (11–15) ☐ High (16–25)	☐ Staff ☐ Volunteers ☐ Attendees ☐ Other [specify]		
Total risk rating:					

Some of the most common hazards to consider are:

• **Trip and equipment hazards:** Examples include cables, steps, flooring and equipment that people could trip over.

• **Electrical equipment:** What generators or electrical equipment could participants, staff and volunteers come into contact with? Are they trained to use them? Has the equipment been tested? Is there a chance it could get wet? (See www.hse.gov.uk/work-equipment-machinery for more information.)

• **Glass:** What glass equipment or structures might people come in contact with? What is the risk of breakage?

• **Crowd management hazards:** Is there any risk of overcrowding, crushing or bottlenecks? How would any aggressive or drunken behaviour be managed? What is the proximity to roads and car parks? Speak to the police for details on traffic control requirements and road closures.

• **Health and injury:** Could people be injured? What will you do if someone faints or suffers from heat exhaustion? Or if someone has a heart attack or stroke? For sporting events ask people when they apply to confirm that they have consulted a doctor and do not have medical issues that should prevent their participation. Provide guidance on appropriate fitness levels for the type of activity and ensure that first aid staff (such as St John Ambulance) are present at all sporting and mass participation events. A member of your team should also be trained in first aid.

- **Fire:** A key provision of legislation is that a defined responsible person must be in charge of fire risk assessments and the implementation of an emergency plan. All participants must know the evacuation procedure and the locations of assembly points and signed and unobstructed exits. The team must know of any special requirements for elderly and disabled people. Check that fire extinguishers and detectors work. Note that the fire service must be informed of any firework displays. Decide on your smoking policy and risks associated with equipment such as electricals, lighting and candles.

- **Food safety:** For in-house events, you will need to know who is preparing food, whether they have a food safety certificate, how allergies will be handled, what the risk from ovens and hot-water urns is, and so on. Any food being supplied must comply with the Food Safety Act 1990 and the Food Safety (General Food Hygiene) Regulations 1995. You will also need to give guidance on food safety to volunteers who are running events in aid of your charity. For further details, see www.food.gov.uk or contact the relevant local authority.

- **Lifting and handling:** How will staff and volunteers be trained, supervised and/or informed about safe handling and lifting? Visit www.hse.gov.uk for guidance.

- **Weather conditions:** Could the weather create risks, such as rain causing slippery floors or ground or making equipment wet? Could the wind have an impact on structures or the sun cause equipment to overheat?

- **Environmental risks:** What are the risks of noise and/or light pollution? How might the event's activities or any rubbish generated affect wildlife or contaminate land?

- **Children:** Will your staff need a DBS (Disclosure and Barring Service) check? Consider whether there is a risk of children getting lost and who is responsible for them. How might all of the above factors in this list affect children differently from other participants?

- **Theft and security:** How will you ensure any cash is kept securely? What is the risk of theft? Stress to staff and volunteers that they should never put their personal safety at risk if threatened with theft.

You will need emergency plans in place for fire, adverse weather, accidents, medical emergencies and so on, with roles allocated to named, trained individuals. All staff and volunteers should know how to record an incident and keep both written and photographic records.

Insurance

Events organised by your charity should be covered under your public liability insurance. Make sure that the maximum amount payable under the policy is sufficient for all events and their level of risk and check in good time that it is not prohibitively expensive (high-risk activities are costly to insure). Staff need to be covered by your employee liability insurance. A third-party event organiser will need its own public liability insurance, and it should confirm in writing that it has such insurance. Ensure participants are aware of whether or not they are covered by your insurance. If they are not covered, consider including a disclaimer in your materials.

Your suppliers should also have equipment insurance, and all contractors must be covered for any cancellation or harm caused by them. While expensive, it is possible to take out insurance for theft, damage and bad weather in the case of an outdoor event's cancellation. Check whether venues have their own insurance and whether this covers your event (and at sufficient levels). Ensure that there is a 'waiver of subrogation' in place – this is an agreement between your charity and the venue that ensures the venue's insurance company cannot target the charity to recover any costs.

Licences, laws and regulations

Alcohol and entertainment

Most UK venues that host events have a premises licence under the Licensing Act 2003. This covers the supply and sale of alcohol, different forms of regulated entertainment (including live and recorded music), and the supply of hot food and any drinks late at night. If your event is not covered by a premises licence and will have under 500 people attending, you can apply for a temporary events notice (in England and Wales) or occasional licence (in Scotland) from the local licensing authority. You will need to apply at least ten working days in advance of the event.

Music

If live or recorded music is to be played at your event, you will need a licence from the Performing Rights Society and/or Phonographic Performance Limited. To find out more about when you need a licence, visit www.gov.uk/licences-to-play-background-music and www.gov.uk/live-music-licence.

Raffles at events

A raffle is a form of lottery. It does not require a licence or permission from either the Gambling Commission or the local authority if it qualifies as an 'incidental lottery'. In an incidental lottery, tickets are sold only during the event and on the premises where the event is held, the draw takes place at the event, there is no rollover, and the raffle does not exceed £100 in costs and £500 in prizes. For more information on raffles and lotteries see section 12.0 of the Code of Fundraising Practice at www.fundraisingregulator.org.uk.

Data protection

Any personal information gathered during the marketing and running of an event needs to adhere to GDPR (the General Data Protection Regulation; for details see 'Data protection legislation and fundraising regulations' on page 156).

Collections

For information on when a licence is needed for collections, see 'Types of collection and necessary permissions' on page 302.

Accounting for funds

Income and expenditure for all types of event should be clearly accounted for:

- **Restricted income:** Funds raised from an event must be spent on the purposes for which they were solicited. If your event is in support of a specific project, by law, if you raise more than the project requires or not enough for the project to take place, you must contact the donors and offer to return the funds or request to use them for alternative purposes. You may choose to state on your promotional materials that in such circumstances funds may be used for general charitable purposes.
- **Separate records:** Each fundraising event must have its own records. These must provide enough detail to identify its gross takings and the costs incurred.
- **Ticketing:** Ensure that:
  - all tickets sold are numbered;
  - you keep a record of who has been allocated which ticket numbers to sell;
  - you collect all money from tickets and any unsold tickets;
  - a reconciliation is made of receipts against tickets sold.

Cash handling

If staff and volunteers handle cash, you must have a policy and processes in place to adhere to section 4.0 of the Code of Fundraising Practice ('Processing donations') and any applicable insurance policies.

Cash must be collected, counted and recorded by two members of staff who are not related to each other and then safely locked away. Risk assessments should identify risks associated with cash handling and how these will be mitigated. Unsecured cash must not be left unattended, so you might use a locked private room to store money, or even a locked boot of a car if you are at an event in the middle of a field.

Cash should be counted in a secure environment and banked as soon as possible. If your event takes place over a weekend, you must return any cash to your office or charity headquarters and lock it away until it can be banked the next working day. It will not be insured if it is kept overnight at a staff member's home. If it is impossible to return cash to your office immediately, you must identify in your risk assessment what security measures you will take in the intervening time. A reconciliation of cash banked and income summaries must also be completed at the earliest possible time.

Post-event activation and evaluation

Gather feedback from staff and volunteers on the various elements of the event. Particularly, ask what could have provided a better supporter experience:

- Did staff have enough information to execute tasks?
- Did the timings work?
- Were the briefing and training adequate?

Provide people with the option to give feedback face to face, as a group or even anonymously – feedback is only as useful as how honest it is. Ensure that you also thank all staff and volunteers.

It is important to measure your success against the original event objectives and relevant key performance indicators (see 'Key performance indicators' on page 91). Finally, collate all evaluations into a recommendations report indicating who will be responsible for delivering what changes, with what impact and by when.

Post-event actions

If you have decided to repeat an event, you may want to open registration for the next event immediately as this can:

- capitalise on positive post-event energy;
- take advantage of online traffic to pages giving the results of events such as races (often when event pages receive their highest traffic);
- give more time for participants to promote your event to peers;
- even out cash flow with a steady stream of incoming registrations, which can alleviate the burden of some operating expenses.

Research by the Institute of Fundraising found that while 83.3% of event participants said they would definitely or possibly take part in another event for the same charity, 44.2% had not been asked to do so. Furthermore, only 9.3% did not want to be contacted again, suggesting that charities which continuously seek to understand the types of event participants are interested in have a real opportunity to generate repeat support.[22]

Conclusion

Events are an important staple of community fundraising and offer a means of achieving a range of objectives. Provided they are well planned, they can deliver powerful engagement opportunities and recruit new supporters with the potential of providing further support.

Notes

1 Sally Falvey, 'Infographic: Big event fundraising trends' [blog post], JustGiving, https://blog.justgiving.com/infographic-big-event-fundraising-trends, 4 July 2017.
2 *Successful Events Fundraising: The motivations behind event fundraising and how charities can better support their fundraisers*, Charleston, Blackbaud/Everydayhero, 2015, p. 2.
3 *Sports Fundraising Market Snapshot* [PDF], massive, 2019, www.wearemassive.co.uk/insight/sports-fundraising-market-snapshot, accessed 8 July 2019.
4 'What's next for events?' [presentation slides], JustGiving, presented by Sally Falvey and Keith Williams for JustGiving at the IoF Convention, July 2017, www.slideshare.net/JustGiving/whats-next-for-events-80211419, slides 16 and 18, accessed 13 February 2019.
5 *What Creates Virtual Event Success?* [PDF], Everydayhero/More Strategic, 2017, http://hub.blackbaud.co.uk/peer-to-peer/what-creates-virtual-event-success, p. 4, accessed 13 July 2018.
6 'Great British Bake Off inspires millions to bake for charity' [press release], Charities Aid Foundation, www.cafonline.org/about-us/media-office/great-british-bake-off-inspires-millions-to-bake-for-charity, 5 August 2015.
7 'What's next for events?' [presentation slides], JustGiving, presented by Sally Falvey and Keith Williams for JustGiving at the IoF Convention, July 2017, www.slideshare.net/JustGiving/whats-next-for-events-80211419, slide 10, accessed 13 February 2019.

8 'Great British Bake Off inspires millions to bake for charity' [press release], Charities Aid Foundation, www.cafonline.org/about-us/media-office/great-british-bake-off-inspires-millions-to-bake-for-charity, 5 August 2015.
9 'Fundratios 2014' [web page], Centre for Interfirm Comparison, 2015, www.cifc.co.uk/Fundratios14.html, accessed 30 June 2018.
10 *Closing the Loop* [PDF], Institute of Fundraising, 2015, www.institute-of-fundraising.org.uk/library/closing-the-loop, p. 14, accessed 13 July 2018.
11 'Trends in mass participation events fundraising' [web page], massive, 2017, www.wearemassive.co.uk/insight/trends-in-mass-participation-events-fundraising, accessed 13 March 2018.
12 Adrian Sargeant and Harriet Day, *Great Fundraising Events: From experience to transformation* [PDF], Hartsook Centre for Sustainable Philanthropy, Plymouth University, 2017, http://studyfundraising.com/wp-content/uploads/2017/08/Events-Fundraising-Final-Report.pdf, p. 3, accessed 13 July 2018.
13 See Karin Cox, 'Fundraising Events', in *Fundraising Principles and Practice*, edited by Adrian Sargeant and Jen Shang, San Francisco, Jossey-Bass, 2010, pp. 519–39, for details on these primary purposes of fundraising events, as identified by Cox.
14 Adrian Sargeant and Harriet Day, *Great Fundraising Events: From experience to transformation* [PDF], Hartsook Centre for Sustainable Philanthropy, Plymouth University, 2017, http://studyfundraising.com/wp-content/uploads/2017/08/Events-Fundraising-Final-Report.pdf, p. 45, accessed 13 July 2018.
15 Frederick Herzberg, 'One More Time: How do you motivate employees?', originally published in *Harvard Business Review*, vol. 65, no. 5, 1987, pp. 109–20; available with a retrospective commentary by the author in various locations online and in print.
16 *2015 Event Planning Guide for Classes & Conferences* [PDF], Eventbrite, 2015, www.eventbrite.com/blog/academy/2015-planning-guide-classes-conferences, p. 5, accessed 19 July 2018.
17 Daniel Webber, 'Understanding Charity Fundraising Events', *International Journal of Nonprofit and Voluntary Sector Marketing*, vol. 9, no. 2, 2004, pp. 122–34.
18 'A guide to Gift Aid' [web page], JustGiving, 2015, https://help.justgiving.com/hc/en-us/articles/200670391-A-guide-to-Gift-Aid, accessed 8 March 2018.
19 Dan Brockington and Spencer Henson, 'Signifying the Public: Celebrity advocacy and post-democratic politics', *International Journal of Cultural Studies*, vol. 18, no. 4, 2015, pp. 431–48.
20 Emma Samman, Eilish McAuliffe and Malcolm MacLachlan, 'The Role of Celebrity in Endorsing Poverty Reduction through International Aid', *International Journal of Nonprofit and Voluntary Sector Marketing*, vol. 14, no. 2, 2009, pp. 137–48.
21 Kyle Findlay and Kirsty Alberts, 'Gamification: The reality of what it is and what it isn't' [presentation], 2011, www.slideshare.net/TNSGlobal/gamification-the-reality-of-what-it-is-and-what-it-isnt-9471654, slide 8, accessed 17 May 2019.
22 *Closing the Loop* [PDF], Institute of Fundraising, 2015, www.institute-of-fundraising.org.uk/library/closing-the-loop, p. 15, accessed 13 July 2018.

CHAPTER SEVEN

Developing do-it-yourself fundraising

Sam Rider and Gill Jolly

Introduction

Do-it-yourself (DIY) fundraising (another term for supporter-led fundraising) is where individuals or groups of people, rather than the beneficiary charity, take responsibility for initiating, planning and running a fundraising activity themselves. The charity's role is to support this fundraising to help participants have the best possible experience of fundraising by providing personalised and appropriate guidance, advice and stewardship.

Over recent years there has been an increased focus on the value and benefits of DIY fundraising. Recent research indicates that DIY fundraising generates the largest proportion (24%) of charities' community fundraising income, with high returns on investment. It is therefore hardly surprising that charities are highlighting DIY fundraising as a key source of future growth.[1]

This chapter explores the nature of DIY fundraising and how it benefits both participants and charities. It also takes into account the idiosyncratic nature of DIY fundraisers to suggest which tactics can enable them to raise as much as possible for the issues they are passionate about.

The benefits of DIY fundraising

Higher levels of donation

Research by the University of Warwick suggests that among those using online giving platforms to support their fundraising, fewer people undertake DIY fundraising compared to those who engage in mass participation events; however, these DIY fundraisers tend to raise more money and receive a higher number of donations.[2] In addition, the THINK Community Forum Benchmarking Survey reported that the average amount an individual DIY fundraiser raised for each DIY activity was £400, compared to an average of £100 raised per event by mass participation event fundraisers.[3] This may be due to a number of reasons.

One factor is that the top three fundraising motivations of DIY fundraisers (as reported in the University of Warwick research) all focus on a desire to raise money and awareness for a charity and/or its cause. The researchers speculate that mass participation fundraisers, by contrast, are more likely to be attracted by the fundraising event itself (for example, the draw of having a good time with friends at a coffee morning). The researchers conclude that

DIY fundraisers' high level of commitment to a cause may be why they raise higher amounts than mass participation fundraisers do.[4]

The same research reports two further potential reasons why DIY fundraisers raise more than mass participation fundraisers: the desire to raise money for a cause connected to a life event that has affected the fundraiser or someone they know, and the desire to raise money in memory of someone.[5] Some research in the USA found that people with a clear personal link to a cause, such as supporting a cancer charity after a family member has died of cancer, are more likely to gain support than people without such a connection. This is because potential sponsors find it much harder to say 'no' to these types of fundraiser than they do to someone without a personal connection to the issue.[6]

Another reason why DIY fundraisers raise more than mass participation fundraisers, as suggested by the University of Warwick researchers, is that mass participation fundraisers face more competition than DIY fundraisers when competing for funds from their social network. For example, it is often the case that a mass participation event is likely to attract similar people who have shared social networks, with the result that several fundraisers may each be asking for sponsorship from the same pool of people, including those who have already donated to another fundraiser.[7]

Finally, the nature of DIY fundraisers' activities, which tend to require significant effort or physical exertion, may also influence the higher levels of money they raise. According to Christopher Olivola,[8] who analysed data on endurance cyclists and runners who raised money for two US charities (respectively), the greater the distances the participants undertook, the higher the amounts they raised. Olivola found that when a fundraiser communicates to supporters that they anticipate their fundraising experience will be painful and expect it to involve substantial effort (relative to their ability), sponsors are willing to give more to that individual than they are if the fundraiser expects the event to be fun and easy. Furthermore, people are willing to donate more when the fundraiser reports having a difficult experience during the event than when they enjoy it. People are also more willing to give more when the cause is related to human suffering (such as helping people living in poverty) rather than when it is linked to enjoyment (such as supporting an arts centre). This phenomenon, which the researchers call the 'martyrdom effect', appears to occur directly because of the pain and effort associated with an event, not purely because the sponsors feel empathy for their friend who is fundraising. It may be that sponsors appreciate how special it feels to donate when there has been sacrifice and suffering involved.

Lower costs

DIY fundraising is usually comparatively inexpensive for a charity to support. Whereas a charity incurs upfront costs when it organises its own events or purchases event places, DIY fundraisers generally require a lower investment. Given their high level of commitment to the cause and/or charity, they tend to put a significant amount of time and energy into ensuring an activity's success, while at the same time covering their own costs. For example, a DIY fundraiser who chooses to devise their own fundraising trek will incur and cover the costs of organising, booking and promoting this activity to raise money from their friends and family.

Wider audiences and fundraising options

DIY fundraising provides ways to give that may appeal to people who wouldn't normally have supported a charity based on its traditional offerings. For many potential supporters, a charity's own fundraising activities may simply not appeal, and it is unrealistic for charities to design events that meet the needs of all possible participants. DIY fundraising is an opportunity for people to do what they wish to do rather than being pushed towards existing initiatives that don't inspire them. In the current age of customisation, this gives people the choices they increasingly expect around the time, place, format and fundraising target they wish to commit to. And, thanks to online giving platforms and social media, which allow people to create their own content about their fundraising activities, DIY supporters have the tools they need to raise significant sums on their own terms.

By meeting supporters on their own terms rather than relying on proprietary fundraising products, charities can attract a wider diversity of fundraisers. For example:

- By undertaking their own personal challenge or event, many supporters can raise more than they would be able to give as a personal donation to the charity.
- Those who have participated in multiple mass participation events, but now wish to do something different, have the option to create their own personal challenge that fits their interests, resources, motivations and circumstances.
- In-memory fundraisers can determine which activities best link to their own unique experiences of bereavement and remembrance.
- Those raising funds to achieve challenge event targets may also undertake some DIY fundraising, such as a bake sale at work, to supplement their donations from sponsors.

Directing these types of supporter towards your DIY programmes can give them the ideas, support and confidence they require to be successful.

Younger audiences

DIY fundraising has the potential to be particularly attractive to millennials and generation Z. As avid social media users, they tend to have wide online social networks to fundraise through and they actively create their own shareable content. The inherently social aspect of peer-to-peer DIY fundraising meets the need of these generations to express, through their online identities, who they are and what they care about.

Being prepared for DIY fundraising

Before embarking on a DIY programme, consider whether it is right for your fundraising portfolio (see 'Analysing your portfolio of products' on page 56).

- **What are you seeking to achieve?** Are you aiming to reach a demographic that does not engage with your existing activities? What will motivate them to make the time and effort required to fundraise?
- **What are your timescales?** Consider the time it takes to develop a programme, market the opportunity and support those who participate.
- **Do you have a high enough profile?** DIY programmes require a strong online presence and need investment in advertising and search engine optimisation.
- **Do you have the right staff and skills to support and steward DIY fundraisers?** You will need the input of someone with marketing or communications skills to develop the materials and tools DIY fundraisers will need to promote your cause to their peers.
- **How will you track relationships?** With multiple supporters undertaking different activities with different needs at different times, you will need to have a database which enables you to track and develop individual supporter journeys. (For details on how to plan supporter journeys, see page 137.)
- **Will DIY fundraising complement or compete with your other community fundraising programmes?** Donor research can help you to answer this question. Are there groups of donors already asking for different fundraising options? Are existing events in decline?
- **How will you monitor the success of your DIY programme?** In addition to tracking relationships (noted above), you will need to define the metrics against which performance will be measured. (For details on the types of metric you can use, see 'Monitoring and reporting' on page 95.)

Getting started with DIY fundraising

If your organisation decides to go ahead with a DIY fundraising programme, you will need to demonstrate to potential supporters that DIY fundraising is something you value and explain the impact of fundraisers' efforts upon your mission and beneficiaries.

Distinguishing the DIY option

Charities can distinguish the DIY option as a product within their fundraising portfolio, branding it separately from their own events. For example, as shown in figure 7.1, Alzheimer's Research UK branded its DIY option as 'I fight dementia'.

FIGURE 7.1 ALZHEIMER'S RESEARCH UK'S 'I FIGHT DEMENTIA' DIY FUNDRAISING OPTION[9]

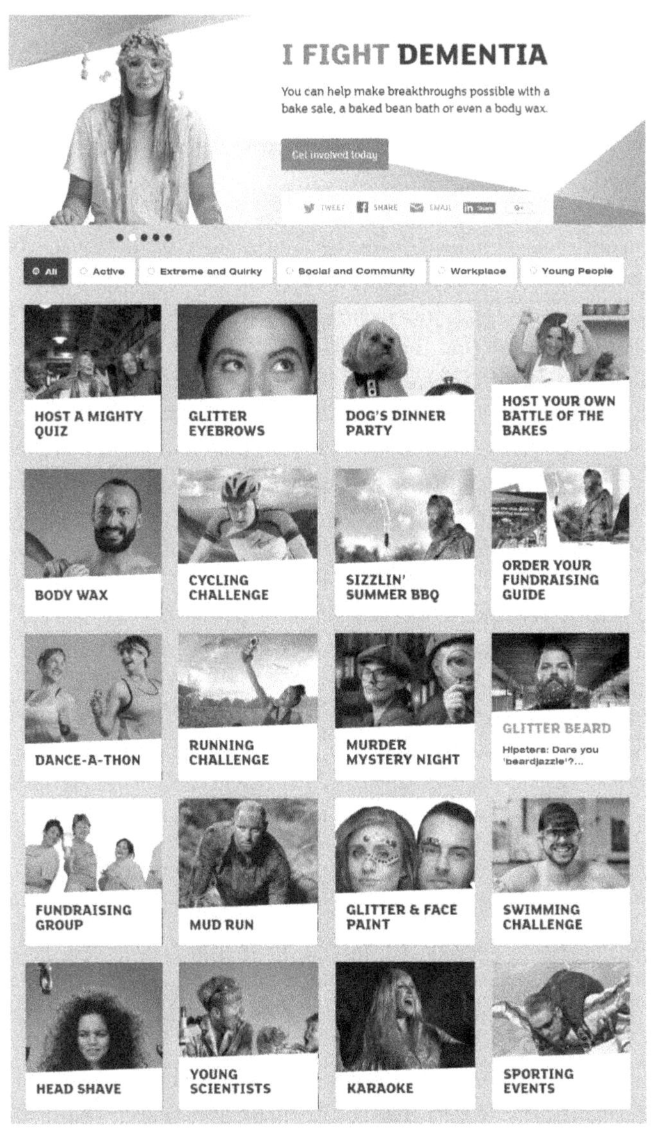

Another way of creating a tangible DIY fundraising hook is to suggest a broad umbrella concept that allows participants to undertake any of a range of activities within a certain timeframe. For example, for the American Alzheimer's Association's Longest Day, supporters undertake a fundraising activity of their choice on the summer solstice.

Promoting the DIY option

Unlike hosted events, DIY programmes don't have to follow a set calendar, so you need to promote the DIY option when and where people make fundraising decisions. For example, if most of your DIY fundraisers are raising funds in memory of others, consider promoting this option via channels such as funeral directors and solicitors as well as on Facebook – the primary social medium used to remember loved ones.[10] Also consider common types of DIY activity (bake sales, abseils, weight loss, runs, etc.) and the websites, Facebook pages, Pinterest boards, retailers, clubs, venues and other online and offline channels through which you might reach people with related interests. Use social media to pinpoint indicators of interest, such as relevant likes, shares, posts, hashtags and comments related to your cause, to enable you to start conversations with potential supporters who might have an interest in your charity's work. Promote posts to those familiar with the cause, as well as your charity's existing followers.

Ensure asks for support are relevant. For example, ask for support within the context of a response to a news event, promotion of an awareness day, wider campaigns, project updates, or other annual, seasonal or high-profile public events. Include a call to action and ensure that people can sign up online by taking as few steps as possible.

Finally, don't forget the people you know. Ensure donors and community and employee fundraisers are all aware of the DIY opportunity by including it in website banners, email footers, features in offline and online newsletters, and so on.

For details on how to communicate effectively with your supporters, see chapter 4.

Championing the champions

When people make decisions in group situations, they are influenced by 'social information', i.e. other people's judgements. They look to see what others are doing and often revise their own judgement based on what other people believe.[11] Showcasing the ideas of and amounts raised by other DIY fundraisers can help people decide to go ahead with their fundraising ambitions. It can also help those who have made the decision to feel confident both in their activity and in knowing they too will be supported and appreciated by your charity. These fundraising stories can feature on your DIY web pages, across your social media platforms, in supporter newsletters and in local press and media.

Critical things your DIY fundraisers need to know

DIY fundraisers are 'in-aid-of' fundraisers (see also 'In-aid-of (or DIY) volunteers' on page 262) so, although they are raising funds for your charity, they do not represent it, have no authority from your organisation and are acting on their own initiative. To manage this status, provide guidance to help fundraisers identify how to stay within the law and act according to best practices.

Materials

Help fundraisers to make their in-aid-of status clear in all communications in which they promote and solicit funds. Provide pro forma materials that include a statement that funds are being raised in aid of your charity. Many charities also provide in-aid-of logos that fundraisers can download and add to their own materials.

Collections

Ensure that fundraisers are aware that collections on private property require the landowner's permission and that any collections in public places require a local authority permit. As long as you have made it clear that they should have the right permissions in place, you can encourage DIY fundraisers to organise collections at offices, parties and other events on private property. Supply collecting tins or flat-packed self-assembly collection boxes and ensure they are sent out quickly so fundraisers can react to collection opportunities as they arise. Make it clear on tins and boxes that the collection is in aid of your charity and keep a record of the number of the box or tin, when it was issued, to whom it was issued and when it was returned. Do not forget to provide details of how and when boxes can be returned and monies can be paid to the charity (see 'Managing and tracking tins' on page 312).

Raffles and lotteries

Raffles and lotteries should be limited to incidental lotteries (see 'Raffles at events' on page 214).

Competitions

Fundraisers must not link donations to your charity to entry into a competition. For example, you cannot ask people to send a donation in order to enter into a prize draw.

Events

DIY fundraisers should be advised of the following:

- Any event they organise should be run safely and your charity takes no responsibility for its organisation or participants.
- They should undertake risk assessments – you can provide a pro forma to assist with the process.
- They should consider having appropriate insurance in place.
- They need licences for certain event activities, such as the sale of alcohol and musical performances.
- Events need appropriate supervision and participants must be briefed on any risks, fitness levels, standards of behaviour or special equipment required.
- Any children involved must have appropriate adult supervision and permission from their parents or guardians to attend. People who supervise children during the event may need Disclosure and Barring Service clearance.
- While a food hygiene certificate is not a requirement for a volunteer fundraising event, fundraisers are responsible for ensuring food hygiene standards are upheld (visit the 'Business guidance' section of www.food.gov.uk).
- Fundraisers should seek general first-aid advice from organisations such as St John Ambulance and should also check whether a first aider should be present at the event (for more details on event planning, see chapter 6).

Data protection

Any electronic or paper records fundraisers keep about people involved in a fundraising activity they are running must comply with the General Data Protection Regulation (GDPR).

Funds

All funds raised must be passed on to the charity. If a fundraiser is unable to complete an event for which they are sponsored, they should offer to return the funds or ask donors' permission for the monies to be donated to the charity. Reinforce this point by displaying a statement on any sponsorship forms or online giving pages. If a fundraiser is running an event where all profits are being donated to the charity (and so they are using a proportion of the funds they raise to cover their costs), they should keep receipts for the costs they have incurred.

Identifying supporters' activities

One of the challenges of stewarding DIY fundraisers is knowing when someone is fundraising for you. Online giving platforms can generate reports on who has set up a page for your charity and, if the supporter has given permission to be contacted (via the platform concerned), contact them to see what support they might like. Monitoring hashtags used in social media is another means of spotting supporters you might want to make contact with. Many charities also include a point of registration on their DIY fundraising website pages where they capture contact details, when activities are planned, locations, fundraising targets and the nature of the activity. This can help with:

- acknowledging support and initiating a conversation as part of a personalised stewardship programme;
- gathering insight into what type of support, advice, guidance, materials, encouragement and recognition you need to provide;
- predicting likely income, allocating appropriate levels of support and assessing whether fundraising targets are realistic;
- monitoring the numbers of DIY fundraisers over a period of time to plan staff workloads;
- coding different activities to improve and streamline support – for example, you may find that 60% of your DIY fundraisers are holding bake sales and therefore that it would be cost-effective to develop a support package that is specific to this activity.

Welcoming and stewarding

Once you have identified your DIY supporters, you can take action to welcome and steward them through the fundraising process. To set the tone of the relationship, contact your fundraisers at the earliest opportunity to thank them for their support, and reassure them that you will help them to get started with their fundraising. Welcome them by phone, email, mailing packs or short videos. Some charities, such as Shelter, have involved their beneficiaries in welcome calls, which helps to connect the fundraiser directly to the cause. Use this opportunity to explore the story behind the fundraiser's support of your charity and encourage them to share this with those from whom they are seeking funds. Also establish and record each individual's communication preferences to ensure you are compliant with GDPR and to confirm that you are permitted to record any details of their motivations and other relationships with your charity in your database.

After this initial contact, provide ongoing personalised support to ensure individuals have a positive fundraising experience and maintain the momentum of their fundraising efforts by:

- checking in regularly to see how fundraising (or training, preparations for an event, etc.) is going;
- congratulating supporters on their progress towards sponsorship targets;
- sending news about the projects that motivated them to support you;
- wishing them good luck the day before a key activity and asking how they got on afterwards.

Using automated personalisation software can enable you to customise communications to individual fundraisers or segments of fundraisers depending upon their characteristics and touch points. This allows you to communicate on the basis of the unique nature and stage of activity the fundraiser has reached. You also need to react flexibly by, for example, responding as soon as you hear about any setbacks or significant milestones. Ensure staff know how to answer questions and solve problems as they occur. If supporters are local, you might hold information sessions or, for those further afield, you can offer regular webinars. (See also 'Planning supporter journeys' on page 137.)

Enabling DIY fundraisers' success

While each fundraiser may be undertaking a different activity, there are some generic ways of guiding and signposting them. Having a dedicated DIY fundraising section on your website with clearly written guidance and means of downloading and ordering support materials is a low-cost way of giving individuals a range of tools to organise and promote their activity.

Helping with ideas

Whereas many DIY fundraisers have their own ideas, others may seek inspiration. To provide fundraising food for thought, list possible activities on your DIY web page, from the most simple (such as donations in lieu of a celebration) to how to organise a larger-scale event. Provide guidance on the time commitment and complexity of organising different types of activity: for instance, a collection in the office is quick and easy whereas organising a golf day is far more time-consuming and costly.

Setting targets

Targets motivate fundraisers, and those who set a fundraising target raise an average of 46% more than those who do not.[12] Online fundraising pages with high targets raise more than pages with low targets, but donors also tend to give less once a target has been reached. Fundraisers can use target-setting strategically, however, by raising a target once it has been reached.[13]

People are more likely to set targets if you provide defaults, although these should be relevant to the different types of fundraising activity people are undertaking.[14] To avoid disappointment, it is important that fundraisers set realistic targets – for example, a bake sale at £1 per cake might raise a couple of hundred pounds, whereas a major personal physical challenge may raise several thousand. To determine what target levels to suggest, track the previous performance of DIY fundraising by type of activity. In your fundraising pack, include case studies on how past participants have reached their targets by featuring the different activities they undertook and the amounts they raised. You can also translate the targets into what they could mean in terms of impact for your beneficiaries, as this will give the targets greater significance. Finally, you can also encourage fundraisers to pass this information on to potential sponsors (see 'Tools to help DIY fundraisers promote their activities' on page 235).

Seeking sponsorship

As early as possible in the relationship, provide DIY fundraisers with a link to online donation platforms and offer simple tips on how to make the most of online giving pages. Participants can:

- **personalise pages** by telling the story of why they are fundraising;
- **include photographs** – JustGiving's research has shown that those who add a photo to their page tend to raise 14% more;[15]
- **give their activity a simple name**, such as 'Sue's Berlin run' or 'Sanjee's party';
- **personalise their fundraising page's web address** – for example, if a supporter is running a 10k for Oxfam and is called Jim, he could set his web address as www.justgiving.com/JimsOxfam10k;
- **email friends, family and colleagues** with the link to their page and your charity's website or a video to explain your work (it can help to provide a pro forma email to structure their ask) – analysis by Blackbaud identified that participants who send emails raise between 2 and 11 times more than those who don't;[16]
- **target their most generous supporters first;**
- **start their approach for support with family** – as a person's closest family members are the most likely to respond positively to a sponsorship

ask[17] – before targeting their wider network of friends, colleagues and acquaintances;

- **promote online giving page links on their own Facebook page:** the vast majority of visits to JustGiving come from Facebook;[18]
- **link their Twitter account to online giving pages** and use tools such as giv2 to invite people to tweet a donation (for more details, see www.giv2.it);
- **include links to their online giving page in their email signature;**
- **publicise their fundraising page** on any intranets, workplace or community newsletters, or notice boards to which they have access, as well as approaching clubs or groups to which they belong;
- **keep their sponsors informed of progress:** they should temper their requests for sponsorship with details of how hard they are working towards their goal (you can send your DIY fundraisers fun and interesting examples of how other fundraisers have achieved this);
- **personalise email thank yous** to encourage sponsors to spread the word about their fundraising efforts, such as forwarding links to their online giving page and sharing their Facebook posts (give examples of how to do this);
- **update fundraising pages with post-event photos and results** and thank people via email and social media – as well as being hugely important to do in itself, this can serve to raise more funds, given that around 20% of online donations are received after an event (additionally, if they have met their target, advise your DIY fundraisers that a small increase in the target can help to boost the final amount they can raise[19] – see also 'Setting targets' on page 228).

Ensure that you have a homepage on the various fundraising platforms (JustGiving, Virgin Money Giving and so on) that is branded with your charity's logo, colours, strapline, etc. Depending on the set-up of the giving platform, a charity-branded online giving page may have a feed on its home page that can enable fundraisers to see what other DIY fundraisers are doing for your organisation. This might include photos of supporters, stories about why they are supporting your charity, messages about progress on their training or event preparation, and notes of support from sponsors and amounts raised. This feed can additionally help you to keep a check on messages about your charity, signpost fundraisers to guidance and develop a community of supporters. It can also be a means of cross-selling other events or campaigns. There is some evidence that donors are significantly more likely to give permission for future contact if a donation page is branded by the charity, as opposed to being branded purely by the giving platform.[20]

Some platforms facilitate team pages for DIY fundraisers undertaking similar activities or raising money for the same project or campaign. JustGiving has found that people raise on average 10% more when they link their fundraising page to a team page.[21]

Offline sponsorship is still an important option, and one study identified that 55% of people's most recent experience of being asked to sponsor someone had been via a sign-up sheet.[22] Paper forms can work well on office noticeboards, at events, at face-to-face social gatherings, and with friends and relatives (often among the older generations) who prefer to give cash. Ensure that downloadable forms are available from your website and included in hard-copy fundraising packs.

Using Facebook

If a DIY fundraiser is creating their own event, you may want to encourage them to set up a Facebook event page or create a Facebook group. This is one way in which they can provide updates to their supporters and have discussions with them about their fundraising activities by sending messages and sharing content.

If your charity has its own Facebook page and is signed up to receive donations directly (see https://donations.fb.com/en-gb), you can advise DIY fundraisers on how to set up their own Facebook fundraiser page directly from their Facebook profile page via www.facebook.com/fundraisers. (The method of doing this is liable to change, so ensure the information on your website or in your fundraising advice packs is always up to date with step-by-step instructions on how to set up a page.) Once a DIY fundraiser has set up their page, their friends who sponsor them on Facebook will be able to do so without needing to leave the site, providing a seamless means of sponsoring your charity via social media. The page will allow fundraisers to display, for example, their own photographs, their story of why they are fundraising, a donate button and how many people have donated to the charity via their page.

Setting up unique text codes

Donating by text message is an easy, convenient and increasingly trusted means of giving. Fundraisers can set up their own unique text codes via online giving providers, and the donation is automatically added to the fundraiser's online fundraising page. Encourage fundraisers to personalise their code (for example, by asking donors to 'Text SUE66 £5 to 70070') and include it in online and offline promotional materials.

Encouraging giving using Gift Aid

Explain the importance and value of Gift Aid. Knowing that 25p can be claimed on every £1 donation (if your organisation is a charity or community amateur sports club) can be particularly motivating for sponsors (see also 'Gift Aid' on page 196).

Boosting amounts with matched funding

Matched funds can significantly boost the total amount a fundraiser can raise. Some charities have been successful at using matched-funding schemes (run by companies, grant-making charities and/or government) as part of their DIY fundraising programmes, and research has shown that, on average, donors give 2.5 times more when they know their donation will be matched.[23]

Helping in-memory fundraisers

Fundraising in memory of someone is a powerful motivator that can have a significant impact on the value of donations. In the case of events, in-memory online pages raise 54% more than other event pages.[24] In-memory donations usually take the form of direct donations from bereaved family and friends, funeral collections, or a multitude of DIY events and personal challenges.

The driver for in-memory support is primarily the desire to remember and celebrate the life of the deceased and the emotions related to this relationship, rather than the fundraiser's passion for the charity or cause. According to Elizabeth Kessick, people select a charity based on one or more of the following reasons:[25]

- The charity supports people who suffer from the same condition that the deceased person suffered from (58%).
- The person who died had direct experience of the charity towards the end of their life (26%).
- The deceased person directly benefitted from the charity's work during their lifetime (8%).

These personal connections should be reflected in communications with the in-memory fundraiser. While traditional donor communications tend to focus on stimulating sympathy or empathy, interactions with in-memory donors should reflect their need to sustain a memory and find meaning in loss. When a fundraiser contacts your charity about fundraising in memory, seek to understand the connections between the person who died and your charity – i.e. the reason behind why the bereaved person chose your organisation. By doing so, you can reflect in your communications the areas of your work that hold the greatest meaning for them. Furthermore, you may be able to provide the fundraiser with opportunities to link their fundraising to aspects of your charity's work that relate to the deceased's interests.

In a small percentage of cases, the person who died supported the charity,[26] so check your database in case you need to recognise this in your communications. Ensure that you capture the name of the deceased so that your communications are personalised to recognise them. If a range of activities are being carried out in memory of a person, try to identify the main co-ordinator of the remembrance giving and provide them with updates on the amounts raised from all activities undertaken in memory of their loved one.

Tribute funds

A tribute fund (or tribute page) is usually a webpage that acts as an online space where people can remember and celebrate the life of a loved one. A person close to the deceased normally sets up the page and then invites family and friends to visit it to upload photos, videos and music and to share memories, thoughts and stories with each other. They can also give donations or set up events to collect sponsorship money in aid of the fund. People sometimes communicate practical details such as where and when the deceased's funeral or memorial service will be held and remember special days such as birthdays and anniversaries. A tribute fund or page can be kept private to a particular person or group of people or can be accessed by anyone online who would like to see the tributes, share memories, donate to the fund or attend an event.

Bereaved people can set up their own remembrance page directly on a website such as MuchLoved (www.muchloved.com) and may choose a charity (possibly as one of several charities) that way. Alternatively, they may consult a charity's website directly to find out how to set up a tribute fund. A cost-effective option for charities is to create a tribute home page that is branded with the charity's logo, colours, etc. via services such as Fundraising in Memory (www.fundraisinginmemory.org, operated by MuchLoved) and everydayhero (www.everydayhero.com/uk/charities). Otherwise, if it is strategically and financially viable, a charity may use a web developer (such as http://tributefunds.com) to create its own tribute fund platform on which people can create their tribute pages directly.

Charities' promotion of tribute funds tends to emphasise their value as a positive lasting record of a loved one and a means of doing something truly special in their memory. Most charities, however, naturally highlight the option to make a donation to the fund and the impact that the donation will have on their beneficiaries. Some charities suggest options such as giving a gift on a special date or raising money at a family gathering – indeed, there are no limits to what people can choose to do to raise funds, and all activities contribute to an overall total that provides a real-time record of monies raised. Other charities prefer to express the fundraising side of a tribute page as optional and focus instead on remembrance.

A tribute fund can be managed offline by providing the main contact or next of kin with regular updates on how much their and their family and friends' fundraising activities have raised in memory of their loved one. This may be appropriate for those who are not familiar or comfortable with what has become the standard (online) option.

While an individual or group of family and friends may fundraise over some months in memory of a loved one, people should be thanked for donations as the charity receives them. They can be thanked within the tribute fund page itself, directly by emailing the organiser or both.

Most in-memory fundraisers are close family members and they often begin fundraising within the first three months of a death.[27] This means you need to respond quickly to fundraising enquiries to facilitate the types of fundraising that occur soon after a bereavement, such as collection envelopes, online and offline gifts in lieu of flowers, tribute pages, or donations towards a tangible means of recognition (such as a plaque, a brick, a tree, etc.). Have a dedicated web page for in-memory giving that allows people to order and download materials and gives the opportunity to set up a tribute-fund page, and suggest useful links to bereavement organisations and support.

All those in contact with in-memory DIY fundraisers need the skills and emotional resources to provide the level of calm and compassion this vulnerable group of donors needs and deserves. First and foremost, ensure that all staff members' actions in relation to in-memory fundraising adhere to the standards outlined in section 1.0 of the Fundraising Regulator's Code of Fundraising Practice, 'Behaviour when fundraising', regarding dealing with people who are in vulnerable circumstances. Furthermore, ensure that you have a written policy on protecting people who are in vulnerable circumstances. It is also important to equip staff with the skills to feel comfortable talking with bereaved fundraisers about the deceased, the bereaved fundraiser's relationship with them and their motivation to fundraise. Finally, ensure staff are sensitive to the fact that in-memory DIY fundraisers are likely to behave in ways other DIY fundraisers do not. For instance, some people will throw themselves into fundraising activities as they try to make sense of their loss and then run out of energy during the process. Others may find that the normal speed of the charity's fundraising processes feels too fast or too slow for them. So, while encouraging fundraisers in their efforts, staff must manage the process carefully and kindly, giving fundraisers the space to fundraise in their own time.

There is considerable potential for longer-term support from in-memory donors, given that 98% of those giving in memory say they would support a charity again.[28] These supporters need their own donor journey, and some charities have developed specific in-memory products to further these ongoing relationships (including memory walks; donations for dedications via plaques, bricks, tree-planting, etc.; and, depending on the cause, schemes to sponsor a nurse, child, animal, and so on, in memory of the deceased).

Supporting DIY fundraisers' activities

Training support

For those undertaking a physical challenge, provide training advice via emails, blog posts or videos, such as a training calendar, nutrition advice and guidance on how to stay safe. Larger charities might choose to partner with a service such as runningwithus.com to provide this advice, and smaller charities could seek the services of a local personal trainer or signpost to existing online training sites (such as runforcharity.com) and materials. Suggest training playlists or ask fundraisers to share their favourite training tracks via social media to build interaction and engagement. Provide hashtags for people to use in posts about their own training and event preparation (for example, people may wish to share bake-sale recipes or preferred workouts). There are also apps you can promote that provide help with training motivation. You can create a page or pages on your website to put all your training advice in one place. See, for example, Cancer Research UK's online events training hub (www.cancerresearchuk.org/support-us/find-an-event/training-for-an-event), which offers advice for various types of activity including marathons, obstacle races and swimming events.

Tools to help DIY fundraisers promote their activities

Unlike mass events, which your organisation will almost certainly promote in order to drive participation, DIY fundraisers' events are reliant on their own promotional efforts. Fundraisers need the choice to promote their activity through whichever medium works best for them and their peers. Some people, for instance, may not be comfortable with online options and others, because of their fundraising activity and the audience they want to reach, may want to do both online and offline promotion.

Following are some of the tools you can offer to help fundraisers in their efforts.

Online promotion

- **Templates:** Provide email and social media templates containing details on the impact your organisation makes for its beneficiaries and the difference that different levels of donation can make.
- **Sharing:** Retweet fundraisers' tweets and share their posts to show your support of them and your acknowledgement of their efforts.
- **Twibbon:** Twibbon is a microsite that allows you to provide images and content for people to use on their own Facebook and Twitter pages (see twibbon.com). This not only makes it simple and undemanding for DIY fundraisers to promote their support of your cause but also gives you some control over their presentation of your charity's message and brand. You can offer:
  - options for Facebook cover photos and other images that fundraisers can add to their timelines;
  - Facebook updates that they can post with links to online giving pages;
  - Twitter backgrounds and messages to tweet;
  - automatic tweets they can use to let their contacts know they can make a donation.
- **Video:** With 57% of donors watching a video before donating,[29] and Facebook videos shared seven times more than links,[30] video is a powerful tool for telling a compelling fundraising story. Encourage people to create their own videos and provide videos about the impact of donations which they can share on social media, through online giving platforms and via email.
- **Blogs:** Offer tips on setting up a blog using free tools such as WordPress, blogger, tumbler, etc. Encourage fundraisers to share their fundraising experience more widely by linking their blog to their online giving pages and promoting it via social media.

Offline promotion

- **Printed resources:** Most fundraisers will be happy to download and print resources, which they can customise to support their activity, including:
  - flyers;
  - invitations;

- tickets;
- posters;
- signs and banners;
- cards and postcards;
- photographs, infographics and images.

• **Merchandise:** Branded items provide a tangible association with your charity and raise awareness of your organisation and cause. Decide which items you might give away for free and which to sell. Quirky, fashionable and celebrity-endorsed designs can gain attention and become another income generator. There are now website plug-ins to allow participants to customise charities' merchandise with their name, text-to-donate code, messages, photographs, etc. You can develop merchandise kits for specific types of DIY event (such as a baking pack with recipe cards, cupcake holders, tablecloth and bunting). Fundraisers can encourage family and friends to buy these kits – adding friends' or family members' sales amounts to their offline fundraising figure helps towards achieving their overall fundraising target.

• **Press:** Local papers often look for human-interest pieces and local radio stations frequently seek small fillers for breakfast and drive-time shows. This can help with an individual's event recruitment or support from local companies. Encourage fundraisers to email local media, community bloggers and neighbourhood newsletter editors explaining why, when and how they are fundraising.

Updating and thanking

Help DIY fundraisers to thank their donors, whether face to face, on social media or by email, phone or letter. This might include providing thank-you images and videos for them to share on social media; downloadable thank-you cards and certificates for fundraisers to give to people who have participated in an activity the fundraiser has organised; or templates for emails and letters. Remind them to re-engage with those who have not yet given to provide news of their progress and when they reach milestones, such as reaching 25% and then 50% of a target.

Collecting and paying in funds

As more than half of people in the UK (55%) prefer to give cash,[31] fundraisers need information on how to safely collect, store and pay in the cash they raise (see also 'Cash handling' on page 216). There is also an element of trust that DIY fundraisers will pay in the funds they have raised.

Sponsors and donors can send their funds to your charity in a variety of ways. For example:

- They might pay the monies they have collected into their bank account and then transfer the total amount to your charity via an online payment, telephone or cheque.
- You can provide paying-in slips so that fundraisers can pay cash directly into your charity's account via their local bank.

You will need to ensure that you support all the payment options that people may want to use. Provide forms to be completed and returned with any cheques sent by post, including the fundraiser's name and contact details, consent for future contact, the type of activity, the total number and value of cheques, and any Gift Aid declarations (the fundraiser will need to send the charity any paper sponsorship forms for it to be able to claim Gift Aid on these donations).

Thanking DIY fundraisers

DIY fundraisers are challenging to retain and they are less likely than mass participation fundraisers to fundraise again within the next 12 months.[32] However, thanking your fundraisers is the simplest and easiest way of strengthening their bond with your organisation and encouraging them to fundraise for you again. You should thank fundraisers frequently throughout the course of their efforts. Furthermore, thank them promptly after you have received their funds – this reassures them that you have received the money and that they are of value to you.

Consider the following questions when evaluating the effectiveness of your stewardship and thanking processes:

- **Are you creating a sense of belonging?** For example, do you give fundraisers a title, such as Movember's Mo Bros and Mo Sistas?
- **Who is involved in each step of the thank-you process?** Is it always the fundraising staff or do you include beneficiaries, service staff and board members?
- **What is your gift acknowledgement policy?** What happens from the moment a gift arrives? Does the value of the amount raised determine how you thank someone and who sends the thank you? For instance, when would a high-value gift warrant a thank you from your CEO or an invitation to attend a thank-you event?

- **When do you thank donors?** For example, do you thank them daily, weekly or monthly? Do you acknowledge them at the point of enquiry? When they sign up? When they receive their first online donations? Before, during or just after the fundraising activity?

- **Where do you thank fundraisers?** Is it across all channels? Do you recognise them via social media 'shout-outs' to provide public acknowledgement? Do you publish all of your fundraisers' names on web pages, in newsletters, on Twitter feeds, on naming boards, etc.?

- **What options do you have for thanking?** Do you have, for example, thank-you phonathons, videos, certificates, events, GIFs,[33] hand-written notes and/or live Facebook broadcasts?

- **Are thank yous always appropriate?** Are thank yous relevant and specific to the activity the fundraiser has undertaken, their reasons for fundraising and their wider relationship with your organisation?

- **Is your message as effective as it could be?** Does your language focus on the fundraiser's achievements, talents and efforts and the impact they will create?

To build long-term relationships, make sure that you:

- **Follow up after thanking fundraisers:** Provide news on results, what the money they raised accomplished, whose life it changed and so on. Rather than always asking people to fundraise again, make some of your communications simply about sharing progress.

- **Get to know fundraisers:** What other interests do they have? How could these be facilitated through other forms of fundraising participation?

- **Build fundraisers' sense of belonging:** Encourage them to sign up to your blogs, newsletters and so on.

- **Learn from fundraisers' experience:** What could your DIY fundraising programme do better? What advice do fundraisers have for you?

- **Value fundraisers' experience:** Would they like to help your charity find more supporters? Find out whether they are interested in acting as an ambassador by tweeting and sharing your events and news or undertaking talks in their community.

Bearing in mind the Pareto principle (also known as the 80/20 rule, which predicts that about 80% of effects are a result of 20% of inputs), ensure that you focus on retaining your most engaged fundraisers and those who raise the highest amounts for your cause. Design a stewardship process specifically to look after this group. For example, the British Heart Foundation has an exclusive 500 Club for challenge event participants who raise over £500. Such initiatives provide a sense of reward, and their exclusivity can make them aspirational.

Evaluating the sustainability of your DIY options

As with any fundraising programme, it is crucial to reflect on how your DIY fundraising is performing and how sustainable it is. Understanding where the greatest value lies, who supports you, their motivations and the impacts of the wider external environment are all essential to a DIY programme's ongoing planning. Consider the following questions:

- What are the average values raised?
- How much time do you spend on supporting fundraisers, and is this proportionate to what they raise?
- Are you supporting those who are generating the greatest value?
- Are there patterns in the types of activity supporters undertake?
- Are you gathering feedback on how participants feel about their experience?
- How easy is it to navigate your DIY pages?
- How many views convert to registration?
- Is there a particular participant demographic and how might you reach more of this audience?
- Is there a particular trigger for support?
- What technological changes might add ease and value to fundraisers' experience?
- What are your competitors doing?
- What elements of your marketing campaigns are driving support?

For more information on how to evaluate your overall fundraising programme, see 'The fundraising audit process' on page 33.

Conclusion

DIY fundraising is perhaps the most democratic form of fundraising. Its growth reflects people's desire to choose how they support a cause and to customise their fundraising to their interests, their concepts of what a personal challenge represents, what their social networks will give, and their available time and talents. Professional fundraisers are increasingly conduits to the cause, providing the storytelling and evidence of impact. Rather than controlling those who fundraise, the focus is to enable people to have uniquely meaningful experiences. This requires staff who respond flexibly, databases that can track relationships, and investment in the technologies that empower DIY fundraisers to reach and engage with their networks.

Notes

1 'Community fundraising benchmarking 2018' [web page], THINK, 2018, www.thinkcs.org/community-fundraising-benchmarking-2018, accessed 10 September 2018.

2 Abigail Payne, Kimberley Scharf and Sarah Smith, *Online Fundraising: The perfect ask?* [working paper], University of Warwick Department of Economics, no. 194, 2014, https://warwick.ac.uk/fac/soc/economics/research/centres/cage/manage/publications/194-2014_scharf.pdf, pp. 8–9, accessed 3 August 2018. (Note that all page numbers noted in Payne *et al.* 2014 references correspond to the PDF numbering in the particular version of the file that this URL leads to. The pages of the report itself are unnumbered.)

3 'CDE project 11d community section 2' [web article], Commission on the Donor Experience, http://sofii.org/article/cde-project-11d-community-section-2, 27 April 2017.

4 Abigail Payne, Kimberley Scharf and Sarah Smith, *Online Fundraising: The perfect ask?* [working paper], University of Warwick Department of Economics, no. 194, 2014, https://warwick.ac.uk/fac/soc/economics/research/centres/cage/manage/publications/194-2014_scharf.pdf, pp. 7 & 9, accessed 3 August 2018.

5 *Ibid.*, p. 7.

6 Rebecca Ratner, Min Zhao and Jennifer Clarke, 'The Norm of Self-Interest: Implications for charitable giving', in *The Science of Giving: Experimental approaches to the study of charity*, edited by Daniel M. Oppenheimer and Christopher Y. Olivola, New York, Psychology Press, 2011, pp. 113–31.

7 Abigail Payne, Kimberley Scharf and Sarah Smith, *Online Fundraising: The perfect ask?* [working paper], University of Warwick Department of Economics, no. 194, 2014, https://warwick.ac.uk/fac/soc/economics/research/centres/cage/manage/publications/194-2014_scharf.pdf, p. 9, accessed 3 August 2018.

8 Christopher Y. Olivola, 'When Noble Means Hinder Noble Ends: The benefits and costs of a preference for martyrdom in altruism', in *The Science of Giving: Experimental approaches to the study of charity*, edited by Daniel M. Oppenheimer and Christopher Y. Olivola, New York, Psychology Press, 2011, pp. 49–62.

9 'I fight dementia' [web page], Alzheimer's Research UK, 2018, www.alzheimersresearchuk.org/support-us/fundraise/fundraising-ideas, accessed 15 October 2018.

10 *In-Memory Briefing* [PDF], Legacy Foresight, 2017, www.legacyforesight.co.uk/resources/In-Memory%20Briefing%20May%202017.pdf, accessed 10 September 2018, p. 2.

11 Seongmin A. Park, Sidney Goïame, David A. O'Connor and Jean-Claude Dreher, 'Integration of Individual and Social Information for Decision-Making in Groups of Different Sizes', *PLOS Biology*, vol. 15, no. 6, 2017, doi:10.1371/journal.pbio.2001958.

12 'Boost your fundraising / Fundraising for a charity checklist: Are you using all of the features?' [web page], JustGiving, 2014, https://help.justgiving.com/hc/en-us/articles/200669391-Fundraising-for-a-charity-checklist-are-you-using-all-of-the-features, accessed 26 July 2018.
13 Abigail Payne, Kimberley Scharf and Sarah Smith, *Online Fundraising: The perfect ask?* [working paper], University of Warwick Department of Economics, no. 194, 2014, https://warwick.ac.uk/fac/soc/economics/research/centres/cage/manage/publications/194-2014_scharf.pdf, pp. 10–11, accessed 3 August 2018.
14 Presentation by Sarah Smith, 'Do targets matter?', Rotterdam, EUR Micro Seminars, 22 May 2015.
15 'Personalising your fundraising page' [web page], JustGiving, 2015, https://help.justgiving.com/hc/en-us/articles/200669521-Personalising-your-Fundraising-Page, accessed 31 August 2017.
16 *2016 Blackbaud Peer-to-Peer Fundraising Study* [PDF], Blackbaud, 2017, http://hi.blackbaud.com/p2p/2016-Peer-to-Peer-Report-pub2017.pdf, p. 4, accessed 24 April 2018.
17 Abigail Payne, Kimberley Scharf and Sarah Smith, *Online Fundraising: The perfect ask?* [working paper], University of Warwick Department of Economics, no. 194, 2014, https://warwick.ac.uk/fac/soc/economics/research/centres/cage/manage/publications/194-2014_scharf.pdf, p. 6, accessed 3 August 2018.
18 'Nine reasons why social and mobile are the future of fundraising' [blog post], JustGiving, https://blog.justgiving.com/nine-reasons-why-social-and-mobile-are-the-future-of-fundraising, 9 September 2013.
19 'Event fundraising tips for your marathon runners' [blog post], JustGiving, https://blog.justgiving.com/how-to-motivate-your-marathon-fundraisers, 29 July 2013.
20 Jesper Juul Jensen, 'Branding, trust and donor contact permission' [blog post], BetterNow, www.betternow.org/blog/branding-trust-donor-contact-permission, 26 January 2017.
21 'Five reasons to encourage team fundraising' [blog post], JustGiving, http://blog.justgiving.com/five-reasons-to-fundraise-as-a-team, 20 February 2015.
22 'Is the public getting tired of sponsoring fundraising events?' [blog post], nfpSynergy, https://nfpsynergy.net/blog/public-getting-tired-sponsoring-fundraising-events, 15 January 2018.
23 Catherine Walker, *A Great Match: How match-funding incentivises charitable giving in the UK and unites funders and donors in tackling social issues* [PDF], The Big Give, Charities Trust and RBS, 2016, https://cdn.thebiggive.org.uk/static/docs/A-Great+Match-EVersion.pdf, p. 6, accessed 17 August 2018.
24 Howard Lake, 'In memory event fundraising is worth £15m to charities, says JustGiving' [web article], UK Fundraising, https://fundraising.co.uk/2013/07/04/memory-event-fundraising-worth-15m-charities-says-justgiving, 4 July 2013.
25 Presentation by Elizabeth Kessick, 'Creating a digital legacy', London, Institute of Fundraising Event Fundraising Conference, 19 May 2014.
26 *Ibid.*
27 *Ibid.*
28 *Ibid.*
29 'Google survey reveals patterns of how we donate money online' [web article], Fast Company, www.fastcompany.com/3016088/google-survey-reveals-patterns-of-how-we-donate-money-online, 21 July 2013.

30 Lucia Moses, 'Publishers' Facebook videos are shared 7 times more than links' [web article], Digiday UK, https://digiday.com/media/publishers-facebook-videos-shared-7-times-links, 31 March 2016.
31 *CAF UK Giving 2018: An overview of charitable giving in the UK* [PDF], Charities Aid Foundation, 2018, www.cafonline.org/docs/default-source/about-us-publications/caf-uk-giving-2018-report.pdf, p. 15, accessed 17 August 2018.
32 Abigail Payne, Kimberley Scharf and Sarah Smith, *Online Fundraising: The perfect ask?* [working paper], University of Warwick Department of Economics, no. 194, 2014, https://warwick.ac.uk/fac/soc/economics/research/centres/cage/manage/publications/194-2014_scharf.pdf, p. 9, accessed 3 August 2018.
33 A GIF (which stands for graphic interchange format) is an image format that compresses images to reduce their size without losing their quality. This format is often used to present short videos that repeat on loop.

CHAPTER EIGHT

Developing mass participation events

John Tasker and Hannah Redmond

Introduction

Mass participation events are fundraising events that involve participants undertaking a common and straightforward activity (such as holding a tea party, wearing a Christmas jumper, running a race or growing a beard), normally at the same time and/or in the same place and for the same cause. They are based on simple concepts that are replicable and scalable, and can work successfully for organisations of any size, regardless of whether the event is seeking to have niche or wide appeal.

Since the mid-2010s, some UK-based mass participation events have started to be delivered in a virtual context, where supporters raise money for a charity remotely, usually within a period of time (such as a particular month), rather than in the same place at the same time. For example, the British Heart Foundation's MyMarathon involves people running a marathon distance, but participants are free to complete it over the course of a month in any way that suits them.

The 25 biggest mass participation events in the UK (as shown in figure 8.1) are estimated to have raised more than £135.5 million in 2017.[1] Most sizeable UK charities run at least one mass participation event on an ongoing basis, but larger charities may own and operate multiple events, each delivering to a different segment of their audience and the events market.

Great mass participation fundraising events come in various shapes and sizes. Examples include:

- **physical events**, such as Alzheimer's Society's Memory Walk;
- **community-focused campaigns**, such as Macmillan Cancer Support's World's Biggest Coffee Morning;
- **virtual events**, such as the British Heart Foundation's MyMarathon;
- **social campaigns**, such as Movember.

Each event is based on a different activity and delivery model, with each engaging and inspiring different audiences to participate and fundraise.

FIGURE 8.1 THE MASSIVE TOP 25[2]

1	£37,100,000	∨	Race For Life	Run /Walk	Cancer Research UK
2	£27,000,000	∨	World's Biggest Coffee Morning	Social	Macmillan Cancer Support
3	£7,700,000	∧	Memory Walk	Walk	Alzheimer's Society
4	£5,800,000	∧	Mighty Hikes	Walk	Macmillan Cancer Support
5	£5,000,000	∧	Kiltwalk	Walk	Kiltwalk
5	£5,000,000	∧	Movember	Social	The Movember Foundation
7	£4,900,000	∨	Moonwalk	Walk	Walk the Walk
7	£4,900,000	∨	Brave The Shave	Social	Macmillan Cancer Support
9	£4,450,000	∨	Go Sober	Social	Macmillan Cancer Support
10	£4,000,000	∨	Christmas Jumper Day	Dress	Save the Children
11	£3,950,000	∧	Shine	Walk	Cancer Research UK
12	£3,650,000	∧	Sleep In The Park	Other	Social Bite
13	£3,000,000	∧	BHF London To Brighton	Cycle	BHF
14	£2,700,000	∧	Relay For Life	Walk	Cancer Research UK
15	£2,600,000	∨	Walking All Over Cancer	Social	Cancer Research UK
16	£1,800,000	–	The Marsden March	Walk	Royal Marsden Hospital
17	£1,700,000	∧	Wear It Pink	Dress	Breast Cancer Now
18	£1,400,000	∧	Cupcake Day	Social	Alzheimer's Society
19	£1,100,000	∨	ByteNight	Other	Action for Children
20	£1,050,000	∧	BHF Dechox	Social	BHF
21	£1,000,000	∨	Longest Day Golf Challenge	Golf	Macmillan Cancer Support
21	£1,000,000	∧	Dryathlon	Social	Cancer Research UK
21	£1,000,000	∧	London Legal Walk	Walk	London Legal Support Trust
24	£970,000	∨	Palace To Palace	Cycle	Princes Trust
25	£960,000	∧	Jeans For Genes	Dress	Jeans for Genes

It is often the simplest campaigns – the ones that can be integrated into everyday life, with cause, motivation and community spirit at their heart – that achieve the most success. These are the events that bring people together, that create conversations, that bring about a shared moment or experience, and that give the feeling of being part of something much bigger.

In addition to generating income, these events can be incredibly beneficial for building your charity's brand by attracting advocates for your cause who will subsequently recommend and talk about you and the value of what you are doing.

How to create a successful mass participation event

Successful mass participation fundraising events align three key areas: the activity, the audience, and the cause that the event supports (see figure 8.2).

FIGURE 8.2 ALIGNING ACTIVITY, AUDIENCE AND CAUSE

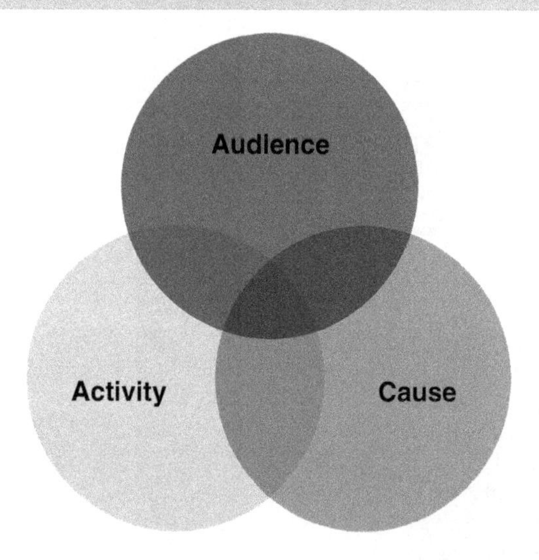

If you create an event that is centred on a popular, desirable or fashionable activity, then you're laying the foundations for a highly successful event. In the commercial events world, knowing the audience that your event is likely to appeal to enables you to reach out to your target demographic and recruit large volumes of participants cost-effectively. However, in the fundraising world, you need to go a step further and ensure that the fundraising activity is also aligned with your cause. If you don't communicate this to your audience, it will be difficult to drive high levels of fundraising or sustain longer-term support.

Organisations that intelligently link all three of these elements create a recipe for success. Movember, which raised over £490 million globally between 2004 and 2017,[3] is a good example: it perfectly connects an audience (men) with a simple activity that is likely to appeal to many of them (having a moustache-growing contest with their mates) and a cause that is relevant (supporting the fight against men's cancers).

Another good example is Tommy's – a charity that is focused on preventing miscarriages, stillbirths and premature births. Tommy's delivers fantastic results with its Splashathon event. The event aligns an audience (mothers with young children) with an activity that is likely to appeal to many of them (swimming with their babies) and a cause they are likely to directly relate to (saving babies' lives).

When you decide that you want to bring a new concept to market, there are many challenges for which you will need to plan. However, using the three-stage process outlined in the following sections can help you to navigate your journey successfully. By working through each stage, asking and answering a series of simple questions first (rather than waiting until you have an event to test), you can validate your thoughts, ideas and assumptions before you begin, and create a bespoke solution that achieves a participatory fundraising objective. This model is always applicable, whether you're working with an external agency or your internal team. Kept simple, this method can be applied to any organisation or opportunity.

Stage one: Defining the opportunity

Coming up with ideas for events is easy; it is coming up with the *right* ideas that is hard. At the outset of any product development process, begin at the end. By defining the end goal first, you can work out specific criteria for each project and build a picture of what successful delivery will look like. This enables you to focus both your creativity and your resources more effectively, so that you can arrive at your destination as quickly and cost-effectively as possible.

1. Who is the audience for your event?

If your answer is 'everyone', stop now and take some time to think about this question. It can be tempting to want to attract a very broad audience. However, while you won't want to alienate anybody, almost all successful products are designed with a target customer in mind, and almost every great event has achieved success through knowing who its target audience is and appealing to them.

Yes, it can sometimes feel like you're cutting out potential participants, but in fact, by following this principle, your event will have a stronger appeal. Whatever you define your audience by – motivation, attitude, relationship to your organisation, gender, age, social grouping, etc. – you need to create a tight focus in order to attract a specific group of participants.

2. What does the event need to deliver?

What is the primary aim of your event? Is it about acquiring new supporters or re-engaging existing ones? Is your aim primarily fundraising or is it to increase brand awareness?

Charity events work well as tools to acquire new supporters and audiences, who can then be cross-sold other fundraising offers. For example, up to 90% of participants in virtual running events marketed by charities such as the British Heart Foundation and Macmillan are new to the organisation.[4]

Crohn's & Colitis UK wanted to raise awareness of inflammatory bowel disease, so it created WALK IT, a series of city-centre walking events. The events feature 'event villages' at the finish line, which are places where people can find information on the condition, the support available and the work the charity does, alongside refreshments and entertainment. This, combined with a crowd of hundreds of branded cause-aware supporters travelling around the city, delivers a cost-effective solution to 'activate' the charity's brand and engage new supporters while offering a way for those closest to the cause to get involved with fundraising activity.

Of course, events can deliver more than one benefit for an organisation, but many projects are hampered from the outset by an extensive shopping list of expectations. Narrowing down your objectives from the outset will give your project focus, subsequently increasing the chances of a successful outcome.

Brand activation goes beyond general brand marketing. It is the process of moving a brand from OK to great: either making a new brand known to people or reinvigorating one that's lost momentum or become a bit stale. This is achieved via activities that increase people's awareness of a brand by changing their experience of it and/or their engagement with it.

3. What resources are available to you?

Be realistic about what resources you have to deliver your chosen event. Whereas events marketed to and by your current supporter base are less costly to deliver, if you are looking to recruit *new* supporters then you will need to invest significantly in your marketing activities. Mass participation events tend to be regarded as successful if they break even in their first year, and over the longer term very few major events will achieve anything greater than a 3:1 return on investment.

Outside financial resources, review all of the available assets that could be used for your event. For example, do you have strong celebrity support, well-connected supporters, or media or corporate partners that can leverage exposure or add value to your event?

The value unlocked by Race for Life's transformational partnership with Tesco in the early 2000s was not purely financial; the greatest value came from the outreach delivered through the company's store network and from exposure to the event's core audience through the retailer's predominantly female customer base. Similarly, Alzheimer's Research UK's Running Down Dementia campaign leveraged its existing partnership with parkrun (an organisation that organises free weekly outdoor runs all over the world) to deliver a new and relevant fundraising offer to parkrun's membership and beyond, with relatively limited marketing investment.

4. Are people going to support your idea?

Launching something new is always challenging and labour intensive, so it is crucial to have high levels of support for your idea. To evaluate whether you have the right level of support both internally and externally, ask yourself:

- Do your senior stakeholders agree with and support your idea?
- Who needs to facilitate your event internally?
- Are the people and departments you will depend on to support and deliver your event (marketing, digital, PR, etc.) all involved and supportive?
- Are these people and departments aligned with the aims and objectives of your event?

It almost always makes sense to invest time to get their input and buy-in at an early stage.

Stage two: Designing the solution

Once the opportunity has been defined, you need to begin developing ideas that you can explore, refine and develop into a solution that meets the needs of your organisation and your audience, and make sure that it fits into the current market.

1. How well do you know your audience?

What insights into your audience do you have? What do they need from an event? Is it about people demonstrating achievement through challenging themselves? Or supporting the cause in a social and community-spirited way? How will the event fit in with people's lives? And what puts people off doing one activity and draws them to another?

A good example of an insight-based solution is the NSPCC's family mud-run event, Messathon. The event design was based on two key insights: first, kids enjoy getting messy – and enjoy it even more when their parents get covered in paint, mud or gunge – and, second, parents want opportunities to play with their children and have fun with them more often, shunning any notions of being 'responsible' and 'boring' parents. These insights shaped every single element of the final event, from the design of the obstacles to the creative execution and marketing strategy, and even the event name itself.

To keep your mass participation campaign on track and keep your target audience at the forefront of your mind, one useful design method is to create supporter profiles (written summaries of your ideal supporters, known as 'personas' or 'pen portraits' in the business and marketing worlds) based on the knowledge and insights you have gained through your research. This helps to remove the temptation to develop ideas based on your personal tastes and subjective preferences. (For details on how to create personas, see page 107.)

The behaviours and tastes of your target demographic will shape your 'route to market' – i.e. how you plan to promote your new product and which channels of promotion you will choose. For example, you might know that the supporters who are likely to take part in your next running event are predominately women aged 45 or over, have children who have left home, shop in Marks & Spencer or Waitrose, and are primarily motivated by finding a sociable way to exercise with their friends. These and similar insights can help you to shape your campaign to appeal to the audience you want to target. Channels for this audience might include advertising in retailers' magazines and Facebook advertising based on demographics and interests.

Case study: How the World's Biggest Coffee Morning was revitalised

Macmillan's World's Biggest Coffee Morning is one of the largest mass participation events in the UK and one of the longest running. Heritage, tradition and simplicity are at its core. However, there have been periods of decline and growth in the campaign's history.

In 2011, the World's Biggest Coffee Morning was in a third year of income plateau at around the £8 million mark. We were successful in retaining hosts who had previously run coffee mornings but it was challenging to acquire new hosts: it was unclear who was responding to our advertising campaigns, and the impact of our advertising activity was therefore questionable.

Creatively, we moved the campaign in a number of directions, looking to appeal to a broader market by including more men in imagery and expanding beyond coffee and cake to quiz nights, events in pubs and multiple other ideas and settings. The result was a highly confused campaign and, without a clear target market in mind, media buying became a challenge ('media buying' is the standard term for purchasing advertising from a media company). In stretching the event to these new areas and not just focusing on coming together with friends over coffee and cake, we inadvertently caused the original concept to lose its simplicity, and the new approach was misunderstood by new audiences and potentially alienated those who had taken part before.

To refocus the campaign, we commissioned qualitative and quantitative research to understand the demographics, behaviours and motivations of our existing and potential World's Biggest Coffee Morning supporters. We also considered the propensity of new audiences to take part in this type of event and narrowed our targeting further. This gave us absolute clarity on our target market, which not surprisingly was predominately female, middle class, aged 45 or over and with a connection to cancer.

We discovered that our audience's core motivation was getting together in a social and fun way to support people living with cancer. These insights drove a new campaign proposition which, rather than focusing on 'Making it the biggest ever', became 'Make time for what really matters'. This new proposition articulates the desire of our new and potential audience to do something good, for a cause they care about, with people they care about. We reinvigorated the campaign's visual identity by moving away from single-colour illustrations that lacked emotion and instead using full-bleed photography – of cakes, tables of treats and real-life supporters holding events – to inspire and enthuse others.

The marketing strategy was also overhauled. For our existing supporters, we revised the mix of marketing activity in terms of our chosen communication channels and the frequency of our communications. This involved moving from a very email-heavy campaign to using a greater number of direct mail communications and directing more telemarketing to past participants asking them to sign up again. Critical to the success of the campaign was our approach to above-the-line media (i.e. advertising in the mass media) to attract hosts who had not taken part before. Previously, we had primarily relied on partnerships with radio and print media to attract hosts. This approach was reviewed and replaced with a direct response TV campaign as the primary channel, supported by digital, targeted print and radio channels. Taking the proposition to a mass-market channel through an insight-driven proposition for a specific target audience caused awareness of the campaign to peak and registrations trebled.

Another vital element of the campaign was the Coffee Morning Kit – our fundraising pack sent to all registrants. In previous years, this had been delivered both through email and as a physical pack. Included were balloons (in the physical pack) and a few leaflets. We realised this was a huge branding opportunity that had the potential to be a very desirable item which would encourage people to move from signing up to converting to hosting an event. In developing the items included in the Coffee Morning Kit, we considered the following core questions for each item:

- Is it useful? (For example, a Gift Aid form or reply envelope for donations.)
- Does it decorate in a way that enhances our brand? (Such as bunting or a table cloth.)
- Does it increase the average gift amount? (For instance, a donation box or a game.)

In order to suit our supporter demographic, the items we included needed to be attractive yet also fit within a budget per pack. We achieved this by sending our leaflets to print early (allowing the printer to process our job during quiet periods and us to negotiate a lower price as a result) and using smart printing (where text and graphics may be changed from one printing to the next) for economies of scale. We tested various types of pack, including online and offline versions and with differing contents. As a result, the kit has become an icon of the event and something we know supporters value.

The World's Biggest Coffee Morning grew from generating £8 million in 2011 to almost £30 million in 2016. By 2017, Macmillan cumulatively raised £200 million for people living with cancer as a direct result of the hundreds of thousands of coffee mornings that have taken place in our event's 30-year history. The event is also a great example of how the fundamentals of good mass participation lie in keeping things simple and being driven by an understanding of supporter motivations.

2. Who else knows your audience?

Gathering insight doesn't have to be expensive or involve commissioning your own research. There may be other people or organisations that share your target audience and already have insights that you can learn from.

Ask yourself: is there an existing brand or company that specialises in offering products or services to the audience that you're targeting? Is there a product or event out there in the market already that delivers what you need and could be borrowed or adapted for your audience? Marie Curie's Blooming Great Tea Party may not have the scale of the World's Biggest Coffee Morning, but it uses a concept that has already proved to be successful. Many of the biggest mass participation events in the UK are directly lifted or even licensed versions of existing successful events (such as Race for Life and Brave the Shave).

Consider too whether there are people within your organisation who have already worked with your target audience before and have personal experience in understanding them. Or can you speak directly to the people you are looking to target and involve them in any element of the event's design?

A successful example of this direct kind of approach can be seen in the initial concept for the sobriety campaign Dry July, which originated from discussions with fellow drinkers in an Australian bar and eventually made its way to the UK as Dryathlon and Sober October. While not all ideas developed in the pub will come to fruition, it is worth starting conversations and opening up dialogues in social situations to get to know how your audience thinks – inspiration can be found in surprising places.

3. Which idea works best?

Once you've gathered insights into your audience and created multiple ideas, the next step is to select which ones you're going to build on and which ones you're going to set aside. Use the criteria you created in stage one to slim down your choices. Take the four best ideas and create a more detailed proposition for each, sketching out how the event will actually work, starting with what need it meets for your target audience and why they would want to take part. Then build a high-level budget and outline how each concept will be delivered. Test reactions from your target audience (via social media or whichever channel is most appropriate for that audience) and internal stakeholders. Finally, based on your research and feedback, pick one or two ideas to take forward.

4. When should I test?

There is always a temptation to wait until you have a perfect business case or a finished concept before you share your thinking, but don't wait until you're ready to launch until you test out your ideas. The right time to do this is in development. For example, you can test concepts on social media by asking people to register their interest to gauge audience reaction to your propositions. This is an easy and cost-effective method to gain insight into your audience, and you get results quickly, helping you to decide which proposition is the strongest and most appealing to potential participants.

Stage three: Delivery

Let's be honest: groundbreaking new event concepts are few and far between – but don't let this dishearten you. An event doesn't need to be completely new and unique to stand out and be successful. Many of the biggest and most successful events are not particularly innovative, but they have strong concepts that are supported by creative thinking and an excellent campaign delivery. A seemingly average concept delivered well will generally trump a brilliantly thought-out concept event that is delivered badly.

1. Do the delivery plan and business case stack up?

Take time to accurately estimate the costs of bringing your concept to market. How realistic are the numbers and assumptions in your business case? Are they overly optimistic? Look at how much other similar events generate through fundraising and be objective about how your cause compares when it comes to inspiring fundraisers. Which entry platform (for example, Eventbrite or Active Network) is best for your organisation? How will it integrate with your website and online giving pages?

While you are committed to and fully behind your own idea, remember that consumers will see it against a backdrop of hundreds of other events, so consider the following questions:

- Have you researched who your competitors are?
- How do your offering and pricing compare to those of your competitors?
- When you intend to launch, what else will be competing for attention and participants in the marketplace?
- Have you given yourself enough time to deliver?
- Have you considered what makes your event stand out and what sets it apart from other organisations in the marketplace?

Building your business case and delivery plan is an iterative process: start with an outline case to prove the concept, and then move into more detailed delivery planning and finalise your budget.

2. Where do I need support?

Carefully consider where your skills lie and the gaps in your capabilities and knowledge. Work with agencies, such as ones focusing on event design and management, to supplement your understanding of the market and bring in expertise (such as an events management partner) when required to ensure all elements are realistic and will deliver the right results. If budgets are tight, consider what you could deliver in-house against the cost of the time and energy you and your team will spend on it. For example, is your time best spent fulfilling requests for information packs or delivering strong fundraising PR through conversations with your supporters? Ask where a supplier can add most value, where they can deliver faster or more efficiently, and where they can provide a more effective solution, so that your time is getting you the best results.

3. What is the route to market?

Deciding where and how to market your event is dependent on many variables, such as your audience and budget, but it is often best to choose a mix of marketing channels and PR activity. You may want to start with a very targeted approach and then build outwards from there.

Begin with supporters who have previously shown an interest in mass participation – this is a low-cost way to acquire new supporters. Then, depending on the type of campaign, it can also be cost-effective to enlist the help of staff and local networks. If you are organising a local running event, ask volunteers to promote it through community venue posters and flyers. Consider how to gain support from local corporate partners and encourage regional fundraisers to engage members of the local business community in face-to-face conversations about your campaign. (For details on how to gain support from local corporate partners, see chapter 12.)

If you want to take your campaign up a level, you will need to use above-the-line media. You can buy media through an agency or a broker, particularly for larger-budget activities, such as TV or radio advertising or for specialist channels such as social media. However, if your budget is small, you can easily buy media directly from local press, and you can buy search terms (e.g. Google AdWords – terms and phrases that are used to match your adverts with the terms people are searching for) and advertising directly from social platforms. If you're targeting people on social media, you might consider approaching audiences who are similar to one another, who are in close proximity to your event, or who engage with the same causes, events or activities. For example, you could target people on Facebook who 'like' charities and the genre of campaign you are promoting, such as baking.

Ensure you are making the best use of your resources. For example, if you are targeting schoolteachers for a mass participation event for young people, a broadly targeted above-the-line campaign may not be efficient. Instead, it would be a better choice to target communications only to named schools and contacts or to reach your target audience via the trade press.

4. Are people excited about the event?

Successful events excite and engage internal stakeholders and delivery partners. Are people talking about the event? Have you created a sense of excitement? Are people proud to be involved with it? Get your colleagues enthused and inspire them to talk to others about the event. Hold briefings to keep momentum, throw a launch party to build motivation, and build a team ethos across all of your internal partners to inspire community and camaraderie. This is a test in itself: if you can't excite those closest to the cause, then you need to ask why anybody outside your organisation is going to be excited about your event.

5. What should I test?

It is not always possible to pilot your idea, meaning that launch and delivery is the only test that really matters. However, your marketing campaign will provide ample opportunities to test and learn as you go. Monitor performance and track the results of every campaign element along the way, vary and adjust your digital activity to continually fine-tune and refine your campaign method, and compare performance and recruitment against your forecasts. Ultimately, you need to be flexible, reactive and prepared to modify your plans and approach in order to deliver the results that will make your event a success.

Conclusion

To create a successful mass participation event, you need to be clear about who you are targeting and what you want to achieve: an event intended for everyone and with too many aims will be a recipe for disappointment. Equally, the better you get to know your audience and their needs, the more likely you will be to come up with effective ideas that you can then test, as you go, by directly gauging the interest of your external supporters and internal stakeholders.

Remember that your event doesn't need to be completely new to stand out and be successful. If you have a seemingly average concept but you deliver it with both internal and external support and an excellent campaign, you are more likely to succeed than if you bring a brilliantly thought-out concept to market badly.

Notes

1 *The Massive Top 25* [PDF], massive, 2019, www.wearemassive.co.uk/insight/mass-participation-top-25-2, p. 1, accessed 30 July 2019.

2 *Ibid.*

3 'Our financials' [web page], Movember Foundation, 2018, https://uk.movember.com/about/money, accessed 25 April 2018.

4 *What Creates Virtual Event Success?* [PDF], Everydayhero and About More Strategic, 2017, http://hub.blackbaud.co.uk/peer-to-peer/what-creates-virtual-event-success, p. 4, accessed 21 June 2018.

CHAPTER NINE

Managing volunteers and in-house fundraising groups

Jane Galloway

Introduction

Community fundraising is reliant on people power, in terms of both participants and the essential volunteers that help to organise and run participatory fundraising activities for charities. Volunteers are often the lifeblood of a community fundraising programme – they act as a vital resource across myriad roles, from marshalling events to helping with administration and running volunteer fundraising groups. Without this human resource, many community fundraising initiatives would simply be uneconomical.

In 2017/18, over a third of adults (38%) in England engaged in volunteering at least once a year.[1] The most popular activity undertaken by volunteers is organising or helping to run a charity event or activity, followed closely by raising or handling money or taking part in a sponsored event. Nearly two in five of those who have volunteered regularly have undertaken activities to get others involved.[2]

This chapter looks at the best practice for managing all types of fundraising volunteer, from those running committees to individuals helping with administration or logistics. It also focuses on the value, benefits and means of harnessing volunteer support in the form of in-house fundraising groups. Using established volunteer management models, the chapter advises on how you might plan to identify, recruit, recognise, retain, motivate and support community fundraising volunteers.

Why do people volunteer?

To match volunteer experiences to the meanings that people are seeking from them, it is vital to understand the different reasons why people choose to volunteer.

Volunteering is best understood as a journey over someone's lifetime, where their reasons for volunteering change in relation to their life stage and wider external influences. The reasons why people volunteer also vary according to personal, cultural, structural and environmental circumstances and there is considerable research into both psychological and social drivers.

One model identifies ten key motivational categories, with people often motivated by more than one of these needs or goals when engaging in volunteering:[3]

1. **values:** to act on or express a belief in the importance of helping others;
2. **reciprocity:** to bring about a benefit for themselves or for family members, such as a service they may need in the future;
3. **recognition:** to be recognised for their skills and contribution;
4. **understanding:** to learn new information, experiences or skills;
5. **self-esteem:** to increase feelings of self-worth and self-esteem;
6. **reactivity:** as a form of therapy to address issues in the past or present;
7. **social norms:** because they are influenced by the behaviour of friends or family;
8. **self-protection:** to address personal problems or reduce negative feelings about themselves, such as guilt;
9. **social interaction:** to build social networks and because of the enjoyment of interacting with others;
10. **career development:** to gain experience, skills or contacts that improve employability.

There is also a tendency for motivations to change with age – older volunteers are often more interested in social contact and younger volunteers are more likely to be seeking skills and work experience.[4]

Why do people stop volunteering?

High turnover of fundraising volunteers can present a major barrier to achieving growth within a charity, demoralise staff and other volunteers, and consume managerial energies in the continual need to replace volunteers. Your ability to retain volunteers is likely to be affected by the quality of your organisation's recruitment practices, where poor fits with roles or unrealistic expectations can cause people to leave.

Volunteer programmes have widely varying retention rates, which reflect large differences in types of volunteering activities, lengths of programmes and levels of management support.[5] People stop volunteering for both controllable and uncontrollable reasons. Uncontrollable reasons include changes in personal circumstances (such as when someone gets a new job or goes into further/higher education), or family circumstances and moving out of a locality. Common controllable factors, as revealed by reviews of the research literature,[6] include volunteers:

- experiencing poor volunteer management practices where they felt that the charity or group was disorganised, badly managed or lacking direction;
- feeling that they were not able to accomplish what they hoped, the charity was not using their time or talents well or they were not asked to do worthwhile tasks;
- receiving an inadequate amount of orientation, training, support or supervision;
- having badly defined tasks or unclear expectations about what they are supposed to be doing;
- having too much expected of them or feeling overburdened due to either the intensity or quantity of demands or responsibility placed upon them;
- not being treated well by disorganised management or indifferent staff and feeling a lack of respect for supervisors or co-workers as a result;
- feeling unappreciated or unrecognised for their efforts;
- sensing that their help was not really wanted or that they were not progressing or making a difference;
- seeking flexibility and autonomy but feeling demoralised by the formality of a role;
- finding themselves out of pocket;
- finding that volunteering is too time-consuming.

The following section looks at ways you can prevent or solve issues such as these.

What helps people to keep volunteering?

> 'Retention is about making sure your volunteers are motivated and stay motivated and achieve what you want them to achieve.'
>
> Rob Jackson, 2002[7]

People will usually continue to volunteer if their experience proves to be a positive one. The factors that make this positive will vary by different types of volunteer, in different situations and in different types of organisation, but they can be summarised as volunteers experiencing:[8]

- the organisation to be explicit around expectations and providing clear job roles;
- the organisation to be flexible around hours, location and the ongoing shaping of roles and responsibilities;
- management that is developmental and supportive, giving people space and autonomy within their roles and opportunities to take initiative, including tasks where they can express themselves, develop their skills and feel a sense of achievement;
- a sense of gratitude from the people within the organisation and a feeling that they genuinely care about the volunteers' efforts and well-being;
- a social element to their volunteering, via the friendships made and networks joined through the volunteering experience;
- a sense of confidence that the organisation and work are worthwhile and deserving of feelings of pride;
- development opportunities when career-related factors are important;
- self-esteem or personal growth from a role.

Research on Girl Scout volunteers in the USA suggests that, as people continue to volunteer, they tend to become more committed to the organisation, its cause and its personnel (both paid staff and volunteers).[9] The research found that long-term volunteers continued volunteering when the role became a part of how they saw themselves. This integration of self-image and role occurred when volunteers became invested in the role and the organisation, developed an attachment to others in the organisation, and felt that what they were doing, fitted with who they want to be.

For details on what to monitor to help ensure your programme offers volunteers a positive experience, see 'Monitoring and evaluating your programme' on page 280.

The two types of fundraising volunteer

The glossary of the Code of Fundraising Practice defines two forms of fundraising volunteer: on-behalf-of volunteers and in-aid-of volunteers.[10]

On-behalf-of volunteers

On-behalf-of volunteers are volunteers who have been authorised by an organisation to fundraise on its behalf. The organisation knows the volunteers are raising money for it and provides help in the form of support, advice, training and resources. You have more control over these volunteers' activities but you are also responsible for how those activities are undertaken. These volunteers should be covered under your organisation's insurance.

Many types of on-behalf-of fundraising volunteers can be critical to a community fundraising programme, including those who:

- perform **administrative duties**, such as doing data entry, answering phones, undertaking research and offering social media support;
- carry out **logistical tasks**, such as driving, catering, event marshalling, first aid, running stalls, stock management and collection of funds;
- have **organisational and advocacy roles**, such as being community champions or ambassadors, running events, recruiting and managing other volunteers;
- **manage members** of the fundraising group they are a part of.

In-aid-of volunteers

In-aid-of volunteers (often referred to as DIY fundraisers) are volunteers who raise funds and act independently of a charity. This means they have often not been authorised by the organisation they are supporting and are acting on their own initiative. Often, the charity only learns about this fundraising activity when it receives the fundraiser's donation. The organisation has no (or little) control over these volunteers, and they are not covered by the organisation's insurance. However, if in-aid-of volunteers use methods that the organisation disapproves of, as a last resort, it is possible to take legal action to prevent their fundraising. Seeking to engage constructively with potential volunteers is always preferable. Furthermore, a charity can positively influence the actions of in-aid-of volunteers by developing a relationship with them by offering support and advice and providing information packs, thereby reducing the chances of these volunteers using inappropriate fundraising methods.

Differences between the two types of fundraising volunteer

These are two important definitions of volunteer status, with different implications for their management. It can sometimes be challenging, however, to identify which category of volunteer a supporter fits into.

Generally speaking, the more you are directing a volunteer's activities and asking them to actively represent you, the more likely they are to be acting on behalf of your charity. Table 9.1 gives examples of the two types to help clarify the delineations between them.

TABLE 9.1 IN-AID-OF VOLUNTEERING VERSUS ON-BEHALF-OF VOLUNTEERING

Example	Type of volunteer
Danika is helping with a street collection that your charity is running	On behalf of
George and his friends have organised a pub quiz to raise money for your charity	In aid of
The Lions Club is holding a dinner dance for your charity	In aid of
Suzie and Becky are running a stall at a fete as members of your friends group	On behalf of
Sinita has asked her Zumba group to run a sponsored Zumbathon for your charity	In aid of
The local golf club has agreed to run a charity golf day with you	On behalf of
Jonas is doing a sponsored silence at school for your charity	In aid of

This chapter focuses on on-behalf-of volunteers and friends groups. For detailed information on in-aid-of (or DIY) volunteers, see chapter 7.

Organising a volunteer programme

Volunteer programmes vary – from those where staff closely manage volunteers (for example, volunteers entering data or undertaking research) to those organised by other volunteers (friends groups and collectors). However, in all cases the effective involvement of volunteers requires a planned and organised process. The process outlined in this section (illustrated in figure 9.1) is structured using an adapted version of the management model for designing effective volunteer programmes, proposed by McCurley, Lynch and Jackson.

FIGURE 9.1 DESIGNING EFFECTIVE VOLUNTEER PROGRAMMES[11]

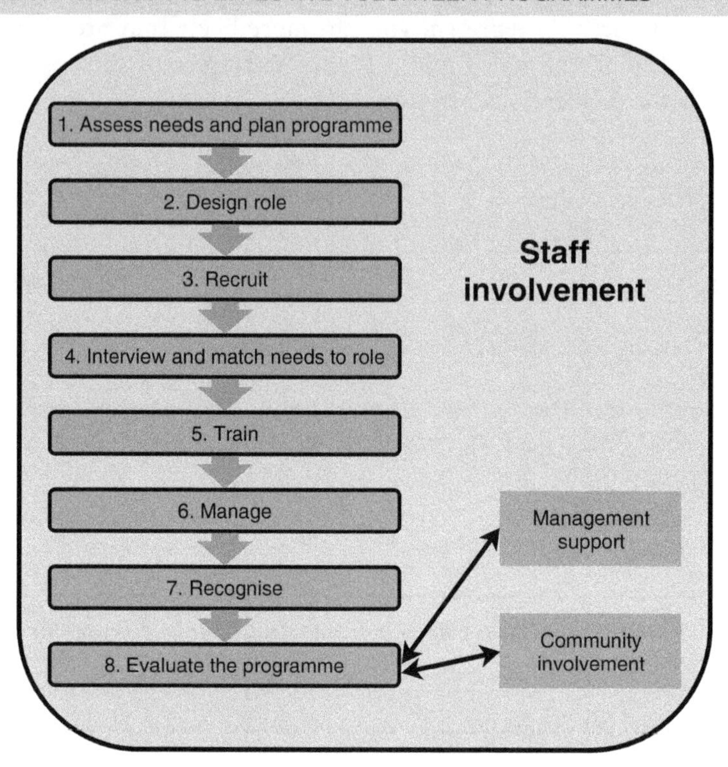

1. Assessing needs and planning the programme

The business case for volunteers

Establish which activities are appropriate volunteer roles and your rationale for using volunteers over paid staff. This may seem obvious, but the time and costs of managing volunteers need to be weighed against the results of their contribution. Possible rationales for using volunteers might include:

- creating networking opportunities to access new sources of income and support;
- ensuring fundraising reflects a community's interests so as to increase participation;
- providing key skills needed to meet income targets, when resources are not available to make a staff appointment;
- providing a more personal touch to communications to improve supporter recruitment and retention;
- increasing the cost-effectiveness of fundraising activities.

To help you determine your rationale for involving volunteers, you can also ask team members the following questions:

- What are some things you would like to see done that no one currently within our team has the skills to do?
- What are the parts of your job that you really like to do?
- What are the parts of your job that you dislike?
- What other activities or projects have you always wanted to undertake but never had time for?
- What are some areas which we have never had the opportunity to develop which would add value to what we do?

The answers to these questions can help to form the basis for developing volunteer work that really needs to be done, that can be integrated with the team's workload, and that will be appreciated and supported by the staff. As a consequence, the potential for staff–volunteer difficulties, such as staff forgetting to thank volunteers for their efforts or feeling threatened, will be greatly reduced.

Enlisting staff and senior management support

Positive relationships between staff and volunteers are also reliant on staff valuing volunteer input. It is worth understanding staff members' attitudes by finding out:

- what experience they have of working with volunteers;
- whether there are roles they feel volunteers should not be undertaking and why;
- whether staff could take up volunteer roles themselves with the right training;
- whether using volunteers raises concerns about the security and scope of staff members' own roles;
- whether there are other gaps in skills or resources where they would like to see volunteers contributing.

In order to ensure that what your colleagues would like volunteers to do is realistic, it is important to work with them and to manage expectations. Clearly establishing what volunteers can be asked to do – and what they cannot be asked to do – should save you from being bombarded with impossible requests for volunteers to undertake certain activities. To assist in this effort, you can employ a number of tools to show staff what will be possible, including:

- a list of the types of positions or functions that community fundraising volunteers have done in the past or are currently performing;
- a list of types of positions or functions that volunteers perform in other organisations in the community or in similar programmes across the country;
- a skills list and descriptions of available volunteers.

These lists may provide ideas to staff who do not have a clear understanding of the potential ways to involve volunteers within the team. They can serve to broaden the perspective and improve the creativity of staff in developing interesting and challenging volunteer positions.

As well as enlisting staff support, it is critical to get senior management on board if the right levels of resources are to be allocated to volunteers. Having a clear rationale that quantifies the benefit of using volunteers to further your organisation's mission will enable you to develop the business case for this investment.

Placing the programme in context

To plan your volunteering programme effectively, you need to have a defined volunteer strategy that ties in with your overall organisational and fundraising plans. This will be based on:

- your organisation's remit and scope, and how you operate;
- your plans for the future – for example:
  - are you likely to be constant in your need for volunteers?
  - are there any changes in the pipeline that might require more volunteers?
  - are you likely to be changing your remit and require fewer volunteers?
- your organisation's place in the market and the level of competition for volunteers.

Volunteering works best when you have a clear vision of how the role of volunteers contributes towards your organisation's mission. Involving volunteers in defining this vision will enrich their experience and make the vision more relevant.

A volunteer vision

The elements of a volunteer vision might include:[12]

- All volunteer roles will be linked to achieving our charity's overall vision and mission.
- Our staff and volunteers work together as equals.
- Staff are empowered to identify and create volunteer roles.
- Volunteers are supported with appropriate training, policies and guidance to enable them to clearly understand their roles and responsibilities, to perform effectively and to derive the maximum satisfaction from their role.
- All reasonable steps are taken to protect volunteers' health and safety and ensure they are covered by our insurance arrangements.
- Volunteers' legitimate expenses are reimbursed promptly.
- We learn from our volunteers' experiences with our charity.
- We recognise the value of volunteers in mission-critical activities.
- There is a central point for volunteer management in the organisation.
- All staff play a role in developing roles for and in supervising volunteers.

Volunteers and the law

When planning any volunteering programme, you must pay close attention to what can and cannot be done from a legal point of view.

The legal status of volunteers is a complex area. Volunteers do not have the same legal rights as employees (for example, protection from unfair dismissal, statutory sick pay, minimum wage, and four weeks' paid holiday a year) as they are not contracted to work for an organisation in the way an employee is. However, even where neither a charity nor a volunteer has explicitly stated they intend a contract to be created, the nature of the relationship with the volunteer may be judged to be contractual.

While tribunal cases are very rare, there have been instances where a contract was considered to exist. For example, in *Armitage v. Relate* (1994), a Relate volunteer was obliged to work a certain number of hours and pay the charity back for training if the hours were not fulfilled. The tribunal decided that a contract of employment had been created owing to the obligations agreed between the parties plus the expectation of a paid job at the end of the volunteering period. Furthermore, in *Migrant Advisory Service v. Chaudri* (1998), a volunteer was paid regular expenses even when on holiday or off sick, and despite living within walking distance of where she was volunteering (and therefore needing to incur very few expenses). The appeals tribunal saw this as a simple, clear-cut case of payments in return for work amounting to an employment contract.[13] If a volunteer is found to have employee status, the consequences can be serious, with a potential requirement of backdated pay and fines.

Volunteers must not be paid for any services they provide but they are entitled to be reimbursed for out-of-pocket expenses, such as travel expenses. Using expense claim forms, with copies of receipts, provides a clear record of what people have been paid. The only benefits volunteers should receive are:

- **training specific** to improving their ability to do the work they are carrying out;
- **subsistence** and/or **accommodation**, if this is reasonably required to complete their task.

Your charity has a duty of care relating to volunteers' health and safety, so you should take reasonable steps to reduce the risk of injury by providing information, training, safety clothing, supervision and so on. When working with volunteers, it makes sense to have an overall risk assessment for the volunteer programme and smaller risk assessments for individual roles. Although the law does not compel organisations to insure volunteers under employers' liability, it is advisable for your organisation to do so, otherwise it may be open to negligence claims. As public liability policies vary, it is important to check whether they cover your volunteers. Even if your charity doesn't employ staff, you may still decide to take out employers' liability cover for volunteers – see Charity Commission guidance on this. Check whether your insurance policy:

- includes volunteers;
- covers the activities the volunteers will be doing;
- states any age limits for volunteers.

Volunteers who have unsupervised contact with children (such as those involved in schools fundraising and youth programmes) or vulnerable adults need to be checked through the Disclosure and Barring Service (DBS). All volunteers should adhere to your organisation's safeguarding policies.

Consider providing safeguarding induction and training sessions to ensure that all volunteers are fully aware of your policies and procedures.

As with all data, volunteers' records should be processed in accordance with data protection legislation. Having a volunteer database can help you to categorise your volunteers according to their roles and interests, record their training and supervision, and ensure your communications are targeted and relevant.

Some volunteers may be involved in producing ideas and materials, so it is important to remember that copyright normally belongs to the person who created a piece of work. You may therefore need to ensure that your volunteers transfer copyright to your organisation or agree a licence whereby your organisation can use the work within agreed limits.

For more information on legal and best practice requirements, see section 5.0, 'Volunteers', of the Fundraising Regulator's Code of Fundraising Practice at www.fundraisingregulator.org.uk.

Budgets

Finally, when planning any volunteering programme, you will need to consider the financial viability of your proposed programme. Volunteers and volunteer groups come with costs, and these need to be evaluated against the returns generated by their time. You may have the costs of a designated volunteer manager as well as the costs of the time spent by fundraising staff in recruiting, training, supervising, supporting and recognising volunteers. Depending on volunteers' roles, you may also need to ensure part of the budget is allocated for clothing (including T-shirts, tabards, sweatshirts and safety wear), travel expenses, refreshments, additional computers and licences, insurance, etc.

2. Designing the role

Your volunteer recruitment objectives need to match your fundraising objectives. For example, if you know that you are about to run a large campaign requiring significant help with data entry, or if you are about to launch a series of local events for which you need marshals, or if you have an annual programme of street collections, you will need to design recruitment strategies to support these.

Start with SMART (specific, measurable, achievable, realistic and time-bound) objectives which quantify how many volunteers you will need by when, for what activity and at what cost. For example:

> 40 event marshals by October 2022 to complete training in time for our December 2022 challenge event at a cost of £1,000.

To clarify your purpose, you can also put your objectives in the following format:

> **Who:** 40 volunteer event marshals
>
> **What:** To complete health and safety, logistics and first-aid training
>
> **When:** By October 2022 – in time for our December 2022 challenge event
>
> **Why:** So we have adequate cover at all stages of the event
>
> So all volunteers are fully trained to deal with all eventualities
>
> **How much:** At a cost of £25 per volunteer (max budget allocated: £1,000).

Role descriptions

Volunteer role descriptions not only help with recruiting the right person but should also be motivational and prevent any misconceptions or misunderstandings about their remit. Role descriptions are very similar to job descriptions, but it is important not to use the term 'job'. Talk about 'expectations' and 'intentions' rather than 'requirements' and 'obligations'. You must also avoid or in any way imply that your charity is receiving services in exchange for money or offering the same legal rights as those offered to paid, contracted members of staff. Written agreements do not need to be signed by volunteers as they are purely indicative, not binding.

To develop volunteer positions that support the team's work and that volunteers want to do, volunteer role descriptions should be developed in consultation with staff and existing volunteers. Volunteer role descriptions generally include:

- **title;**
- **purpose:** what the role is intended to achieve;
- **results** (definable);
- **tasks:** the activities that need to be undertaken;
- **measures:** how you will tell whether the results have been achieved;
- **qualifications,** including experience and skills;
- **time frame:** hours, days of the week, times and duration of role;
- **location;**
- **supervision:** relationship with staff and other volunteers;
- **benefits,** such as what experience can be gained from the role;
- **training** required and provided.

As well as skills, consider the personal qualities you are seeking for the role, bearing in mind the personal qualities of existing staff and volunteer teams. For example, you might be looking for someone to support a member of staff who lacks confidence about the financial aspects of their job. You might look to recruit someone with good financial skills who previously held a position of authority and who has a non-confrontational manner.

When designing and promoting the roles, take account of the common barriers to volunteering and how you might overcome these barriers.

Perceived barriers

Consider the barriers potential volunteers might be concerned about and potential solutions, such as:

- **not having enough time:** offer flexible options and short chunks of time for volunteers who don't want to make a regular commitment;
- **not being valued:** share existing volunteers' experiences of being recognised;
- **not having the right skills:** offer training;
- **being pigeon-holed in a role:** show a diversity of volunteers in a range of roles;
- **being judged as not the right kind of person to volunteer:** emphasise openness to people from all backgrounds.

Practical barriers

Consider the actual barriers you may be creating and how to remove them, such as having:

- **an overly formal application process:** offer a simple application process with opportunities for taster days;
- **a bad recruitment process:** provide a seamless process, request only relevant information and give timely responses to enquiries.

Additionally, ensure you remove any practical barriers surrounding:

- **expenses:** make budget available to pay expenses;
- **caring responsibilities:** be flexible around when people can volunteer.

From the role description, you can start to identify who may have the skills you require (or whose skills may transfer to the role). It might be difficult to find some skill sets in a single individual, so tasks may have to be divided into multiple roles. Also ensure that new roles are offered to existing volunteers as this can be a way of maximising retention among those looking for new challenges.

3. Recruiting volunteers

There are many ways you can plan your recruitment campaign, but five recommended methods are:[14]

- warm body;
- targeted;
- concentric circles;
- ambient;
- event-based.

Understanding your existing volunteers

Understanding who your existing volunteers are will help you to determine how to recruit more of similar kinds of volunteer. Audit your existing volunteer base to gain a clear understanding of:

- where your volunteers live and how far they are prepared to travel;
- their ages and life stages;
- why they chose your charity;
- why they chose particular roles;
- other connections with your charity;
- how long they have been with you;
- how they were recruited;
- whether they volunteer for other organisations.

Warm body

Warm body recruitment is essentially a numbers game where you need many helpers but they don't need to have specific skills. The main aim of warm body recruitment is to spread the message widely. Ways of doing this include:

- distributing leaflets or posters house to house, at a local event or at your own events (such as an annual open day), taking the opportunity to speak to people face to face;
- using more traditional forms of advertising, such as low-cost or free adverts in your local newspaper or on the radio;
- contacting organisations and community groups with wide networks of people, such as universities or the Guides or Scouts;
- using the various local and national agencies that promote and broker volunteering, such as local volunteer centres, corporate volunteer programmes and youth programmes;
- using social media, such as putting out a call to action on Facebook or Twitter.

Targeted

A targeted volunteer recruitment campaign is required when you are seeking specific skills or types of people. You will need to consider:

- what needs to be done;
- who would be the right person to do it and where you can find them;
- what their needs are likely to be;
- how you can communicate with them and what you will say.

For example, if you require a volunteer to help with catering at an event, you might consider approaching students at a local catering college. Alternatively, if you need a video to support a mass participation campaign, you might target media students looking to gain experience in real (rather than academic) projects. Targeted recruitment can also be useful if you are looking to diversify your existing volunteer base.

By considering volunteers' needs when promoting roles, you can emphasise the benefits that your prospective volunteer is most likely to be seeking. For example, if you are recruiting young volunteers, they are likely to be seeking work experience, so be specific in your advertising about the skills they will gain and why your event or organisation is best able to deliver these. Remember also to address any of the real and perceived barriers to volunteering (as discussed above).

Concentric circles

This method encourages people already volunteering or connected to your organisation to approach their family and friends to volunteer. A peer-to-peer ask from your volunteers can be an effective form of recruitment, as they will be in the best position to determine what roles might be motivating to their family and friends. A downside of this method is that, because existing volunteers are likely to be surrounded by people who are very similar to themselves, it is unlikely to help with increasing diversity.

Ambient

Ambient recruitment targets existing groups or communities where there is a strong belief in or culture of volunteering. This might be a group such the local Soroptimist group or Rotary Club, where volunteering is part of the organisation's service mission. A common tactic is to identify influencers who are already sympathetic to your charity within these groups who can ask members to take on volunteering roles you have available.

Event-based

Event-based recruitment aims to attract people using events to engage the attention and short-term involvement of large numbers of volunteers. The key to this type of recruitment is that current volunteers should be a prominent part of the event. This type of recruitment can be organised around any activity that:

- is worthwhile doing so that the volunteers feel they have made a difference;
- can introduce volunteers to your cause, beneficiaries and how your organisation operates;
- involves large numbers of people in a variety of tasks or projects;
- doesn't require any substantial training or preparation to do;
- is fun and exciting and allows people to work with others;
- is photogenic and, as such, can potentially attract publicity.

Examples include clean-ups (of a beach, for instance), community education (such as a corporate fair), a 'something-a-thon' fundraiser, or any other activity which meets these requirements.

Ask existing volunteers who are friendly and outgoing to lead the activity and to encourage the new volunteers to re-engage with your organisation after the event has ended. Ask them to keep a note of those people they have asked to volunteer and/or those they think have the potential to become volunteers. Hold a debriefing following the event to discuss who might be receptive to further involvement, what types of volunteer work they have shown an interest in and the best way to encourage them further into your organisation. The most effective approach is to get the same volunteers (rather than someone they don't know) to re-contact them.

4. Interviewing volunteers and matching their interests to the right role

There is no one-size-fits-all approach to interviewing volunteers. How you should interview, including whether it is in the form of a brief chat or something more formal, will depend on the nature of the role and whether you are recruiting individuals or groups of people.

In the first instance, it might be worth inviting the prospective volunteer to one of the community fundraising activities one of your groups is organising. This will allow them the chance to meet other volunteers and get a feel for what is involved. (Ensure that you choose an established, well-organised group or you may put them off.) Then, if they feel comfortable with proceeding, suggest that you meet to discuss what's involved in more detail.

In the majority of situations, a fairly basic interview with prospective volunteers is likely to be sufficient for your team's needs. Volunteers themselves may play a valuable role in the interview process, as they can share their own experiences of volunteering for your charity and may be able to relate to common concerns that prospective volunteers might have.

Where to interview

Where the interviewer will conduct the interview will vary depending on your organisation's set-up and how formal the interview should be. In any case, the main aim should be to find a site that allows volunteers to feel a sense of privacy and enables them to discuss their abilities and concerns openly. If it is not possible to conduct the interview in person, a video call may suffice, but this option is not ideal if the role requires a significant time commitment, if you need volunteer skills that are out of the ordinary or if the position is a sensitive one (in terms of the nature of the work or the relationship with your beneficiaries).

Matching interests

During the interview or chat, the interviewer should aim to match the interests, motivations and experience of the potential volunteer with the available roles (see 'Why do people volunteer?' on page 258). The interviewer should try to see whether there is a natural fit between the potential volunteer and your organisation, its style of operating and its mission (in terms of how likely the volunteer is to work well with your beneficiaries, other volunteers and staff). They should also aim to detect any unexpected talents in the volunteer and use that information to match them with an appropriate role. Finally, the interviewer should let the volunteer know what will be expected of them and explain why the role is important to the interests of your organisation and its beneficiaries.

You can offer a trial period to make it easier to encourage volunteers to try out roles. This will also make it easier to identify any mismatches or other problems early and to correct them quickly.

Concluding the interview

If the interview concludes with an agreement to go ahead, the interviewer will need to get the volunteer's permission to conduct any necessary references or background checks, including DBS checks if appropriate (in England and Wales). The interviewer should also explain the process for what will happen next, the timeframe and what your charity needs the volunteer to do during this process.

Once the interviewing and matching process has been satisfactorily concluded, you may wish to enter into an agreement with the volunteer. A volunteer agreement is not a formal legal document but is the acceptance by both your organisation and the volunteer of what they are mutually agreeing to. The agreement might specify the tasks that the volunteer will perform, how long they are agreeing to volunteer for, and the support that your organisation agrees to provide to the volunteer, but all of this should be stated in indicative terms rather than as binding commitments. The purpose of the volunteer agreement is to clarify the volunteer's role and relationship with your organisation; it is not intended to convey a sense of legal responsibility and obligation and this should be made clear both in writing and directly to the prospective volunteer.

On some occasions, you may find that the person is not suitable for your organisation. In these instances, be as clear as you can about why they are not a match and refer them to another organisation or onto a volunteer brokering agency. It is preferable to identify and deal with issues at this early stage, but they may not become clear until after a volunteer has started in the role. (For advice on how to deal with suitability problems after a volunteer has started, see 'What to do when relationships break down' on page 281.)

5. Training volunteers

Welcome and orientation

To make volunteers feel welcome, you need to ensure you have the right organisational climate. A positive climate will be one where volunteers feel:

- **accepted:** connected to the overall purpose of their role, and the department and team in which they will be working;

- **appreciated** for their unique contribution to the purpose of your organisation and fundraising programme.

When volunteers start their role at your organisation, you should assign them a dedicated contact person or supervisor who can set goals, explain tasks and provide ongoing support. You should have a clear induction programme with introductions to colleagues (staff and other volunteers) and other teams the volunteer may need to communicate with, and an overview of your organisation's work. If your projects are local to the volunteer, provide them with opportunities to see the effects of the work they will be doing and how this contributes to your charity's mission.

Training

To decide what training volunteers may require you need to answer three questions:

1. What information do they need to successfully perform the role?
2. What skills do they need to successfully perform the role?
3. What attitudes or approaches do they need to successfully perform the role?

You can provide this information, develop these skills and engender these attitudes via formal training sessions or on-the-job training.

You will also need to provide training on how to use all the systems and processes they will be part of, as well as copies and explanations of relevant policies and procedures.

6. Managing volunteers

To complete a task effectively, volunteers should have clear lines of authority, but they also need to have a sense of autonomy. They should feel in control, unhindered by overly bureaucratic processes and in possession of the skills and tools to do the task. They should also feel that they have the full backing of the organisation. The overarching goal here is to offer a guiding hand, rather than aiming to control. This is especially the case for on-behalf-of group events, where volunteers are taking the lead.

Becoming involved at the planning stage is the best way of striking this balance. The level of involvement required will be quite different depending on the complexity of the event. For example, more can go wrong at a mass participation event than at a quiz night, so you would be correspondingly more or less involved. You should also participate more during post-activity evaluations, so that you can express appreciation to the volunteers involved and also build on what was learnt during the activity to allow the next one to be even more successful.

Regular reviews

You should have frequent reviews with your volunteers so that you can check whether:

- the role is meeting their expectations and interests;
- they feel the training is adequate;
- the hours still fit around their other commitments;
- they feel respected by the team;
- they are seeking further development opportunities.

Getting to know your volunteers well might reveal other skills that could make an even more valuable contribution to your organisation. Build feelings of belonging as early as possible. Ways of doing this include mentoring, buddying new volunteers with experienced volunteers, opportunities to make contact with other volunteers, and relevant symbols of belonging (badges, business cards, clothing, etc.).

Policies and procedures

Volunteers require consistent support to feel inspired and valued. Formal policies and procedures will be needed to govern your relationship with them. These documents should be developed and communicated in such a way that they do not crush volunteers' enthusiasm, creativity or sense of ownership of their role. A comprehensive volunteer policy will cover:

- recruitment, including equality and diversity;
- induction and training;
- expenses;
- supervision and support;
- health and safety;
- confidentiality and data protection;
- problem solving and complaints procedures.

7. Recognising volunteers

It is vital to thank volunteers and regularly show your appreciation. There are many ways of doing this, such as celebrating anniversaries of service. For some people volunteering is a recreational activity, so help to make the experience more social with volunteer and staff get-togethers.

Ensure volunteers know the impact of their efforts – for instance how:

- their data entry enabled a campaign to raise significant sums;
- much the event they sold tickets for raised;
- much was generated from the raffle prizes they sourced;
- re-organising the electronic diaries saved time and improved efficiencies;
- working with staff has helped them understand their role and improved their job satisfaction.

The critically important point is to demonstrate the difference they are making for your beneficiaries and mission.

Try to involve volunteers in the decisions that affect them and invite them to relevant meetings. If you can, try to make sure that you recognise volunteers on a daily basis (via text messages, face-to-face thanking at the end of the day, feeding back on tasks, asking for opinions, etc.) as well as at key milestones (using Facebook live at an event to name and thank event volunteers, citing people's contribution in articles in newsletters, etc.). Consider saying thank you in more tangible ways too, such as by giving out certificates to recognise attainment, providing references, or nominating for local or national awards.

Help make communication between volunteers easy by creating their own Facebook page or WhatsApp group. This will help them to build belonging, foster ideas, share knowledge and provide feedback.

Recognition takes different forms for different people, depending on their motivations and personalities. Those who are achievement orientated might want a more challenging role, whereas those motivated by affiliation to the cause and colleagues might seek recognition by the organisation in the presence of peers. All recognition should therefore be appropriate to the individual and their particular achievements.

While volunteers will come and go, it is always worth considering how you might keep them connected to your organisation. For example:

- for those who give your organisation short chunks of time, ask for more short chunks of time;
- gain feedback on volunteers' experience and ways your organisation could work better;

- encourage volunteers to follow your social media pages;
- provide email updates on your work and other volunteering roles;
- send volunteers invites to social functions;
- encourage existing volunteers to stay in touch with past volunteers.

8. Monitoring and evaluating your programme

Whatever activities your volunteers are undertaking, you should evaluate the success of your programme to continually find ways of improving your volunteers' experience. This includes monitoring and evaluating:

- response rates on different recruitment methods with different audiences;
- the types of respondent and skills you are able to attract;
- drop-out rates and feedback on why people leave;
- number of returners;
- whether your role descriptions represent the reality of the tasks and responsibilities that volunteers will undertake;
- volunteers' motivations, experiences and perceptions of their role;
- satisfaction levels in relation to support, communication and sense of team;
- your organisation's performance and behaviour towards volunteers;
- whether volunteers are meeting the targets you are setting (be that by income or activity);
- whether volunteers are happy with their tasks and whether there are other roles they might prefer;
- how well volunteers recruit other volunteers;
- how many volunteers take on new roles or more responsibilities;
- volunteers' attitudes to staff;
- volunteers' perceptions about the quality of feedback they receive on their contribution and how valued they feel;
- volunteers' goals and the setting of new goals;
- reimbursement of volunteers' expenses.

Face-to-face discussions are an effective means of monitoring many of these points. Set meetings and reminders, such as trigger dates in your volunteer database, to make sure you have these conversations.

What to do when relationships break down

While a recruitment process that matches motivation to roles and a retention programme that is based on mutual respect, common goals, communication and recognition will both help to foster strong relationships, sometimes things do go wrong and a volunteer's behaviour or attitudes can start to be perceived as challenging. This is usually driven by issues relating to:

- **Capability:** a volunteer's ability to undertake the role. This may be addressed by offering the volunteer additional training or identifying a different role for them.
- **Performance:** how well a volunteer is performing their role. This may be linked to capability but also to low confidence, a mismatch between the volunteer's and the organisation's understandings of what is expected of the volunteer, difficult relationships with staff or other volunteers, and how motivated the individual feels about the role.
- **Conduct:** the volunteer's behaviour when taking part in volunteering. This may be rooted in whether the role is meeting the volunteer's expectations, their understanding of boundaries, their feelings about appropriate recognition, their response to wider decisions made by the organisation, or relationships with colleagues.

You need to have a process in place to ensure that volunteers are treated fairly. Complaints must be dealt with openly and quickly, and all parties should be treated with respect. Many issues can be dealt with informally, with regular meetings to discuss issues raised by or about a volunteer. What may initially seem to be a serious issue could in fact be a need for more information or training. A volunteer may not realise that something they are doing is a cause for concern. When any concerns are raised, meet with the volunteer as soon as possible to discuss the facts, and agree the changes expected, the timescales for actions and the follow-up dates. Ensure that you keep written records of these details.

If problems persist, you might want to consider other options, such as:

- reassigning a volunteer to a role that better suits their motivations, sustains their enthusiasm and retains their skills;

- providing more training, bearing in mind that some volunteers may take longer to learn new skills or process information;
- revitalising their energies, perhaps by offering a break if they are overly committed, suffering from burnout or dealing with difficult personal circumstances;
- if appropriate, referring them to another organisation where their skills and interests might prove a better match;
- jointly deciding on releasing them from their role, but making the exit positive to ensure they leave feeling appreciated.

There may be times, such as when there has been a case of gross misconduct or there is an ongoing lack of change in performance, when dismissal becomes the only option. You must have a clear volunteer disciplinary and grievance policy in place, and relevant members of senior management should be involved in any dismissal proceedings. Asking volunteers to leave is rare and the process has to be fair. You will need to be mindful of reputational risk and of the support that other volunteers and staff may need during such circumstances. It may be advisable to have an exit interview so that lessons may be learned.

Developing and managing community fundraising volunteer groups

Fundraising groups provide an infrastructure that can be essential to delivering a wide range of community fundraising initiatives, from centrally organised events to mass participation campaigns, collections and corporate partnerships.

What are volunteer groups?

The status of a volunteer group is determined by whether it is an official part of a charity or a separate, legally disconnected group. The distinction between the different types of group has implications for how they are managed and where responsibilities lie, especially if anything goes wrong at an activity or event.

Your charity's (on-behalf-of) groups

An on-behalf-of volunteer group is a subgroup of your organisation, with no separate legal identity, where volunteers fundraise on behalf of your charity.

National and regional charities tend to have local on-behalf-of groups to give them a presence at a community level. Other charities set up on-behalf-of groups to spearhead a time-bounded project with a target amount to be raised, such as a capital appeal. A group of this sort would have its own committee with a nominated chairperson. Having a representative on that committee from the charity board or staff helps to keep things on track and ensure that the right hand knows what the left hand is doing.

External (in-aid-of) volunteer groups

An in-aid-of volunteer group is a separate organisation in its own right, where the group fundraises in aid of a charity (or charities). Like individual in-aid-of volunteers, these groups have no authority from the organisations they are fundraising for and they act on their own initiative. Charities tend not to encourage new in-aid-of groups, although groups were often set up this way in the past and may still continue to fundraise for the charity and require guidance.

Given in-aid-of groups act independently, issues can arise. For instance, a group might run an activity that brings a charity's name into disrepute (such as holding a white-collar charity boxing match for a brain injury charity). Although there are legal steps that can be taken to get a group to cease what they are doing, you may be able to prevent problems from arising by keeping in regular contact with any in-aid-of groups you are aware of. Stay in the loop regarding their fundraising plans, ensure that they are fully aware of your organisation's values and provide guidance on appropriate fundraising activities and practice (for details, see 'Critical things your DIY fundraisers need to know' on page 225). You might also encourage in-aid-of groups to disband and reform as on-behalf-of groups.

Why set up on-behalf-of volunteer groups?

While the rise of social media and online giving have changed the face of community fundraising, allowing for more independent, self-determined fundraising, there are still a number of strategic benefits to having on-behalf-of fundraising groups:

- Fundraising and friends groups can provide regular sources of income, particularly as their activities become more established over time. In 2018, groups and committees run by national charities raised an average of £14,000 per group, and larger charities may have dozens or hundreds of such groups.[15] Macmillan's volunteer groups and committees, for example, generated £8 million between them in 2016.[16]

- Effective, established groups can operate with little financial input relative to their return – one benchmarking study has shown that groups have a high average return on investment.[17]

- Group members can lever their contacts to recruit fundraising participants and act as advocates across the fundraising mix by identifying potential corporate partners, grant-making charities, major donors and legacy pledgers.

- A network of groups can provide the capacity to do bigger, better or different events or campaigns.

- Groups provide a local infrastructure to support cash collections, corporate partnerships and charity shop stock collections. They can also promote centrally coordinated campaigns and signpost potential beneficiaries to services.

- To have legitimacy, charities need to engage with their communities. Friends groups, which are often integrated within the local community, can act as ambassadors that are able to shape local perceptions of your organisation.

- For national charities without local services, groups provide a visible local presence.

- Group members will accumulate fundraising knowledge and relationships with the community, and they can pass this information down to newer members of the group to sustain skills and knowledge.

Do you need to set up new groups?

Setting up on-behalf-of groups or committees of volunteers can be an effective way of fundraising, if they are managed well. If they are not, they can be a serious drain on resources. It is therefore important to choose the right group structure for your organisation and the right group members.

Consider your organisation's needs. Do you need a new group or could you expand an existing group's size, remit or geographical scope? What is your reason for wanting to set up or expand a group? Would it be to reach new audiences, to provide new skills or fresh ideas, or to access new locations? What would the group's purposes be? Potential purposes include:

- to access support in a new region or town;

- to facilitate a wider range of local fundraising activities;

- to raise funds for a time-bound project, such as a capital appeal;

- to provide the infrastructure for other income sources, such as corporate fundraising;
- to facilitate the community engagement needed to develop a new local project or service;
- to reach a new demographic.

Consider the characteristics of the geographical area in question and how these might influence the traction of a new group. For example, do you have awareness or service users in the area? How might local facilities, demographics, a sense of community and levels of competition have an impact on a group's activities?

Developing a group

New groups can take many months to develop. When setting up a new group, if you don't have any existing volunteers with the right skills, capacity and enthusiasm, you will need to start by identifying active leadership. The chairperson of your new group has such a pivotal role in a group's success (as informed by the specific remit of the group) and requires qualities such as:

- passion for the cause;
- an ability to make the necessary time commitment;
- willingness to use their own home or office for initial recruitment meetings or social gatherings;
- an extensive network of contacts that they are happy to approach;
- an ability to work on their own initiative;
- a sociable, confident, likeable manner and good communication skills.

As we have seen throughout this chapter, it is important to ensure that a volunteer's motivations match the requirements of the role they will be carrying out. As such, you will need to understand what experience any potential chairperson is seeking. Finding the right person will involve networking among your existing volunteers, contacts and other community influencers. You can also talk to supporters you meet at your events and within the wider fundraising mix (corporate supporters, major donors, event participants, DIY fundraisers, etc.).

Harry Brown's model for developing groups (see figure 9.2) moves from identifying potential leaders and members to setting very clear purposes and aims. The next step is to organise an initial event, where early group members enlist the support of friends. Some of these friends may then go on to become group members who create and promote more events themselves.

FIGURE 9.2 COMMITTEE RECRUITMENT[18]

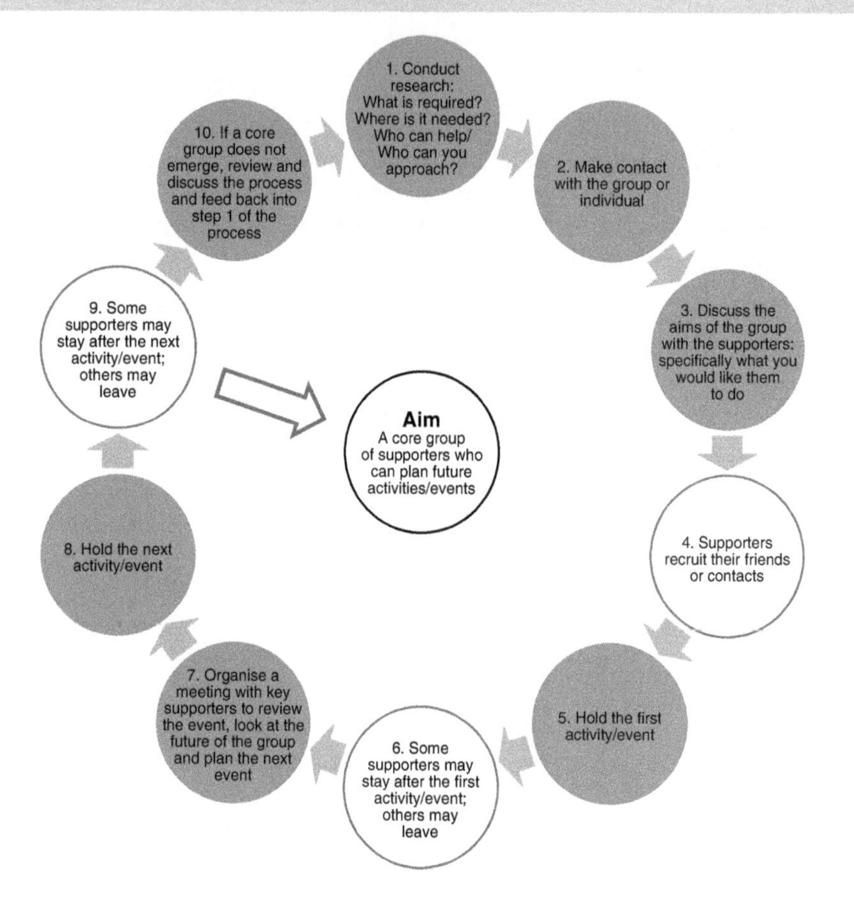

On-behalf-of volunteer group members need to be supported in the ways already outlined in this chapter. To help them achieve as much success as possible, provide them with some basic fundraising training on how to:

- organise events;
- set budgets;
- present your case for support;
- develop basic materials;

- work with suppliers;
- adhere to relevant regulation and fundraising codes of practice.

Encourage groups to meet with each other and share best practice. You also need to ensure that you set clear boundaries with them, such as which organisations they can approach, types of income and projects they should focus their fundraising on, your brand guidelines, requirements for working with third parties, what activities insurance does or does not cover, responsibilities for promoting activities, etc. Make sure you keep them fully informed of key organisational developments and other campaigns and partnerships you are running to ensure there is synergy between all your fundraising messages and activities.

You should help each group to develop a plan for its activities, including helping it to set targets and schedules. You will need to allocate a portion of your departmental budget to support these groups, and individual groups may also require their own budgets in order to fulfil their remits.

Conclusion

Volunteers are vital to community fundraising and effectively harnessing their time, talent and enthusiasm can enable you to raise more funds more profitably. However, volunteers are not without costs, some of which are often hidden – such as staff management time. Careful thought therefore needs to go into the planning and resourcing of volunteer management. Fully understanding volunteer motivations and ensuring that the roles and experiences you offer match what volunteers want to do is critical to successful volunteer relationships.

Notes

1 *Community Life Survey 2017–2018: Statistical bulletin* [PDF], Department for Digital, Culture, Media and Sport, 2018, www.gov.uk/government/statistics/community-life-survey-2017-18, p. 15, accessed 5 March 2019.

2 'UK Civil Society Almanac 2018: Volunteering activities' [web page], NCVO, 2019, https://data.ncvo.org.uk/a/almanac18/volunteer-profiles-2015-16, 2018, accessed 5 March 2019.

3 Judy Esmond and Patrick Dunlop, *Developing the Volunteer Motivation Inventory to Assess the Underlying Motivational Drives of Volunteers in Western Australia*, Perth, CLAN WA, 2004, pp. 7–8.

4 Joe Saxton, Tim Harrison and Mhairi Guild, *The New Alchemy: How volunteering turns donations of time and talent into human gold* [PDF], nfpSynergy, 2015, https://nfpsynergy.net/free-report/new-alchemy-how-volunteering-turns-donations-time-and-talent-human-gold-part-1, p. 54, accessed 5 March 2019.

5 Steve McCurley and Rick Lynch, *Keeping Volunteers*, London, DSC, 2007, pp. 8–10.

6 *Ibid.*, pp. 3–6; and Michael Locke, Angela Ellis and Justin Davis Smith, 'Hold On to What You've Got: The volunteer retention literature', *Voluntary Action*, vol. 5, no. 3, 2003, pp. 81–99.

7 Rob Jackson, 'Recruitment, Retention and Development of Volunteers', in *Community Fundraising: The effective use of volunteer networks*, edited by Harry Brown, London, DSC, 2002, pp. 107–43 at p. 119.

8 Michael Locke, Angela Ellis and Justin Davis Smith, 'Hold On to What You've Got: The volunteer retention literature', *Voluntary Action*, vol. 5, no. 3, 2003, pp. 81–99.

9 Linda Ann Brandt, *Girl Scout Volunteer Leader Retention: An issue of self-role merger*, South Dakota State University, 1998; cited in Donald R. Self, Walter W. Wymer and Teri Kline Henley, *Marketing Communications for Local Nonprofit Organisations: Targets and tools*, Abingdon, Routledge, 2013, p. 100.

10 The Code of Fundraising Practice was fully revised by the Fundraising Regulator in 2019. See section 5, 'Volunteers', and the glossary, which defines the two types of volunteer, at www.fundraisingregulator.org.uk.

11 Adapted from Steve McCurley, Rick Lynch and Rob Jackson, *The Complete Volunteer Management Handbook*, London, DSC, 2012, p. 32.

12 Based on the concept of creating a vision of how volunteers will contribute to the achievement on an organisation's mission in Rob Jackson, Mike Locke, Dr Eddy Hogg and Rick Lynch, *The Complete Volunteer Management Handbook*, London, DSC, manuscript in preparation, 2019.

13 Mark Restall, *Volunteers and the Law*, London, Volunteering England, 2005, pp. 8–9.

14 Rob Jackson, Mike Locke, Eddy Hogg and Rick Lynch, *The Complete Volunteer Management Handbook*, London, DSC, manuscript in preparation, 2019.

15 'Community fundraising benchmarking 2018' [web page], THINK Consulting, 2018, www.thinkcs.org/community-fundraising-benchmarking-2018, accessed 5 March 2019.

16 'Your awesome achievements in a nutshell' [web page], Macmillan, 2017, www.macmillan.org.uk/get-involved/volunteering/volunteer-news/2017/summer/mac-in-a-nutshell.html, accessed 5 March 2019.

17 Claire Daniels and Sam Rider, 'Community Fundraising Snapshot', manuscript in preparation, 2017.

18 Adapted from Harry Brown, 'Developing fundraising groups/networks', in *Community Fundraising: The effective use of volunteer networks*, edited by Harry Brown, London, DSC, 2002, pp. 144–62 at p. 154.

CHAPTER TEN

Engaging and supporting community groups

Lianne Howard-Dace

Introduction

Community groups, clubs and associations are means through which a charity can extend its fundraising networks. These groups are hugely diverse entities and can range from small Girlguiding or Scout groups to international membership organisations. In addition to opening up access to new audiences through their networks, community groups have organisational skills, experience and resources that can be particularly suited to fundraising. Many groups identify themselves as being part of civil society with the potential to engage with charities around shared values. Such visible support of your charity can help to add legitimacy to your organisation's place in the community.

Community groups can contribute in many ways. For example, they can run their own ad hoc fundraising events, adopt your charity for a year, or support your in-house fundraising by providing volunteers, teams of participants, equipment, venues and promotional opportunities. Even when community groups are not actively fundraising for you, having a good relationship with them can enable you to access members' local knowledge and contacts.

With these benefits come challenges, including competition for support and the cost of building relationships and servicing these groups, where the costs sometimes outweigh the returns. As many groups face their own funding challenges, identifying points of mutual benefit beyond the straightforward philanthropic proposition of helping a charity has become increasingly important in securing their support. This chapter provides an overview of some of the main community groups and how to build and manage relationships with them.

Types of community group

The broad spectrum of community bodies that a charity might engage in fundraising can be categorised as follows:

- **sporting groups**, such as teams and classes covering everything from rugby and running to dance and rambling and professional and semi-professional sporting teams;
- **business and civil society groups**, such as Inner Wheel, Lions, Freemasons, Rotaract, Rotary, Round Table, WI (Women's Institute), village and neighbourhood groups, and social clubs;
- **hobby and activity groups**, including amateur dramatics, choral societies, book clubs, owners' clubs, gardening clubs, supper clubs and slimming clubs;
- **youth-related groups**, such as university RAG (Raising and Giving) groups, Girlguiding, the Scout Association and Young Farmers;
- **service groups**, including the police, the fire brigade and the Army Reserve;
- **places of worship**, for instance churches, mosques and synagogues, and related organisations such as parochial church councils;
- **public bodies**, such as schools, universities, GP surgeries, hospitals, councils and mayoralties;
- **commercial bodies**, including gyms, pubs and small businesses (see chapter 12).

As populations have become more transient, as lifestyles have become more diverse and as society has come to occupy new kinds of spaces, more virtual groups have formed around people's shared interests. However, as social engagement still acts as a driver, real-life (as opposed to online) events remain part of these groups' mainstay. For example, an online crafting community might host quarterly meet-ups in local areas.

Evaluating and prioritising which groups to approach

Identifying the most appropriate groups to engage will be determined by the synergy between a group's needs and the nature of your charity. This will require a nuanced approach, based on research which considers how your charity, cause or activity can or might support the group in any of the following ways:

- **Help to deliver the group's mission:** For example, if a gardening club is concerned with developing knowledge and skills, could these be showcased by it running open garden events? Could your fundraising activities help a teacher to deliver elements of the curriculum? Would completing a challenge event help to build youth club members' confidence?

- **Fit the interests of members:** For example, could your sporting events provide new fitness activities for gym or slimming club members?

- **Help a group to secure more members or raise its profile:** For instance, Rotary club volunteers could help you with a street collection, providing them with an opportunity to talk to people about their own organisation.

- **Provide social opportunities:** Some groups might be looking for enjoyable social activities, which could be provided by participation in your events or by making fundraising part of their own events.

- **Help a group with its funding needs:** In return for your support and ideas, some groups might be happy to split funds they raise between your charity and their organisation.

- **Cooperate in relation to a geographical interest:** Does your work cover the same locations? Or, if yours is a national charity, could you partner with national groups?

- **Help to develop a group's knowledge and expertise:** For example, you could help a group to run their events more effectively.

- **Cooperate with members' existing aims:** Is your cause one of concern to group members? Is there a crossover between their members and your supporters?

Consider also whether you have any existing contacts with groups. Staff or trustees may have a personal contact with a group, or you may know a community influencer (for example, a councillor, bishop, head-teacher or other community group leader) who could make an introduction for you. You may have some very engaged supporters who can give you access to a group to which they belong. The value of these supporters can be considerable as, although they themselves may not be able to make a large gift, the collective value of the network they can access may be on a par with a major gift. The Charities Aid Foundation estimates that just 9% of the UK public carry out 66% of charitable activity, including donating, raising money and other types of volunteering.[1] So, the fact that someone is already engaged in a community group could be one of the strongest indicators that they are likely to support other causes.

After considering these possibilities, you can then start to assess which organisations might have the greatest synergy with your organisation and fundraising activities. Putting this into a table format can be useful, as shown in table 10.1.

TABLE 10.1 PRIORITISING ORGANISATIONS TO CONTACT

Group	Cause link?	Geographical link?	Charity supporters are members?	Charity provides social activity?	Warm contact?	Group skills can be developed?	Shared fundraising opportunities?	Provides awareness for group recruitment?	Priority rating
WI	No	Yes	Yes	Yes	No	Yes	No	No	Medium
Church of England	No	Yes	No	No	Yes	No	Yes	No	Low
Girlguiding	Yes	Yes	Yes	Yes	Yes	Yes	No	No	High
Ramblers	No	No	No	No	Yes	Yes	No	Yes	Low

Criteria: 0–3 Yeses: Low; 4–5 Yeses: Medium; 6–8 Yeses: High.

If you do not have a contact who can introduce you to the organisation you want to target, get to grips with its structure. Does it have a chairperson you can start building a relationship with or someone whose role links in with the activities you might want to promote to the organisation? To start a conversation with your chosen person, invite them to events you are running, or introduce them to your projects and link with them on social media. Keep abreast of the trends and issues affecting relevant community groups, and take advantage of initiatives which you could piggyback on to make a timely approach. For example, if the WI is running a campaign on loneliness, your cause might fit its agenda in relation to this specific theme. Alternatively, you might hear about a new addition to the National Curriculum that crosses over with your work, creating an opportunity to re-engage schools in your database.

If yours is a national charity, you might engage with more structured community groups at a national or regional level to develop a partnership. However, it is worth noting that the predominantly voluntary nature of the groups in a national network means that each will have a degree of autonomy and may engage with local charity initiatives differently.

Engaging and supporting community groups

Most community groups are run entirely by volunteers and, even when there are paid staff, they are likely to be very time poor. While you may have identified shared values that will motivate people to work with you, it is important to make supporting your charity as easy as possible. Which benefits or useful contacts can you offer the busy teacher, vicar or Rotary chair to help them meet their needs? What can you bring to the party to help inspire and mobilise the members of their group? Possibilities include a speaker, a ready-made group session, a pack of resources that helps a teacher to deliver the curriculum, or an event that challenges a sports group.

A starting point for developing a relationship is often giving a talk to members. This can happen in various ways. In some cases, a group that is already running a fundraising event for your charity, such as a coffee morning, may invite you to introduce your cause before the activity begins. In other cases, a fundraising activity may arise as a result of a talk you give to a community group (for instance, after you deliver a talk to your local Brownies group, the children may be inspired to raise money for your charity).

As not all talks will result in fundraising, however, it can be worthwhile to ask volunteers, such as members of your own groups, to do presentations for you. Some charities train people who have previously raised money for them to become their community ambassadors or champions and to make presentations to community groups on their behalf. If you have a contact who can introduce you to a particular group, meet with them first to learn about the group's current priorities and challenges before developing your ask. If you have engaged one or two groups within an organisation or network, consider how you might leverage that support by asking for an endorsement, testimonial or referral that will allow you to engage with similar groups and therefore widen your reach.

Checklist for planning fundraising with groups

- Which groups does my organisation have the greatest synergy with?
- What existing contacts and connections do we have?
- What more do I need to find out about their needs and interests?
- Who am I going to ask?
- How am I going to reach out to them?
- How am I going to record their engagement?
- What am I going to ask them to do?
- How will I support them?
- What is the stewardship journey? (That is, how will I engage with the members of the group throughout their fundraising activities? What follow-up communications will I have with them and what will I ask them to do next?)
- How will I thank them and recognise their support?

Whether you can maximise income from these groups will depend on whether your fundraising meets the needs and motivations you have identified in your research. To make the most of your role as a facilitator, share your professional expertise to help the groups raise the most funds possible.

Creating bespoke resources for every individual group is not the best use of your team's time. Instead, consider the common needs of different types of group (schools, religious groups, youth groups, Rotary clubs, ramblers, etc.) and develop appropriate materials that they can customise. Accumulate a pool of resources that includes poster templates, how-to guides and FAQs, rather than starting with a blank sheet of paper for each new group you engage (for more details, see 'Supporting DIY fundraisers' activities' on page 235). This will save a lot of time. You might also sometimes run mass participation events that have enough generic appeal to offer to a cross-section of different groups.

Some of the groups that support you may be experienced in fundraising and may already run their own activities that require little input from you. However, to ensure these groups represent your brand consistently, you may wish to give them guidance on how to present your organisation. Ensure you regularly check in with their progress and maintain stewardship by, for example:

- seeking feedback to better understand how you can improve your support of the group;
- updating and sharing with the group the impact their fundraising efforts have on your mission and beneficiaries;
- finding out how the group would like to be thanked and acknowledged publicly.

See chapter 7 for more guidance on stewarding DIY fundraisers.

Approaching different types of community group

While there are a multitude of types of group and informal grassroots organisations, the following sections focus on the main groups engaged in community fundraising programmes and the differences between them that might affect how you approach them.

Membership organisations and activity groups

Membership organisations and activity groups are what might be referred to more colloquially as 'clubs'. There is almost certainly a social element to their activities and they are often formally structured, are part of a bigger organisation, or, particularly in the case of sports groups, have a paid person leading the group. Of the types of group listed on page 290, sporting groups, business and civil society groups, and hobby and activity groups all fall into this category.

These groups are likely to have a focused set of activities and/or a strong governing constitution. They are highly likely to be registered charities in their own right. To tailor your initial approach, gain some useful insights into your chosen group by researching its vision, mission and history and ascertaining its membership numbers.

Determining the best way of maximising your income from these groups will depend on what activities they carry out in aid of your charity and whether they are taking part in your initiatives or devising their own fundraising activities. Framing your role as a facilitator will help you to find ways to share your professional expertise so as to help them raise the highest amount of money possible. Methods for doing so might include offering a pre-developed resource, providing bespoke advice or creating space for sharing learning between your supporters.

Schools and youth groups

Fundraising can be a fun and engaging way for young people to investigate issues and be empowered to feel they can make a difference in the world. While schools will have much clearer targets and objectives to reach than the more informal goals commonly found in a youth group, there is much crossover in devising initiatives and resources for both.

Whether state run or private, primary or secondary, schools have long provided valuable fundraising opportunities for charities. In a survey of 200 secondary schools published in 2013, 70% of teachers stated that their schools undertook fundraising for charities and 78% thought they should do more to teach children about the role of charities.[2]

Schools often organise their fundraising as school-wide initiatives but they also place value on children being involved in deciding which charity to support. Teachers see fundraising as motivating to students, teaching social and team skills which can raise a child's self-esteem and attainment.[3] However, it is important to acknowledge that schools are facing their own funding challenges. In the case of primary schools, over half rely on fundraising to support their activities,[4] and some state schools have started to hire their own professional fundraisers. Some evidence suggests that, while the average value of charitable giving by schools has been dropping (from an average school donation of £3,541 in 2012/13 to £3,030 in 2013/14 and £2,896 in 2014/15),[5] young people are still raising millions of pounds for charities, and schools 'lie at the heart of the bond between children and charities'.[6]

While most school fundraising activities are traditional events such as non-uniform days and bake sales, schools also value class-based activities using good-quality educational materials that allow students to take the initiative and forge links with the community.[7] Depending on your cause, fundraising can be linked to a wide range of subjects from geography to citizenship and PSHE (personal, social, health and economic) education, and you can send teachers both printed packs and materials to download.

Youth groups constitute many forms, both local and national. Some groups – such as the Scout Association, Girlguiding, Cadets and Woodcraft Folk – have national programmes of activities delivered locally by volunteers. Familiarising yourself with their objectives and priorities – both central and local – will help you to find mutually beneficial areas for carrying out joint activities. You may also have independent groups that offer services in your local area.

If you have locally based services, you can offer schools and youth groups the opportunity to visit your charity to see what you do and introduce children to your cause in an inspiring way. If a visit would not be appropriate, it can also be very effective to give a talk at a school and answer any questions the children and young people have. You can complement this with packs of resources, videos, and games and activities with educational links for teachers and group leaders to use in their own sessions. For a range of useful resources, see Giving Nation (an organisation which teaches about charitable giving and social action in education settings): www.g-nation.org.uk.

Once you have introduced the children to your organisation, you will need to convert the interest you create into action and fundraising. Offer fundraising activities which ask for a small donation from a lot of children (such as a bake sale or non-uniform day) or tap into the generosity of their extended family (such as a sponsored challenge or family event).

There are particular ethical and safeguarding considerations to keep in mind when working with children and young people, and you will also need to understand what kinds of fundraising activities a child can legally take part in. If you work with children in the UK, you should be familiar with section 6.0 of the Code of Fundraising Practice, 'Fundraising involving children' (www.fundraisingregulator.org.uk). Some key elements of best practice and compliance include:

- **Safeguarding:** Staff and volunteers involved in fundraising from and running events with children should receive safeguarding training. In addition, anyone who has unsupervised contact with children must have a Disclosure and Barring Service check. Note that these checks can take some weeks to process and there is a cost attached. Parental consent is also required if you intend to take or publish photographs of participating children. Take care to ensure that any photographs are only used strictly in accordance with the consent that has been given and do not use for future events unless authorised.

- **Data:** While there is no legal age set for when children are deemed to have the capacity to give informed consent for the collection of their data (some organisations set this at the age of 12, others at 14 or 16), it is best practice to get consent from parents or guardians. Any information collected from anyone under 14 years of age must never be disclosed without consent from a parent or guardian.

- **Communications:** Presentations to children should be age appropriate and should not have any political content. It is advisable to talk through the educational content of talks with an appropriate person of authority, such as a teacher or youth group leader. Think carefully about how you are presenting your charity's beneficiaries to your audience, as these are formative years for young people and you have the power to influence their worldview. Find out what they already know about your cause and make links between their lives and the lives of the people your money could help to support. Be thoughtful about the backgrounds of young people and how the issues you are discussing might directly impact them and their families; speak to teachers and youth leaders to ensure you are aware of any individual sensitivities. Consider the children's age and levels of understanding, so that you can appropriately build empathy. As with all types of fundraising, ensure that you are clear about how the funds raised will be used. Show the impact that low-value gifts have on your beneficiaries and ensure that all children, teachers and youth leaders are thanked for their efforts.

- **Fundraising:** If children are securing and collecting sponsorship, they should be encouraged to talk to their parents about whom they might approach. In fundraising talks and written materials, give examples of how children can approach sponsors safely by, for example, approaching family friends and other people known to them and not by approaching strangers or knocking on doors. All material should be written in appropriate, simple language, and bear in mind that for some children English may be their second language. To avoid any impression that children and young people are being harassed by your charity to collect sponsorship money, provide clear instructions that set a time limit and date on which a teacher or someone from your charity will collect the funds. You may offer gifts as prizes to encourage young people but they should be made available to all participants and not given as rewards for particular individuals' efforts.

The following case study is an example of how fundraising in schools must be developed around the needs of children and the time constraints of the curriculum.

Case study: Children with Cancer UK – increasing income from schools and children's groups

In 2015, Children with Cancer UK decided to explore the possibility of beginning a new fundraising campaign to increase income from schools and children's groups. To assess the potential of this avenue, we studied the market to identify children's groups and schools' appetite for a new fundraising product.

We looked at whether our licence of the Mr. Men and Little Miss characters would appeal to younger children, evaluated the organisations and activities that schools currently supported, determined the weaknesses of our previous campaigns, and identified adequate budget and staffing. We piloted a Mr. Men and Little Miss challenge, where, as part of their fundraising, children could colour in a Mr. Man or Little Miss, design a new character, or write a new story. Each school or group would enter a UK-wide competition, with the winner receiving Mr. Men and Little Miss goodies. Feedback showed that the pilot organisations liked the theme but found the challenges complicated and the competition element too time restrictive.

As a result, we tweaked our campaign, launching the Mr. Men Little Miss Marathon Challenge in 2016. This challenge involves asking children to create their own 'marathon', consisting of 26 activities for which they can be sponsored, such as 26 laps of the playing field or spelling 26 words. This approach has the flexibility for groups and individual children to choose what type of activity most inspires them and is supported by a range of online and offline materials. Within six months, over 800 schools and youth groups were participating.

Ben Twyman, Head of Events, and Emily Roff, Sports and Community Fundraising Manager, Children with Cancer UK

Faith groups

Most major religions have service to the poor and generosity among their key tenets. Faith-based donors are also some of the most generous donors.[8] Different faiths have different times in the calendar – at major festivals or during the preparation time preceding them – when giving and philanthropy are particularly encouraged (for example, during Lent or Ramadan). Different faiths may also have different practices of charitable giving, such as *dāna* (in several religions, including Buddhism and Hinduism), tithing (in Christianity) and *zakat* (in Islam).

To create a targeted approach, you will need to be aware of the preferred donation methods and areas of support of specific religious groups. A basic understanding of the theological motivations behind a faith group's philanthropy and of the best times of year to reach out will help you to approach the group in the most appropriate way.

Your organisation may be faith based and have a particular remit within a certain faith community, or it may have historical links to particular religious groups, even if it is now a secular organisation. Secular charities without these pre-existing ties can still gain strong support from faith-based groups, particularly if the charity supports a cause with few (or no) existing faith-based charities already working in that area – this is the case in the medical research sector, for instance. If there are several faith-based charities working in the same cause area as you, however, faith groups are naturally more likely to prefer to support these charities. The key here, though, is to be authentic in the relationship. In managing the relationship, you might consider involving a team member who shares the faith. Do not try to pretend that you know more about the community's beliefs than you do, as you will easily be found out. Rather, focus on values which you share and where your work meets the altruistic needs of the community. Ask lots of questions, seek guidance about what goals the group is aiming to achieve and don't overextend yourself theologically!

Many faith leaders are very time poor and may be juggling their commitments to their faith community with secular employment, so many of the same principles detailed in the rest of this chapter apply to approaching them. Make participation easy, enjoyable and mutually beneficial. For instance, simply having a chat over coffee with a faith leader can help you to understand their needs. Perhaps they want to engage more with the local community, be more visible in the local area or encourage members of their community to take on a sponsored sacrificial challenge. This could involve community members giving up something they enjoy for a given period (for example, consuming no sugar or alcohol for a month) or imposing a restriction on themselves to highlight the plight of people living in poverty, such as living on a small food budget for a week or fasting for a day.[9] What do you have in your portfolio of offerings which could help the faith leader to achieve these goals? For example, could they run a stall at one of your events, host a refreshment stop on your sponsored walk, or take on your abstinence challenge during a time of fasting?

It can be difficult to navigate the structures and procedures of different religious groups. For instance, it is estimated that there are over 250 Protestant Christian denominations in the UK (as opposed to Roman Catholic or Orthodox denominations),[10] and they vary from hugely hierarchical to having a very flat structure. Keeping a curious mindset and asking lots of questions will help you to ascertain who the influencers are in different groups and how you may be able to best nurture relationships.

It can be beneficial to focus on one religion or denomination at a time rather than taking a broader approach.

Conclusion

Fundraising from community groups can provide an economy of scale for your activities by accessing a closed community which often has a culture and experience of fundraising for other organisations. Visible support by such groups can enhance your charity's status and legitimacy and provide a means of wider community engagement. A rewarding and meaningful experience of participating in fundraising for your charity, and greater awareness of the impact you deliver for your beneficiaries, could also lead group members to support you individually in other ways. It is therefore vital that these opportunities are integrated into your communications with these groups.

Notes

1 *Britain's Civic Core: Who are the people powering Britain's charities?* [PDF], Charities Aid Foundation, 2013, www.cafonline.org/docs/default-source/about-us-publications/caf_britains_civic_core_sept13.pdf, p. 5, accessed 15 June 2018.

2 'Schools and Charities' [infographic], Charities Aid Foundation, 2013, www.cafonline.org/docs/default-source/about-us-publications/caf_education_infographic_final.pdf, accessed 15 June 2018.

3 *Ibid.*

4 Alison Body, Kerry Holman and Eddy Hogg, *To Bridge the Gap? Voluntary action in primary schools*, Canterbury, Canterbury Christ Church University, 2017, p. 7.

5 *Charitable Giving by Schools 2014* [PDF], The Classroom Voice, 2014, http://classroomvoice.co.uk/crv/wp-content/uploads/2014/11/Charitable-Giving-CV-1.21.pdf, p. 16, accessed 15 June 2018.

6 *Growing up Giving* [PDF], Charities Aid Foundation, 2013, https://www.cafonline.org/docs/default-source/about-us-publications/growing_up_giving.pdf, p. 8, accessed 15 June 2018.

7 *Charitable Giving by Schools 2014* [PDF], The Classroom Voice, 2014, http://classroomvoice.co.uk/crv/wp-content/uploads/2014/11/Charitable-Giving-CV-1.21.pdf, pp. 7, 10 and 15, accessed 15 June 2018.

8 Lucy de Las Casas, Matt van Poortvliet, Rob Abercrombie and Sally Bagwell, *Money for Good UK: Understanding donor motivation and behaviour* [PDF], New Philanthropy Capital, 2013, www.thinknpc.org/publications/money-for-good-uk, p. 45, accessed 15 June 2018.

9 See, for example, the Hunger Project at www.thehungerproject.org.uk and World Vision's 30-hour famine at www.30hourfamine.org.

10 'UK church statistics no 3 2018 edition' [web page], Brierley Consultancy, 2017, www.brierleyconsultancy.com/growth-decline-1, accessed 30 July 2018.

CHAPTER ELEVEN

Planning and managing cash collections

Lianne Howard-Dace

> Throughout its existence, the collection tin has served as a visual cue that there is a need to remain charitable. It is a symbol of the philanthropic culture within the UK and remains a continual reminder that giving is an important part of life.
>
> Sam Butler, 2016[1]

Introduction

Public cash collections are one of the oldest forms of fundraising and it is thought that the original collection tin was placed outside the first temple of Jerusalem. Collections are the ultimate in high-volume, low-value gifts. While the odd person may kindly put a note in your collection tin, the majority will add whatever small coins they have to hand, meaning that it will usually take many contributions to fill your tin. However, collecting can be cost-effective, with each tin generating an average of £260 over a year and costing between £1 and £2.70.[2] Collections are the simplest way for people to contribute and can mobilise large numbers in a light-touch and easy way. There is high public awareness of this form of giving, and cash donations through street collections are cited as the most preferred way to give.[3] As most donors still give by cash,[4] collections remain a valuable source of income, with an estimated £620 million raised annually from tin and bucket collections in the UK.[5]

This chapter considers the different forms of collection, how to ensure collections are legally compliant, the importance of good planning and logistics, and the vital role of volunteers. (See also section 8.0 of the Code of Fundraising Practice, 'Collecting money and other property'.)

Benefits of collections

The barrier to entry for collections is low for both charities and donors; even charities in their infancy can easily benefit from various types of collection, and it is relatively inexpensive to get started. Collections provide a visible presence in the community and street, and house-to-house collections offer opportunities to talk to donors about the importance of your charity's work. Collections can generate a fairly constant source of income, which is usually unrestricted. Collections are scalable and can be increased to match the size of your charity's operations – from a few collection tins in shops in one city to large nationwide street and house-to-house appeals with collectors in every community. Collections can engage and deepen relationships with volunteers, and provide opportunities to extend their organisational responsibilities. Collections are also a valuable mechanism through which to generate secondary sources of income within other forms of participatory fundraising activity, such as at an event.

Types of collection and necessary permissions

Broadly speaking, there are four types of cash collection. However, as we will see in the next section, with the growth of contactless payments, the number of potential categories of collections are expanding. Each type of collection is governed by a different part of the Fundraising Regulator's Code of Fundraising Practice, and require various types of permit.

- **Street collections** – as opposed to street fundraising, which seeks to sign donors up to give regularly – involve a bucket or tin collection where volunteers collect one-off gifts from passers-by in public areas, such as streets, roads, bridges, public squares and courtyards. To undertake a street collection in England, Wales or Scotland, a charity must apply to its local authority (or, in the case of Greater London, the Metropolitan Police) for a permit. In Northern Ireland, a charity must apply to the Police Service.

- **House-to-house** collections involve volunteers going door to door collecting from residents. Often this will involve dropping off an envelope with information about the charity and going back to ask for a donation in person a few days later. Permission must be sought from the same bodies as for a street collection. Some charities qualify for national exemption orders if they have had house-to-house collection licences in at least 70 to 100 local authority licensing areas. As good practice, these charities should still liaise with their local authorities about the dates and locations of their collections. Exempt charities are listed on the Department for Digital, Culture, Media & Sport's website.

- **Static collections** generally consist of countertop collection tins left in shops and other consumer-facing sites but also include more elaborate collection devices such as free-standing collection boxes and even some interactive contactless installations. Boxes and tins must be secure and tamper-proof and, while you do not need a licence to place these, you do need permission from the business owner or landlord.

- **Private collections** are bucket or tin collections which take place on private property such as supermarkets, offices, pubs, football grounds and train stations. These require permission from the business owner or landlord.

Using technology and research to improve collections

As recommended in chapter 2, it is strategically wise to keep up to date on the trends affecting community fundraising and to use secondary research findings to back up your in-house research and testing. The following sections outline how changes in payment technology are likely to transform charities' collections in the future. They will also examine how you can use research findings as inspiration to experiment with ways of increasing donations.

Trends on maximising donations using payment technology

Payment technology is developing exponentially. In the late 1980s, debit cards came into the UK marketplace, with internet banking appearing in the late 1990s and contactless technology emerging in the UK in 2007.[6] The speed at which people are willing to adopt new technologies is getting quicker, and in terms of payment technology this means more diversity in the ways we can pay for things – contactless cards, mobile phone payments, SMS – and less need to carry around cash. Indeed, cash is no longer the most popular method of payment: more than half of consumers in the UK are using cards for in-store payments, partly due to the wider use of contactless payments.[7] Contactless technology itself is reaching high levels of adoption – over a third of all card payments in the UK in 2017 were made contactlessly[8] and, of all in-store transactions processed by Worldpay in 2017/18, contactless payments overtook chip-and-pin transactions in the UK for the first time.[9] At the time of writing, however, contactless collection devices can cost as much as ten times more than traditional donation boxes. They also incur payment processing charges and payment units are not as low maintenance as tins (in that they need charging, they need a data connection, they might stop working, etc.). These issues were highlighted in a 2018 survey which found that 74% of UK charities had not yet tried any contactless payment systems to take donations, with charities citing the cost of the technology as a barrier.[10]

The convenience provided by contactless giving for donors cannot be overestimated, however, with over a third of people saying that if they were able to give contactlessly they would be more likely to give to street collections.[11] Furthermore, research by Barclaycard shows that charities lose out on £80 million in donations each year because it was not possible to donate through collections by card.[12]

On a practical level for charities, contactless devices are an effective option when there is the potential for higher-value gifts (such as a collection at an event or in a place of worship) and where staff or volunteers are available to look after each unit. Furthermore, cashless methods often allow additional functionality that other payment methods do not. For example, some smartphone payment methods include built-in Gift Aid declarations and an opportunity to share contact details with charities.[13] Some devices have card slots and keypads as well to allow chip-and-pin payments in case a donor wishes to give more than the £30 limit currently set for contactless payments in the UK. Cashless technology allows for campaign innovation in that physical objects, from cars and benches to window displays and posters, can become collection points. In 2016, the Blue Cross introduced the world's first example of dogs functioning as fundraisers: these Tap Dogs, as they have been affectionately named, wear contactless payment devices in their jackets that can accept donations of £2 per tap from a mobile phone.[14]

Whatever the situation your charity finds itself regarding the latest technology, ensure that you carefully monitor your ongoing returns from the traditional cash collecting tin and consider investing in contactless devices (payment machines, freestanding collection boxes, posters, etc.) or other emerging cashless technologies.

As with all consumer-facing technology, there will likely be a tipping point in the not-so-distant future when the technology becomes cheaply scalable. So, if you are already testing different technologies and building a culture of readiness in your organisation, you will be able to capitalise on this more quickly than your competitors. A complex picture weaving together payment devices, related developments such as battery life, and other factors such as cryptocurrencies mean it is likely that payment options we can't conceive of now may quickly go to market in the coming years, potentially changing the face of the collections market.

Research on maximising donations during charity collections

The following two sections introduce examples of how research from the field of behavioural economics can inform new ways of stimulating giving during charity collections.

Use of eye images on collection buckets

A 2011 UK study sought to test the effect of using images of eyes in a charitable donation setting, based on a number of previous studies showing that displaying eye images in public settings encourages people to increase 'prosocial' behaviours. In other words, these studies found that, when presented with images of eyes, people are more likely to behave in a way that benefits other people relative to how they would normally behave under the same circumstances with control (non-eye) pictures displayed. For instance, in one study, researchers displayed posters in a cafeteria that featured either eye images or images of flowers. They found that the pictures of eyes caused people to be more likely to remove litter from their tables.[15]

In the context of collection buckets at checkouts in a supermarket, UK researchers in 2012 found that when the buckets displayed small cartoon images of eyes on the sticker that covered the lid of the bucket (see figure 11.1), donations increased by 48% compared with when the buckets displayed control images (i.e. images without eyes).[16] The researchers suggest that this effect may be thanks to humans having evolved to be sensitive to the positive social consequences associated with being viewed to be generous. Even though the eye images were cartoon-like and not naturalistic, this cue was sufficient to produce a positive effect on giving behaviour.

FIGURE 11.1 RECREATION OF THE EYE IMAGE (LEFT) AND CONTROL IMAGE (RIGHT) DISPLAYED IN THE SUPERMARKET[17]

The researchers also found that the increase in donations was most pronounced during quiet periods in the supermarket. Other researchers propose that this higher effect may occur because people are less likely to notice the eye images in a busier context.[18]

Effects of direct face-to-face requests

In 2016, American researchers examined people's responses to Salvation Army collection methods at the entrances of supermarkets to compare the act of ringing a bell (one of the standard approaches of Salvation Army collectors) with directly asking passers-by to 'please give'. They also compared having a collector at just one supermarket entrance with having collectors at two entrances.

Directly asking shoppers to 'please give' increased the number of people donating by 55% and the total amount donated by 69%. The addition of a second collector, meaning that both doors at a store were attended, increased the number of people donating by 65% and the total amount donated by 80%. However, the researchers estimated that directly asking for a donation may also have had an actively off-putting effect on some people. When collectors rang their bell rather than directly engaging shoppers and making eye contact, shoppers did not make efforts to actively avoid them; when collectors asked shoppers to 'please give', 25% to 33% of people actively tried to avoid the collectors. The researchers did not suggest that this aversive effect implies fundraisers should not directly solicit donations, rather that the act of asking magnifies the effect in both directions: people who are not going to give anyway will more actively avoid the need to say 'no', whereas people who are open to giving are more likely to do so when asked.

Why does asking have such a powerful impact on people's behaviour? The researchers postulate that it is not because people gain more knowledge about the fundraising, since in the supermarket scenario the request did not include any explanatory information. Nor, the researchers say, is it a result of any enhancement of people's image of themselves as morally good people, since the non-verbal version of the ask would have worked similarly well in that case. Rather, it is because passers-by feel an emotional response when another person directly requests that they give – their sense of empathy is stimulated. This also explains why some people actively dodge the ask: it is a way of controlling their emotional response – if they aren't directly addressed, they can avoid feeling bad about ignoring the collectors.[19]

Similar results were found over 40 years ago by a different team of researchers, who compared a direct request to 3,000 passers-by ('Excuse me, would you like to contribute... please?', using eye contact) with a more passive request ('Give to the children', using only brief eye contact). In this case, the personal request was considerably more effective. Furthermore, in a similar vein to the research on the use of eye images at supermarket checkout collection buckets, donors gave larger donations during quieter periods (when there were fewer pedestrians passing by). Light pedestrian traffic did not cause there to be a higher overall number of givers, however. This disproved the researchers' original theory that a direct appeal to passers-by in a lightly populated environment would increase the number of givers. Instead, the results implied that people in crowded and quieter environments are similar in the degree to which they feel compelled to give. Nevertheless, the larger size of the donations given during quieter periods implied to the researchers that people feel more commitment and a higher sense of being monitored when there are fewer passers-by around.[20]

The evidence from both these studies on making direct requests suggests that encouraging your collection volunteers to politely ask passers-by to donate to your beneficiaries, while making eye contact, will increase donation levels. This approach is preferable to rattling buckets or tins, which (even if it is not illegal, as it is often stated to be) may annoy people. Informed by research such as this and, naturally, your charity's own experience of which techniques increase levels of giving, it is important to provide verbal or written advice on phrases that are suitable for volunteers to say and that are in line with your charity's values to ensure collection volunteers are communicating appropriately and effectively with the public. (For more information on communicating appropriate collection behaviour, see 'Behaviour expectations' on page 310.)

Planning and managing collections

While collections offer a simple mechanism for soliciting and securing donations, they bring with them a number of risks which require careful planning and attention to all logistical considerations.

Where and when

Whether you are organising a street, private venue or static collection, consider where you will find a heavy footfall of people who are likely to give money. With static collections, identify where people are likely to be making cash transactions as well as where you can find people who are likely to be sympathetic to your cause. For street and house-to-house collections, be mindful of the time of day you go out collecting and when people might have time to engage with you. For example, you are unlikely to be welcome on someone's doorstep if they are about to sit down and eat. Timing will depend upon the nature of the location, when there are likely to be a high number of people available to donate and when your volunteers are most likely to be available. For example, charities tend to prefer to run collections on Fridays and Saturdays (when retailers are busiest) and at the beginning of the month (when people have been paid). Holding a collection on the same day as a major local event, where local pedestrian footfall to and from venues is heavy, can provide an ideal opportunity to reach large numbers of people. If your charity runs awareness days or weeks, collections could help with raising their profile.

For both house-to-house and street collections, it is good practice to establish a clear annual programme of collections around which to plan volunteer recruitment. All charities should avoid a conflict in collection dates (for instance, two similar local charities collecting in the same week) and those with national exemption orders should let other exemption-order holders know where and when their collections will be taking place. Exemption-order holders should also avoid booking large blocks of time which prevent other charities from collecting in the area.

Permits and permission

Collection permissions are in high demand and often allocated many months in advance for popular spots and times of year. The Code of Fundraising Practice requires that you apply for permits from local authorities or police at least one month prior to the collection, but in practice you will often need to apply many months in advance in order to secure the block of time you desire. An online search is the best place to find out what each local authority's permit procedure is, and most now offer an online application. If you are a humanitarian aid organisation, it is worth asking both local authorities and corporate supporters whether they have any special arrangements in place to allow you to collect quickly when a natural disaster strikes. Local authorities increasingly require collectors to have Disclosure and Barring Service (DBS) checks, so this needs to be built into your scheduling for seeking permissions. Often a local authority will give you some sort of letter of authorisation for collectors to carry on their person and will have their own guidelines on how to carry out a collection.

To ensure that it is clear to the public that collectors have local authority or police permission, collectors should be issued with badges which include the charity's name and registration number, and the collector's signature. They must also have certificates to show on request that include the charity name, address and number; the name and address of the collector; the place of collection; the authorised period of collection; and the collector and promoter's signatures. Fundraisers should ensure that they are familiar with the Code of Fundraising Practice for collections and monitor any changes or updates. Badges and certificates must be returned after the collection is completed.

If you are collecting on private property, you must have written permission from the owner. Supermarket chains and public transport stations, which deal with large numbers of charity collections, will have their own systems for applying for permits. If you are using static collecting tins, you should also issue certificates of authority and identity badges to the collectors who site and service the boxes.

Volunteer collectors

While relatively simple, collections require peoplepower to either carry out or maintain them. Collections are a low-skill activity which is unlikely to be profitable enough to warrant the time of paid staff, except in a supervisory capacity. You will therefore need a mixture of volunteer roles to support collections, bearing in mind how labour intensive they can be. The tasks of securing permits, carrying out the collection, managing static tins and counting the money all provide flexible volunteering roles. These may be more or less formal, from a collection tin coordinator in a geographical area to ad hoc participation in street collections. The role of staff is usually supervisory and involves tasks such as recruiting and training volunteers, providing certificates and badges, and processing DBS checks. If you have your own in-house groups of fundraising volunteers, this may be something they take responsibility for. This approach can work particularly well because it creates some sort of structure, however informal, where lead volunteers can coordinate other volunteers.

You may also be able to capitalise on other forms of partnership to take the onus of managing your collections away from your staff team. A corporate partner may maintain countertop collections in its retail outlets or provide teams of street collectors. You may also have strong links with community or other groups – such as rotary clubs, students, faith groups or business networks – which can rally together collectors on your behalf.

Encourage your existing collecting volunteers to recruit other collectors through word of mouth, perhaps providing a leaflet or postcard they can use. Further recruitment can take place through your owned communications channels, such as your newsletter and website, and, if the scale of your activity warrants it and you have budget available, you can supplement this with paid advertising. Paid social media adverts can be particularly cost-effective as they can be targeted towards specific demographics and focus on particular geographical areas (and turned off if they aren't working, unlike costlier channels such as print adverts).

Different countries have different legal requirements regarding the minimum age of collectors (although in many countries the age is 16), so you must check this with your local authority and the relevant best-practice fundraising guidance or code in that area. Children below the minimum legal age may be able to collect with a supervising adult.

Promoting the collection

If you are running a house-to-house or street collection, it is always worth ensuring that your local groups and corporate partners are aware that the collection is taking place so they avoid organising other activities that might clash with it. You can also inform local supporters through your social media channels and raise a wider profile through local media announcements.

Seeing your collecting tins may add to people's general awareness of your cause, so it is important to make the most of these devices by displaying clear branding and a call to action which emphasises the impact of people's donations. Providing volunteers with branded T-shirts or tabards can help to increase their visibility and people's recognition of your cause. To recognise gifts, you may also want to have badges, stickers, pins, etc. to hand out when a donation is made. Ensure that the cost of producing these small tokens does not outweigh the value of the gifts you are receiving, and you may want to consider suggesting different minimum donations depending on the cost of the items. (See 'Gift Aid' on page 196 for information on Gift Aid benefit rules.) This form of low-value merchandise helps with awareness and, when well designed, can become a popular fashion item which stimulates further gifts and gives tangibility to what can be a low-engagement transaction. Depending on the location of your collection, there may also be an opportunity to have a stall and further materials about your organisation and ways of supporting it.

Managing collectors

Health and safety

The health and safety of volunteers who collect on behalf of your charity are your organisation's responsibility. Collectors should be given guidance on ensuring their own personal safety and you should ensure you make contact with them before a collection and ask them to let you know they have returned home safely afterwards. You should also hold phone numbers of volunteers' next of kin in case of emergency. People should collect in pairs and should do so in safe areas which are well lit. Make sure you tell volunteers that if someone attempts to steal a tin, they should not put themselves in any danger to resist the theft.

Behaviour expectations

Collectors should also be briefed on what is expected of them in terms of their behaviour. For example:

- being courteous and always thanking donors;
- knowing how to answer questions about the charity and follow complaints procedures;
- not harassing the public into making a donation;
- not smoking or using alcohol or drugs;
- respecting no-cold-calling zones and notices;
- remaining stationary when street collecting and at the advised distance apart from other collectors, as stipulated by the regulations in your area (for example, the Street Collections (Metropolitan Police District) Regulations 1979 require collectors to remain further than 25 metres away from one another);[21]
- ensuring they do not cause any danger, obstruction or inconvenience to the public.

All collectors should be trained and briefed to ensure they understand their legal obligations and the best practice required by your charity, such as your safeguarding policies. It is a requirement of legislation and the Code of Fundraising Practice that a collector is a 'fit and proper' person. While there is no specific definition of this term, broadly it relates to ensuring collectors have not been involved in fraudulent activity. You may consider seeking a reference, asking them to sign a declaration and, when required, carrying out a DBS check.

Coordinating large numbers of collectors and ensuring that they have a positive experience should be a priority for collection staff. Volunteers should feel supported and valued throughout their involvement, and thanked and updated on how much their efforts have raised. The following case study describes how Marie Curie Cancer Care has used an online platform which interfaces with its database to support its collectors' experience.

Case study: Marie Curie Great Daffodil Appeal

As our annual Great Daffodil Appeal at Marie Curie grew in popularity, the number of volunteer collectors was becoming too high for our regional fundraising teams to be able to give them the desired level of support. At the same time, in 2014, the number of people registering to volunteer online became greater than the number applying through offline methods, so it was the ideal time to start digitising some of our processes.

We created a bespoke online platform which allowed volunteers to sign themselves up to specific collecting shifts near them. The platform also helped regional fundraising teams to steward collectors, follow up on their collecting experience and thank them. The platform has multiple benefits:

- increasing volunteer conversion from registering interest to completing a collection;
- ensuring a consistent and seamless supporter experience;
- freeing up the time of regional fundraisers to focus on the big picture of facilitating the appeal.

We piloted the platform in London in 2014 and rolled it out across the UK in 2015. Each year we take the opportunity to optimise the platform as the appeal grows and new technologies develop. Volunteers can sign up straight away for the best collecting shifts for them, and they are kept up to date with any changes and thanked for how much they raised after the event. Regional fundraisers and lead volunteers, such as local group chairs, can update the system with the latest slots and monitor and promote those which need additional volunteers. The online platform has played an important role in ensuring the sustainable growth of our Great Daffodil Appeal, and we have made use of the platform during other busy periods of collecting, such as Christmas.

Mark Winton, Head of Community Fundraising UK, Marie Curie

Managing and tracking tins

You will need to maintain a stock of collecting equipment: tins, buckets, boxes, envelopes, etc., for rotation with your activities. All collecting tins and buckets need to be secure and have seals to ensure that you know they have not been tampered with. Static collecting tins also need security chains. Each tin should have its own unique number and, when it is issued to a collector or static site, the collector or location should be recorded against the tin number to ensure that the location and use of all tins is always being monitored. All tins used at events and in street collections should be returned to the charity. In the case of house-to-house collections, the number of envelopes issued to the collector and returned must also be recorded, and all collection devices must bear the name and address of the charity and its registered number. Street, house-to-house and static site collectors should be issued with certificates of authority and identity badges.

Cash handling

The time it can take to count and bank large amounts of collection cash shouldn't be underestimated, and you will need to factor into your planning appropriate numbers and types of volunteers to undertake this.

For all forms of collection, it is best practice that at least two people who are not related to each other are present for any counting. This practice protects your charity against fraud, makes it easier to double-check totals and saves time at the bank, as it is less likely that counting will have been inaccurate. A variety of devices, from relatively cheap to more complex and expensive units, can be purchased to help with counting and may be worthwhile, depending on the volume of collections your organisation deals with. Counting should be undertaken in a secure place, with the monies kept safely and banked as soon as possible. All donations should be placed in tins or sealable envelopes.

In situations such as static collections, where you might be reliant on a site holder (i.e. the owner, manager or occupier of the premises) to open collection tins and bank monies, the site holder should be provided with materials to record and bank proceeds, along with paying-in slips and a counterfoil to return to the charity as proof of counting and banking. You should issue a formal acknowledgement, such as a receipt, to the site holder for monies received from static sites, and you should also keep records of what has been received from each tin and ensure the site holder has the necessary materials to reseal the box. If your in-house volunteer fundraising groups carry out street, private-property and event collections, you may also wish to provide them with paying-in books so they can deposit money directly into the bank on your behalf.

You should keep separate accounting records for the different forms of collection you run. When issuing collection licences, local authorities will require you to submit a return showing the gross income raised from a collection and the costs incurred. Proceeds from static box collections ought to be separately available, detailing gross income for the year, direct expenses incurred and any fees paid in connection with collections. It is the responsibility of a collections promoter to maintain accurate, up-to-date records so that income and direct expenditure for individual boxes can be traced.

Data protection

Many collection techniques, such as bucket collections and countertop collections, are entirely anonymous, and so asking a supporter to Gift Aid their donation or opt in to further communications when they are giving such small donations is neither appropriate nor cost-effective. However, if you have collections taking place in more engaged settings, such as at an event or a stall where you are having conversations with people and are seeking higher average gifts, then it is worth considering capturing these people's data. One of the most effective ways to do this is through envelopes, where donors can supply contact details, give permission to be contacted and complete a Gift Aid declaration. In the UK, the Small Donations Scheme allows charities to claim Gift Aid on some of the low-level, anonymous gifts which they receive.

You also need to consider any requirements of your volunteers when they are handling data. If a volunteer is handling data on behalf of your organisation, such as data relating to supporters or fellow volunteers whom they coordinate, you have an obligation to ensure that they are doing so legally. You should have clear guidelines that reflect the latest data protection legislation in this area and provide induction and training on how to capture, enter, update and use data (see 'Data protection legislation and fundraising regulations' on page 156). Likewise, any data collected by third parties via contactless devices must adhere to data protection legislation, and you are responsible for checking third parties' practices (as outlined in section 7.0 of the Code of Fundraising Practice: 'Professional fundraisers, commercial participators and partners' – see www.fundraisingregulator.org.uk for details on how to do this).

Conclusion

On the whole, collections offer a scalable, simple and effective way for charities to raise voluntary income. By investing in efficient processes for maintaining and reconciling collections and securing volunteer support, charities can maximise their return on effort for the income raised.

Collections can stand alone or be added to other fundraising activities, such as events. To add value and appeal, enhance collections with activities such as carol singing or fancy dress, or by giving tokens such as badges to increase visibility.

Keep abreast of the latest regulatory factors related to collections and scan the horizon for how technology is changing collections in an increasingly cashless society. At the heart of most collections are the volunteers who make them possible, and so you must pay close attention to how this vital resource should be cultivated, stewarded and thanked throughout the process, to ensure the experience is safe, easy, rewarding and enjoyable.

With a little thought and planning, this income stream can form a regular and reliable source of often unrestricted funds for your cause.

Notes

1 Sam Butler, 'The Collection Tin' [case study], SOFII, http://sofii.org/case-study/the-collection-tin, 10 February 2016.

2 *Ibid.*

3 *Charity Awareness Monitor 2015*, London, nfpSynergy, 2015.

4 *CAF UK Giving: An overview of charitable giving in the UK* [PDF], CAF, 2018, www.cafonline.org/docs/default-source/about-us-publications/caf-uk-giving-2018-report.pdf, p. 15, accessed 3 August 2018.

5 *Charitable Giving and Gift Aid: Research report for HM Revenue and Customs September 2016* [PDF], HM Revenue and Customs, 2018, https://assets.publishing.service.gov.uk/government/uploads/system/uploads/attachment_data/file/690609/HMRC_Report_482__GiftAid_Research_Report.pdf, p. 17, accessed 3 August 2018.

6 'History of cards' [web page], UK Cards Association, 2018, www.theukcardsassociation.org.uk/history_of_cards/index.asp, accessed 21 June 2018.

7 *Payments Survey 2016* [PDF], British Retail Consortium, 2016, https://brc.org.uk/media/179489/payment-survey-2016_final.pdf, p. 8, accessed 21 June 2018.

8 *UK card payments* [PDF], UK Finance, 2018, www.ukfinance.org.uk/system/files/UK-Card-Payments-2018-Summary.pdf, p. 3, accessed 23 April 2019.

9 Claire Hardy, '"Tap and Go" tipping point: Contactless overtakes Chip and Pin for instore card payments' [press release], Worldpay, www.worldpay.com/uk/about/media-centre/2018–10/tap-and-go-tipping-point, 16 October 2018.

10 *Cash and Digital Payments in the New Economy: Call for evidence response by the Institute of Fundraising* [PDF], Institute of Fundraising, 2018, www.institute-of-fundraising.org.uk/library/hm-treasury-call-for-evidence-on-cash-and-digital-payments-in, p. 2, accessed 17 April 2018.
11 *Charity Giving 2017* [PDF], yougov, 2017, https://reports.yougov.com/reports/charitablegiving17/files/CharitableGiving2017, p. 23, accessed 21 June 2018.
12 'Charities miss out on more than £80m a year by only accepting cash donations' [press release], Barclaycard, www.home.barclaycard/media-centre/press-releases/contactless-donation-boxes.html, 5 March 2017.
13 Howard Lake, 'Cashless giving added to traditional charity collection boxes and buckets' [blog post], UK Fundraising, https://fundraising.co.uk/2017/04/20/cashless-giving-added-to-traditional-charity-collection-boxes-and-buckets, 20 April 2017.
14 Howard Lake, 'Blue Cross uses dogs for mobile contactless fundraising' [blog post], UK Fundraising, https://fundraising.co.uk/2016/05/19/blue-cross-uses-dogs-mobile-contactless-fundraising, 19 May 2016.
15 Max Ernest-Jones, Daniel Nettle and Melissa Bateson, 'Effects of Eye Images on Everyday Cooperative Behavior: A field experiment', *Evolution and Human Behavior*, vol. 32, 2011, pp. 172–8.
16 Kate L. Powell, Gilbert Roberts and Daniel Nettle, 'Eye Images Increase Charitable Donations: Evidence from an opportunistic field experiment in a supermarket', *Ethology*, vol. 118, no. 11, 2012, pp. 1–6.
17 These images are illustrative of the original photographs displayed in the Powell, Roberts and Nettle research paper.
18 See Mathias Ekström, 'Do Watching Eyes Affect Charitable Giving? Evidence from a field experiment', *Experimental Economics*, vol. 15, no. 3, 2011, pp. 530–46 and Max Ernest-Jones, Daniel Nettle and Melissa Bateson, 'Effects of Eye Images on Everyday Cooperative Behavior: A field experiment', *Evolution and Human Behavior*, vol. 32, 2011, pp. 172–8.
19 James Andreoni, Justin M. Rao and Hannah Trachtman, 'Avoiding the Ask: A field experiment on altruism, empathy and charitable giving', *Journal of Political Economy*, vol. 125, no. 3, 2017, pp. 625–653.
20 Svenn Lindskold, Robert A. Forte, Charles S. Haake and Edward K. Schmidt, 'The Effects of Directness of Face-to-Face Requests and Sex of Solicitor on Streetcorner Donations', *The Journal of Social Psychology*, vol. 101, no. 1, 1977, pp. 45–51.
21 'The Street Collections (Metropolitan Police District) Regulations 1979', www.legislation.gov.uk/uksi/1979/1230, section 12.

CHAPTER TWELVE

Engaging with business in the community

Andrew Peel

Introduction

There is a level of crossover between corporate and community fundraising, where community fundraisers have responsibility for engaging corporates in events and campaigns or for supporting the local delivery of corporate partnerships. The volunteer networks and events which are the bedrock of community fundraising can also attract the support of local, regional and national companies. The wide-ranging audiences that can be engaged by community fundraising may, for example, represent companies' potential customers and provide good opportunities for cause-related marketing and sponsorship. Similarly, companies' employees can provide a vital source of volunteers for charities, while mass participation fundraising events can usually be adapted to meet employee fundraising, team-building and other staff development goals. As this chapter will highlight, there are many ways in which community fundraising activities can be tailored to accommodate companies' objectives and raise additional income for your charity.

Corporate relationships can be challenging to secure and execute effectively, however, even for the most experienced practitioners. Approaching a company, negotiating a suitable partnership and then managing the process to reach a successful conclusion can be daunting, and enough to deter many smaller (and even some larger) charities from investing in this income stream. Furthermore, there are legal issues to contend with – a company's aims and objectives are likely to diverge significantly from a charity's. To avoid breaching charity law (regarding potential conflicts of interest, risks to reputation and so on), this contrast must be kept firmly in focus. As long as there is clarity and compatibility on this point, however, the relationship can work well for both parties.

While corporate fundraising can be a slow and labour-intensive process, involving long periods of research and analysis, relationship-building and negotiation, it is feasible for charities of all shapes and sizes to develop an effective and coherent approach. If you have little or no corporate fundraising experience, the following guidance should equip you to feel better able to:

- spot opportunities for corporate engagement;
- feel more confident about approaching businesses;
- be better placed to negotiate and develop fruitful, fulfilling partnerships that benefit all parties.

Trends in corporate philanthropy and their implications for charities

The level of corporate giving is startlingly low in the UK, accounting for around only 2% of charitable income.[1] Despite attempts over the years by customers, staff, charities, pressure groups, the media, government and more enlightened shareholders to encourage more corporate giving, the figures on corporate philanthropy make depressing reading. For instance, in 2016 the Charities Aid Foundation (CAF) found that only 26% of FTSE 100 companies donated at least 1% of their pre-tax profits[2] – the level generally deemed a respectable benchmark of corporate giving. CAF also discovered that in 2016 total donations by FTSE 100 companies were at their lowest level since 2009.[3] In addition, significant giving is concentrated among a few large companies, with 20% of all UK companies donating 90% of the cash. Furthermore, the majority of this giving benefits a narrow range of causes – educational, community and social welfare, and children and young people, with fewer than 10% of companies supporting causes such as human rights, inner cities, women's issues and equal opportunities.[4]

Furthermore, many companies that have traditionally provided financial support to charities have shifted their focus from straightforward philanthropy (i.e. donations of money) towards what might be termed 'skillanthropy' and relationships of a more strategic nature, where they invest their resources, expertise and other assets in furthering good causes. This change of emphasis has been driven, in the main, by the need for companies to be seen to be behaving responsibly; by the need for more tangible business benefits to come out of such projects; and because consumers now expect so much more from businesses, including meaningful social and environmental impact.

This is underlined by a 2015 study which revealed that 91% of shoppers worldwide expect companies to do more than make a profit and 90% would switch to brands that supported a good cause, given similar price and quality. Furthermore, the research found that businesses that are not socially responsible run the risk of alienating their customers, with 90% of those surveyed saying they would boycott companies found to be engaged in irresponsible business practices.[5]

Clearly, corporate–charity partnerships should no longer be viewed simply from a financial perspective but rather in terms of the wider value that can be gained by both parties and wider society. It follows, then, that fundraisers who think of themselves simply as 'raisers of corporate funds' are going to be destined for frustration and possibly failure. Some might even argue that the very term 'corporate fundraising', while it remains a useful generic term, has become something of a misnomer because of the need to think about this income stream in a broader, more strategic way.

Fundraisers (but also trustees and senior managers) now need to regard a corporate partner not as the proverbial cash cow to be milked as rapidly as possible but as a multidimensional resource that, if managed skilfully, can present a plethora of opportunities for both organisations. For the charity, as well as being a potential source of income, a company might represent a route to achieving heightened public awareness, a source of invaluable pro bono support or gifts in kind, or a new audience for challenge events. Mass participation fundraising events, for example, can be adapted for employee fundraising, thereby increasing overall participant numbers. For the company, the charity can provide benefits such as access to new markets and policymakers, positive PR, staff development opportunities and new experiences for existing customers.

However, research carried out for C&E's *Corporate–NGO Partnerships Barometer* muddies the waters somewhat by revealing that companies' motivations for charity partnerships usually differ from charities' motivations – 92% of businesses stated that their key reason for partnering was the reputational benefits, whereas 93% of charities stated that their leading reason was to access funds. So the key challenge for fundraisers is: how can this difference in motivations be reconciled? The answer is that charities and corporates must work together to identify areas of mutual interest and use these drivers as a basis for initial discussions and joint working. Indeed, the main areas of mutual interest, as reported in the 2017 C&E *Barometer* reports, are the opportunity to gain access to people and contacts, innovation, and long-term stability and impact.[6]

There is little doubt that charities which target the corporate sector face a range of challenges and tough decisions. Yet, for creative, astute and commercially minded fundraisers, this new climate means that there is almost no limit to the ways in which a charity can engage with a company. (There are, of course, legal limits. For example, a charity must comply with its governing document and must not expose its assets or reputation to undue risks.)

Examples of corporate engagement in community fundraising products or campaigns

The following examples showcase the range of ways in which companies can partner with charities' community fundraising initiatives:

- **In support of a themed campaign:** In 2018, Haven holiday parks supported RNLI's yellow-themed annual fundraising campaign, Mayday, by encouraging staff, holiday home owners and holiday makers to participate in a range of fundraising events.[7]
- **By sponsoring local events:** In 2018, travel agency Flight Centre sponsored the third annual Flight Centre Schools Triathlon, a series of events for 7–13-year-olds to raise money for the social change charity for young people, Restless Development. The children raised £320,000 at events hosted at schools in Berkshire, London, Surrey, and Wiltshire.[8]
- **By taking part in and sponsoring mass participation events:** ScottishPower raised £20 million over a six-year partnership with Cancer Research UK that began in 2012. Among various fundraising activities, the company sponsored mass participation campaigns Race for Life, Shine Night Walk and Stand Up To Cancer and promoted employee and supplier fundraising.[9]
- **Via in-kind support for a challenge event:** Anchor Vans supported cyclists taking part in the Felix Fund's Tour de Troops – a five-day endurance ride from Land's End to John O' Groats – by lending the organisers two large vans as support vehicles.[10]
- **By developing cause-related marketing products to support a mass participation event:** In December 2018, online retailer Zavvi made a donation to Save the Children for every Christmas jumper it sold, to raise funds for the charity's Christmas Jumper Day appeal.[11]

Ten guiding principles

Whether you are new to corporate fundraising or a seasoned professional, it is useful to bear in mind certain rules and principles which apply to this area of fundraising. These apply regardless of whether you are seeking funding for a new project, a Charity of the Year partnership with a supermarket, event sponsorship from a regional engineering company or a gift in kind from a local brewery.

1. There's no substitute for thorough prospect research

'Warm' companies

As is the case with most fundraising streams, the starting point should be to get to know your 'warm' supporters, if you have any, or those companies that have supported your charity in the past.

If you are a fundraiser in a larger charity, it is imperative to understand what national supporters your charity already has, the nature of those relationships and whether the companies involved have either local or regional offices. Establish, from your corporate fundraising manager or equivalent, if there is the potential for you to engage with the company locally and, if so, agree some rules of engagement that frame how you can work with the company, how your involvement will complement the broader partnership and how any resultant income will be credited internally.

If you are a fundraiser in a smaller charity that has no significant existing corporate relationships, you should review your supporter database to identify which, if any, companies have supported you in the past. Familiarise yourself with those names and the nature of their support, rank their donations in order of size, and carry out further research into your best prospects. Go back as far as records allow, resisting the temptation to impose a random cut-off date. (More recent supporters are likely to be your best prospects, but I know of several significant donations and partnerships that have come about through the sensitive rekindling of connections with long-forgotten supporters.)

'Cold' companies

Regardless of how many warm supporters you have, the time will come when you must make some approaches to 'cold' companies: those that don't currently support you and, at the coldest end of the spectrum, those that don't even know of your charity's existence. Where possible, start with those closest to you, such as your charity's current suppliers, trustees' contacts and beneficiaries' contacts (if appropriate), and perhaps your own friends and networks.

Next, examine your local area and consider:

- Who are the biggest employers?
- Which are the fastest growing businesses?
- Which have the highest turnover or biggest profits?
- Who are the highest-profile movers and shakers in each industry?
- Which businesses have a track record of charitable support?

- What form do those relationships take and when might they be coming to an end?

This stage is simply about investing time in comprehensive desk research – establishing who is out there and what opportunities exist, and then prioritising accordingly.

Think sectors rather than companies

One effective scoping strategy is to consider your charity's potential sphere of influence – both geographically and in terms of business sectors that fit naturally with your cause. It is then easier to refine your options and to research companies within those categories. For example, a national eye-care charity might list its priority sectors as opticians, sunglasses brands and pharmaceutical companies. Meanwhile, an outward-bound centre for disadvantaged young people might consider targeting the outdoor retail sector, travel and tourism, outdoor clothing brands and businesses with large workforces that might be attracted by volunteering opportunities.

Familiarise yourself with each target

Once you have identified a range of relevant industries or sectors and narrowed down your targets to a manageable number of individual warm and cold companies, the next step is to carry out deeper research in order to better understand each business. By delving into a company's activities, culture, language, structure, markets, brands, sub-brands and even its competitors, you will be in a better position to target it effectively.

Such information can usually be garnered from any of a variety of sources, such as the company's website, Companies House, *The Guide to UK Company Giving*,[12] Google, social media, local or trade press, or even a friendly receptionist. Alternatively, your database might reveal useful connections, such as a payroll giver, event participant or volunteer who works for the company in question, or you may identify another corporate supporter who can shed light on the company's culture and operations, or who would be prepared to facilitate an introduction.

Keep in mind at all times that the relationship will need to work both ways. Your charity's reputation should be enhanced by the corporate relationship and any risks will need to be minimised. Keep a close eye on the bigger picture of how the company operates. Are its commercial ethics at odds with those of your charity? A corporate-charity relationship should not be sought at any cost, however tempting the potential financial rewards. (For details on legal and regulatory issues and how to carry out due diligence on a potential corporate partner, see *Corporate Fundraising and Partnerships* at www.dsc.org.uk/cfr.)

2. 'Friend-raising' comes before fundraising

As well as conducting desk research, you must be prepared to invest sufficient time in networking and 'friend-raising' in order to turn a cold company into a warm (or at least a lukewarm) one. You need to be regularly out of the office, raising your charity's profile locally and building relationships within the business community. It can be particularly helpful, for example, to:

- join business networks, such as the local Chamber of Commerce, in order to attend their networking events;
- offer to give talks at business breakfasts;
- attend Rotary, Round Table and Lions Clubs events.

You will need to be comfortable operating in such an environment and be capable of building strong relationships, and you will usually need to wait several months before broaching the subject of financial (or other) support. The old adage that 'people give to people' (and particularly to people they like) holds true, even when you are dealing with hard-nosed business executives.

In short, by taking time to identify and thoroughly research prospective sectors, partners and products, as well as 'winning friends and influencing people' (in the words of the famously titled book), you will find it easier to decide whether a particular company would be a suitable partner for your charity. If it would, you should also make sure you have a clear sense of which part of the business to target – whether that be the corporate social responsibility (CSR) team, the marketing team, the sponsorship team or the human resources team – in order to stand the best possible chance of success.

3. When you know what companies want, offer it to them

The more research and homework you do, and the more you understand a company's business, markets and challenges, the more likely it is that you will be able to develop a relevant and impactful proposal that will make the company sit up and take notice. To frame your thinking, consider:

- What might this company need from its CSR or charity partnerships?
- What problems or challenges is it facing?
- What role can my organisation play in providing a solution to any such problems or challenges?
- What value can my organisation add?

Benefits your activities might offer a corporate partner include:

- access to existing or new customers;
- access to new audiences (e.g. via channels such as social media pages, newsletters, surveys and events);
- attracting media coverage and providing access to new communication channels;
- brand enhancement and product differentiation;
- improved staff engagement, team-working, internal communications, skills development and employee relations;
- enhanced ability to attract – and retain – employees;
- help with researching, developing, testing or launching a new product or service;
- assistance with community consultation and engagement;
- stronger relationships with suppliers;
- access to policymakers.

At this point, carefully audit your own assets and the ways in which you might position them to companies. What channels, events or activities (shops, local groups, fundraising events, consultancy services, volunteering opportunities, etc.) does your charity own or operate that might provide a fundraising, marketing or staff engagement hook for a business? Which of the typical corporate fundraising and engagement mechanisms – philanthropic support, formal adoptions (such as Charity of the Year), cause-related marketing, sponsorship, payroll giving, pro bono support, gifts in kind, etc. – could best be employed to help the company achieve its objectives? By turning the tables in this way – focusing more on *what you can do for them* than on *what they can do for you* – your proposal is far more likely to stand out from the crowd.

It is also worth noting that, if you are targeting larger companies, charitable support and community investment can fall within the remit of a range of departments. It can therefore help to consider how many corporate boxes your proposal can tick, rather than just aiming to tick one. In other words, does your proposal appeal to the company just from the point of view of PR (for example)? Or does it also look attractive from the perspective of CSR, communications, marketing, HR and so on?

It can help your cause even more if you consider using a less conventional route into a target company. For example, if you have developed an event that could offer strong employee engagement or a volunteering opportunity, you may find that it receives a warmer response if you channel it via the HR team than if you direct it at the CSR or community affairs department. In this case, you may also find that, because you are dealing with people less used to working directly with charities, you experience fewer of the usual barriers and standard rejections.

4. Take time to develop a strong proposition

To engage businesses and set yourself apart from other charities, your 'offer'[13] needs to be simple, tangible, emotive and, if possible, local or regional in nature. It is vital to select the right product, project or fundraising mechanism; to pitch it at the right price and to the right audience; and to make it clear how the target company can support you and what you can offer them. Moreover, make sure the pitch stays in line with your charity's objectives and that your offer only features things that you can deliver.

The prospect of engaging with companies can certainly be intimidating, but keep in mind that all companies are run by people. They are most likely to be interested in the same aspects of the charity's work that engage your individual supporters[14] – whether that be the opportunity to fund the training of a cute guide dog puppy, a sight-restoring cataract operation or a holiday for a terminally ill child. Play to your strengths by focusing your offer on what your charity does best, what it is best known for, and what differentiates it from the competition. Use everyday language to convey passion and emotion in a way that tugs at the heartstrings and makes people want to take action, without getting overly soppy or sentimental. Aim to develop a product that will instantly engage the company and make its employees feel that their support – in whatever form – is going to have a sustained impact on your work and your beneficiaries, while also enabling them to meet their own objectives.

This approach has worked well for Whoopsadaisy, a small Brighton-based charity that supports children with cerebral palsy and other motor disorders. The charity has developed a strong corporate offer relating to the annual cost of providing a child with a place in its under-fives groups. At £3,500, this clear and inspiring 'product' can act either as a focus for longer-term corporate support or as a platform for staff engagement (such as via a mass participation event or a DIY fundraising campaign). The proposition can also easily be scaled up or down to take into account a company's CSR or charity budget, fundraising target, timescales, and other business constraints and objectives.

5. Ensure you're 'pitch perfect'

Once you're clear about the rationale for your approach and the best engagement angle, and once you've identified the right person to contact, you should spend time honing and rehearsing your pitch, verbally and on paper, even if you're only preparing for a phone call. Ask a friend or colleague to review your approach and business case to see whether they are coherent and stand up to scrutiny, and then amend accordingly.

While it is generally fairly straightforward to pick up the phone to a supporter, it can be a real challenge to approach new prospects, because completely cold approaches rarely work. Although this is an extreme example, the potential scale of the task is demonstrated by the fact that, in a typical year, HSBC receives around 10,000 unsolicited sponsorship proposals, of which no more than four (0.04%) are successful.[15] The challenge when approaching companies, then, is to do whatever homework is required to make your approach stand out for all the right reasons. For you, as the fundraiser, this means meticulously examining, understanding and mapping the target company; engaging its people in dialogue; and then creating a focused and tailored proposition. This kind of ongoing, market- and customer-led background work and preparation can mean the difference between a well-targeted approach and one that falls on fallow ground.

6. Adopt a strategic, integrated mindset

Community-based corporate fundraising has a tendency to be rather ad hoc, uncoordinated and opportunistic, and this is rarely a recipe for success. This is often the case within larger charities, where there may be several regional corporate fundraisers and many more community fundraisers. In this scenario, the fundraisers' natural inclination will be to achieve their individual income targets, so it is important to continually encourage them to work together for the greater good. Furthermore, in many charities, there is confusion about where exactly corporate fundraising ends and where community fundraising begins, with blurred lines between the two teams that inevitably leads to confusion, ill-feeling, duplication of effort and missed opportunities.

The solution is for each fundraiser's plans and priorities to be informed by the wider fundraising strategy and for there to be strong management and clear rules of engagement to frame any fundraising activities.

There also needs to be an open, pragmatic ethos of teamwork instilled across your fundraising team that enables all fundraisers and volunteers to see and appreciate the bigger picture. This is, of course, easier said than done, but it can sometimes be achieved through the use of financial reporting arrangements that encourage staff to work together and that present a truer reflection of each fundraiser's contribution within the team.

Two possible techniques include:

1. **The finder's fee arrangement,** whereby a percentage (such as 25% of the value of a corporate donation or partnership) is attributed to the income target of the community fundraiser who made the initial introduction, before the corporate account is passed to the corporate fundraising team to manage. (Conversely, where a corporate fundraiser seals a deal that needs to be managed by a regional or community fundraiser, the finder's fee might be attributed to the corporate fundraiser's income target.)
2. **A soft-crediting system** whereby some or all of the income that an individual fundraiser has helped to raise for a different department is recorded against their performance targets but is still allocated to the different department's income budget within the management accounts. This approach acts as an incentive for fundraisers to work collaboratively across their team or between departments, in the knowledge that their contribution is being recognised. Furthermore, it can provide managers with a useful informal performance-management tool as well as a clearer sense of the true return on investment and added value of different fundraising activities.

I have had experience of using both of these tactics (and a combination of the two) within several charities, and they helped to improve performance and avoid the turf wars and silo-working that can be a feature of corporate–community fundraising. It is important to note, however, that such targets and incentives only work well in organisations where there is an established culture of effective performance management and sound financial management processes.

7. Volunteers can be your best fundraisers

It is essential to appreciate the role of volunteers within the context of corporate fundraising and the way in which they are often able to help you reach the parts of the community that other fundraisers can't reach. There are few more inspiring things than hearing a volunteer with a personal connection to a cause speaking passionately about their experience of a charity's impact and, as such, volunteers can play an invaluable role in raising awareness and opening doors. It is also the case that, while such grassroots, community-level fundraising can sometimes provide a poor return on investment if done by paid staff, it can be a highly cost-effective strategy if such work is delivered by volunteers and leads to new corporate partnerships.

Of course, while volunteers can undoubtedly be a huge asset when it comes to facilitating business relationships, particularly if they have a strong connection to your cause, they can be a considerable challenge to manage, motivate and incentivise given that they are not on the payroll. Nevertheless, it is vital that you invest appropriately in training and supporting volunteers so that they are aware of – and buy into – the bigger picture, and are able to approach and engage with businesses as effectively as your salaried team members do. (For more information on supporting volunteers, see chapter 9.)

8. Invest appropriately in the partnership and manage it professionally

Once the scope and terms of a new corporate partnership have been agreed, it is vital that it is managed professionally from day one. A corporate partner who is gaining any form of commercial benefit is classified by the Charities Act 1992 (as updated in 2016) as a 'commercial participator'.[16] To this end, the best starting point is to draw up a letter of agreement or a contract between the parties (which may also involve the charity's trading subsidiary, if it has one and if there is a commercial angle to the relationship).

While, legally, the onus is on the company to put a contract in place, it is good practice for the charity to take the lead in this process and to finalise the legalities of the relationship as quickly as possible. You will also need to follow section 7.0 of the Code of Fundraising Practice, 'Professional fundraisers, commercial participators and partners' (see www.fundraisingregulator.org.uk).

If your charity is fortunate enough to have secured a major national partnership, there may be a need to restructure and recruit additional staff to cope with the increased workload and make the most of the opportunities available. In most cases, though, managing your new relationship may simply be a question of using the resources you have more effectively.

As a new partnership gets underway, the most likely scenario is that you will be asked to support companies with employee-led fundraising, perhaps in the context of a regional or national Charity of the Year relationship. This role can take many forms, but, typically, you might be required to:

- be on hand to provide **information** to the company about the work of the charity;
- make regular **presentations** to groups of staff about the importance and impact of their support;
- produce good-quality **fundraising materials** (perhaps incorporating an A–Z of fundraising ideas, blank posters for promoting events, sponsorship forms, press release templates, etc.);

• take the lead in organising and running suitable **local fundraising activities** (family fun days, Christmas jumper days, bake sales, etc.);

• identify and promote opportunities for staff to get involved in the charity's **centrally organised activities** (sky dives, parachute jumps, overseas challenges, etc.);

• identify and build a **good working relationship** with the company's fundraising committee or 'champion' (the person who acts as an ambassador for your charity within the company and as a liaison between the two organisations) – this may involve agreeing a partnership plan and ensuring that it is followed, building support across the company (while ensuring that fundraising fatigue does not set in), trouble-shooting, and generally keeping everyone happy;

• **engage the company's management** in the charity's work by arranging project visits or meetings with beneficiaries;

• **meet with the company's marketing or communications team** to understand the internal communication channels, agree internal messaging and identify angles for promoting the partnership externally, such as via social media, the local press and relevant trade publications;

• provide regular **thank yous and feedback** to the company;

• **maintain a relationship and dialogue** with the company after the adoption of your charity has formally ended, keeping them abreast of the longer-term impact of their support on the charity's beneficiaries – and looking for opportunities for further engagement.

9. Think long-term partnerships, not short-term flings

If your charity's finances are under pressure, corporate fundraising is unlikely to provide the swift cash injection required. Lucrative, strategic business relationships can take months, if not years, to broker, and immediate, large donations are increasingly rare. It is usually futile investing in corporate fundraising over the short term – it is investment in the 'long game' (i.e. a partnership of five years or more) that will generally pay off.

This is also the case with individual partnerships, where it is usually the case that the longer the association, the greater the benefits. The best advice is to resist short-term flings with companies, regardless of how attractive they seem, and instead aim to negotiate long-term relationships. In my experience, working with a company for a limited period of time – less than one year, for instance – can lead to frustration on both sides, missed opportunities and a waste of valuable resources. This is simply because it can take a year or more to get to know each other properly and to align both organisations effectively behind a campaign or appeal.

10. Major partnerships are a distraction

Major blue-chip companies and brands are regarded as the holy grail of corporate fundraising, for the simple reason that partnerships with them can present unrivalled opportunities for income generation and awareness. A major adoption by a supermarket, for example, can now generate in excess of £18 million for the partner charity,[17] taking a charity's fundraising and profile to unprecedented levels.

Such relationships are, however, very much the exception rather than the rule and, arguably, something of a distraction for the vast majority of charities. The reality is that, rather than investing considerable resources in trying to land a major partnership, most corporate and community fundraisers are better off focusing their attention on their local or regional business environment. By doing so, they are likely to enjoy far greater success while avoiding the myriad stresses, strains and growing pains that usually go with a major corporate partnership.

The rationale for this stance is twofold. First, there are thousands more small companies than large ones, so you will have far more choice and chance of success by targeting these smaller companies. In fact, government figures reveal that, of the 5.5 million private sector businesses in the UK in 2016, large businesses (i.e. those with more than 250 employees) accounted for only 0.1% of all businesses.[18] With more than 5 million small and medium-sized enterprises located around the UK, the vast majority of which will never have been asked to support a charity in a strategic or mutually beneficial way, this sector represents a huge, virtually untapped resource for corporate and community fundraisers.

Second, it makes sense for the vast majority of charities to seek partnerships with small and medium-sized enterprises rather than major brands and businesses for the simple reason that most charities themselves are small or medium-sized. NCVO figures show that, in 2015/16, charities earning under £100,000 accounted for 47.6% of organisations and 1.5% of the sector's income, while charities earning over £10 million accounted for 0.4% of organisations and 49.6% of the sector's income.[19] This makes the business case for developing partnerships between charities and small and medium-sized enterprises all the more compelling.

There is certainly no rule which holds that charity–corporate partnerships should be the preserve of the larger, household-name charities. In fact, a small, well-run voluntary organisation (such as Whoopsadaisy, highlighted above) with impactful local or regional services can make just as strong a partnership proposition as a national charity if it takes the time to package its strengths and assets.

Case study: Age UK and innocent's Big Knit – corporate partnership with participatory fundraising

A West London smoothie company, a charity for older people, thousands of community craftivists and 5 million miniature woolly hats. This is the story of how a community fundraising activity of crafting to raise funds has provided the infrastructure for a cause-related-marketing promotion where innocent makes a donation for every smoothie drink sold with a knitted woollen hat.

In 2003, innocent, an emerging UK drinks brand with a unique brand personality and values of doing good and keeping it fresh, developed an off-the-wall idea to top its smoothie bottles with little hand-knitted hats in winter. Innocent approached us at Age UK (Age Concern at the time) with a proposition: ask the older people you support to knit the little hats and we'll make a donation from every be-hatted bottle sold.

The appeal of the Big Knit spanned both older donors, some of whom are also service users, and a younger generation inspired by a resurgence in crafting and the explosion of social media. In turn, social media also provided a cost-effective platform to reach millennials. Together, we and innocent smoothies generated playful, interactive content that encouraged audiences to get involved, knit a hat and share their stories. For us at Age UK, this has provided our widest community engagement campaign to date and has developed a rewarding relationship with a new audience of younger supporters. With over 6 million mini woolly creations knitted to date, the campaign has also so far raised £2 million. The initiative furthermore meets innocent's positioning of helping people to live well while creating a fun experience for customers. In turn, it creates deeper connections with consumers than traditional marketing does and helps innocent's smoothies to stand out of the crowd.

Hannorah Lee, Head of Corporate Partnerships and Community Fundraising, Age UK, and Daniel Stewart, Corporate and Community Fundraising Manager, Age UK

Conclusion

The aim of this chapter has been to provide a broad and objective view of the challenges that fundraisers face in raising funds from companies and to advise on what you need to do to realise sustained growth from this income stream. Corporate–charity partnerships can be challenging to secure and execute effectively, even for the most experienced practitioners, and there are few quick wins.

It takes time to identify and research supporters and prospects, to refine propositions, to prepare applications and proposals to the required standard, to negotiate suitable terms, to ensure that your charity does not compromise its own ethics and objectives, and to build long-lasting, meaningful relationships. That said, despite the many challenges and potential pitfalls, if you are a creative and commercially minded fundraiser, there are few limits to the ways in which you can engage with companies at the local, regional or national level. Given sufficient planning, investment and internal support, the impact of corporate fundraising on your charity, your beneficiaries *and* your corporate partner can be profound and can usually be achieved without prohibitively high costs.

Notes

1 Catherine Walker, *The Company Giving Almanac 2013*, London, DSC, 2013, pp. xiii–xiv. Data was collected from the latest available company accounts; most year ends were 2011 (74%), followed by 2010 (19%) and 2012 (7%).
2 *Corporate Giving by the FTSE 100* [PDF], CAF, 2018, www.cafonline.org/about-us/publications/2018-publications/corporate-giving-by-the-ftse-100, p. 9, accessed 23 July 2018.
3 *Ibid.*, p. 8.
4 Catherine Walker, *The Company Giving Almanac 2013*, London, DSC, 2013, pp. xiii–xiv.
5 *Cone Communications/Ebiquity Global CSR Study 2015* [PDF], Cone Communications, 2015, www.conecomm.com/research-blog/2015-cone-communications-ebiquity-global-csr-study, pp. 7, 10 and 22, accessed 23 July 2018. Interviews were conducted with 9,709 shoppers in nine countries: Brazil, Canada, China, France, Germany, India, Japan, the UK and the USA.
6 *Corporate–NGO Partnerships Barometer 2017* [PDF], C&E Advisory Services, 2017, www.candeadvisory.com/barometer, p. 8, accessed 26 July 2018.
7 Melanie May, '6 corporate fundraising partnerships helping UK charities' [web article], UK Fundraising, https://fundraising.co.uk/2018/12/28/6-corporate-fundraising-partnerships-helping-uk-charities, 28 December 2018.
8 Melanie May, '12 corporate fundraising partnerships' [web article], UK Fundraising, https://fundraising.co.uk/2018/06/19/250494, 19 June 2018.
9 Howard Lake, 'ScottishPower raises £20m for CRUK in six years' [web article], UK Fundraising, https://fundraising.co.uk/2018/12/17/scottishpower-raises-20m-cruk-six-years, 17 December 2018.
10 Melanie May, '12 corporate fundraising partnerships' [web article], UK Fundraising, https://fundraising.co.uk/2018/06/19/250494, 19 June 2018.
11 Melanie May, 'Christmas fundraising & corporate support round-up' [web article], UK Fundraising, https://fundraising.co.uk/2018/12/17/christmas-fundraising-corporate-support-round, 17 December 2018.

12 See www.dsc.org.uk/gcg for the book and www.dsc.org.uk/funding-website for the searchable subscription website, which contains a company giving arm. Both the book and the website offer detailed information on over 400 companies, including who to contact, any application processes, the company's financial details and number of employees, and examples of organisations the company has supported in the past. They also offer details on companies' preferred methods of giving, including cash donations, in-kind support, employee-led support, sponsorship and/or commercially led support.

13 In both business and fundraising, the term 'offer' describes the full package being offered to a customer. It includes the physical product, if there is one, and other factors which together make up the sum total of what is on offer. In fundraising and direct marketing, the offer refers not only to how much is being asked for but also to the rationale for giving, such as what the money will be used for and how the donor will feel as a result of giving. In corporate sponsorship, the offer might be made up of tangible benefits along with the expectation of good customer service from the charity and the less tangible warm glow from being involved with a good cause.

14 Beth Breeze, *Corporate Philanthropy on the Shop Floor: What drives employee fundraising?* [working paper], Centre for Charitable Giving and Philanthropy and the University of Kent, 2013, www.kent.ac.uk/sspssr/philanthropy/documents/CP-from-the-shop-floor-Beth-Breeze-May-2013.pdf, p. 5, accessed 23 July 2018.

15 Figures noted by HSBC speakers at the European Sponsorship Association's Future Sponsorship Conference, as reported in 'Future Sponsorship 09 split over impact of recession as biggest shake up for the industry for 25 years predicted' [press release], SportCal, www.sportcal.com/News/PressReleases/36170?size=50, 27 November 2009.

16 'Charities Act 2016: New fundraising rules' [web page], Charity Commission, 2016, www.gov.uk/government/news/charities-act-2016-new-fundraising-rules, accessed 1 August 2018.

17 Taku Dzimwasha, 'Diabetes UK partnership with Tesco raises £18.6m in less than two years' [web article], Third Sector, www.thirdsector.co.uk/diabetes-uk-partnership-tesco-raises-186m-less-two-years/fundraising/article/1336034, 27 February 2015.

18 Chris Rhodes, *Business Statistics (Briefing Paper no. 06152)* [PDF], House of Commons Library, 2017, http://researchbriefings.parliament.uk/ResearchBriefing/Summary/SN06152#fullreport, p. 5, accessed 23 July 2018.

19 'UK Civil Society Almanac 2018: Income data' and 'UK Civil Society Almanac 2018: Scope data' [web pages], NCVO, 2018, https://data.ncvo.org.uk/a/almanac18/income-data-2015-16 and https://data.ncvo.org.uk/a/almanac18/scope-data-2015-16, accessed 16 August 2018.

CHAPTER THIRTEEN

Recruiting, leading and developing community fundraisers

Liz Haigh-Reeve and Claire Singlehurst

Introduction

The competition for good fundraisers is intense, with many organisations struggling to find people with the right skill sets. Community and event fundraisers are in particular demand[1] and over 50% of community fundraising managers find it difficult to recruit.[2] Yet, once appointed, fundraisers have the highest turnover rates of staff in the voluntary sector.[3] This poor level of retention is costly in terms of lost learning, re-recruiting and potential damage to relationships with supporters. However, when the right teams are in place and they gain experience of performing successfully together, learning to blend each other's different skills and strengths, fundraisers will remain longer in their roles.[4] In this chapter, we consider what makes a great community fundraiser, how to identify and recruit them, and how to develop a high-performance team by managing talent and developing leadership.

What makes a great community fundraiser?

While community fundraising looks different in every charity, with varying combinations of participative fundraising activities and geographical reach, the role of the community fundraiser requires a broader range of skills than ever. Communities are becoming ever more diverse, with multicultural and multifaceted groups providing rich sources of ideas, talent and fundraising. In this context, community fundraisers need to know how to flex their fundraising models to inspire and engage both geographically bounded fundraising committees and new communities based on an array of social groups (such as gym members, cycling clubs, car enthusiasts, music lovers or artisan producers). They need to address the needs of hard-pressed and time-poor schools and local businesses, facilitate the support of traditional groups such as Rotary clubs and Freemasons, and engage digital communities, new business hubs and even the coffee shop community.

To ignite the interest of these networks, a great community fundraiser needs to be able to research potential participants' needs and motivations, plan effectively, implement those plans, review the outcomes, and adjust their strategies and tactics accordingly. They need to be able to judge when to step in to work with their volunteers and when to step back, how to evaluate where they can achieve the best returns for their efforts, and by what means they can develop a multitude of relationships. Often working remotely from central fundraising teams, they need to be resourceful, creative and independent decision makers who can confidently bring to life – often for vastly differing audiences – the case for supporting their organisation. They need to have strong interpersonal skills, be talented verbal communicators, be able to write engaging copy and have the ability to create shareable content for a variety of digital platforms. They must be facilitators who help supporters achieve their goal of making a difference to the people or cause that they care about, and to do this they need to judge the levels of help or assistance different individuals and groups will require to make their experience successful and meaningful.

While the key technical skills of a community fundraiser are usefully summarised in the Fundraising National Occupational Standards,[5] mastering these skills alone is not enough to make a great community fundraiser. Successful fundraisers also display a particular mindset. They tend to be people who are open to gaining new experience, are able to consider and evaluate various solutions, have passion for the cause, and are enthusiastic about testing new fundraising approaches.[6]

How to recruit the best community fundraisers

To recruit the best people, you will need to demonstrate that your charity is a great employer that cares about its staff and is clear about its expectations of them. This starts with producing a clear job description and a person specification that accurately describes whom you are looking for. Think through the role:

- Who are the key stakeholders?
- What do you expect from the post holder? What skills, competencies and personal qualities or attitudes are essential?
- How much time can you give your new recruit? Are you looking for an experienced charity professional or will you consider someone with transferrable skills but who will require more training time initially?

One of the destructive demons for fundraisers is silo-working. When drawing up the job description, you need to think through how your fundraisers will work together and support each other to ensure that each of your supporters is treated holistically across all fundraising teams.

Once you have a clear job description and person specification, consider what else will be in the recruitment documentation that will help you to promote your charity to the potential applicant:

- What makes your charity a great place to work?
- What benefits does it offer?
- What are the options for flexible working?
- How do you reward success (additional leave days, experience days, bonuses, etc.)?

Some charities will have a standardised procedure, laid down by the HR team, for what is included in the recruitment pack, but in smaller charities this often falls to the fundraising manager. Here are some materials you could consider including:

- a welcome letter from the chief executive or department head summarising the role's purpose and what the person who gets the role will need to achieve;
- the job description and person specification;
- an annual review;
- an organisation chart;
- testimonials from other members of staff about why your charity is a great place to work;
- information about how your charity is committed to training and staff development;
- a message from a service user;
- some links to online videos about your work.

To develop your recruitment packs, test on colleagues those being used by other charities to prompt feedback on what your colleagues like and dislike about the approach taken. As with every piece of material, this documentation is a window onto your charity, so check that your pack:

- reflects your charity's values;
- demonstrates the difference that your charity makes;
- differentiates between your charity and others;
- highlights the benefits of working with your charity;

• shows a commitment to all stakeholders: beneficiaries, supporters, staff and volunteers.

Where to find your new team member

Finding the right person – someone who has the skills and competencies you need and also fits in well with your team – can be daunting. There are plenty of options open to you, some more expensive than others and some that require more time. Table 13.1 summarises some of these options.

TABLE 13.1 RECRUITMENT SOURCES

Recruitment method	Advantages	Disadvantages and risks	Comments
Advertising in publications read by those working in fundraising, such as *The Guardian*, *The Sunday Times*, *Third Sector* and local press.	• This provides an opportunity to promote your charity to a wide audience and reach those who have not previously considered a fundraising role.	• It can be expensive and there are no guarantees – you pay even if your recruitment is unsuccessful. • You will be bombarded by agencies seeking to help you.	• Try to negotiate on price. • An advertising package will usually include both the print publication and the associated website.
Advertising on online recruitment sites only.	• This is less expensive than advertising in publications. • Many candidates seeking new roles will check online sites. • It is a cost-effective way of reaching a wide audience.	• You have to pay regardless of success. • You will reach only those who are aware of specialist recruitment sites.	• It is worth checking with fundraising peers to find out which sites they have used successfully.

Advertising on social media sites, such as in the Fundraising Chat group on Facebook, or on LinkedIn or Twitter.	• Many opportunities are free of charge. • These adverts can reach wide audiences through shares. • This route can particularly reach millennials.	• There is limited space to sell a role, so ensure you include links for candidates to click on to see more information about the role and its requirements.	• It is always worth including the free sites in your recruitment efforts – you only need to find one person, and you could be lucky and find that one person through a free route.
Using a specialist fundraising recruitment consultant.	• Building a relationship with the agency of your choice means they get to know and understand your charity and who will be the best fit. • The agency will usually undertake some initial screening, check references and schedule interviews for you. • If the recruitment is unsuccessful, there is either no fee or a reduced fee.	• A successful appointment is usually charged as a percentage of the salary to be paid, so it can be expensive.	• It is worth negotiating: most consultants have some wriggle room on the fee. • If your candidate doesn't work out and leaves within the first few weeks, you can usually negotiate a refund or a free replacement.

Networking through your own personal contacts, on social media sites, at conferences, etc.	• The only cost is your time (but this may also be a disadvantage). • Peer-to-peer recommendations can be a powerful source of good candidates.	• It can be time-consuming. • There is the risk of producing limited diversity if you are only reaching out to people you already know.	• Institute of Fundraising conferences usually have a jobs board. • Look out for other networking opportunities and special interest groups.
Using CV database searches.	• This method provides access to a wide base of candidates.	• It can be time-consuming. • You need to ensure you are using the right keywords for searches. • There is a subscription fee. • CVs may not be up to date.	• Targeting those not currently looking to change roles with the right opportunity can encourage them to consider a career development opportunity earlier than they had planned.

Ensure that the application process is not overly complicated and decide whether you are going to use application forms or CVs. Asking candidates to use application forms ensures more consistency and allows you to get answers to specific questions about their skills and experience. This process is more time-consuming for applicants, so it may put some off, but not those who are serious about the role. Application forms are also an easier means of comparing candidates against your criteria. Requesting CVs makes the response quicker for candidates and the looser format provides an opportunity for them to show more of their personality, but this format makes evaluating candidates more onerous.

Interviewing candidates

First decide on the format of the interview process:

- Do you plan to have a single interview stage and then make a decision on whom to appoint immediately, or will you see a long list and hope to find two or three strong candidates whom you want to invite to a second interview? (A one-stage interview is risky, as nerves can skew a candidate's performance; a second interview can help you to make a more complete judgement.)

- Will you set any sort of test for your candidates?
- Will you use psychometric testing to see how individuals may fit within a team?
- Do you plan to introduce candidates to team members during the interview process to judge potential team dynamics?
- Will you include a tour of your charity so as to give candidates an opportunity to see its work and/or a chance to meet beneficiaries? (This can be very motivating for candidates but is time-consuming for staff, so it may be best saved for second-interview stage.)
- Who will conduct the interviews? (The interviewers should be the people who are best placed to judge candidates' competencies against the role, the team and the fundraising objectives. Some organisations always include a member of the HR team, but it can be helpful to include a stakeholder, such as the chair of a local fundraising group or another key volunteer.)
- Do you want to have a different interview panel at second interview? (While a mix of perspectives can be helpful, it is vital that all those involved in the interview are clear on the requirements of the role.)

Once you have judged applications and/or CVs against the required key skills and competencies and created a shortlist of people to invite to interview, you will need to plan the interview questions.

Competency-based interview questions

Competency-based interview questions include the STAR technique, which stands for situation, task, action and result. For example, a candidate might be asked to describe a situation where they had a communication problem, what their responsibility was, the action they took to solve the problem, and what the result was and whether they would do anything differently in hindsight. Go through the person specification and job description pulling out what you consider to be the most important competencies and frame some questions based on these.

Value-based interview questions

Combining value-based interview questions with competency-based questions can help you to establish whether your candidate is a good fit for your charity. For example, if trust is one of your core values, you might ask a candidate how they would respond if they knew for certain that a colleague was misleading a supporter.

Before and after the interview: prepare and evaluate

Make sure you give yourself and the colleagues you are interviewing with sufficient time before and after each interview to prepare and evaluate. For example, you may need to discuss the results of any specific tests you have set before the candidate comes into the room. Recruiting a great candidate can be enormously satisfying, and recruiting the wrong person will be demoralising for you, the team and your new appointment. It is very costly to make a bad decision, so time spent in preparation will pay off in the long run.

Once you have found your ideal candidate, communicate their success as quickly as possible both informally by phone and formally by letter and contract. This shows your enthusiasm for them to be a part of your team and reduces the risk of them taking up another role if you delay. Appointments should be subject to checking references to ensure the validity of claims about experience and qualifications. You might choose to check these before conducting second interviews.

Welcoming new staff

The factors that determine how well a new member of staff will perform start even before someone's induction. Make sure that the practical issues have been dealt with efficiently and that your new team member knows who to ask about pension issues, travel season tickets, their contract and their own specific needs. Who will meet them on their first day? Should they bring lunch or will you be taking them out for lunch that day? Do they know your office dress code? Is their desk clear and clean with empty drawers? Will they be hot-desking? Is any equipment – such as a computer, laptop, mobile or car – ready?

It's worthwhile getting existing staff to brainstorm what could be added to the induction plan to make new employees feel welcome. Also consider training existing staff to buddy up with new starters so as to provide a friendly face and point of contact for information and advice. In the first few days, help everyone to get to know each other and consider social opportunities such as a team lunch.

Table 13.2 can be used as a checklist for what might be included in an induction period to help new staff understand the mission they are working to achieve, the goals of the team and how their role is interdependent with other roles in the organisation.

TABLE 13.2 INDUCTION CHECKLIST

<table>
<tr><th>Meetings</th><th>Training</th><th>Practical information to be provided</th></tr>
<tr>
<td>Depending on the role and seniority of the new employee, consider arranging meetings between the employee and the following people and departments:
• Department heads: overview of each department and their role and goals.
• HR induction: sickness reporting, holidays, working hours, training opportunities, claiming expenses, requesting holiday, time off in lieu, etc.
• Team members: job-specific introductions.
• Handover meeting either with previous post holder or with line manager.
• Chief executive: to explain the charity's vision and mission and current priorities.
• Line manager: agree key milestones, key performance indicators (KPIs), targets, budgets, etc. This may include the finance team.
• Key supporters and volunteers.</td>
<td>Arrange training to cover all of the following areas that are relevant:
• IT: computer systems, database and internal information management.
• Health and safety.
• First aid.
• Mandatory training, e.g. safeguarding.
• Skills training (e.g. training on using the charity's database, training in working with volunteers, training in managing difficult people, etc.)
• Learning about the organisation's work.
• Support with professional qualifications such as the Institute of Fundraising's Certificate in Fundraising and Diploma in Fundraising.</td>
<td>Provide all of the following that are relevant:
• Organisation chart with photos.
• Floor plan of the building.
• Glossary of any acronyms used by the charity.
• Simple map of the local area, shops, cafes, etc.
• Important passwords, security codes, etc.
• Copies of the:
– vision, mission and values of the charity;
– organisational strategy;
– business plan;
– fundraising strategy;
– budget.
• Policies and procedures on probation period, performance management, grievances, disciplinary, locking up, and what to do if a person is the first in or the last to leave for the day.
• Handover notes.
• List of dates of key meetings, and dates papers (i.e. a document containing a new idea, such as the case for a new database) are due.
• Dates and format of key regular reports that will be required.
• Codes of practice and internal fundraising policies and procedures.</td>
</tr>
</table>

Managing staff performance

New staff will have a probationary period that has been specified in their contract of employment. They should be clear about what they are expected to achieve during their probation. Managers should set up regular one-to-ones to assess progress. A probationary period gives both the employer and the employee a chance to assess whether they have made the right decision. One-to-ones enable both parties to raise any concerns, set up additional support and reflect on what is going well.

For existing staff, the programme of regular monitoring and review of performance should be embedded in business planning, as illustrated in figure 13.1.

FIGURE 13.1 PERFORMANCE MONITORING AND REVIEWING WITHIN THE OVERALL BUSINESS PLANNING CYCLE

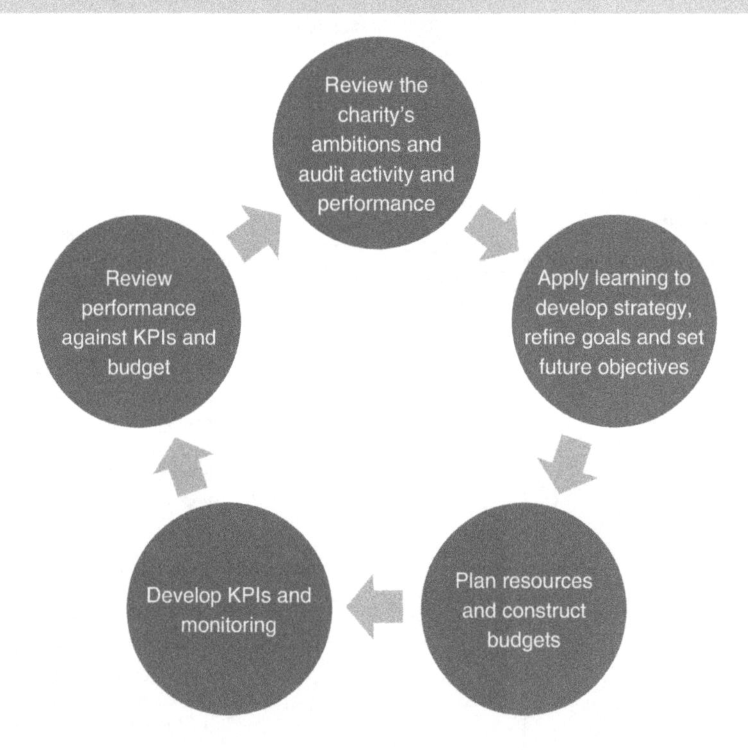

Excellent performance management starts with clarity of expectation. If staff are involved in every stage of the planning cycle and understand the challenges and opportunities that the charity and senior managers face, they will feel included and motivated. No one enjoys being kept in the dark and having targets and objectives imposed upon them without any consultation. Both during the period of business planning and throughout regular performance management, individuals and teams should be encouraged to reflect on and learn from all previous activities as well as to question current practice and explore new ideas.

Meetings

One-to-ones and performance reviews

One-to-one meetings and the annual performance review meeting are where a manager and team member can look more deeply at what is working well and where adjustments should be made. Generally, there should be no surprises from either side. Managers should recognise and address both good news and problems as they arise rather than waiting to talk about them at these meetings. Such meetings are not only an opportunity for managers to monitor progress against KPIs and budget but also an opening to understand the wider team issues, spot talent and get to know the ambitions and ideas of their staff.

Both managers and team members should prepare for one-to-ones and performance reviews in advance. In addition, reviews and one-to-one meetings need a structure, which could include elements such as those outlined in the following box.

Operational performance

- A review: what has gone well this month?
- KPIs
- Budget versus actual
- Learning points
- New opportunities
- Current challenges and concerns

Team performance

- Successes
- Changes, leavers and joiners
- Team dynamics
- Skills, training and special recognition
- Current challenges and concerns

Individual performance and development

- Staff member's own career aims
- Training and development opportunities: courses, job shadowing and mentoring
- 360-degree feedback
- Workload

Keeping written records of meetings removes ambiguity around feedback and agreed actions. Six-monthly and annual reviews should be documented to an agreed format, with key points usually prepared in advance by the post holder as a starting point for discussion. These are more formal meetings which form part of an employee's employment record. One-to-ones, which help the team member to keep on the right track and the manager to understand the issues faced by employee, occur frequently – usually monthly or fortnightly, depending on the level of support needed. One-to-ones should be documented. Some managers prefer to make notes at the meeting and to send them to their staff member, but experience suggests that it is more effective to ask the staff member to write up notes and agreed actions which the manager then signs off. One-to-one notes can be used as part of a performance management process if the team member is not performing well.

Giving feedback, both positive and negative, is a skill. By dealing with issues and giving praise as situations arise, you can prevent future problems, but even the most assiduous manager will sometimes have to address poor performance. The process is made easier by ensuring that everything that is discussed at each meeting is clear, documented and agreed.

Team meetings

A good leader will use a variety of meetings to keep their team on track and motivated, including:

- regular team meetings;
- planning meetings;
- creative brainstorms that drive innovation and solve problems;
- away days and off-site sessions.

The following section expands on how to develop exceptional teams.

Developing a high-performing team

A review of a vast number of theories and experimental data on leadership approaches was conducted by Stagl, Salas and Burke to detail the characteristics that make up high-performing teams.[7] The authors of the review focus on the conditions required to ensure effective team performance. Below, we have summarised the aspects of their review that we believe are most useful in a community fundraising context and have adapted them to fit that context:

1. **Team leaders should ensure team members' roles are interdependent by clearly defining shared goals and creating roles that rely on each other in order to achieve successful outcomes.** The studies cited within the report all demonstrate the importance of mutual reliance for creating a high-performing team. This interdependence works best when everyone in the team is pursuing the same goals and receiving feedback from the leader on how well the whole team is achieving both its tasks and its overall objectives. Furthermore, the team leader must ensure there is a clear structure so that everyone knows what outcomes they are accountable for and the expected overall performance of the team. This is particularly important in cases of cross-departmental work, where members of different teams work alongside each other on a particular project.
2. **Decision-making processes should be clearly determined regarding who has the authority to do what** (from setting the overall direction within the team to monitoring performance) to reduce the risk of team members making inappropriate decisions or failing to show initiative where a situation requires it. By communicating the standards that need to be achieved and considering who has the appropriate capabilities and levels of expertise, leaders can assign team tasks and delegate authority to team members to handle additional responsibilities. In a fundraising context, team members should understand in which cases authority ultimately lies with the trustees and therefore when the team is carrying out delegated responsibilities on their behalf. As a result, team members should know when they should be keeping the board informed and in what format the trustees require that information. For instance, some events and activities can present a high level of risk, both operationally and financially, and these should be included in the risk register and reports to the board.
3. **The membership of teams should remain as stable as possible, recognising that it takes time for members to learn to work together at an optimal level.** According to the research cited in the report, teams tend to achieve higher levels of performance the longer their

members work together. As outlined in the introduction to this chapter, given that fundraisers have the highest turnover rates of staff in the voluntary sector, this level of stability may be difficult to achieve. The case study on page 349, however, contains practical advice on how to reduce staff turnover.

4. **The team should have a clear and compelling shared direction, in line with the charity's overall mission; this will have the effect of engaging each member of the team to make the most of their capabilities.** When a team has a clear shared direction, it will be able to align its performance strategies with its overall purpose, and it will be able to see the direct links between each member's actions, the team's collective achievements and the results for the organisation's beneficiaries. In this way, members can see beyond their individual tasks and feel they are working both for the team and towards a higher purpose. (See the case study on page 349 for details on the importance of creating a vision and strategy, and linking individuals' objectives to that vision and strategy.) Team members should feel that their shared goal has a level of difficulty and a weight of importance that is challenging without being overwhelming.

5. **Team leaders who brief their teams at the start of a project in a 'transformational' way create a sense of mission that inspires members to achieve organisational objectives rather than focusing on their own.** The term 'transformational leadership' was originally coined by James V. Downton in 1973.[8] A transformational leadership style is primarily characterised by promoting the development of others in terms of their growth and levels of achievement within the context of a group or organisation. Transformational leaders have an inspiring, authentic and ethical leadership approach that inspires people to work for the greater good.[9] One way leaders can do this is to discuss and agree team values that are in line with the organisation's overall values. These then act as guiding principles whenever any member of the team creates a strategy, chooses how to behave in a given situation, decides which action to choose over another, etc.

6. **Effective leaders allow both the team as a unit and the individual members to set their own goals and monitor their own progress to achieve both personal and group goals.** Effective team leaders encourage a sense of ownership in other members of the team by giving them a clear desired end result but empowering them to decide the best means of achieving it and then letting them manage it themselves. They also allow team members to carry out full projects (rather than disconnected elements of a project) that contain a

combination of tasks requiring a variety of skills, and may also give team members extra management responsibilities. In community fundraising, volunteers in the community should also have a sense of ownership, and it is the role of the community fundraiser to empower volunteers and support and inspire them. This can often require good negotiating skills in cases when volunteers want to delegate responsibility to the community fundraiser.

7. **Team leaders should aim to optimise the composition and size of the team.** It is the leader's responsibility to balance the range of skills, personalities and abilities that are necessary for high performance – through spotting the potential in and developing existing staff, appointing new members, employing external experts for specific projects, or a mixture of these ways. The research analysed in the report also suggests that the size of a team can have an influence on its performance. When a team is growing, it becomes more difficult to keep its members motivated, well equipped, well co-ordinated and sufficiently rewarded. Consequently, effective leaders tend to have smaller numbers of well-chosen team members, with the optimal number of people in a team being between four and seven.

8. **There should be a balance between offering performance-related rewards for the team and recognising individual members of the team.** It is important to both recognise individual achievements and hold people accountable for their actions; however, leaders should avoid concentrating on an individual team member as a cause of either success or failure of a team, since this will undermine the sense of mutual dependence that is so important for high-performing teams. This tension can be relieved by consistently linking rewards not only with individual growth but also with performance as a team and as an organisation. In this way, individual achievements are acknowledged but in the context of how they contribute to the overall team's and organisation's performance.

9. **Team leaders should lead or arrange training programmes** for team members to develop the knowledge and skills they need to carry out their roles successfully and manage any challenges they face. Even the most well-formed teams need to review and update their skills base to address changing circumstances and new challenges.

10. **Team leaders should establish a culture of continuous improvement by coaching members so as to help them identify where team performance can be improved and prompting them to find specific actions for development.** Leaders should seek opportunities for learning at naturally emerging critical points in time, taking into

account the team's workload and ability to take in learning points as well as the pertinence of the learning point itself at any particular moment. The research in the report identifies that giving coaching-style feedback is most relevant at the beginning, midpoint and end of a task or project (although feedback can be given at any appropriate point).

– **Beginnings:** At the beginning, coaching serves to motivate the team, establish the desired conditions for teamwork, and agree shared expected behaviours and routines for the task. For example, team members might discuss and agree (with reference to the Code of Fundraising Practice) shared expectations for behaviour and then set these down in writing. This would be important to do with regard to working with potentially vulnerable people, such as bereaved supporters. Coaching also provides an opportunity to hold a discussion to gather members' thoughts, suggestions and concerns and get them engaged in the decision-making. The leader should facilitate constructive discussions by being open, rather than defensive, when responding to queries. In this way, the leader's aim should be to create an environment where innovation is supported and where members feel safe to take risks and feel open to considering and constructively questioning ideas and approaches before they begin the task.

– **Midpoints:** At the midpoint, coaching can be used to review and reflect on the team's performance so far and to tweak the current approach to help them achieve their objectives or in light of any required changes to goals. The leader's role here is to guide the team members to consider and anticipate potential opportunities and challenges that may affect their strategy, and help with solutions where necessary.

– **Ends:** At the end of the task or project, regardless of its outcome, leaders should encourage team members to analyse the team's performance with a view to improving future efforts; here the focus is on getting team members to think about the rationales for the decisions they took throughout the project, consider how these decisions unfolded and plan how they could be improved in future tasks. Crucially, feedback must be focused on the overall team performance, not individual members' achievements; it should also be clearly linked to the team's goals. (See also 'Managing staff performance' on page 342.)

Case study: Macmillan Cancer Support's approach to developing its community fundraising team

The challenge of low staff retention

In 2012 at Macmillan we identified that annual staff turnover in our community fundraising team was 30%. We attributed this in part to a period of change that had seen a shift from our community fundraisers being office-based to being mobile workers, based in their local communities. But we also recognised that we needed a plan to give a consistent experience in the induction, performance coaching and development of new and existing members of the team.

Such a high turnover was more than an inconvenience to our recruiting manager, as any gaps in a community fundraising team can result in supporter attrition and a drop in income. We identified that the average term of a community fundraiser was 18 months, and the reasons for leaving that they gave on exit interviews were:

- a lack of development opportunities;
- having no clear progression path within the organisation;
- a lack of opportunities to be involved in cross-organisational work;
- feelings of isolation from being in a mobile role;
- feeling like a poor fit for the role and having an inability to adjust to mobile ways of working.

The impact of this high level of turnover on performance and the wider team included:

- a drop in income;
- a loss of volunteers and donors;
- an increased workload for other team members during recruitment of replacement fundraisers.

The length of time in the role had a direct correlation with sustained income growth and the recruitment and retention of volunteers. The cost of losing a community fundraiser and recruiting a replacement was, on average, equivalent to six months of income from the fundraiser's income stream. This takes into account the delays experienced in recruiting a suitable replacement and them getting sufficiently up to speed to deliver their objectives in their role.

We approached this issue of high turnover by:

- promoting a focus on leadership;
- creating a vision and a strategy;
- clearly linking individuals' objectives to the vision and strategy;
- introducing a comprehensive induction programme;
- starting a talent management and development programme;
- establishing succession planning.

A focus on leadership

We identified a gap in leadership capability within our community fundraising team, with line managers spending too much time on operational detail and too little time developing clear plans and leading their teams to deliver against them. For any strategy to succeed, you need the right people, with the right capabilities, doing the right things. For this, you need leaders who nurture and develop other leaders at all levels.

With this in mind, we created a new leadership development programme that focused on building a community of leaders, with a vision for the future and a plan of how to engage the team to get there through:

- creating a shared vision of the opportunity for community fundraising with a strategy that focused our teams on the four areas of community fundraising that had the highest potential to deliver income growth;
- developing plans, milestones and processes to enable delivery;
- setting objectives linked to the strategy, with clear performance expectations;
- using performance measures;
- training our leaders to become performance coaches so as to enable community fundraisers to achieve at the very highest level;
- holding all staff to account through coaching and measurement of KPIs.

This new approach had a significantly positive impact for community fundraising, including:

- over 20% year-on-year improvement in employee engagement (measured using internal employee engagement metrics and results of staff surveys);
- reduced attrition at the leadership level of over 50% over two years;
- reduced attrition across the team by over 30% over two years;
- increased income by over 30% over three years.

A vision and a strategy, with individuals' objectives clearly linked

To create a shared vision and strategic plan, leaders within the community fundraising team formed project groups to focus on the areas that they had identified as having the potential to grow. While it was not possible to have the input of everyone into every area of the strategy, having representation from across the team helped to engage and get buy-in from the wider team. Once we had agreed the strategy, the team leaders and fundraisers linked the fundraisers' performance objectives to the vision and strategy and to the fundraisers' own objectives.

A comprehensive induction programme

We realised that we were inadvertently setting up our new community fundraisers to fail due to the absence of a consistent induction programme. To address this issue, we established an approach based on feedback from existing fundraisers on what team members really wanted and needed to enable them to hit the ground running and, importantly, settle happily into their roles. High-performing community fundraisers led the delivery of this new induction programme, which focused on:

- getting to know Macmillan and how post holders fit into the organisation;
- building a support network for new recruits;
- building an organisational case for support for community fundraising;
- communicating which tools and support are available to do the job;

- teaching specific technical skills, such as using the organisation's database and reporting tools;
- conducting a training needs analysis and signposting new recruits to additional coaching, training and support.

Talent management and development programme

Given our recognition of the fact that the high attrition rate was in part due to the lack of opportunity for development within the community fundraising team, we decided to focus on talent management. Talent management is designed to:

- identify staff with exceptional skills whom you wish to nurture to support the development of the organisation;
- develop one (usually, but perhaps more) particular aspect of the organisation, such as leadership or diversity;
- support the succession planning needs of the organisation;
- fast-track staff into senior positions;
- be linked to existing and future strategic organisational objectives;
- support the motivational levels of talented staff, and encourage loyalty and retention.

We established a development programme that included 10 training days over 12 months. To qualify to take part in the programme, fundraisers need to have:

- been in the role for over 12 months;
- a proven ability to operate at a high standard, assessed as those achieving the highest rating in their previous performance review;
- demonstrated an ability to maintain a high level of performance in their role.

The programme covers a variety of topics, including:

- leading beyond authority;
- coaching;
- strategy development;
- developing others as leaders;

- project management;
- budgeting.

Leaders give unsuccessful applicants comprehensive feedback on the reason they have not been selected, with a development plan to help them work towards a place in the following cohort of selected staff.

An element of the programme involves the chosen cohort of staff identifying an issue within the organisation and forming a project group to involve stakeholders from across the organisation to solve the issue. Internal experts facilitate and run the sessions and, as the programme develops, previous participants take a role in developing and delivering content. The results of this approach are that now:

- over 80% of the talent programme participants are retained three years after participation;
- over 70% have been promoted into new roles within the organisation;
- Macmillan has saved an estimated £100,000 or more in facilitation and training fees by using internal staff;
- participants are positive about the opportunity to learn directly from colleagues;
- over £1 million of income is attributed to reducing turnover and increasing employee motivation, engagement and performance.

Succession planning

We placed an emphasis on home-grown talent and set about identifying our rising stars, alongside mapping key roles and the critical skills needed to perform those roles. Once we had identified the individuals with high potential at every level, we pinpointed any gaps in their knowledge, skills and experience and created development plans to address these gaps. Three years after the introduction of our talent management and development programme, every appointment at a senior level within the community fundraising team was an internal promotion, and we have a continued focus on development to ensure retention and a talent pipeline to fill critical roles as they arise. This has contributed to a reduction in attrition at all levels, as talented fundraisers can see that they are rewarded with development opportunities and career progression.

Conclusion

Perhaps more than any other fundraisers, community fundraisers are the face of an organisation, presenting it to myriad networks and driving participation through peer-to-peer recruitment. It is not only a charity's income but also its profile and the perception of its brand that are influenced by the quality and performance of community fundraisers. The cost to recruit is high, in terms of time invested in the process, advertising and fees, and the lost opportunity costs of replacing an existing team member. It is therefore vital that the right mix of talent is recruited through a thoughtful and effective process, and that this talent is nurtured and developed through a culture of leadership that provides clear and shared goals, space for innovation and reward, and development that is motivational and sustained.

Notes

1 *2017 Salary Survey* [PDF], Harris Hill, 2017, www.harrishill.co.uk/cms-uploaded/Harris_Hill_2017_Salary_Survey.pdf, p. 9, accessed 11 June 2018.
2 Claire Daniels and Sam Rider, 'Community Fundraising Snapshot', manuscript in preparation, 2017.
3 Andy Hillier, 'Female charity staff twice as likely as men to work part time' [web article], Third Sector, www.thirdsector.co.uk/female-charity-staff-twice-likely-men-work-part-time-report-says/management/article/1366512, 30 September 2015.
4 Adrian Sargeant and Jen Shang, *Great Fundraising: What makes fundraising truly great?* [PDF], Clayton Burnett, 2013, http://studyfundraising.com/wp-content/uploads/2016/07/Great-Fundraising.pdf, pp. 10–11, accessed 11 September 2018.
5 *Fundraising National Occupational Standards* [PDF], Institute of Fundraising, 2013, www.institute-of-fundraising.org.uk/library/fundraising-national-occupational-standards/fnos-web-version-052013.pdf, accessed 13 February 2018.
6 Adrian Sargeant and Jen Shang, *Great Fundraising: What makes fundraising truly great?* [PDF], Clayton Burnett, 2013, http://studyfundraising.com/wp-content/uploads/2016/07/Great-Fundraising.pdf, pp. 8–9, accessed 11 September 2018.
7 Kevin C. Stagl, Eduardo Salas and C. S. Shawn Burke, 'Best Practices in Team Leadership: What team leaders do to facilitate team effectiveness', in *The Practice of Leadership: Developing the next generation of leaders*, edited by Jay A. Conger and Ronald E. Riggio, San Francisco, Jossey-Bass, 2007 pp. 172–98.
8 James V. Downton, *Rebel Leadership: Commitment and charisma in the revolutionary process*, New York, Free Press, 1973.
9 David Waldman, Bernard M. Bass and Francis J. Yammarino, *Adding to Leader–Follower Transactions: The augmenting effect of charismatic leadership*, New York, Center for Leadership Studies at Binghamton University, 1988, pp. 3–4.

Index

Page numbers in *italics* refer specifically to figures; those in **bold** refer to tables.